By One Man

By One Man

A compilation of evidence from Scripture
and Christadelphian writers demonstrating
that Evolutionary Creation is incompatible
with Bible teaching and the BASF

Colin Byrnes and Matthew Jamieson

2021

First Published 2021

Copyright © 2021 by Colin Byrnes and Matthew Jamieson

ISBN 978-0-6489926-2-2 (print edition)
ISBN 978-0-6489926-3-9 (electronic edition)
ISBN 978-0-6489926-4-6 (*Supplementary Material*, electronic edition)

Cover Design: Hannah Jamieson

Unless otherwise stated, all Scripture quotations are from the Authorised Version of the Bible (The King James Bible).

Any proceeds from this book will go to the Asia-Pacific Christadelphian Bible Mission (acbm.org.au).

Abbreviations Occurring in *By One Man*

ACBM	Asia-Pacific Christadelphian Bible Mission
ABP	Apostolic Bible Polyglot © 1996, 2013, by Charles Van der Pool.
ANE	Ancient Near East
AUA	Australian Unity Agreement, or the booklet *"Christadelphian Unity in Australia - The Accepted Basis"*, 1963
BASF	Birmingham Amended Statement of Faith
CBM	Christadelphian Bible Mission (UK)
CCA	Cooper-Carter Addendum *(a statement regarding clauses 5 &12 of the BASF, included in the AUA). Originally this was an "addendum" to a letter written by brethren Cyril Cooper and John Carter to Australian brethren and sisters in 1956*
COD	Christadelphian Origins Discussion website, and with reference to the anonymous authors promoting the content of this website.
EC	Evolutionary Creation
ESV	ESV® Bible (The Holy Bible, English Standard Version®), copyright © 2001 by Crossway, a publishing ministry of Good News Publishers. Used by permission. All rights reserved
NASB	New American Standard Bible®, Copyright © 1960, 1962, 1963, 1968, 1971, 1972, 1973,1975, 1977, 1995 by The Lockman Foundation. Used by permission. www.Lockman.org
NET	New English Translation, NET Bible® copyright ©1996, 2019 by Biblical Studies Press, L.L.C. http://netbible.com. All rights reserved
NIV	New International Version®, NIV®. Copyright © 1973, 1978, 1984, 2011 by Biblica, Inc.™ Used by permission of Zondervan. All rights reserved worldwide. www.zondervan.com
OENC	Old Earth New Creation
TE	Theistic Evolution
YEC	Young Earth Creation
YLT	Young's Literal Translation
WNT	Weymouth New Testament

Contents

SECTION 3: VITAL ASPECTS OF THE ATONEMENT WRESTED BY EC

SECTION 4: THE DOCTRINES OF TWO EC VIEWS COMPARED

SECTION 5: EC BREAKS MANY LINKS IN THE BASF CHAIN

SECTION 6: CHRISTADELPHIAN WRITERS ON CREATION AND THE ATONEMENT

SECTION 7: FURTHER READING

Foreword

A book of this sort is long awaited and much needed for those eager to defend the truth of Scripture. Living in an age where knowledge is increasing ever more quickly and scientific discoveries take mankind into uncharted areas, it seems that today almost nothing is beyond reach. Knowledge has brought many benefits such as higher living standards, better health, increased life expectancy and broader access to education, all of which has improved the lives of many, at least throughout the developed world. But increased knowledge it seems goes hand in hand with a growing confidence and self-assurance, which could easily be regarded as arrogance. Much of the scientific world has concluded to its own satisfaction that this world came into existence through evolutionary processes and regards with some disdain those who build their faith on the foundation chapters of Genesis which describe simply and clearly that all things were miraculously brought into existence through the work of a creator God.

On the face of it one has a binary choice. It must be accepted that either the Genesis account of creation is true or that the evolutionary processes promoted by scientists brought about the earth and all that it contains. Either the Biblical record explaining how God created all plant and animal life "after their kind" in well-defined miraculous steps is true, or chance mutations and incremental developments over many millions of years brought about the majestic, complex, beautiful, fruitful, finely-tuned world we are all privileged to inhabit. Creationists and evolutionists both need faith, the former in the Biblical account, the latter in the miniscule odds that chance events took place at just the right time, in just the right place and in just the right way to bring about this world.

Such a binary choice was never easy. Plenty of scientists believe in God and at times creationists can find it difficult to hold on to a belief system which apparently runs contrary to the thinking of the scientific world. A compromising third approach therefore, which apparently offers some kind of middle ground has some attraction. Could it be possible that evolutionary processes were the means by which the earth came about because God was behind it, either directing the various stages of development or at least starting the whole thing off at the outset? Such an idea is appealing, marrying the Bible record with scientific discoveries. It enables a believer in God to maintain his or her faith, whilst accommodating current scientific thinking. After all, hasn't this been done in the past with the acknowledgement that not everything moved around the earth but that planet earth was itself just one part of a heliocentric Solar system?

But is it reasonable or indeed possible to mix creation and evolution in this way? Is it possible to do so without dishonouring the great Creator? And if this compromise were adopted, are there any consequences to faith?

By One Man is a clear and carefully reasoned response to these questions, showing that it is not possible to blend the Bible principle of God's creative power with man's theory of human evolution from lower life forms without undermining the key principles of faith. If this compromise approach is adopted then the creation account of Genesis has to be 'reinterpreted'. And if Genesis is 'reinterpreted' then wholesale changes have to be made to the entirety of Scripture, for prophets, poets, psalmists, apostles – even the Lord Jesus himself, declare their belief in creation. With so many 'reinterpretations' being required the principle of the Bible being God's inspired word is lost. Where does that leave faith, if the very book on which it is based is demeaned? Similarly, if the world evolved over many millions of years Adam cannot have been the first man, and death cannot have entered as a consequence of disobedience but was just part of the evolutionary process. Where does that leave the value of the sacrifice of Jesus, the very centre of faith?

The authors of this book address these points showing clearly and thoroughly that acceptance of evolution in any guise, atheistic or theistic, damages the very fabric of God's truth as revealed in His word. This is not a science book and is not intended to be. It is written to show that a real faith, as taught from our earliest days, requires an acceptance of God as the Almighty Creator who "in the beginning…created the heaven and the earth" and created Adam and Eve as the sole progenitors of humanity.

Andrew Bramhill
Birmingham, UK
April 2021

Introduction

By One Man is a compilation of evidence from Scripture and Christadelphian writers demonstrating that any form of Theistic Evolution (TE) or Evolutionary Creation (EC)[1]—which asserts that Adam and Eve are not the sole progenitors of our human race—is incompatible with Bible teaching and the Birmingham Amended Statement of Faith (BASF). It is provided as a resource to enable brothers and sisters to clearly see the consistency of Christadelphian teaching on this subject, from Bro Thomas to the present.

Essentially, ***By One Man*** is two books in one. The first half (Sections 1 to 5) demonstrates the incompatibility of EC with the BASF. It also counters many scriptures wrested by promoters of EC to support their view. The second half (Section 6) presents the Bible-based views of leading Christadelphian authors on first-principle subjects wrested by EC advocates.

There is nothing new in this book. It is not an attempt to foist upon the ecclesial world a unique teaching. Rather, ***By One Man*** is designed to uphold Bible teaching, Christadelphian teaching (on creation, the first man and woman, the nature and consequences of the fall, the devil, the atoning work of our Lord Jesus Christ and the purpose of God with mankind) and the BASF (including, in Australia, the Unity Agreement).

It says no more, and no less, than has been stated in the past by many respected Christadelphian writers in numerous standard Christadelphian works and our leading magazines. The material in ***By One Man*** provides easy access to the views expressed by these writers. It assures readers that the foundation beliefs that they firmly accepted at the time of their baptism remain Christadelphian teaching despite recent challenges to them.

By One Man has also been written as a ready reference for future generations to consult, whenever subjects of this nature arise, to give them an understanding of Bible and Christadelphian teaching and the confidence to not be *"carried about with every wind of doctrine"* (Ephesians 4:14).

By One Man's ultimate aim is to glorify our Heavenly Father and our Lord Jesus Christ by helping to maintain true ecclesial unity. ***By One Man*** reinforces those core Bible doctrines that Christadelphians worldwide believe are essential for salvation. These doctrines, set

---

[1] In this book, the term Evolutionary Creation (EC) covers all views which assert that certain ancestors of humans on the earth today evolved from lower animals as part of God's creative method. See Evolutionary Creation (EC) Defined on page 5.

out in the BASF, conflict with EC teaching. The authors' prayer is that *By One Man* will encourage those who have embraced EC to return to Bible truth.

Any comment on fellowship matters in *By One Man* is based on Scripture, the Birmingham Amended Statement of Faith, the Australian Unity Agreement, the Ecclesial Guide and Christadelphian precedent.

We are indebted to those who have reviewed draft versions of *By One Man* over the past three years, in part or fully, and made many helpful suggestions towards the improvement of its content — Brethren Bruce Bates, Andrew Bramhill, James Larsen, James McCann, Tecwyn Morgan, Mark Taunton, and Mark Vincent. Their contributions are greatly appreciated.

Thanks to Sisters Gisela Larsen and Keren Jamieson for their keen eyes, finding many mistakes that we had typed into the manuscript and making many helpful suggestions.

We would also like to thank Sis Kay McGrath for her help finding some of the material cited in *By One Man* and the *Supplementary Material*. Kay directed us to various comments by past writers that make an essential contribution to this book.

Finally, we thank our wives Janette Byrnes and Priscilla Jamieson for their patience, understanding, input and support during the production of *By One Man*.

All Bible quotations in *By One Man* are taken from the King James Bible (KJV), unless otherwise noted.

Our prayer is that truth, wisdom, patience and love will prevail in resolving an issue that should never have surfaced in the first place.

Colin Byrnes and Matthew Jamieson
Sydney, Australia
April 2021

Guide to Reading *By One Man*

Section 1: How Evolutionary Creation (EC) Undermines Christadelphian Faith and Fellowship

Section 1 is for those readers who want a solid overview of this subject without having to delve into the many detailed arguments covered in Sections 2 to 5. This section concisely explains how Evolutionary Creation conflicts with core Bible doctrines and our basis of fellowship. It outlines Bible/Christadelphian teaching as expressed in the BASF, the differences between Christadelphian and EC teaching and the spiritually destructive ramifications for our faith and fellowship of adopting a belief in EC. Sections 2 to 5 consider the minutiae of EC claims and can be read according to readers' needs or level of interest.

Section 2: Unnatural Readings of Genesis

Section 2 explains how belief in evolution inevitably produces the need to re-interpret Scripture and undermine its intended meaning. It discusses the difference between operational science with its many benefits for mankind and historical science that attempts to reconstruct the distant past without regard to the normal scientific method. Section 2 then answers a number of the tired old arguments of past Bible critics that EC advocates have revived in an effort to support EC teaching.

Section 3: Vital Aspects of the Atonement Wrested by EC

This section responds in more detail to numerous arguments that EC advocates have raised. Each chapter can be read independently as a specific answer to a particular EC argument related to the atonement. This means that readers can go directly to any Biblical issue covered in *By One Man* that is concerning them and find a response to it.

Section 4: Two Different EC Views Compared

The fourth section contains relevant quotations from specific Evolutionary Creationist writers, arranged under the headings of eight core doctrinal questions. This section contrasts EC views to Christadelphian belief on these crucial subjects.

Section 5: EC Views Break Links in the BASF Chain

The fifth section explains how EC views conflict with more than ten clauses in the BASF.

Section 6: Christadelphian Writers on Creation and The Atonement

The sixth section is a compilation of quotations from past Christadelphian writers up to the 1990s, demonstrating that it is impossible to harmonise EC views with Christadelphian teaching. This section serves as an important resource and will reduce the need to scour past books and magazines for relevant material on these subjects.

Section 7: A Further Reading List

This section provides a list of authors and titles of recent Christadelphian books and magazine articles opposing EC.

By One Man: Supplementary Material

By One Man is supported by *Supplementary Material* that provides the full context of all the articles by various writers cited in Section 6 of *By One Man*. Also, where possible, further quotations are included that affirm each writer's view on creation and the atonement to enable readers to understand more fully what they believed. The *Supplementary Material* also includes all the Watford Ecclesial statements published in the Christadelphian Magazine.

The *Supplementary Material* is available in pdf format from either of the following websites:

cbmresources.org/forums/index.php?/topic/1156-by-one-man/

lulu.com

Evolutionary Creation (EC) Defined

What is Evolutionary Creation?

In this book, the authors use the term Evolutionary Creation (EC) to cover major views which assert that the ancestors of all or a proportion of humans on the earth today evolved from lower animals as part of God's creative method.

Since the 1990s, evangelical advocates have increasingly preferred the term "Evolutionary Creation" over "Theistic Evolution" (TE) to describe their acceptance of *evolutionary* science as the best explanation for how all life upon this earth was *created*.[2] The terms God-directed Evolution (GDE) and God-guided Evolution are also sometimes used to designate these views. To our knowledge, most advocates arising from within the Christadelphian community prefer the "EC" designation. Accordingly, we use EC in this book, but we acknowledge that certain advocates may still prefer to describe their belief as TE.

The theory of neo-Darwinian evolution attempts to explain how humans evolved upwards from lower simple animal organisms entirely by natural means and without appealing to any involvement from God. When it comes to Evolutionary Creation, there is little or no practical disagreement with neo-Darwinian evolution over the mechanism. However, Evolutionary Creation asserts that God was somehow the hidden instigator behind the whole evolutionary process, and that God's "mechanism" of creation was evolution.

To what extent was God involved?

While EC proponents unanimously agree that God is the Creator of all life, and hence behind the evolutionary process, they seem very reluctant to clarify to what extent God was involved and how He directed the evolutionary process.

Francis Collins, a famous Evolutionary Creationist, asserts that *"evolution is real, but that it was set in motion by God".*[3] He believes God's existence explains certain aspects of humanity, such as self-sacrificing morality, as well as the fine-tuning of the fundamental physical constants that allow life to exist. [4] A similar definition by anthropologist Claude E. Stipe characterises it as accepting *"that evolution occurred as biologists describe it, but under the direction of God".*[5]

---

[2] biologos.org/common-questions/what-is-evolutionary-creation.

[3] Collins, Francis, *The Language of God*: A Scientist Presents Evidence for Belief, 2006

[4] Collins, Francis, *Building Bridges*, Nature, vol. 442, 2006, p. 110.

[5] Stipe, Claude E. *Scientific Creationism and Evangelical Christianity*, American Anthropologist, March 1985, vol 87, No. 1, 149.

Perhaps the most informative explanation by EC proponents within our community is Bro Ken Gilmore's statement: *"we can see a Divine hand at work in natural history, intervening at key times to nudge evolution in the right direction to bring about the evolution of the human race".*[6]

EC advocates consider the evolutionary process itself testifies to the glory of God. However, evolution is the poster child of the atheist movement. This is because evolution does not testify to a creator, and therefore has no need for a creator. EC advocates claim that a sufficient understanding of God's word is a prerequisite to an appreciation of how evolution can declare the glory of God. EC, therefore, attempts to glorify God as the author of a mechanism that secular evolutionists maintain excludes God. Unsurprisingly, secular evolutionists see EC as a lame attempt to introduce the assumption that God was involved.

Regardless, it is important to keep in mind that EC believers form their world view by accepting an interpretation of history published by today's non-theistic[7] evolutionary scientific academies, where the possibility of God being involved is not even allowed to be considered. EC believers simply overlay the explanation that "God did it" or "God was in control", or "God nudged evolution when necessary" without being specific so as to limit any possible conflict with the neo-Darwinian historical narrative. With this non-theistic historical filter in place, they re-interpret the Bible accordingly.

Three different EC explanations of Adam and Eve

Based on a foundation belief in evolution, EC promoters subject the Bible to several different interpretations designed to reconcile the Bible and evolution. Specifically, concerning Adam and Eve, there are at least three different explanations with which advocates align themselves[8]:

---

[6] Gilmore, Ken, *Issues in Genesis 1-11*, September 2011, p. 13.

[7] Non-theism is silence towards the concept of God, as opposed to atheism, which is hostile to that concept. Non-theism is relevant to the various branches of evolutionary science, where some scientists either believe in God, or are agnostic, and are therefore not atheists However, they embrace the evolutionary world-view and remove God from consideration when researching or publishing material that concerns the origins of the universe and life. 'Non-theistic' is an umbrella term that describes all scientists committed to the evolutionary paradigm, as it accommodates all of their personal views of God.

[8] Evolutionary Creationists appear to disagree among themselves about whether or not Adam and Eve were historical figures, and then whether Adam and Eve were miraculously created. The Evolutionary Creationist website, Biologos, notes *"BioLogos does not take a firm position on the historicity of Adam and Eve, but welcomes a range of perspectives … We view the historical details of Adam and the physical details of the Fall as secondary matters of belief and not core beliefs on which all Christians must agree".* biologos.org/articles/series/southern-baptist-voices/southern-baptist-voices-expressing-our-concerns, accessed April 2020.

(i)   That Adam and Eve were fictional characters. Therefore the story of the fall is not actual history, but a myth or allegory supposedly used by God to provide spiritual enlightenment.

(ii)   That Adam and Eve were part of a race of mortal humans that had evolved from primaeval animals. From among these 'evolved' humans, God appointed Adam and Eve as the first two humans through whom spiritual concepts could be introduced.

(iii)   That Adam was miraculously created from the dust and Eve from his side, as the Scripture teaches, but God made them mortal (subject to death) and sin-prone from the outset, and they existed alongside many other 'evolved' humans. The condition of evolved human nature was identical to that of Adam and Eve, and Adam and Eve's children intermarried with these evolved humans.

A small minority of Christadelphians have adopted one of the above explanations regarding Adam and Eve's origin. In the 1960s, Bro Ralph Lovelock proposed explanation (ii). This book mainly focuses on explanation (iii) because it is held by most Christadelphian advocates of EC today. In contrast, most Evangelical EC advocates align themselves with either explanation (i) or (ii).

What is common is that all EC views propose that:

1. **God, in some unclear way and to varying degrees, guided evolution over a long period of time to produce human beings from lower animals.**

2. **The condition of human nature that God allowed to evolve, well before the time of the real or symbolic Adam, is exactly the same as the condition of human nature today.**

3. **Adam and Eve were not the sole progenitors of our human race.**

4. **God did not change the hereditary condition of human nature to become subject to death, vanity, disease and suffering in consequence of Adam and Eve's sin.**

Two different EC views quoted in this book

By One Man specifically addresses two different Christadelphian EC views that fall under EC explanation (iii) – that God miraculously created Adam and Eve. Throughout *By One Man*, these two views are referred to as *EC View A* and *EC View B*. The table on the following page summarises the similarities and differences. Excerpts from these writers are included in Section 4. The main differences between the two views concern how one becomes *"in Adam"* and subject to the *"eternal death"* introduced by Adam, and what the devil is.

Two EC Views Quoted in *By One Man*

Similarities	EC View A[9] & EC View B[10]
First humans of our race, and mortality	Came into existence by God's evolutionary creation of humans from lower animals, well before Adam and Eve. Countless humans were already mortal and hence dying before Adam.
Adam & Eve	Adam was miraculously created from the dust and Eve from his side, as the Scripture teaches. From the outset they were made mortal and prone to sin, and in the same condition as all evolved humans. Their sin resulted in no change to the condition of their nature, and their children intermarried with the evolved humans.
What "death" did Adam introduce?	"Eternal death", which is distinct from or overlays as a legal or judicial condemnation the normal death associated with mortality.
Was Christ subject to this "death"?	No

Differences	EC View A	EC View B
Who is *"in Adam"* and hence subject to the "eternal death" Adam introduced?	Only those who have sufficient knowledge of God's laws and break them.	1) Those who have sufficient knowledge of God's laws and break them; and 2) Based on Adam's sin, all living in ignorance (both before and after Adam) are "accounted" as sinners and legally condemned to eternal death. All living before Adam were retrospectively condemned to eternal death, on the basis that Adam demonstrated that all men would sin once exposed to God's laws.
When did/will the death Adam introduced occur?	At the judgment seat of Christ for the unworthy responsible.	1) At the judgment seat of Christ for the unworthy responsible; and 2) Cessation of mortal existence in the case of the ignorant.
What is the Devil?	A state of mind conflicting with God's ways, that can only arise when a person has sufficient understanding of God's laws.	Personification of human nature.

[9] EC View A: Bro Ken Gilmore, Bro Jonathan Burke - see Section 4.

[10] EC View B: Bro. Mike Pearson, and the anonymous brethren writing articles on the Christadelphian Origins Discussion (COD) website. See Section 4.

SECTION 1

HOW EVOLUTIONARY CREATION UNDERMINES CHRISTADELPHIAN FAITH AND FELLOWSHIP

*O Timothy, guard what has been entrusted to you,
avoiding worldly and empty chatter and the opposing
arguments of what is falsely called "knowledge"
(1 Timothy 6:20, NASB)*

Chapter 1
The Issue Briefly Stated

Consistent Christadelphian Belief and Teaching

- The first man of our human race was Adam, who God miraculously created from the dust of the ground.

- Eve, the first woman, was miraculously created from Adam's side.

- Adam and Eve are the sole progenitors of our entire human race.

- God created them with a *"natural body of life"* that was *"very good in kind and condition"* (BASF 4), i.e. not an immortal body incapable of death, but a natural body capable of death, but not yet subject to it.

- Their sin resulted in a physical change in the condition of their natural bodies that made them prone to sin and subject to death, as confirmed by God's just and necessary sentence in Genesis 3:15-23.

- All of Adam and Eve's posterity (i.e. our entire human race) inherit from them the death-stricken and sin-biased condition of their nature.

- Christ was born subject to and died the same death that was introduced by Adam and Eve's sin.

- The devil, which has *"the power of death"* (Hebrews 2:14), is the Bible's way of personifying the sin-biased and mortal condition of our nature.

- *"The appearance of Jesus of Nazareth on the earth was necessitated* by *the position and state into which the human race had been brought by circumstances connected with the first man"*; and *"the first man was Adam"* (BASF clauses 3 and 4).

As is the case for all of Adam's descendants, the condition of Christ's nature was his misfortune and not his crime. By his life of perfect obedience and his ultimate sacrifice on the cross, he voluntarily declared God's righteousness by demonstrating that the nature he bore was *"by divine appointment rightly related to death"*.[11]

1. By our own actions, we become sinners and require forgiveness of sins before we can be acceptable to God.

2. If we have faith in what God has done in Christ, confess our sins and recognise that *"as members of Adam's race we are rightly related to a dispensation of death"*,[12] then God is willing to forgive our sins and ultimately reward us with immortality.

3. The gift of salvation is freely given. We can do nothing to earn it.

4. We need to respond through faith to God's grace, by baptism into the saving name of Jesus Christ.

5. We will be rewarded with immortality when Christ returns if we continue to abide in Christ's vine. We should try our best to allow God's word to influence everything we do or say, to crucify *"the flesh with the affections and lusts"*, and to produce spiritual fruit for the benefit of others.

Jesus will rule over the earth for a thousand years with the objective of completely removing the problems of sin and death introduced into the world *"by one man"*. At the end of the Millennium, after the final judgment, the fellowship with God that was originally lost will be completely restored for faithful members of our human race from every age. Sin and death will be no more, all will be immortal, and God will be all in all.

EC challenges to these Christadelphian beliefs

These vital doctrines of how sin and mortality entered into the world, and God's plan for removing both, have been challenged by a number of brethren. In an effort to reconcile evolution with the Scriptures, these brethren have propagated worldwide, mainly via the Internet, the view that a race of humans evolved from primordial animals. They take their cue from leading evangelical promoters of EC.

Advocates of EC who seek to reconcile their views with Christadelphian beliefs need to explain:

a) What death did Adam's sin introduce, did Adam die this death, and did Christ die this death?

b) The devil's origin and meaning, including what is the death that the devil holds power over (Hebrews 2:14-15)?

---

[11] See the Australian Unity Agreement on page 30.

[12] Ibid.

Those who hold the view that Adam and Eve were selected among evolved humans, or that Adam and Eve were miraculously created, both agree that 'evolved' humans existed both before and alongside Adam and Eve and their offspring. Furthermore, Adam's offspring supposedly married into this evolved human populace, the genetic condition of whose nature was identical with that of Adam and Eve's children, thereby allowing procreation. Therefore, they claim that human nature, afflicted by mortality, with its predisposition toward sin, disease and suffering, was in the world long before Adam and Eve. Hence, they argue that the origin of our human race is merely shared with Adam and Eve, and there was no physical change, even after Adam and Eve sinned, in the condition of the nature that all their descendants inherit.

Because of their view that death was already in the world, they need to assert that the *"death"* that Adam introduced into the world (Romans 5:12; 1 Corinthians 15:22) is not the natural death associated with mortality. Rather it is a "spiritual" or "eternal" death that is either distinct from, or overlays as a judicial or legal condemnation, our natural death (see page 8 for a summary of the two EC views, and Section 4 for a detailed review).

These EC views would mean that in the case of Christ:

1. The mortal and sin-prone nature with which Christ was born and came to destroy, was unrelated to the physical consequences of Adam's sin. This is because they assert that God made all humans mortal and sin-prone from the outset, irrespective of whether they were created or evolved by God.

2. Christ was not subject to the death Adam introduced, as he never sinned. EC advocates propose that Adam's sin introduced "eternal" death and this applies to unrepentant sinners at the judgment seat (and the ignorant when they die in the case of EC View B).

3. The reason God required Christ to die on the cross was a) to provide forgiveness of sins; b) to potentially release us from "eternal" death at the judgment; and c) as the ultimate example of how to overcome the nature with which God evolved/created us.

If the above three points are correct:

- How could "death" have dominion over Christ (Romans 6:9) if he never sinned and was not subject to the death that Adam introduced?

- How could Christ, by partaking of flesh and blood, destroy the devil through his own death, if he was not subject to the death the devil holds power over (Hebrews 2:14)?

- How could Christ, in putting the flesh to death on the cross, declare God to be righteous and just (Romans 3:25-26) if the condition of Christ's flesh was not a consequence of Adam and Eve's sin, but rather the way God evolved/created all humans from the outset?

If EC proponents are right, why did God not reward the sinless Christ with immortal life without having to die, as would have been the case for Adam and Eve if they had remained obedient? The tree of life in the garden promised immortality (Genesis 3:22). But after they sinned, God drove them out of the garden, away from this tree, and placed cherubim to keep the way (Genesis 3:22-24).

Christadelphians teach that Christ is our representative because he came in the same fallen nature that all human beings inherit as a result of Adam and Eve's sin. Only by sharing in this nature could he both, in his life, and by his death, overcome it, and thus save himself and believers from the problem of death. The EC view is substitutionary. It rejects Christadelphian teaching that, in saving us, Christ himself obtained eternal redemption (Hebrews 9:12; 13:20) from the nature to which sin and death belong (see BASF 8 and 10).

Christadelphians have always believed that Christ himself was born subject to and died the same death that Adam introduced.

- *"Wherefore, as by one man sin entered into the world, and **death** by sin"* (Romans 5:12)

- *"… by one man's offence **death** reigned by one; much more they which receive abundance of grace and of the gift of righteousness shall reign in life by one, Jesus Christ"* (Romans 5:17)

- *"Knowing that Christ being raised from the dead dieth no more; **death hath no more dominion over him**. 10 For in that he died, he died unto sin once: but in that he liveth, he liveth unto God"* (Romans 6:9-10)

- *"But we see Jesus, who was made a little lower than the angels for the **suffering of death**, crowned with glory and honour; that he by the grace of God should taste **death for every man."** (Hebrews 2:9)

- *"… that **through death** he might destroy him that had **the power of death**, that is, the devil; 15 And deliver them who through fear of **death** were all their lifetime subject to bondage."* (Hebrews 2:14-15)

- *"Whom God hath raised up, having **loosed the pains of death**: because it was not possible that he should be holden of it."* (Acts 2:24)

- *See BASF clauses 8, 9,10 and 12.*

Evolutionary creationists make God directly responsible from the very beginning for the prevalence of sin and our death-stricken state. In contrast, Scripture states that it was *"by one man sin entered into the world, and death by sin"*. It could not be said that Christ rose after *"suffering the death required by the righteousness of God"* (BASF clause 9) if God's requirement was to rectify a problem that God Himself introduced from the outset. And then, having introduced His laws to men subject to the weak condition that He created them in, He caused them to fail.

The life and death of Christ could not declare God to be just, and the justifier of all who believe in Jesus (Romans 3:21-26) if from the beginning, before sin even entered into the world, God had willingly made His creation *"subject to vanity"*, under *"bondage of corruption"* and *"groaning and travailing in pain"* (Romans 8:20-23).

God did not evolve a world that was under bondage to sin, disease and death, with most of humanity excluded from fellowship with Him, as EC advocates propose. We know that at the conclusion of His creative acts, God, from His own perspective, declared that everything He had made, including man, was *"very good"* (Genesis 1:31). At the very least, this means that human death and sin-bias, which are both God's enemies (1 Corinthians 15:26; Revelation 20:2-3, 9-10), could not have been part of His original creation. What God declared to be *"very good"* cannot be harmonised with the current state of humanity where we all *"live in fear of death"*, are *"all our lifetime subject to bondage"* (Hebrews 2:14-15) and struggle with a nature in which there *"dwelleth **no good thing**"* (Romans 7:18).

In contrast to this, God created Adam and Eve in a state where they were to *"have dominion"* over everything He had created (Genesis 1:28). They were not physically subject to the *"law of sin and death"* prior to sin (Romans 7:23,25; 8:2). They only became *"afraid"* (Genesis 3:8-10) and only lost the dominion *after* they sinned (Genesis 3:15-24).

We know that in their *"very good"* state Adam and Eve enjoyed direct fellowship with God in the garden of Eden. The way to the tree of life was not guarded by cherubim with a flaming sword. They had the prospect of eternal life without the need for any suffering or the sacrifice of Christ. But we also know from Genesis 3 that God subsequently introduced into the world enmity, sorrow, death, thorns and thistles, curses on the ground and the animals as part of His just and necessary sentence on Adam and Eve. They were evicted from the garden, and God placed the cherubim to guard and keep the way to the tree of life. Although, because of sin, God subjected His creation to vanity, at the same time He provided a way, foreshadowed and typified by animal sacrifices, whereby sins could be forgiven and ultimately eternal life could be obtained. The apostle Paul comments on this in Romans 8:

> *"For the creation was subjected to futility, **not willingly**, but because of him who subjected it, **in hope** that the creation itself will be set free from its bondage to corruption and obtain the freedom of the glory of the children of God."* **(Romans 8:20-22, ESV)**

This subjection of His creation to futility, not willingly, but in hope, occurred immediately after Adam and Eve sinned. Genesis 3:15 reveals that God then *"put enmity"* into the world but at the same time promised that the seed of the woman would fatally crush the serpent. Likewise, when He slew an animal to provide garments of skin as a covering for their nakedness (Genesis 3:21) and placed the cherubim to keep the way to the tree of life (Genesis 3:24), God signalled His intention to provide a means whereby sins could be forgiven, the problems of sin and death removed and direct fellowship with God could be restored.

This was initially achieved through the life, death, resurrection and glorification of Jesus Christ, after he completely overcame and destroyed his sin-biased nature, and thus opened the way back to the tree of life for all who faithfully identify with what God accomplished in him. Through the work of the millennial reign of Christ, God intends to remove the curses He imposed across His entire creation at the time of the fall (Isaiah 11:1-9; 65:17-25; Revelation 22:3), culminating in the complete abolition of the twin enemies, sin and death (Isaiah 25:6-8; 1 Corinthians 15:25-26; Revelation 20:2,10, 13-14; 21:4). Christ will reward those judged faithful, whether at his return or the end of his millennial reign, by enabling them to eat from the tree of life (Revelation 2:7; 22:14).

In this way, God will restore the human race to fellowship with Himself so that He may both (i) be "all in all", at one with His creation (1 Corinthians 15:28) and (ii) realise His unalterable purpose of filling the earth *"with the knowledge of the glory of the LORD, as the waters cover the sea"* (Habakkuk 2:14).

The EC view is that our human race did not solely originate with Adam and Eve, and that the physical condition of our nature has nothing to do with their sin. They claim that countless human deaths, along with untold disease and suffering, were all part of God's *"very good"* creation before the entry of sin and death through Adam (Romans 5:12-21). This is a serious challenge to the foundation teaching of the Bible, Christadelphian teaching and our basis of fellowship – the BASF and (in Australia) the Australian Unity Agreement (AUA) (see Chapter 2).

Chapter 2
The Purpose of *By One Man*

Whenever brethren attempt to impose error on the Christadelphian body, it is a tragedy. It is a tragedy from their perspective because they believe that adopting their new "truth" is essential to save the brotherhood from itself and prevent it from being lost in a no-longer-acceptable paradigm of ignorance and ineffectiveness in the modern world.

It is also a tragedy for those who stand fast and hold on to Bible truth because they witness beloved brethren abandoning saving truth. It is a tragedy that they find themselves, in the process of defending Christadelphian teaching, in conflict with brethren with whom they have had many years of sweet fellowship in Christ. Despite appeals to those in error to return to believing essential Bible truth as expressed in our Statement of Faith, and to consider the damage they are inflicting on the peace of the Christadelphian world, such appeals usually go unheeded, and conflict is the inevitable result. The alternatives of either accommodating the new "truth" or burying our heads in the sand cannot be sustained when the issue comes knocking at our family's or ecclesia's door.

We, the authors, would much prefer to be writing about more positive scriptural subjects. Of necessity, this book discusses sin, disease, death, fallen human nature, what caused them and how Christ's sinlessness overcame them. In reading *By One Man*, some may get the impression that we believe that human beings are incapable of doing anything other than sinning. However, humans are created in the image of God, and although the fall greatly marred that image, humans still have the capacity to display divine characteristics such as logic, love, justice, compassion, joy, sacrifice and so forth. The purpose of our Lord's life was not just to be sinless. As vital as his sinlessness was, he also came to be a complete manifestation of his Father's glorious character to mankind.

There is positive and essential material presented in *By One Man*. However, the subject we are dealing with by its very nature is embroiled in controversy that detracts from the enjoyment of reading about, without distraction, those great Scriptural truths that Christadelphians agree form the foundation of our faith.

Unfortunately, not only do EC proposals conflict with more than ten clauses of the BASF, they also are at variance with the large number of standard Christadelphian books and articles that support our understanding of the atonement outlined in our basis of fellowship.

In keeping with this, *By One Man's* purpose is to direct attention to the Bible's teaching, consistent Christadelphian foundational teaching on this subject and the precedent set by the Watford Ecclesia in 1966 (see page 39) relating to the first man and the fall. In Section 6, eighteen Christadelphian commentators from John Thomas to Michael Ashton are quoted extensively on both creation and the atonement. Although they expressed different views on the six days of creation and the age of the earth, their teachings were consistent on the first man and woman and how their sin affected the whole of humanity.

The quotations in Section 6 are arranged under three main topical headings, and summarised in the table *"Christadelphian Authors – Creation and the Atonement"* on page 44. This should be sufficient to clearly illustrate each writer truly believing that Adam and Eve were the sole parents of our human race, and that sin and mortality entered into the world as a result of their sin.

The information contained in *By One Man* is vital from a doctrinal perspective as it demonstrates the consistency of Christadelphian teaching on the atonement from the time of John Thomas through to the present. If EC views were to be accepted in the Christadelphian world, it would necessitate a re-writing of sections of the Statement of Faith and the Australian Unity Agreement. The acceptance of EC views would require such a radical change to the Christadelphian understanding of the atoning work of Christ that it would eradicate what our forebears in the Central Fellowship, who have fallen asleep in Christ, relied upon and regarded as essential saving truth.

The alternative would simply be to accommodate these false doctrines. However, this would reduce the BASF (and AUA) to meaningless documents to which we would give lip service, but, in reality, ignore. If a brother proposed baptising or accepting into fellowship someone who still firmly believed in a false doctrine such as the Trinity or the immortal soul, the extent of the clash with the BASF would make his proposal indefensible. How then can we justify accepting EC beliefs, which conflict with a third of the BASF, and treat them differently?

The warm and precious spirit of fellowship that brothers and sisters enjoy all over the world is thanks to a Bible-centred community that respects the written expression of the Bible's core doctrines contained in the BASF. As the Christadelphian Committee's statement on fellowship in 1972 pointed out (see page 28), it is not honourable to enjoy this warm spirit of fellowship without accepting and upholding the very basis that makes it possible.

Chapter 3
The Conflict With Christadelphian Teaching

How EC Conflicts with Christadelphian Core Beliefs

EC views conflict with fundamental Christadelphian beliefs by teaching:

- That Adam was not the first man of our human race and that God created the ancestors of many humans living on the earth today via an evolutionary process from primaeval animals (compare BASF 3,4).

- That Adam was not miraculously created, nor Eve created from his side. Some EC view holders do teach the miraculous creation of Adam and Eve, in contrast to all other 'evolved' humans, but maintain that Adam & Eve's children intermarried with the alleged evolved humans (compare BASF 3,4).

- That the mortal and sin-biased physical condition of our nature did not arise post Adam and Eve's sin as part of God's just and necessary sentence (compare BASF 5,6). Instead, EC advocates believe this is how God created all humans from the outset, whether by evolution or miraculously.

- That the death introduced by Adam's sin into the world was not the death that is the end result of mortality. Instead, EC believers assert that Adam introduced "eternal" death, which is distinct from or overlays as a legal or judicial condemnation the normal death associated with mortality.

- That all who are "in Adam" does not refer to Adam's progeny who inherit by descent from him the death-stricken and sin-prone condition of human nature that came in consequence of Adams's sin (compare BASF 5,6,8,9,10,12).

- That the death-stricken, sin-biased nature that Jesus was born subject to, and destroyed on the cross, had nothing to do with the physical consequences of Adam and Eve's sin *(compare BASF 10 – Jesus was "a sufferer from all the effects that came by Adam's transgression, including the death that passed on all men"*).

- That the devil (diabolos) with its "power of death" (Hebrews 2:14) is not the personification of the sin-prone and mortal condition of our nature that resulted from Adam's sin.

Evolutionary Creation and Christadelphian teachings

From the early 2000s, a small number of brethren within the brotherhood have relentlessly promoted their belief in EC using various public online Christadelphian social media forums and other Internet sites. This has enabled them to reach many, particularly the younger generation, outside the umbrella of normal ecclesial activities. They argue that the community should accept or accommodate their views, claiming that EC beliefs are compatible with the Bible and what Christadelphians consider to be the Bible's foundational teachings.

EC advocates, and others supporting them, insist that ecclesias should regard these ideas as "uncertain details". It is reasoned that a belief in EC should have *no implication for an individual's fellowship standing*.[13] That those propagating Theistic Evolution or Evolutionary Creationism should be accommodated, given that differing views on the six days of creation and the age of the earth have been tolerated in the Christadelphian world since the days of Bro Thomas.

Although accommodation is a well-meaning approach in that it aims to prevent ecclesial disruption, it would be disastrous for Christadelphian foundational teachings if it went unchallenged. Tolerance of different viewpoints *not* defined in our Statement of Faith cannot justify tolerance of the undermining of teachings that *are* defined in our Statement of Faith. Therefore it is not unreasonable that *By One Man* should address this matter.

What the Bible tells us

The Bible is not silent on God's method of creation

It is important to note that there is nothing throughout the Bible that describes a process of evolution in any sense. God could have done so easily in straightforward terms (just as some ancient Greek philosophers did)[14], but such a description is absent from the record. EC advocates accept that the Bible does not describe the process of evolution. But they go one step further and claim that the Bible is completely silent on God's method of creation to legitimise their acceptance of the naturalistic evolutionary explanation promoted by today's scientific academies.

---

[13] Cited in Chalmers, Ken, *Early Genesis, A review of historical Christadelphian approaches*, January 2016.

[14] For example: 1) Thales of Miletus (640–546 BC) was evidently the first "Greek Philosopher" to advance the idea that life first originated in water [Birdsell, J.B., *Human Evolution*, Rand McNally, p. 22, 1972]; and 2) Aristotle (384–322 BC) claimed that humans are the highest point of one long, continuous 'ascent with modification' of life [Osborn, H.F., *From the Greeks to Darwin*, Charles Scribner's Sons, p. 54, 1929].

However, **the Bible is far from silent on God's method of creation.** While the Bible does not detail all the 'science' behind God's method of creation, it leaves us in no doubt that the various elements of His creative work upon this earth, including the creation of man from the ground, the creation of woman from Adam's side, and the creation of all forms of life *"after their kind"* (Genesis 1:11-12, 21, 24-25), were miraculous and did not evolve over many millions of years.

God will repeat His act of creating man from the dust when He miraculously resurrects the responsible dead from the dust at the return of Christ. We firmly believe and teach that, at Christ's second advent and at the end of the millennium, *"… many of them that sleep in the dust of the earth shall awake, some to everlasting life, and some to shame and everlasting contempt"* (Daniel 12:2), and that the faithful will be changed to immortality *"in a moment, in the twinkling of an eye"* (1 Corinthians 15:52). Why then should we baulk at the idea of God miraculously creating Adam from the dust of the earth?

The Lord Jesus Christ confirms that Adam and Eve were made at the **"beginning** of Creation" (Mark 10:6), not at the **end** of a very long creative process that would have been the case if evolution was truly God's method. Furthermore, the Bible reveals that God created by His Word (Genesis 1:3-26; Psalm 33:6-9; 148:3-5; Hebrews 11:3), and by His infinite wisdom and intelligence (Psalm 104:24; 136:5-8; Jeremiah 10:12; 51:15; Isaiah 40:28). This contradicts the concept of gradual evolutionary development, which would require endless competition for survival, suffering and death.

Genesis is meant to convey real historical events

To Christadelphians, Genesis 1-4 presents historical events that are confirmed by our Lord and the New Testament writers. This includes the miraculous creation of all life upon this earth as we know it, and the creation of Adam and Eve as the first man and woman. Whenever the prophets, the Lord and the Apostles quote Genesis chapters 1-4, they view the Genesis record as historical.[15] There is not the slightest hint of the interpretations employed by EC advocates to accommodate naturalistic evolution. They regard Genesis 1 as a description of the actual or "material" creation of all life upon the earth. It is not about a "functional" creation (or the point in time when "purpose" was established), as some Evolutionary Creationists propose[16].

---

[15] Acts 14:15; 17:24; Romans 1:19-20; Ephesians 3:9; Revelation 10:6; 14:7 (even if symbolic, these last two verses allude to the literal creation); Hebrews 4:4; Matthew 19:4-5; Mark 10:6-8; 1 Corinthians 15:45-47; 1 Timothy 2:13; 1 Corinthians 11:8-9; 1 Corinthians 6:16; Ephesians 5:31; Revelation 2:7; 2 Corinthians 11:3; Romans 5:12-21; 1 Cor 15:21-22.

[16] This view is proposed by John H. Walton in his *"Lost World"* series. See Chapter 15 for a critique of this view.

So why do EC advocates reject a straightforward reading of Genesis as an accurate historical account and the clauses in the BASF that reflect this (particularly BASF 3, 4, 5, 10, 12)?

EC reasoning begins with believing in evolution as taught by naturalist scientists as their foundation starting point. This then forces re-interpretation of all Bible passages concerned with the origin of life upon this earth, and ends up undermining Bible and Christadelphian teaching. They suggest that the extent of what God could convey in His word was restricted by the background culture and limited understanding of the human writers He worked through, while at the same time still insisting that the Bible is inspired by God. It is claimed that evolutionary teaching 'proves' that the way Christadelphians have always read these authors on the subject of origins is at least partially wrong.

So, to understand the Bible correctly, EC promoters are asking us to accept that God's ability to convey historical truths was limited by the unsophisticated worldview held by each of the prophets and apostles He "inspired" to write His word. This particularly applies to the subject of origins in Genesis. See Chapter 7 for a fuller explanation of the EC steps to error and a rebuttal of this reasoning.

Some EC proponents even argue that Genesis chapters 1-11 are comprised of mythical stories that contain spiritual lessons but no real history, and so cannot be taken literally. They claim that the historical portion of Genesis only begins with the life of Abraham in chapter 12.

However, the following points refute such a reading of Genesis 1-11:

1. Christ and the apostles read the whole of Genesis as history, without the slightest indication that they were citing mythical stories. In fact, they knew of and were opposed to citing cunningly devised fables (2 Timothy 4:4; 2 Peter 1:16).

2. Genesis 11 contains Abraham's genealogy – his ancestral line back to Shem – which provides the background to chapter 12 where the promises to Abraham begin. So, there is clear continuity between these two chapters.

3. The genealogy of 1 Chronicles 1-8 runs from Adam through to the period of the exile. The first half of 1 Chronicles 1 (vv 1-27) repeats all of the names found in Genesis 5, 10 and 11 from Adam to Abraham, with no hint of any of the names being anything but historical people. The second half of the chapter (vv 28-54) lists all the real descendants of Abraham's two sons – Isaac and Ishmael. It simply would not make sense to read 1 Chronicles 1 and insist that while the second half contains a list of real people, the names mentioned in the first half, including Adam, Seth and Enosh (v1), were not real people. All the names listed across the genealogies in Chronicles, spanning from Adam to Abraham to David and through to the exiles that returned to rebuild

Jerusalem after the Babylonian captivity, are presented as real people. There are no exceptions.

4. Christ's genealogy in Luke 3:23-38 traces his origins back to Adam, then God, and stops there. The genealogy lists Christ's forbears who lived in the period of Genesis 1-11. If, as some contend, Adam descended from pre-existing men, it is strange that there is no mention of them in the genealogy.

5. Hebrews 11 discusses many faithful people, including four named individuals (Abel, Enoch, Noah and Abraham) mentioned in Genesis 1-11. Hebrews 11:4-10, 39-40 says that these four were among the faithful who died not having received the promise. If these "mythical" people never lived and never died, why are they included among those who will receive the promise and be made perfect?

The genealogies in the Bible list the line of descent from the historical Adam to the historical Jesus Christ. They serve the purpose of confirming the Bible, from Genesis 1 onwards, as a reliable record of historical people and events. We are meant to understand that the people and events of Genesis 1-11 are historical.

EC reasoning is that i) God was limited in His ability to convey accurate historical truths; ii) God worked through widely-held mythological views to express spiritual truths; and iii) we must turn to modern evolutionary science for correct information on how God created life upon this earth. But this undermines the Foundation clause of the BASF by challenging the Christadelphian view of the Scriptures, that they are *"wholly given by inspiration of God in the writers, and are consequently without error in all parts of them"*, and as *"the only source of knowledge concerning God and His purposes at present or extant or available in the earth"*. (See Bro Alfred Nicholls' explanation of the Foundation Clause[17].)

As a Bible-based community, Christadelphians should not feel pressure to follow the "consensus" view of so-called "experts" on historical matters, particularly when their view contradicts the Bible. It is important to note that secular scientists working in the various fields relating to "historical origins" are tied to a "non-theistic" approach. See Chapter 8 for a more detailed discussion of the problems with evolutionary science taught by today's scientific institutions.

---

[17] Studies in the Statement of Faith, *Chapter 1: The Bible – Wholly Inspired and Infallible,* The Christadelphian, Birmingham, 1991.

Chapter 4
The Conflict With Our Basis of Fellowship
EC conflicts with the BASF's atonement clauses

Christadelphians accept the BASF as an apt summary of the Bible's fundamental teachings essential for salvation. As such, it is our basis for baptism and fellowship.

It is true that Clause 1 of the BASF is not specific on "how" [18] God created. Different interpretations of the six days and the age of the earth have never been a matter of fellowship.

However, the **specific EC teachings** listed at the outset of Chapter 3 come into conflict with many other clauses in our BASF which focus on the atonement. Altogether, EC teachings conflict with approximately 30% of the clauses in the BASF [19].

The BASF plainly states that Adam was the first man of the human race, that the appearance of Jesus *"was necessitated by the position and state into which **the human race** had been brought by the circumstances connected with the **first** man"* [20], and as a result of Adam's sin the entire human race is subject to God's *"just and necessary law of sin and death"*.[21] It is impossible for EC concepts to be harmonised with this, as they claim that i) Adam and Eve are not the progenitors of the entire human race, and ii) a state of mortality was already in the world before their sin.

The BASF also clearly conveys that God's *"plan of restoration"*, of ultimately *"rescuing the race from destruction"*,[22] focuses on one man, Jesus Christ, a member of *"Adam's disobedient race"* [23] who was born with a nature suffering *"from all the effects that came by Adam's transgression including the death that passed upon all men, which he shared by partaking of their physical nature"* [24]. Propagators of EC insist that there was no physical change in the condition of human nature in consequence of Adam and Eve's sin, so the death that Christ was born subject to, and died to overcome, has nothing to do with it either.

As a result of Christ's divine begettal and education, in conjunction with his own faithful, willing cooperation and determination

---

[18] Nevertheless, the Bible clearly states "what" God did when He created in a manner that rules out an evolutionary interpretation, and this stands as His own record for us to accept.

[19] Clauses 3, 4, 5, 6, 8, 9, 10, 12, 28 & 30.

[20] BASF 3 and 4.

[21] BASF 6.

[22] BASF 6.

[23] BASF 12.

[24] BASF 10.

throughout his whole life, he overcame the promptings of his sin-biased nature and rendered perfect obedience to his Father's will. In doing so, when he died on the cross he destroyed or condemned *"sin in the flesh"* [25] or *"abrogated the law of condemnation for himself and all who should believe and obey him"* [26] (i.e. Christ destroyed the *diabolos*). In so doing, he declared God to be righteous. This declaration became the basis for the forgiveness of our sins and the hope of eternal life. However, EC advocates hypothesize that God created Adam and Eve mortal, and this mortality has nothing to do with God's sentence of physical condemnation, which, as both Scripture and the BASF [27] teach, came as a result of their sin.

We need to be clear that we do not inherit or receive any legal or moral condemnation from Adam's sin. Rather, the "condemned line" or "condemned nature", referred to in BASF 8 and 9, is a physical condemnation, as defined by the context of BASF 5 – *"a sentence which defiled and became a **physical law of his being"***, and is further clarified by the context of BASF 10 – *"Jesus was … a sufferer, in the days of his flesh, from all the effects that came by Adam's transgression including the death that passed upon all men, which he shared by partaking of their **physical nature"***.

"Condemned nature" simply refers to the sin-prone and death-stricken condition of human nature with which God "condemned" Adam and Eve. It is synonymous with the *diabolos*, which is part and parcel of the "flesh and blood" referred to in Hebrews 2:14-15. This same verse is referenced by the BASF clauses 8, 9 and 10. As it became a physical law of their being, it hereditarily impacted all of Adam and Eve's posterity. To be born into such a physically condemned state (the *diabolos* within) is our misfortune, not our crime, so God doesn't hold us accountable for it. God only holds us responsible for our actual sins. Bro. Harry Tennant expresses the matter succinctly:

> *"The truth is simple: as a result of his transgression **Adam was condemned to die; his "very good" nature became evil. We physically inherit the results, but not the guilt, of that condemnation.** When we sin we come under personal condemnation, and deservedly so. The condemnation in our physical natures cannot be removed by baptism, by faith, by law or by anything other than a change to immortality at the hand of Christ should we be found faithful. The condemnation because of sin, however, can be removed by forgiveness through faithful baptism into the death of the Lord Jesus."*[28]

---

[25] BASF 12.

[26] BASF 8.

[27] BASF 5.

[28] Tennant, Harry, *The Nature of Christ*, The Testimony, vol. 58, 1988 pp. 234-237.

The scriptures supporting BASF 5 confirm that *"God's sentence"* in consequence of Adam and Eve's sin, which ***"became a physical law of Adam's being, and was transmitted to all his posterity"***, refer to all aspects of fallen human nature - subject to death, sin bias, disease and suffering. However, EC advocates believe that God, via evolution or miraculously in Adam and Eve's case, created human nature subject to all of this well before Adam and Eve sinned. Their view undermines the justice of God by making God the author of sin, death, disease and suffering, and hence the devil, all long before Adam and Eve sinned.

Man is the author of both sin and death (the devil), not God, as the apostle Paul states – *"By one man, sin entered into the world, and death by sin"* (Romans 5:12), and *"by one man's disobedience many were made sinners"* (Romans 5:19).

God brings evil in response to sin[29] yet has provided the hope of redemption to immortality through Jesus Christ (Isaiah 45:7, Amos 3:6, Romans 8:20-23, Genesis 3:15-19, Ecclesiastes 1:13-15; 3:10; 6:4; 7:13-14, Romans 5:16-19).

1 Corinthians 15:21 says, *"For since by man came death, by man came also the resurrection of the dead"*. Adam sinned, but only God could impose mortality and sin-bias as a permanent condition of human nature. Likewise, Christ was righteous, but only God could give him an immortal, sin-absent nature.

The final clauses of the BASF state that the purpose of the millennial reign of Christ will be *"to subdue all enemies, and finally death itself"* [30] so that *"the race* [of which Adam was the progenitor] *will be completely restored to the friendship of the Deity"*. [31]

However, believers in EC claim that mortality (a state of being subject to death) is not an enemy, but an essential mechanism used by God to 'create' by means of evolution over millions of years. Thus EC teaching makes mortality God's friend. Moreover, if Adam and Eve were not the sole forbears of our human race, as EC propounds, it would be impossible for our human race to be *"completely restored"* to the friendship of the Deity. This is because, in their view, there was no point in history when the *entire* human race actually enjoyed that friendship.

---

[29] See pp. 269-270 for Bro Thomas' exposition of this matter in Elpis Israel.

[30] BASF 28.

[31] BASF 30

Relevant clauses from the Birmingham Amended Statement of Faith

THE FOUNDATION — That the book currently known as **the Bible**, consisting of the Scriptures of Moses, the prophets, and the apostles, **is the only source of knowledge concerning God and His purposes at present extant or available in the earth**, and that the same were wholly given by inspiration of God in the writers, and are consequently without error in all parts of them, except such as may be due to errors of transcription or translation. (This paragraph was added in 1886.)

2 Timothy 3:16; 1 Corinthians 2:13; Hebrews 1:1; 2 Peter 1:21; 1 Corinthians 14:37; Nehemiah 9:30; John 10:35.

BASF 1 — That the only true God is He who was revealed to Abraham, Isaac, and Jacob, by angelic visitation and vision, and to Moses at the flaming bush (unconsumed) and at Sinai, and who manifested Himself in the Lord Jesus Christ, as the supreme self-existent Deity, the ONE FATHER, dwelling in unapproachable light, yet everywhere present by His Spirit, which is a unity with His person in heaven. **He hath, out of His own underived energy, created heaven and earth, and all that in them is**.

Isaiah 40:13-25; 43:10-12; 44:6–8; 45:5; 46:9-10; Job 38, 39, 40; Deuteronomy 6:4; Mark 12:29-32; 1 Corinthians 8:4-6; Ephesians 4:6; 1 Timothy 2:5; Nehemiah 9:6; Job 26:13; Psalm 124:8; 146:6; 148:5; Isaiah 40:26-27; Jeremiah 10:12-13; 27:5; 32:17-19; 51:15; Acts 14:15; 17:24; 1 Chronicles 29:11-14; Psalm 62:11; 145:3; Isaiah 26:4; 40:26; Job 9:4; 36:5; Psalm 92:5; 104:24; 147:4-5; Isaiah 28:29; Romans 16:27; 1 Timothy 1:17; 2 Chronicles 16:9; Job 28:24; 34:21; Psalm 33:13-14; 44:21; 94:9; 139 7-12; Proverbs 15:3; Jeremiah 23:24; 32:19; Amos 9:2-3; Acts 17:27-28; Psalm 123:1; 1 Kings 8:30, 39, 43, 49; Matthew 6:9; 1 Timothy 6:15-16; 1:17.

BASF 3 — That **the appearance of Jesus of Nazareth on the earth was necessitated by the position and state into which the human race** had been brought by the circumstances connected with **the first man**.

1 Corinthians 15:21-22; Romans 5:12-19; Genesis 3:19; 2 Corinthians 5:19-21.

BASF 4 — **That the first man was Adam**, whom God created out of the dust of the ground as a living soul, or natural body of life, **"very good" in kind and condition**, and placed him under a law through which the continuance of life was contingent on obedience.

Genesis 2:7; 18:27; Job 4:19; 33:6; 1 Corinthians 15:46-49; Genesis 2:17

BASF 5 — That Adam broke this law, and was adjudged unworthy of immortality, **and sentenced to return to the ground from whence he was taken – a sentence which defiled and became a physical law of his being, and was transmitted to all his posterity.**

Genesis 3:15-19, 22-23; 2 Corinthians 1:9; Romans 7:24; 2 Corinthians 5:2-4; Romans 7:18-23; Galatians 5:16-17; Romans 6:12; 7:21; John 3:6; Romans 5:12; 1 Corinthians 15:22; Psalm 51:5; Job 14:4.

BASF 6 —That God, in His Kindness, conceived **a plan of restoration** which, without setting aside **His just and necessary law of sin and death**, should ultimately **rescue the race from destruction**, and people the earth with sinless immortals.

Revelation 21:4; John 3:16; 2 Timothy 1:10; 1 John 2:25; 2 Timothy 1:1; Titus 1:2; Romans 3:26; John 1:29

BASF 7 — That **He inaugurated this plan by making promises to Adam, Abraham and David**, and afterwards elaborated it in greater detail through the prophets.

Genesis 3:15; 22:18; Psalm 89:34-37; 33:5; Hosea 13:14; Isa. 25:7-9; 51:1-8; Jer. 23:5.

BASF 8 — That these promises had reference to Jesus Christ, **who was to be raised up in the condemned line of Abraham and David**, and who, **though wearing their condemned nature**, was to obtain a title to resurrection by perfect obedience, and, by dying, **abrogate the law of condemnation for himself and all who should believe and obey him**.

1 Corinthians 15:45; Hebrews 2:14-16; Romans 1:3; Hebrews 5:8-9; Hebrews 1:9; Romans 5:19-21; Galatians 4:4-5; Romans 8:3-4; Hebrews 2:14-15; Hebrews 9:26; Galatians 1:4; Hebrews 7:27; 5:3-7; Hebrews 2:17; Romans 6:9-10; Acts 13:34-37; Revelation 1:18; John 5:21-22; John 5:26-27; 14:3; Revelation 2:7; Revelation 3:21; Matthew 25:21; Hebrews 5:9; Mark 16:16; Acts 13:38-39; Romans 3:22; Psalm 2:6-9; Daniel 7:13-14; Revelation 11:15; Jeremiah 23:5; Zechariah 14:9; Ephesians 1:9-10.

BASF 9 — That it was this mission that necessitated the miraculous begettal of Christ of a human mother, **enabling him to bear our condemnation,** and, at the same time, to be **a sinless bearer** thereof, and, therefore, one who could rise after suffering the death required by the righteousness of God.

Matthew 1:18-25; Luke 1:26-35; Galatians 4:4; Isaiah 7:14; Romans 1:3-4; Romans 8:3; 2 Corinthians 5:21; Hebrews 2:14-17; Hebrews 4:15.

BASF 10 — That being so begotten of God, and inhabited and used by God through the indwelling of the Holy Spirit, Jesus was Emmanuel, God with us, God manifested in the flesh-yet was, during his natural life, **of like nature with mortal man**, being made of a woman of the house and lineage of David, and **therefore a sufferer, in the days of his flesh, from all the effects that came by Adam's transgression including the death that passed upon all men, which he shared by partaking of their physical nature.**

Matthew 1:23; 1 Timothy 3:16; Hebrews 2:14; Galatians 4:4; Hebrews 2:17.

BASF 12 — That for delivering this message, he was put to death by the Jews and Romans, who were, however, but instruments in the hands of God, for the doing of that which He had determined before to be done, viz., **the condemnation of sin in the flesh**, through the offering of the body of Jesus once for all, as a propitiation to declare the righteousness of God, as a basis for the remission of sins. All who approach God through this crucified, but risen, representative of **Adam's disobedient race**, are forgiven. Therefore, by a figure, his blood cleanseth from sin.

Luke 19:47; Luke 20:1-16; John 11:45-53; Acts 10:38-39; Acts13:26-29; Acts 4:27-28; Romans 8:3; Hebrews 10:10; Acts 13:38; 1 John 1:7; John 14:6; Acts 4:12; 1 Peter 3:18; 1 Peter 2:24; Hebrews 9:14; Hebrews 7:27; Hebrews 9:26-28; Galatians 1:4; Romans 3:25; Romans 15:8; Galatians 3:21-22; Galatians 2:21; Galatians 4:4-5; Hebrews 9:15; Luke 22:20; Luke 24:26, 46-47; Matthew 26:28.

BASF 26 — That the Kingdom of God, thus constituted, will continue a thousand years, **during which sin and death will continue among the earth's subject inhabitants, though in a much milder degree than now.**

Revelation 20:4-9; 11:15; Isaiah 65:20; Ezekiel 44:22, 25; 1 Corinthians 15:24-28.

BASF 28 — That the mission of the Kingdom will be **to subdue all enemies, and finally death itself,** by opening up the way of life to the nations, which they will enter by faith, during the thousand years, and (in reality) at their close.   1 Corinthians 15:24-28

BASF 30 — That the government will then be delivered up by Jesus to the Father, who will manifest Himself as the "all-in-all"; **sin and death having been taken out of the way, and the race completely restored to the friendship of the Deity.** 1 Cor 15:28

The BASF should be read as originally intended

It is impossible to harmonise EC views with the intended meaning of the BASF. All brothers and sisters accept other brothers and sisters at their word when they assent to the BASF as the basis of fellowship. However, when EC proponents express their consent to the BASF, but in reality reject parts of it or adopt their own reading of certain clauses that they know is not what the original writers intended, then their belief conflicts with the basis of fellowship accepted by the vast majority of their brothers and sisters.

In this regard, the Christadelphian Committee in 1972 gave some sound advice in an article entitled *"Fellowship – Its Spirit and Practice"*:

> *If any man would play fast and loose with the Statement of Faith by driving his heretical chariot through "legal" loopholes in the wording, he has missed the meaning of fellowship and the proper use of our common basis. We are not to seek cover for any fundamental differences between ourselves and those with whom we are in fellowship by exploiting flaws in the human wording which gives expression to that fellowship. The warm spirit of fellowship which does exist between brethren throughout the world has grown in a community with the Statement of Faith as its agreed basis. It is not honourable to enjoy the one without accepting the other. If our views are unquestionably and fundamentally at variance with the plain intention of the Statement of Faith, then the honourable thing is to acknowledge this difference and to make it plain that we cannot subscribe to the apostles' doctrine and fellowship as understood by the Christadelphians. We must not mistake laxity for grace. We must uphold in a spirit of love and compassion the Statement upon which fellowship is based, but this does not mean that we need not observe it or call upon others to do so. Galatians 2:21 (R.V.); 1 Corinthians 14:40; 16:14.*

> ### The Need to Uphold the Basis:

> *We do rightly therefore, when interviewing prospective members of our community, to ensure for their sakes and ours that we have a common understanding and belief. It follows that any member who unquestionably departs from this position and does not respond to loving appeals to preserve the unity of belief, has already broken the bond of fellowship with his brethren and the ecclesia confirms this in its reluctant act of withdrawal. The same is true of behaviour unworthy of the name of Christ, if this is not repented of and acknowledged.*

> *Since each ecclesia has agreed to hold as the basis for its existence the written expression of its beliefs as found in the Statement of Faith, it is in honour bound to uphold that. Each ecclesia is the custodian for its own members of that common faith. The members have given willing assent to that faith when seeking fellowship with the ecclesia and the community of ecclesias which form the Brotherhood. No member may teach doctrines clearly inconsistent with that faith nor ought an ecclesia to retain in its fellowship one so acting. It is noteworthy that in*

> *his epistles Paul addresses individual ecclesias as though they were the whole household of God, and in his commendation of his fellow helpers from one ecclesia to another, assumes a spiritual relationship between them. Each ecclesia administers its own affairs, but it does so upon common principles which must be upheld. Our Brotherhood throughout the world exists only because we have agreed to behave in that way.*[32]

EC beliefs versus the Australian Unity Agreement

In Australia, Clause 1 (a) of the Australian Unity Agreement expresses an accepted understanding of Clauses 5 and 12 of the BASF. It does so in a manner that leaves no room for the accommodation of the EC position, by clearly stating that the mortal and sin-prone condition of human nature with which we are born came from Adam's sin.

> *"because of [Adam's] disobedience to God's Law, he was sentenced to return to the dust. He fell from his very good state, and suffered the consequences of sin – shame, a defiled conscience and mortality. **As his descendants, we partake of that mortality that came by sin, and inherit a nature, prone to sin."***

Elsewhere in the Australian Unity Agreement booklet, Bro Carter makes it plain that the "prone to sin" condition of human nature that arose when Adam and Eve lost their "very good state", and the impulses that lead to sin "are the result of sin at the beginning".

> *Through Adam's sin **the original very good state was lost, and his posterity inherit a nature with a tendency to sin to which all have succumbed.** Because this inherited tendency is so evident a characteristic of human nature, and **because it is the result and cause of sin, Paul by the use of metonymy can describe it as sin:** "It is no more I but sin that dwelleth in me." He gives it other names as well, such as "a law – evil present with me", the "flesh", "a law in my members" (Romans 7:14-25).*[33]

> *"But sufficient to notice that they experienced a sense of shame and the sentence was passed that 'dust thou art, and unto dust shalt thou return'. Here death came, as the Apostles say, into the world through sin. But by and by children are born. What is it that they inherit? This nature related to death, that had now become the lot of Adam and his wife…**What is it that is within us, that the apostle describes as sin? Clearly there are the impulses that lead to sin. There are impulses there that are the result of sin at the beginning, which we have by inheritance."***[34]

The condition of human nature with which we are born is metonymically described as "Sin" (or Sin's flesh). (See Chapter 20 for further discussion and examples of the use of metonymy in the Bible).

---

[32] The Christadelphian Committee, The Christadelphian, 1972, vol. 109, pp. 7-13, *Fellowship—Its Spirit and Practice*. See *Supplementary Material* for the full article.

[33] Carter, John, – *Unity Booklet*, 1958, p. 20.

[34] Carter, John, – *Unity Booklet*, 1958, p. 28-32.

The Australian unity basis of fellowship

Christadelphian Unity in Australia – the Accepted Basis, Central Standing Committee, Sydney 1963, pp. 13-15

(1) GENERAL BELIEFS

 (a) We agree that the doctrines to be believed and taught by us, without reservation, are the first principles of the One Faith as revealed in the Scriptures, of which the Birmingham Amended Statement of Faith (with positive and negative clauses and the Commandments of Christ) gives a true definition. **Clauses 5 and 12 are understood in harmony** with the explanations provided by Brethren Carter and Cooper reading:

> "We believe that **Adam** was made of the earth, and declared to be very good; **because of disobedience to God's Law, he was sentenced to return to the dust. He fell from his very good state, and suffered the consequences of sin – shame, a defiled conscience and mortality. As his descendants, we partake of that mortality that came by sin, and inherit a nature, prone to sin.** By our own actions we become sinners and stand in need of forgiveness of sins before we can be acceptable before God. Forgiveness and reconciliation God has provided by the offering of His Son; though Son of God, He partook of the same nature – the same flesh and blood as all of us, but did no sin. **In His death He voluntarily declared God's righteousness; God was honoured, and the flesh shown to be by divine appointment rightly related to death.** To share in God's forgiveness, we must be united with Christ by baptism into His death, rising from baptism dead to the past, to walk in newness of life. The form of baptism is a token of burial and of resurrection, and in submitting to it we identify ourselves with the principles established in **the death of Jesus "Who died unto sin", recognising that God is righteous in decreeing that the wages of sin is death, and that as members of the race, we are rightly related to a dispensation of death.** In all His appointments, God wills to be honoured, sanctified and hallowed by all who approach to Him. **By His promises God sets before man a hope of life and a prospect of resuming those relationships that are lost by sin.** With the setting forth of this hope, there comes a new basis of responsibility. Times of ignorance God overlooks, but with knowledge a man becomes accountable, and a responsible creature with the obligation to believe and obey God."

(b) Acceptance of this basis would not preclude the use of any other adequate Statement of Faith by an ecclesia, **provided this is in harmony with the B.A.S.F.** understood as in Clause I (a) above.

(2) FELLOWSHIP: It is affirmed that:

(a) Where any brethren depart from any element of the One Faith, either in doctrine or practice, they shall be dealt with according to the Apostolic precept and that extreme action would be ecclesial disfellowship of the offender. (Matthew 18:15-17; Titus 3:10-11).

(b) If it is established that an ecclesia sets itself out by design to preach and propagate at large false doctrine, then it would become necessary to dissociate from such an ecclesia.

(c) The course of action necessitated by the above clauses (a) and (b), will be regulated by the principles of the Scripture and follow the spirit of the Ecclesial Guide, Sections 32, 41 and 42.

The Cooper Carter Addendum (CCA) was designed to be in harmony with BASF 5 and 12

Some EC adherents claim that one of the purposes of the AUA, specifically the CCA within the AUA booklet, was to fix the error of certain clauses in the BASF, particularly the wording of clause 5.[35] However, this is not the case. The very first paragraph 1 (a) of the Basis of Fellowship in the AUA emphasizes that the Cooper-Carter reading was designed to be understood in harmony with clauses 5 and 12. It was not written to replace, supersede or correct them.[36]

> *"We agree that the doctrines to be believed and taught by us, **without reservation**, are the first principles of the One Faith as revealed in the Scriptures, **of which the Birmingham Amended Statement of Faith** (with positive and negative clauses and the Commandments of Christ) **gives a true definition. Clauses 5 and 12 are understood in harmony** with the explanations provided by Brethren Carter and Cooper, reading:"*

BASF Clause 5 itself quotes several verses, including Genesis 3:15-19, 22-23; 1 Corinthians 15:22; 2 Corinthians 1:9; 5:2-4; Romans 5:12; 6:12; 7:18-24; Galatians 5:16-17; Psalm 51:5 and Job 14:4, in support of the expression that God's sentence *"defiled and became a physical law of his being, and was transmitted to all his posterity"*. A review of these scriptures makes it evident that BASF 5 is referring to the condition of human nature that is: a) death-stricken; b) biased to sin; and c) subject to disease and suffering.

The term *"physical law of his being"* (Clause 5), is lexically cohesive with the *"law of sin and death"* (Clause 6), *"condemned line"*, *"condemned nature"*, *"the law of condemnation"* (Clause 8), *"our condemnation"* (Clause 9), and *"sin in the flesh"* (Clause 12). They all refer to the fallen condition of human nature (the *diabolos* within).

---

[35] For example, Bro Jonathan Burke, in his interpretation of the BASF included in Appendix 3 of the Taipei Christadelphian Ecclesia Timeline, makes the comment: *"The Cooper-Carter Addendum rewrites this Clause [5] significantly, omitting any reference to Adam becoming defiled, or anything becoming 'a physical law of his being'."* Also, on page 9 of the Taipei Ecclesia Timeline, Bro Jonathan is quoted as stating: *"I have already made it totally clear that the Cooper-Carter Addendum states truth when it says Adam suffered a defiled conscience as a consequence [sic] sin, but that the Cooper-Carter Addendum states error when it says Adam suffered mortality as a consequence of sin. This is little better than the BASF, which states falsely that Adam suffered a defiled nature as a consequence of sin (an error the Cooper-Carter Addendum abandoned, substituting 'defiled conscience' instead), but does not state Adam suffered mortality as a consequence of sin".* *Taipei Christadelphian Ecclesia Timeline*, distributed to all ACBM Regional Committees and the ecclesias they represent, 25 October 2016.

[36] Likewise, any first principle book or notes that we use to preach the one true gospel should be "in harmony" with the plain intended meaning of the clauses in our BASF. What we require baptismal candidates to accept prior to baptism doesn't have to follow word for word all of the clauses in the BASF but it should be in harmony with the doctrines taught across all of the clauses in the BASF. These doctrines should be taught and accepted without reservation.

Placing the wording of the CCA alongside BASF 5 makes it obvious that both accounts are in harmony with each other.

BASF 5 (as written)	Australian Unity Agreement: Cooper-Carter Addendum (re-arranged to match BASF 5)
That Adam **broke this law**	*because of **disobedience** to God's law*
and was **adjudged unworthy** of immortality	*He [Adam] **fell from his very good state***
and sentenced to **return to the ground**	*sentenced to **return to the dust***
from whence **he was taken**	*Adam was **made of the earth***
A sentence which **defiled**	*Suffered the consequences of sin – shame, a **defiled** conscience and mortality*
and became a **physical law of his being**	***mortality** and a **nature prone to sin***
and was **transmitted** to all his [Adam's] **posterity**	*As [Adam's] **descendants, we partake** of that mortality that came by sin and **inherit a nature**, prone to sin* *Jesus partook of **the same nature** … In his death … **the flesh** shown to be by divine appointment **rightly related to death.*** *… God is righteous in decreeing that the wages of sin is death, and that **as members of the race we are rightly related to a dispensation of death***

To argue that the BASF *"…does not state Adam suffered mortality as a consequence of sin"* is false as the BASF says, Adam *"broke the law"* and as a result was *"sentenced to return to the ground"* and this *"sentence…became a physical law of his being"* i.e. mortality.

That this is Bible and Christadelphian teaching is confirmed by the Scriptures on which Clause 5 is based, numerous Christadelphian expositions of the events in Eden, the atonement and studies in the Statement of Faith itself.

The following quotations from Bro HP Mansfield and Bro Tecwyn Morgan clearly express how Christadelphians have understood BASF 5 with respect to the expression *"a sentence which defiled and became a physical law of his being …"*

HP Mansfield, *"Adamic Condemnation: Legal or Physical?"* Logos Magazine, 1971, vol. 37, pp. 134-137

A careful consideration of the evidence will reveal **that Adamic condemnation is physical, and not legal or moral.** If it were the latter, it would imply the imputation of guilt on every person born without him or her doing anything to deserve that guilt. That would make God unjust. **Physical condemnation, however, constituted the carrying out of the death penalty on Adam by bringing him under the curse of mortality. The mortality inflicted on Adam was inherited by his descendants. They are mortal because of sin, and in this weakened physical state, inherit a nature which is dominated by the lusts of the flesh, which were aggravated, or inflamed, by sin in the first instance.**

So mankind is no longer in the "very good" state of original creation (Genesis 1:31), but as described by God in Genesis 8:21, as "evil from youth".

This, as Brother Thomas declares in *Elpis Israel*, is our misfortune not our crime. It is something we must try to conquer in the strength derived through Christ (Philippians 4:13). We are only held accountable when knowing the means devised by *Yahweh* to control its influence, we refuse to use them. When a person knowingly and blatantly rejects the Truth he will be brought up from the dead for judgment.

… Brother Roberts … clearly showed that the nature of the defilement was physical. This, however, had its reaction upon man's mental condition, for, as a result of sin, he inherited "a nature prone to sin." This "proneness to sin" is so strong, that despite all efforts to the contrary, the most faithful have succumbed to it apart from the Lord Jesus. He did not do so, for he was strengthened of God (Psalm 80:17) to succeed, in the mission of mercy initiated by the Father for the salvation of those who will come unto Him in faith.

Tecwyn Morgan, *Clause V*, Studies in the Statement of Faith, 1991, pp. 26-27
… In what sense can the sentence that was passed upon Adam be regarded as something that "defiles" us? …

In addition to the physical condition of his body, making the grave his certain destiny, Adam's sin also created in him something which affected all his future actions. Once he had made a wilfully wrong choice, his "knowledge of good and evil" was awakened. Before, he had known what "evil" was by definition – it was the breach of God's Law. After, he knew about evil by his experience, and it left a bitter after-taste. He could never again have the guileless innocence that existed when he was created. He was immediately ashamed of his actions; they "hid themselves from the presence of the LORD God amongst the trees of the garden" (Genesis 3:8), and this separation from God featured in all of his future life. **Henceforth temptation would arise both from without and from within. Just as mortality became the experience of all human life, the inner tendency or propensity to please self rather than God was also passed on to all his descendants, for Adam's knowledge of good and evil was inherited by all his children:** now it is invariably the case that, "every man is tempted, when he is drawn away of his own lust and enticed" (James 1:14).

For these reasons Scripture styles the nature we bear "sinful flesh". It has been inherited by all mankind, as Scripture testifies frequently. Consider Jeremiah 17:9; Mark 7:20-22; Psalm 51:5; Romans 7:18,24; Galatians 5:17; James 1:14-15

It is important to recognise that we are not to blame because of these tendencies: they are inherited, and not our fault. In the same way, we die because our bodies have an inbuilt obsolescence; we are dying creatures from our birth onwards.

Chapter 5
Christadelphian Precedents

Evolutionary Creation views rejected in the past

A number of current arguments on this subject in Christadelphian circles are not new. These same arguments were addressed decades before both the 1960s and in recent discussions. They were roundly rejected in the past and should be rejected again. History is repeating itself. The table below provides three examples.

Assertion by EC Proponents	Already Addressed In Christadelphian Writings
Adam was not the first man of our human race. Other 'evolved' men were his contemporaries. **Adam was the first man that God revealed His laws to, or the first man to come into a covenant relationship with God.**	In the 1888 Christadelphian Vol. 25, pp. 618- 619, Bro Robert Roberts wrote, *"That there was a first man, from whom the whole race of mankind…have been derived, is among the first things revealed in the Scriptures… the fact that Adam was formed directly from the dust of the ground shows that he was an original creation, and the first of his kind, as Paul afterwards calls him in the words "the first man Adam was made a living soul" (1 Corinthians 15:45). Observe! The first man "made,' not the first man whom God took into covenant-relation. … to say that Adam was not the only man then existing on the face of the earth is to introduce confusion… more than that, it is to introduce an element that is entirely excluded by all the facts of the case." (see page 246)*
Adam was either created mortal or inherited mortality from an evolved pre-Adamic race. **Adam's punishment for sin was not the sentence of returning to dust but 'eternal' death, because he was already mortal.**	This same argument has been made in the past and was answered by Bro John Carter in the 1938 Christadelphian pp. 173-174: *"The theory is being put forward that death belongs inevitably to the body of man as he was created; that Adam in course of time would have died apart from having disobeyed the law of God; and that the sentence of death imposed for sin is the "second death". We die, according to this view, because it is a law of our nature, and not because of any sentence which has been passed by God upon Adam, and which has involved all his descendants. To those who know the Scriptures the simple statement of this theory would almost seem sufficient to condemn it. But Scripture testimony is twisted to fit the idea, and some are deceived." (see page 300)*
Actual sin is only possible when a person knows the law of God	Bro Islip Collyer addressed this question in the 1896 Christadelphian pp. 99-102: *"Because sin is defined as the 'transgression of the law', some have supposed that those who are not under the law in a definite specific sense cannot sin. This is obviously incorrect. In the second chapter of Romans the apostle declares that those who have sinned without law shall also perish without law; while those who have sinned in the law shall be judged by the law (Romans 2:12)." (see page 307)*

Alternative views - age of the earth and days of creation

The assertion is correct that Christadelphians have tolerated different views on the age of the earth and whether the six days of creation were six 24-hour periods or not. Speculations about the earth's physical history, and the relationship of scientific thought to the Scriptures, have been tolerated within the bounds of what the Bible conveys on the origin of our human race and how Adam and Eve's sin impacted all of humanity.

In *Elpis Israel,* Bro Thomas suggested that the angels could have come from a pre-Adamic creation (not a pre-Adamic evolution) on this earth.[37] Later, when he wrote Phanerosis, Bro Thomas believed that the angels *"are not aboriginal to an earthborn race"* and *"to what orb or planet of the universe they are indigenous, is not revealed"* [38]. Importantly, Bro Thomas is very clear in Elpis Israel that even if life had existed upon the earth in a previous creation, it was completely destroyed prior to God's six literal days of creative activity as recorded in Genesis 1. He believed that all life upon the earth, as we know it today, stems from these six literal days of miraculous activity.[39] Most later Christadelphians have followed this line, which can be summarised as an old-earth but new-creation (OENC) view.

Other Christadelphians hold a young-earth creation perspective (YEC). That the earth itself is only 6,000 years old and, in common with the OENC view, the six days of God's creation were six 24-hour periods of miraculous activity from which all life on the earth today originated.

Bro Alan Hayward proposed that the six literal days were days on which the divine fiats were given but with long ages in between, and Bro A. D. Norris theorized that the six literal days were those in which visions of creation were given to Moses. Others have proposed that the six days were long periods of time.

The critical point is that none of these brethren believed in man's evolution from primaeval animals, that humanity today has descended from a pre- or co-Adamic race, or that Adam was a descendant of evolved men.

They all believed and taught that Adam and Eve were miraculously created, and that there was a post-fall change in the condition of Adam and Eve's nature to mortality and bias to sin that the entire human race has inherited from them (see the table overleaf).

---

[37] Thomas, J, Elpis Israel (1866), pp.10-11, 1983 ed.
[38] Thomas, J, Phanerosis (1869), p.56, Logos 1969 ed.
[39] Thomas, J, Elpis Israel (1866), pp.11-12, 1983 ed.

<table>
<tr><td colspan="2">All Christadelphians, despite differing views on the age of the earth and days of creation:</td></tr>
<tr><td>Believed in</td><td>Did not believe in</td></tr>
<tr><td>A real Adam and Eve who were the parents of our entire human race (BASF 3,4).</td><td>Adam and Eve who merely shared in the origins of our human race, but were the first humans with which God entered into a covenant relationship.</td></tr>
<tr><td>A real Adam who was created miraculously from the dust of the ground, and Eve from his side (BASF 4).</td><td>Adam and Eve who were descendants of an evolved pre-Adamic human race.</td></tr>
<tr><td>A real Adam who was created neither mortal nor immortal, but with a natural body that was "very good" in kind and condition[40] (BASF 4).</td><td>Adam who was either created mortal[41] (subject to death) or inherited mortality from the alleged evolved humans from which he descended.</td></tr>
<tr><td>A real Adam who was created without a sin-prone nature (BASF 4,5).</td><td>Adam who had a sin-prone nature before he sinned, whether created by God or inherited from evolved humans.</td></tr>
<tr><td>A real Adam whose sin resulted in a change to the mortality inherited by our entire human race, along with labour, suffering, a cursed earth, and ultimately dissolution in the grave (BASF 5, 6).</td><td>Adam whose sin meant that a) he was left to suffer the natural consequence of his existing mortal body (decay and death); and b) "eternal death" was introduced.</td></tr>
<tr><td>A Lord Jesus Christ whose appearance on the earth was necessitated by the position and state into which the human race had been brought by Adam and Eve (BASF 3).</td><td>A Lord Jesus Christ whose appearance was necessitated by the way God created/evolved all humans from the outset.</td></tr>
<tr><td>A Lord Jesus Christ who came into the world to conquer the effects of Adam's sin – a mortal nature with a predisposition toward sin (BASF 8, 9, 10).</td><td>A Lord Jesus Christ who had the same mortal and sin-prone nature with which God created/evolved all humans from the outset, but was not subject to the "eternal death" introduced by Adam.</td></tr>
</table>

---

[40] See Chapter 17 for an explanation of these words from BASF 4.

[41] While some of the earlier writings of Bro Thomas and Bro Roberts may appear to be ambiguous on this subject it is clear from their subsequent writings that they firmly believed that mortality followed the fall. See Section 6, pages 263 to 290 for Bro Thomas' and Bro Roberts' remarks on this particular point. Those arguing that Adam was created mortal will often quote an article by Bro Roberts in the 1869 Christadelphian (pp. 83-86) and claim that Bro Roberts supports their position. In a number of subsequent articles and later in response to criticism by Bro George Cornish in Melbourne, Bro Roberts makes it clear that he did not believe that Adam was created mortal. The 1869 article and Bro Roberts' subsequent clarification and replies are reproduced in full over pages 65 to 77 of the *Supplementary Material* of *By One Man*. Bro Roberts wrote the bulk of the Statement of Faith, which clearly states that man was not created mortal.

Believed in	Did not believe in
A Lord Jesus Christ whose miraculous begettal in a human mother enabled him to be a sinless bearer of our sin-prone nature (BASF 9).	A Lord Jesus Christ who was uniquely used by God, but whose divine begettal did not strengthen him to overcome sin.
A Lord Jesus Christ who through faith resisted temptation, culminating in his victory over our fallen human nature through his sacrificial death, resurrection and immortalization (BASF 8,9,10,12).	A Lord Jesus Christ who was victorious over the same condition of human nature with which God created/evolved Adam from the outset.
A Lord Jesus Christ whose life, death and resurrection destroyed the physical law of condemnation (the diabolos) for himself and eventually for all who believe and obey him (BASF 8).	A Lord Jesus Christ who died in a substitutionary manner to save all who believe and obey him.
A Lord Jesus Christ who in his death destroyed the diabolos, which is the personification of our fallen sin-biased mortal nature (Hebrews 2:14; Matthew 4:1-11; Genesis 3:15; John 3:14, BASF 8,9,10).	A Lord Jesus Christ who through death destroyed the diabolos, which either personifies a state of mind in opposition to God (EC View A) or the condition of human nature as created/evolved by God before Adam and Eve sinned (EC View B).
A Lord Jesus Christ who came into the world to **restore** the human race to fellowship with God that Adam's sin destroyed (BASF 3, 12, 28, 30).	A Lord Jesus Christ who came to **provide** for the human race fellowship with God.[42]

Hence there are very sharp differences between Christadelphian beliefs and those of Evolutionary Creation. It would be a huge mistake to argue that, because views on issues not central to the means of our salvation have been tolerated in the past, this tolerance can be transferred to interpretations that amount to a system of belief, which undermines what Christadelphians accept as the Bible's essential teaching.

An important case study: the Watford Ecclesia and Brother Lovelock

To move away from these beliefs, upheld by all Christadelphians who accept the BASF, would be destructive of the atonement, the plan and purpose of God as revealed in the Scriptures and long-established Christadelphian teaching.

---

[42] As EC advocates believe in many evolved humans living in ignorance before Adam, it would be impossible under this view for Jesus to "restore" the human race to fellowship with God, as there was never a historic point when the human race was in fellowship with God.

This is why Bro Lovelock's position in the 1960s became untenable, and why evolution or any form of EC teaching that man evolved from animals is just as untenable today.

The Watford Arranging Brethren endeavoured patiently to reach an acceptable middle ground with Bro Lovelock that would not conflict with our BASF. They asked him *"to abandon the relationship he had conjectured between Adam and the man-like creatures"*, so that *"the two views could live together among us to the edification and well-being of the community"*.[43]

They explained why it matters doctrinally: *"The theory concerning the relationship between Adam and the antecedent and concurrent homo sapiens race requires that our need of redemption from sin is irrespective of our descent from Adam, an idea which is irreconcilable with our understanding of Scripture."* [44]

Because Bro Lovelock could not accept that Adam was the progenitor of the entire human race, they concluded that acceptance of Bro Lovelock's views would *"destroy the distinctive characteristics of the Christadelphian community"*. They could *"only recommend to the ecclesia that Brother Lovelock's views…be rejected as contrary to our common faith and understanding, and as ultimately destructive of the well-being of the Brotherhood in true faith and fellowship."*[45]

Similarly, Brother Sargent expressed in the Christadelphian in 1965 that our community's objection to accepting any EC scenario is not just due to a difference in interpreting the early chapters of Genesis, **but because it does not fit with the essential elements of the one true faith** with respect to the fall, the atonement, the nature of revelation, and the character of the Kingdom of God:

> *"Now, it is true that there are devout Christians such as Professor C. A. Coulson who take a strictly uniformitarian view of the universe and believe that evolution can be regarded as God's method in creation. The objection to this does not rest only, or even mainly, on the early chapters of Genesis. It is that an evolutionary view does not fit in with essential elements of the Faith; where it is adopted there must sooner or later be changes in the Biblical conceptions of the Fall and Atonement, in the nature of revelation, in the literal fact of resurrection, and in the character of the Kingdom of God. Of this there is abundant example in the teaching of the churches around us where an evolutionary philosophy has come to be accepted. If adopted among us I am convinced that it would in time pervade the whole of our belief and change it as the doctrine of the Immortality of the Soul changed the belief of the early church."* [46]

---

[43] *Statement from the Watford Ecclesia,* The Christadelphian, vol. 103, 1966, pp. 543-547.

[44] Ibid.

[45] Ibid.

[46] Sargent, LG, *The Origin of Man*, The Christadelphian, 1965, vol. 102, p. 340.

Watford Ecclesia Statement

Watford Arranging Brethren, The Christadelphian, vol. 103, 1966, pp. 543-547

1. We believe that Adam was the physical progenitor of the whole race with whom God's redemptive purpose is concerned.

2. Whilst we do not claim to know in literal detail either the time taken or the methods used by God in creating Adam, we believe that Adam came into being as the purposed result of God's creative activity, and that he was distinct in kind from the animal world, the fishes, the birds, and the beasts of the field, this distinctiveness of kind being indicated by the scriptural record that "God created man in His own image". We understand this to involve that man, unlike the animals, was endowed with moral and intellectual faculties enabling him to receive and respond to divine revelation.

3. We believe that, possessed of this moral and intellectual capacity, in the beginning Adam was placed in Eden under a law, disobedience to which would bring death into his experience; that he disobeyed this law and was in consequence condemned to die; and that he was expelled from the Garden of Eden, henceforth to experience sorrow, hardship and pain.

4. We believe that the disastrous consequences of Adam's transgression were not restricted to himself, but affected all his descendants, so that:

    a. the death which Adam came to know became the natural lot of all his descendants;

    b. we inherit from Adam our own predisposition to sin—a predisposition which is transmitted to us from Adam the sinner as a "law" bound to our physical bodies from which, with Paul, we cry for deliverance; and

    c. we die, therefore, because we inherit Adam's sin-stricken and dying nature, and we confirm death as our proper individual due by each yielding to the sinful impulses transmitted from Adam to all his descendants.

5. We believe that we can be delivered from this situation and reconciled to God only through the saving activity of God Himself through His son Jesus Christ; and that Jesus opened the way to this deliverance:

    a. by sharing the nature which we all inherit from Adam (including its predisposition to sin and its mortality);

    b. by resisting unto death the power of sin in that nature; and

    c. by offering his body upon the Cross once for all as a propitiation for the sins of all men.

6. After the fullest consideration, we find ourselves unable to reconcile with these beliefs a theory which involves that Adam and his descendants preached the revealed God to a race of man-like creatures who were not men, but became men on contact with the revelation, were able to inter-marry with Adam's descendants, and together with Adam's descendants, became the forerunners of the human race as we know it. We have to reject this theory because:

    a. it presents a fundamentally different view of man, and of the human situation before God, from that outlined in paragraphs (1) to (5) above; and

    b. it is not taught in Scripture and can only be accommodated to Scripture teaching by interpretations likely to undermine foundation truths of our faith.

The Watford experience compared with today

Bro Lovelock's false teaching was regarded as a fellowship matter in the 1960s. It is hard to understand why the same false teaching today, of evolved pre-Adamic and co-Adamic hominids or humans that share the ancestry of our human race, should be regarded as matters of uncertain detail with no implications for an individual's fellowship standing.

Back then, brethren appealed to Bro Lovelock to return to believing essential Bible truths as expressed in our statement of faith. [47] Likewise, the material presented in *By One Man* is, in effect, an appeal to those who today follow a similar line to that of Bro Lovelock, to return to believing Bible truths essential for salvation.

By One Man's intention is not to discourage musing on, and discussion of, the subject of creation (such speculation has always happened in the Christadelphian community). Nor is it concerned with those who are genuinely trying to come to grips with this subject.

Rather, *By One Man's* purpose is to contrast Scriptural and consistent Christadelphian teaching, regarding Adam and Eve and the entry of sin and death into the world, to the firm belief and teaching of those who have departed from the doctrinal elements of the "One Faith". Particularly those who "propagate at large false doctrine" and, in so doing, have the potential to rob their brothers and sisters of saving truth (see the AUA's fellowship clause on page 30).

Sometimes those who are inclined to accommodate unsound doctrines use the parable of the *"tares and wheat"* in Matthew 13:24-30, 36-43 to suggest that we should leave the matter for Christ to determine when he returns. They claim that the *"field"* is the ecclesia and the *"tares"* and *"wheat"* are two classes within the ecclesia who remain together until the end of the *"world"*.

This view rejects the Lord's own interpretation that the *"field"* is the *"world"*, the *"tares"* are the *"children of the wicked"* in the world around us *"sown by the diabolos"*, and the *"wheat"* the *"children of the kingdom"* sown by *"the Son of Man"*. The Lord is describing the day-to-day conflict all true believers will have with their own nature and the godless

---

[47] It is interesting to note that a significant proportion of Christadelphian writers wrote on this subject in the 1960s, prior to and around the time of the Watford Ecclesia's decision to withdraw fellowship from Bro Ralph Lovelock in 1966. English brethren John Carter, Islip Collyer, WF Barling, AD Norris, LG Sargent, and the Watford Arranging Brethren, in the 1960s, were all endeavouring to reach an acceptable "common" ground with Bro Lovelock. These brethren acknowledged that different views on God's method of creation could exist providing they did not overthrow the plain teaching of our BASF that Adam was the progenitor of the entire human race as we know it, and that as a result of his sin all inherit a death-stricken nature with a tendency to sin. They had no desire to withdraw from a much loved and respected brother.

environment that surrounds them in the world at large. The idea that false teachers should be allowed to remain, as a disrupting influence in the ecclesia, conflicts with the Lord's own teaching and that of the apostles (see the scriptures listed below).

Therefore, the parable cannot mean that false teachers, openly attempting to *"draw away disciples after themselves"* (Acts 20:28-31), should be allowed to retain a place in the ecclesia. [48] This was the decision very reluctantly arrived at by the Watford Arranging Brethren.

The Warning From Scripture on False Teachers

Matthew 7:15-20 Beware of false prophets, which come to you in sheep's clothing, but inwardly they are ravening wolves. 16 Ye shall know them by their fruits …

Acts 20:28-31 Take heed therefore unto yourselves, and to all the flock … 29 For I know this, that after my departing shall grievous wolves enter in among you, not sparing the flock. 30 Also of your own selves shall men arise, speaking perverse things, to draw away disciples after them. 31 Therefore watch, and remember, that by the space of three years I ceased not to warn every one night and day with tears.

Romans 16:17-19 Now I beseech you, brethren, mark them which cause divisions and offences contrary to the doctrine which ye have learned; and avoid them. 18 For they that are such serve not our Lord Jesus Christ, but their own belly; and by good words and fair speeches deceive the hearts of the simple. …

Galatians 1:6-8 I marvel that ye are so soon removed from him that called you into the grace of Christ unto another gospel: 7 Which is not another; but there be some that trouble you, and would pervert the gospel of Christ. 8 But though we, or an angel from heaven, preach any other gospel unto you than that which we have preached unto you, let him be accursed.

1 Timothy 1:3 As I besought thee to abide still at Ephesus, when I went into Macedonia, that thou mightest charge some that they teach no other doctrine

Titus 3:10-11 (ESV) As for a person who stirs up division, after warning him once and then twice, have nothing more to do with him, …

2 Thessalonians 3:14-15 And if any man obey not our word by this epistle, note that man, and have no company with him, that he may be ashamed. 15 Yet count him not as an enemy, but admonish him as a brother.

1 John 4:1 Beloved, believe not every spirit, but try the spirits whether they are of God: because many false prophets are gone out into the world.

2 John 1:7-10 For many deceivers are entered into the world, who confess not that Jesus Christ is come in the flesh. This is a deceiver and an antichrist. 8 Look to yourselves, that we lose not those things which we have wrought, but that we receive a full reward. 9 Whosoever transgresseth, and abideth not in the doctrine of Christ, hath not God. He that abideth in the doctrine of Christ, he hath both the Father and the Son. 10 If there come any unto you, and bring not this doctrine, receive him not into your house, neither bid him God speed.

---

[48] See Carter, John, *Parables of the Messiah,* pp. 92-99.

Revelation 2:14-16 But I have a few things against thee, because thou hast there them that hold the doctrine of Balaam, who taught Balac to cast a stumblingblock before the children of Israel, to eat things sacrificed unto idols, and to commit fornication. 15 So hast thou also them that hold the doctrine of the Nicolaitans, which thing I hate. 16 Repent; or else I will come unto thee quickly …

Revelation 2:20 Notwithstanding I have a few things against thee, because thou sufferest that woman Jezebel, which calleth herself a prophetess, to teach and to seduce my servants to commit fornication, and to eat things sacrificed unto idols.

See also Matthew 18:15-17; 2 Corinthians 11:3-4,13-15; 2 Thessalonians 2:3,15; 1 Timothy 1:18-20; Titus 1:9-11.

Chapter 6
Defending Christadelphian Foundations

Most Christadelphian authors disagree with EC

The table on the following page is based on Christadelphian expositors who wrote between the 1850s and 1990s, from John Thomas to Michael Ashton. It firstly presents each writer's view on the age of the earth and the days of creation. The remaining columns summarize each writer's belief on the origin of the present human race, and the condition of human nature. Confirmation of what the Christadelphian writers wrote on these subjects is provided in Section 6.

Based on the quotations found, they rejected the idea that humans evolved from animals and taught that the fallen condition of our nature resulted from Adam and Eve's sin. Moreover, they believed that the "devil" is the Bible's way of personifying this sin-biased, fallen condition of human nature with its *"power of death"* (Hebrews 2:14). It follows that none of the authors listed could agree with EC. While some expressed different views on the age of the earth or the six-days of creation, such speculations do not impact our understanding of the atonement or any clauses in the BASF.

Essential truths must be upheld

It is not surprising that our leading magazines, in the past few years and to the present, have all run series of articles opposing Theistic Evolution/Evolutionary Creation and those who promote it (see Further Reading). Once the line has been crossed, from musing and speculation into challenging the fundamentals of our scripturally based faith, the ecclesial world is duty-bound to resist the teaching of such destructive error. Today the Christadelphian community must continue to reject evolutionary ideas that inevitably undermine what Scripture teaches.

Ecclesias are obliged to maintain the BASF. As the AUA states, *"We agree that the doctrines to **be believed and taught** by us, without reservation, are the first principles of the One Faith as revealed in the Scriptures, of which the BASF (with positive and negative clauses and the Commandments of Christ) gives a true definition."*[49]

---

[49] Australian Unity Agreement – Clause 1a.

Summary Table: Christadelphian Authors – Creation and the Atonement

	View on age of the earth and days of creation in Genesis 1	1. No humans have evolved. Adam the progenitor of humanity		2. What Adam's sin introduced, God made a physical law:		3. The Devil: personification of fallen human nature.
		a) Did our human race evolve from lower animal forms?[b]	b) Adam miraculously created and the progenitor of our entire human race?	a) Human nature became mortal (subject to death)?	b) Human nature became prone to sin?	
John Thomas	OE, NC in 6 literal days[a]	No	Yes	Yes	Yes	Yes
Robert Roberts	OE, NC in 6 literal days	No	Yes	Yes	Yes	Yes
LB Welch	OE, NC in 6 literal days	No	Yes	Yes	Yes	Yes
CC Walker	OE, day = age/epoch	No	Yes	Yes	Yes	Yes
Henry Sulley	OE, day = age/epoch	No	Yes	Yes	Yes	Yes
John Carter	OE, day = age/epoch	No	Yes	Yes	Yes	Yes
Islip Collyer		No	Yes	Yes	Yes	Yes
WF Barling		No*	Yes	Yes	Yes	Yes
AD Norris	OE, day = each vision of creation	No	Yes	Yes	Yes	Yes
LG Sargent	OE possible, NC	No	Yes	Yes [c]	Yes	Yes

Watford ABs	OE possible, NC	No	Yes	Yes	Yes	
E Whittaker	NC in 6 literal days	No	Yes	Yes	Yes	
Peter Watkins	OE, day = fiat/edicts	No*	Yes	Yes	Yes	Yes
Alfred Nicholls		No	Yes	Yes	Yes	Yes
Alan Hayward	OE, day = fiat/edicts	No	Yes	Yes	Yes	Yes
HP Mansfield	OE, NC in 6 literal days	No	Yes	Yes	Yes	Yes
H Whittaker	OE, NC in 6 literal days	No	Yes	Yes [c]	Yes	Yes
Harry Tennant		No	Yes	Yes	Yes	Yes
Michael Ashton	NC in 6 literal days	No*	Yes	Yes	Yes	Yes
EC	OE, various interpretations	Yes	No	No	No	No

Note: The blank cells indicate that we were unable to find quotations to confirm the writer's view, one way or the other.

[a] Old Earth, New Creation of all life in six literal days

[b] Partially or fully, and with specific reference to the ancestry of all people on the earth today.

[c] For clarification that Brethren LG Sargent and H Whittaker did not believe that Adam and Eve were created "subject to death", and that the condition of their nature was physically changed post sin, please refer to their writings included in *By One Man*, and to the specific discussion of this point on page 330.

* While we could not find categorical statements by these writers rejecting the notion that humans evolved, this is precluded by their positive assertion that Adam was miraculously created and is the progenitor of our entire human race.

Because EC views undermine core Christadelphian teaching, it follows that the same principles of ecclesial action that would apply to the promulgation and firm belief of any other false teaching (e.g. the Trinity, immortality of the soul, fallen angel devil, kingdom of God in heaven etc.) also apply to the promulgation of EC.

Unfortunately, those openly teaching these unscriptural ideas are brothers and sisters in Christ who are loved. Deep down, the last thing in ecclesial life that anybody wants is to be in conflict with them. We all know how hard it is to bring our young within, and people without, to the waters of baptism, so no brother or sister takes pleasure in seeing any brother or sister leave, much less like Bro Lovelock be required to leave, our community. Therefore, the main aim of anyone defending the Christadelphian view is to convince those promoting a non-biblical and unChristadelphian view to return to Bible truth as it is expressed in our Statement of Faith.

The source of the problem

Why is this subject even being discussed? Why has so much tension, in some parts of the ecclesial world, been created between brethren who hitherto were able "to dwell together in unity"?

Our community's current distress goes back to a group of brethren who have spent many years promoting their EC views, mainly on the Internet. The younger generation is particularly vulnerable to the arguments presented, as it is more involved in the world of cyberspace. That EC views are communicated privately is not of itself an issue. Rather, the active promotion of their unscriptural and unChristadelphian views, on both their own public sites and many popular Christadelphian social media forums, has become a severe issue in the ecclesial world.

So far, the promotion of EC has led to:

- withdrawals of fellowship of some promoters of EC
- the IEAC[50] and some other ecclesias producing reaffirmations of Christadelphian beliefs that oppose EC
- an extraordinary meeting of the ACBM National Committee to discuss disruption in mission areas over this issue
- an Australian Conference motion for the AACE[51] to examine the problem and provide a document for the Australian ecclesias to consider
- tension between brethren, ecclesial splits, strained relations between some ecclesias, interfamily and intrafamily tensions

---

[50] Inter Ecclesial Advisory Committee of South Australia.

[51] Australian Association of Christadelphian Ecclesias.

- the waste of combined hundreds of hours by brethren discussing, debating and writing about EC
- multiple magazine articles countering EC
- the production of a number of books, including this book *By One Man*, that oppose EC

The solution to the problem

At base, *By One Man* addresses a simple issue. Man's interpretation of non-observable and non-repeatable historical science is being regarded as truth, and the Creator's first-hand account in the Bible is being subjected to a variety of interpretations to accommodate it. Those advocating EC are asking our community to accept that the straightforward teachings of an infallible and infinite God should be re-interpreted in light of the declarations of fallible and finite humans who maintain their evolutionary worldview by expressly removing God from the table of consideration. Without a doubt, the modern world is hugely indebted to the application of scientists and their discoveries. But there are basic Bible teachings that are true, vital for salvation and unchanging, and these must be upheld. They will outlast the constantly changing conclusions of the scientific world about the distant past (in which there is no future hope) and bring eternal life to those who embrace them.

Our ongoing focus needs to be on resisting error and establishing unity based on our long-standing, commonly held foundational doctrines. This is of paramount importance given that EC advocates remain adamant that their view is correct, typically do not admit that it conflicts with our Statement of Faith, and proactively continue to influence our community via the platform of the Internet. Happily, the vast majority of Christadelphians worldwide are unaffected by this issue, but it has been a source of tension and heartache for those who have been directly affected. Sadly, the continued promotion of EC within our belief and fellowship systems, for those who do become directly affected, will create consternation. EC should not be allowed to weaken the faithful endeavours of brothers and sisters to uphold long-standing Christadelphian core teachings based on God's word and encapsulated in our Statement of Faith.

Jesus Christ and the apostles warned against allowing false teachers to draw disciples away from saving truth (refer to the scriptures listed on page 41).

As is their wont, EC proponents will criticise **By One Man**. We, the authors, appeal to readers to closely consider whether what they actually believe and write is compatible with the BASF, because EC must ultimately be measured by our accepted understanding of the **core Bible doctrines** that are summarised in it.

SECTION 2

UNNATURAL READINGS OF GENESIS

"But as for you, continue in what you have learned and have firmly believed, knowing from whom you learned it and how from childhood you have been acquainted with the sacred writings, which are able to make you wise for salvation through faith in Christ Jesus. All Scripture is breathed out by God and profitable for teaching, for reproof, for correction, and for training in righteousness, that the man of God may be complete, equipped for every good work." (2 Timothy 3:14-17, ESV)

Overview of Section 2
Unnatural Readings of Genesis

This section answers several EC objections to the way Christadelphians have always read the entire book of Genesis, as a historical narrative.

Chapter 7 shows how belief in evolution as a fixed point demands re-interpretation of the Bible, which in turn inevitably leads away from saving truth.

Chapter 8 discusses the need to recognise (i) the difference between operational and historical science, and (ii) that the consensus scientific approach on all matters to do with the origins of life refuses even to contemplate the possibility of a Creator being involved, despite all the evidence to the contrary.

EC advocates endeavour to prove that the early chapters of Genesis cannot be read literally by alluding to a number of supposed inconsistencies associated with a natural reading of the text. The six objections listed below and addressed in this section are not exhaustive. Still, they are designed to give an impression of EC arguments, and how they can be answered by simply following the Berean approach of treating God's word as the ultimate authority and *"examining the Scriptures daily"* (Acts 17:11).

1. If animals were dying before Adam's sin, why should we reject the notion that men were as well? (Chapter 9)

2. How could Adam have named all the animals and birds in less than one day? (Chapter 10)

3. As God does not allow incest, doesn't this mean that Cain and Seth could not have married their sisters or other close relatives? (Chapter 11)

4. Where did all the people required to help Cain build a city come from? (Chapter 12)

5. Is Paul referring to the origin of the human race or the commonality of all humans in Acts 17:26? (Chapter 13)

6. Don't demons serve as a relevant example to illustrate that Genesis 1-3 should not be read as a literal historical record? (Chapter 14)

Additional EC objections, including the notion that Genesis 2 is an entirely different creation record to Genesis 1, and the use of "unscientific" expressions and figures of speech as an argument to 'prove' that we should not read early Genesis in a straightforward manner, are covered in Chapter 15.

Other EC objections relating to the fall and the atonement are covered in Section 3.

Chapter 7
Steps That Undermine God's Word

Genesis 1-4 presents historical events that are confirmed by our Lord and the NT writers. So why do EC advocates reject this obvious reading and the clauses in the BASF that reflect it?

This rejection involves a series of steps:

1. The foundation of EC teaching is that evolution, as taught by naturalist scientists, is true.

2. The Bible's history of the earth, based on a natural reading of the text, cannot be reconciled with the evolutionary version of the history of the earth.

3. Therefore, to retain their belief in the Bible and believe in evolution, EC adherents are forced to reinterpret the Bible.

4. One method used to achieve this is to argue that God was constrained by human writers who had a limited and often false understanding of origins based on the culture of the contemporary world in which they lived. Most EC promoters believe that the Bible is inspired but claim that God has accommodated the unsophisticated worldview in which each of the prophets and apostles wrote. EC advocates claim that what the "inspired" writers wrote might not have conveyed real historical truths, and we must take this into consideration.

5. To understand the Bible correctly, Bible readers have to discover how the ancients understood the world they lived in and interpret what the Bible's human authors taught against that background. To this end, appropriately qualified experts on Ancient Near Eastern culture, particularly those promoted on major EC websites such as BioLogos, can guide us on how to read the Bible, particularly early Genesis.

6. To supplement this view, EC promulgators adopt much of the source and form criticism[52] that began in the 19th century. It proposes that later redactors, particularly in the Babylonian exile, reshaped the Old Testament Scriptures. For example, EC advocates argue that the basis of the Sabbath law in Exodus

---

[52] Source Criticism is an attempt to find the sources used by authors and redactors to reconstruct the Biblical text and history of Israel. Form criticism seeks to classify sections of Scripture into literary patterns e.g. narrative, poetry, etc., to trace their period of oral transmission. In modern times, tracing oral transmission has faded and form criticism now centres only on genre criticism.

20:8-11, the seven days of creation, was inserted during the exile and was not written by Moses. Therefore the basis of a literal seven days for creation is regarded as invalid.

7. Some EC believers assert that readers can dismiss much of Paul's theology because it has no basis in scientific fact and has little relevance to the atoning work of Christ. They do not see, as fundamental to the atonement, the need to accept Adam as the lone progenitor of humanity. They wrest those passages where the apostle teaches that Adam's sin physically impacted the condition of human nature, and view Christ merely as an exemplar of righteousness and Adam as an exemplar of unrighteousness.

8. Bible students who employ a natural reading, while recognising that figurative language in addition to narrative does occur in early Genesis and New Testament explanations of early Genesis, are nevertheless labelled by EC believers as 'literalists'.

If this elaborate EC approach of interpreting the Bible were to gain traction in our community, it would mean that the average brother or sister would be unable to decipher the Bible's 'true' message by reading the Bible. They would be reliant on external human "experts" as the primary source of information to guide them to the true meaning of the Bible, instead of following the Berean approach of comparing Scripture with Scripture (Acts 17:11), using God's own word as the primary filter, and any human writings as secondary and subservient sources of information.

In response to these EC views on the nature of inspiration and the need to rely on appropriately qualified external experts to inform us how we should read the Bible, the following points can be made:

- Creation witnesses to a Creator, but creation cannot convey in words the process of salvation or what the kingdom of God will be like. Such information can only come to us today from Scripture.

- Of course, there are false statements in the Bible. The serpent lied to Eve; Job's friends spoke wrongly about God; Rabshakeh's words to the people of Judah were false;[53] Peter's words in his threefold denial were untrue. Verbal inspiration, therefore, does not mean that every individual sentence is true independent of context. Inspiration means that God, by his spirit power through his prophets and apostles, has recorded

---

[53] 2 Kings 18:19-25.

those words and events that He deemed necessary for mankind to understand His purpose and be saved.

- The Bible itself informs us how this inspiration operates:

  "All Scripture is God-breathed and is useful for teaching, rebuking, correcting and training in righteousness, so that the man of God may be thoroughly equipped for every good work." (2 Timothy 3:16-17, NIV)

- Scripture originates with God. It is not the product of human minds that God then accommodates to become part of His inspired word:

  "… you must understand that no prophecy of Scripture came about by the prophet's own interpretation. For prophecy never had its origin in the will of man, but men spoke from God as they were carried along by the Holy Spirit." (2 Peter 1:20-22, NIV)

- Contrary to the notion that Scripture accommodates men's minds limited by their contemporary world, Peter, like Paul, is clear that God's spirit alone drove the production of Scripture. Furthermore, in some cases, the prophets did not know the meaning of what they had said.[54] Some of them were forced to speak against their own will[55] or contradict their own apparently good idea.[56] Others are recorded challenging the wisdom and justice of God. Still, we are not left in doubt over what is true – their challenges, along with the Almighty's corrective replies, are recorded faithfully.[57]

- In 1 Corinthians 2:13-14 the apostle Paul states that the natural man cannot receive the things of the Spirit of God as they appear foolishness unto him, contradicting what man's wisdom teaches. Yet the apostle Paul was still able to receive and understand God's word even though it contradicted man's wisdom, and many other believers he taught were able to receive and understand it as well. This means that God is not constrained by man's limited understanding, education, background or culture to accurately convey the truth of any particular matter.

  "Which things also we speak, not in the words which man's wisdom teacheth, but which the Holy Ghost teacheth; comparing spiritual things with spiritual. But the natural man receiveth not the things of the Spirit of God: for they are foolishness unto him: neither can he know them, because they are spiritually discerned." (1 Corinthians 2:13-14)

---

[54] 1 Peter 1:10-12.

[55] Numbers 22:18-19 cp. Balaam's donkey Numbers 22:28-30; Jeremiah 20:9.

[56] Nathan spoke his own mind to David (2 Sam 7:1-3) but was overridden by God (v4-17).

[57] E.g. Moses, Job, Jonah, Habakkuk.

- The prophets and apostles and, more significantly, our Lord Jesus state plainly that what they are preaching is not their own words but those of God.[58]

- Suppose the Scriptures were simply the products of human minds bound by their contemporary world and were not driven by God's spirit. In that case, it is unlikely that David would have exposed his own sin and much less have recorded it for his contemporaries and all following generations. This was God's doing.[59]

- Whenever the prophets, the Lord and the apostles quote Genesis chapters 1-4, the Genesis record is seen as a historical event. [60] There is not the slightest hint of the fanciful interpretations employed by EC advocates to accommodate naturalistic evolution.

- The story of Genesis itself is a historical document all the way through, describing actual events that took place, including the creation of life upon this earth in Genesis 1, the specific description of Adam and Eve in the Garden of Eden in Genesis 2, the entry of sin into the world in Genesis 3. The narrative continues to describe momentous events surrounding Joseph's elevation from the prisons of Egypt to a position of authority second only to Pharaoh, and the subsequent migration of the household of Jacob into Egypt in the latter chapters. The language used throughout the book of Genesis firmly conveys that God intended it to be understood as an accurate, albeit summarised, account of historical events.

- Genesis 1-4 contains figurative language that is detectable and decipherable. A plain reading of early Genesis does not convey to the reader that the entire account is figurative language with no historical basis.

- Paul's view of the atonement, based on the fall of Adam and its effects on humanity, and the reversal of the fall through Christ's righteousness and its effects on humanity, cannot be dismissed as a personal view that suited his times. For example, if we reject Paul's teaching that, *"The first man is of the earth, earthy: the second man is the Lord from heaven. As is the earthy, such are they also that are earthy"* (1 Corinthians 15:46-48a); how can Paul's assurance

---

[58] Deuteronomy 18:14-22; Nehemiah 9:30; Jeremiah 20:7; John 8:28; John 10:35; John 12:49-50; Acts 2:1-13; 1 Corinthians 2:13; 1 Corinthians 14:37; Hebrews 1:1; 1 Peter 1:12

[59] 2 Samuel 11 and 12 cp. Psalm 51.

[60] Acts 14:15; 17:24; Romans 1:19-20; Ephesians 3:9; Revelation 10:6; 14:7 (even if symbolic, these last two verses allude to the literal creation); Hebrews 4:4; Matthew 19:4-5; Mark 10:6-8; 1 Corinthians 15:45-47; 1 Timothy 2:13; 1 Corinthians 11:8-9; 1 Corinthians 6:16; Ephesians 5:31; Revelation 2:7; 2 Corinthians 11:3; Romans 5:12-21; 1 Cor 15:21-22.

that we will receive the same spirit nature as Christ be trusted - *"as is the heavenly, such are they also that are heavenly. And as we have borne the image of the earthy, we shall also bear the image of the heavenly"* (1 Corinthians 15:48b-49)? If God did not create Adam miraculously from the dust, and this was only Paul's belief, what guarantee is there that He will recreate believers from the dust at Christ's return?

- In fact, what trust can we place in any of the inspired New Testament expositions of the serpent, Eve, Cain, Abel, Enoch, Noah, Abraham, Isaac, Jacob, Joseph and so forth? What faith can we place in the heroes of faith in Hebrews 11 if Paul's words are to be trusted in one place but not in another? Indeed, what exegetical rule can we employ to provide any certainty at all?

- In Psalm 8 David refers to man's creation in Genesis 1:26-28 and the promise of dominion over the earth. Paul refers to this Psalm, and therefore the same event, and extends its promise to the Lord Jesus as the one to whom the ultimate fulfilment of that promise applies [61]. Under inspiration, both David and Paul saw the Genesis creation record as a literal historical event, the purpose of which will finally be realised through Christ and those 'in' him when God's Kingdom is literally established on the earth.

- Many conservative scholars have answered the arguments of form and source criticism. Bro John Carter's book *The Oracles of God* is an excellent introduction to this issue.

Importantly, the above EC reasoning undermines the Foundation clause of the BASF by challenging the Christadelphian view of the Scriptures as *"wholly given by inspiration of God in the writers, and are consequently without error in all parts of them, except such as may be due to the errors of transcription or translation"* and as *"the only source of knowledge concerning God and His purposes at present or extant or available in the earth"*.

Bro Alfred Nicholls concludes his article on the importance of the Foundation Clause with the following words:

> In an age of doubt and distress, when prominent churchmen prefer their own opinion to the Bible message, denying the very basis of life and hope, when false brethren assert that there is a distinction to be drawn between revelation and inspiration, or that there are degrees of inspiration and the New Testament is more important than the Old, how vital it is that we look once more at our distinctive faith and its foundations and resolve to become even more truly "the people of the Book." [62]

---

[61] Psalm 8 cp. 1 Corinthians 15:24-28, Hebrews 2:5-12.

[62] Bro Alfred Nichols, *The Bible – Wholly Inspired and Infallible*, Studies in the Statement of Faith, The Christadelphian, Birmingham 1991, pp. 1-9.

Chapter 8
Elements[63]-to-Man Evolution –
Unobserved and Unrepeatable Science

One of the biggest stumbling blocks preventing EC supporters from accepting God's account of His miraculous creation of all independent "kinds" in Genesis 1-2, is their commitment to what evolutionary scientists allege are "demonstrable scientific truths". On top of this, EC advocates often falsely label believers in miraculous special creation as "science deniers" or "science-haters" in an attempt to minimise the "credibility" of their arguments.

The purpose of this chapter is not to "debate" science, but rather to highlight two notable characteristics of modern evolutionary science that separate it from the operational science we rely on every day.

1. That evolution is a "historical" science, so the process of elements-to-man evolution cannot be repeated, tested or observed in the standard scientific way. It involves many assumptions and extrapolations to explain events of the distant past.

2. That the gatekeepers of today's scientific academies will only allow non-theistic and naturalistic assumptions as possible explanations of origins. The data they consider is filtered through the presuppositions of the evolutionary paradigm.

Believers in special creation do not reject operational science. They reject man's evolutionary historical narrative and rely on God's first-hand account of history in the Bible.

Operational Science Versus Historical Science

The study of elements-to-man evolution is a "historical" form of science, very different from normal "operational" science[64] that involves current observation and experimentation. Operational science gives us the confidence to board an aeroplane or undertake an MRI scan. Everyone has confidence that operational science works because we observe it happening over and over again.

But historical science attempts to explain what happened when no one living today was around to observe what actually occurred. It is

---

[63] i.e. basic chemical elements, as per the 118 elements in the periodic table.

[64] "Science is the systematic knowledge of the physical or **material world** gained through **observation and experimentation**" (Dictionary.com).

an entirely different type of science, premised on a "best guess" that the beginning of life on this earth started 3.8 billion years ago from a cauldron of chemicals. [65] The problem with elements-to-man evolution (including macro-chemical and macro-organic evolution) is that it is impossible to follow the standard scientific approach and perform an experiment proving that complex life forms can evolve from basic chemical elements, even if such an experiment could somehow continue over thousands of years. Instead, evolutionists take what evidence they can observe today (e.g. the fossil record), and then, because the evidence in itself is inconclusive, they must apply many assumptions and interpretations to extrapolate a conclusion in line with their evolutionary paradigm. If the assumptions are wrong, then the conclusions will be wrong. This leaves room for significant doubt.

Ernst Mayr, one of the 20th century's leading evolutionary biologists, fully acknowledged that Darwin introduced "historic science" that follows a very different approach to the operational sciences such as physics and chemistry.

> "DARWIN INTRODUCED HISTORICITY into science. EVOLUTIONARY BIOLOGY, in contrast with physics and chemistry, IS A HISTORIC SCIENCE—the evolutionist attempts to explain events and processes that have already taken place. **Laws and experiments are inappropriate techniques for the explication of such events and processes. Instead one constructs a historical narrative, consisting of a tentative reconstruction of the particular scenario that led to the events one is trying to explain.**"[66]

Historical science is akin to forensic science at a crime scene, where certain indications remaining shortly after the crime (e.g. fingerprints, DNA, broken glass) are interpreted and extrapolated to construct a possible narration of how and when the crime occurred. Nevertheless, an eyewitness account or a video recording of what actually happened is always viewed as superior to other forensic evidence. In many cases, the real criminal ends up being different from the person whose fingerprints or DNA were left (or even planted) at the crime scene.

When it comes to the subject of the origin of all life upon this earth, we are attempting to explain events that occurred not just yesterday, as per a typical crime scene, but events that occurred thousands of years ago. Accordingly, it makes sense to accept what God has revealed in His own first-hand account of history as overriding

---

[65] Marshall, Michael, *Timeline: The evolution of life*, New Scientist, 14 July 2009. www.newscientist.com/article/dn17453-timeline-the-evolution-of-life/

[66] Mayr, Ernst, *Darwin's Influence on Modern Thought*, Scientific American, 24 November 2009 www.scientificamerican.com/article/darwins-influence-on-modern-thought/

evidence. The Bible provides the Creator's own reliable record of the methodology and purpose of His Creation.

The issue is not about *"facts for evolution"* versus *"facts for miraculous creation"*, but how we interpret the limited data observable today. The consensus elements-to-man evolutionary view taught in our education system today is not a "scientific fact" that is as certain as humans having 206 bones, the boiling point of water, gravity, photosynthesis, thermodynamics, solar panels converting sunlight into electricity, and mobile phones communicating via radio frequency waves. Evolutionary science observes certain facts in the present, and then tentatively reconstructs a historical narrative that includes making many assumptions, which are often circular[67], based on the evolutionary paradigm. 'Millions of years' is typically built-in as a governing assumption of their research.

Objections such as *"the Bible is not a scientific textbook"* miss the point. The Bible is an accurate version of what happened historically, recorded by the Eternal Father himself. Genesis presents God's majestic, straightforward and compact first-hand account of one-off, unobservable and unrepeatable events – the history of all life upon this earth, as we know it. Evolution proposes a different set of unobserved and unrepeatable events to explain how all life upon this earth came to be. **Evolutionary scientists have no eyewitness accounts to confirm their version of history. No one has ever observed an information-increasing genetic change of one type of organism to another, let alone the whole process of elements-to-man evolution over billions of years.** The basis for the evolutionary interpretation of history is guided by its paradigm, and limited to educated guesses about what might have happened millions of years ago. In the end, it comes down to what individuals believe about the past and what version of history they are going to accept – God's or man's.

It is impossible to describe the origins of a pot without appealing to the potter who created it. This is the error of EC proponents who appeal to the success of operational science but fail to realize the limitations of historical science. This is why the Bible is the best source of knowledge about what happened historically, and why the Foundation Clause of the BASF is correct.

---

[67] For example, the argument that fossils date rocks and rocks date fossils is circular.

Non-theism[68] and Naturalism – No Other Approaches Allowed

Consensus evolutionary science will never appeal to intelligence, design or purpose to explain how life developed upon this earth, even though such a hypothesis is entirely rational given the astounding witness of creation. This is the outcome of non-theism and naturalism.

The vast majority of evolutionary scientists are neo-Darwinian evolutionists. Their academic positions and ability to publish papers in the top scientific journals is only assured if the rationale driving their conclusions remains entirely naturalistic and non-theistic. There would be immediate pressure to remove any editor who allowed any paper referencing a Creator to be published.

Rigorous debate does occur in scientific academies over the "how" of evolution, including disputes and discussion over different possible mechanisms driving macro-evolution over millions of years. However, no debate is allowed over the "whether" of evolution. Naturalistic scientists scorn anyone who dares to suggest evidence of a Creator, and they prevent any such evidence from being published.

There are numerous cases of reputable scientists being discriminated against and losing their academic positions after publicly doubting the teachings of Neo-Darwinism.[69] This discrimination is shown in Ben Stein's documentary movie "Expelled"[70].

In January 2016, a paper published in the leading scientific journal (PLOS ONE) on the anatomy of the human hand was promptly retracted in a furore of criticism over references made to a "Creator"[71]. The study claimed the hand and its ability to grasp objects is *"the proper design by the Creator to perform a multitude of daily tasks in a comfortable way"*.[72] Fellow editors of PLOS ONE expressed their dismay that such a paper "slipped through" the journal's peer-review process. One editor, Dr Michael Seers, commented below the article *"Retract this article or I resign as an editor – there is no room in the*

---

[68] Non-theism is silence towards the concept of God, as opposed to atheism, which is hostile to that concept. Non-theism is relevant to the various branches of evolutionary science, where some scientists either believe in God, or are agnostic, and are therefore not atheists. However, they embrace the evolutionary world-view and remove God from consideration when researching or publishing material that concerns the origins of the universe and life. 'Non-theistic' is an umbrella term that describes all scientists committed to the elements-to-man evolutionary paradigm, as it accommodates all of their personal views of God.

[69] Bergman, Jerry, *Slaughter of the Dissidents*, 2nd Edition, Leafcutter Press, 2011.

[70] *Expelled: No Intelligence Allowed* (2008). [DVD] Chicago, US: Rocky Mountain Pictures, Premise Media.

[71] www.theguardian.com/science/2016/mar/07/hand-of-god-scientific-plos-one-anatomy-paper-citing-a-creator-retracted-after-furore.

[72] Ming-Jin Liu, Cai-Hua Xiong , Le Xiong, Xiao-Lin Huang, Biomechanical characteristics of hand coordination in grasping activities of daily living, *PLOS ONE*, 5 January 2016.

scientific literature for Intelligent Design"[73]. In March 2016, the PLOS ONE staff issued an official retraction and apology for *the "inappropriate language in the article and the errors during the evaluation process"*.[74] The subsequent absence of the particular academic editor's name (Renzhi Han) on the official editorial board listing of PLOS ONE[75] suggests that he lost his position.

Despite evidence that points to life upon this earth being intelligently created, and evidence of God's power and divinity, modern secular science will not even consider such evidence. It may be true that science has not "ruled out" the possibility of miraculous creation, but it will not allow it to be considered, as the following citations from leading evolutionists make plain:

> "If there is one rule, one criterion that makes an idea scientific, it is that it must invoke naturalistic explanations for phenomena … it's simply a matter of definition—of what is science, and what is not." *(Eldredge, Niles, 1982, The Monkey Business: A Scientist Looks at Creationism, Washington Square Press)*

> **"Any statement concerning the existence, nonexistence, or nature of a creator or creators is not science by definition and has no place in scientific discussion."** *(Pine, R.H., 1984, "But Some of Them Are Scientists, Aren't They?" Creation/Evolution, Issue XIV, pp. 6-18)*

> "Our willingness to accept scientific claims that are against common sense is the key to an understanding of the real struggle between science and the supernatural. We take the side of science in spite of the patent absurdity of some of its constructs, in spite of its failure to fulfil many of its extravagant promises of health and life, in spite of the tolerance of the scientific community for unsubstantiated just-so stories, because **we have a prior commitment, a commitment to materialism.** It is not that the methods and institutions of science somehow compel us to accept a material explanation of the phenomenal world, but, on the contrary, that **we are forced by our a priori adherence to material causes to create an apparatus of investigation and a set of concepts that produce material explanations, no matter how counter-intuitive,** no matter how mystifying to the uninitiated. Moreover, that materialism is absolute, **for we cannot allow a Divine Foot in the door."** *(Richard Lewontin, Billions and billions of demons (review of The Demon-Haunted World: Science as a Candle in the Dark by Carl Sagan, 1997), The New York Review, p. 31, 9 January 1997)*

> **"Even if all the data point to an intelligent designer, such an hypothesis is excluded from science because it is not naturalistic."** *(Scott C. Todd, "A view from Kansas on that evolution debate," Nature, Vol. 401:423 (Sept. 30, 1999).*

> "Darwinism rejects all supernatural phenomena and causations. The theory of evolution by natural selection explains the adaptedness and diversity of

---

[73] journals.plos.org/plosone/article/comment?id=10.1371/annotation/7d0b772c-aebe-4664-80f0-d3ec145f7d57.

[74] dx.plos.org/10.1371/journal.pone.0146193.

[75] journals.plos.org/plosone/static/editorial-board.

the world solely materialistically. **It no longer requires God as creator or designer** (although one is certainly still free to believe in God even if one accepts evolution). **Eliminating God from science** made room for strictly scientific explanations of all natural phenomena; it gave rise to positivism; it produced a powerful intellectual and spiritual revolution, the effects of which have lasted to this day." *("Darwin's Influence on Modern Thought" Ernst Mayr [evolutionist scientist], Scientific American, pg. 82-83, (July 2000))*

From these comments, it is clear that only natural and non-theistic factors can be discussed by scientists working in all areas to do with the origin and development of life upon this earth. Anything that might lead to a conclusion on origins other than that life upon this earth spontaneously generated and evolved by itself *"has no place in the scientific discussion"*.

The truth is that the secular academic world is not open to considering the evidence for a Divine Creator. The very concept of any intelligent design is anathema to them. They will stop at nothing to prevent even a hint of a Creator from breaking through the pages of secular scientific literature. This is contrary to what most people who haven't looked into this matter might think. Many have the false impression that evolutionary science is an honest and genuine search for truth irrespective of the conclusions to which that truth might lead.

It is concerning that EC promoters within our community consent, with little reservation, to the conclusions of today's leading evolutionary scientists and their interpretation of history. It is both ironic and tragic that they are taking their cue on God's mechanism of creation, not from God but from the gatekeepers of modern evolutionary science. These gatekeepers will not allow God's power, creativity, intelligence or design as possible explanations for the world in which we live (cp. Isaiah 51:12-13; 66:2).

Are Believers in Miraculous Creation "Science Deniers"?

Often EC proponents refer to those who believe that God miraculously created in a short period of time as "science deniers" or "science haters". This is a fallacy. God created the universal laws that scientists observe and rely on, so how can creationists be science-deniers? That would be akin to denying God Himself. Instead, creationists deny the evolutionary version of history that modern non-theistic scientists use to explain the origin of life upon this earth and accept God's first-hand account in the Bible. This is not a denial of the operational science that most people benefit from in some form daily. It is, though, a denial of the elements-to-man evolutionary paradigm.

Chapter 9
Was There Death in the Garden Before Sin?

Typical EC Objection: If animals were dying before Adam's sin, why should we reject the notion that men were as well?

EC advocates attempt to convince others that animals died during the period between Adam and Eve's creation and their sin, and then use this as a fulcrum to reason that there should be no difficulty in accepting that humans were also dying before Adam and Eve sinned. EC advocates believe God's creation was by evolution, and therefore death and suffering was an essential part of His creative process.

The Bible does not say that animals died before Adam and Eve sinned

The Bible teaches us that *"the life of the flesh is in the blood"* (Leviticus 17:11 cp. Deuteronomy 12:23 and Genesis 9:4). The Bible describes animals as being souls or having life (i.e. Hebrew *nephesh chayiah*). They are not only air (nostril) breathers but also have blood flowing in their veins. Adam became a *"living soul/being"* (*nephesh chayiah*) when God breathed His spirit into him (Genesis 2:7).

The Bible also tells us that it was the same group of creatures – *"all in whose nostrils was the breath of life"* that died during the flood (Genesis 7:21-22). Hence, living creatures (*nephesh chayiah*) were rescued on the Ark.

Since *nephesh* animals are like us in this regard, there is no scriptural basis for assuming that these creatures were dying before Adam and Eve sinned. Before the fall, God's firm rule was that both humans and animals should eat plants – *"I now give you every seed-bearing plant on the face of the entire earth and every tree that has fruit with seed in it. They will be yours for food. And to all the animals of the earth, and to every bird of the air, and to all the creatures that move on the ground – everything that has the breath of life in it – I give every green plant for food"* (Genesis 1:29-30, NET). After the flood, God did permit man to eat animals: *"You may eat any moving thing that lives. As I gave you the green plants, I now give you everything."* (Genesis 9:3, NET)

In all likelihood, before the flood, animals were killed for food due to man's disregard of God's laws. Nevertheless, after the flood, God specifically allowed animals to be eaten for the first time in addition to plants. This confirms that God's dietary instructions for both humans and animals to eat plants in Genesis 1, means that living creatures (*nephesh chayiah*) were not dying from animal carnivory prior to the fall.

Moreover, such a pre-fall state is supported by scriptures that describe the animal world during the millennial reign of Christ, when *"the wolf also shall dwell with the lamb....and the lion shall eat straw like the ox, and the suckling child shall play on the hole of the asp....They shall not hurt nor destroy in all my holy mountain"* (Isaiah 11:6-9 cp. 65:25). Any unnecessary hurting, harming or destroying of animals will not occur during the millennial reign of Christ.[76] Therefore, it is reasonable to suggest that this would have been the case in God's "very good" creation before the entry of sin and death into the world.

Regarding plants, they do not "die" in the Biblical sense[77], and therefore cannot be used to suggest that *nephesh chayiah* died before sin.

It is true that we cannot rule out the possibility of accidental death of creatures with the breath of life (*nephesh chayiah*) prior to the fall, as Adam and Eve and these creatures were not created immortal. However, the Bible is silent on the possibility of accidental death, and it is reasonable to conclude that God would not have allowed it to happen. What matters is that the inspired record does not tell us that animals died before the fall, so we cannot insist that they did.

The Bible tells us that humans did not die until after Adam and Eve sinned

The crux of the matter is that man was made in the image and likeness of God. Animals are not. After the flood, when God first allowed man to eat meat in addition to herbs, Genesis 9:3-6 makes it plain that human death is very different from animal death due to this very reason - that man was made in the image of God.

> *"Whoso sheddeth man's blood, by man shall his blood be shed: for in the image of God made he man."* (Genesis 9:6)

---

[76] The obvious exception will be the case of animals that are sacrificed during the Kingdom age, to vividly teach the mortals of the great work of salvation accomplished through Christ's life, death and resurrection (Ezekiel 44:29-31; 45:15-25: 46:4-15; 20-24).

[77] The death of plants and single cell organisms is not death in the same sense as the death of beings that have the "breath of life" – including animals and especially man who was made in the image and likeness of God. Plants are not described as dying (Heb. *Muth* H4191) in the Bible. Rather plants wither or dry up (Heb. *yâbêsh* H3001). See Psalm 90:6; 104:2,11; 129:6; Isaiah 15:16; 19:7; 27:11; 40:7,8, 24; 42:15; Jeremiah 12:4; Ezekiel 17:10, 24; 19:12; Job 8:12; 15:30, 18:16; Hosea 9:16; Joel 1:12,17; Amos 4:7; Jonah 4:7.

God has a very negative view of human death compared to his view of animal death. God is opposed to humans killing humans because they are made in His image (cp. James 3:9). So it makes no sense for EC advocates to assert that God created or evolved humans in a death-stricken state and that He could simultaneously describe such a creation as "very good". Furthermore, if humans were killing humans long before Adam and Eve existed (the evolutionary view), how can God consider this a part of His "very good", "first-rate" and "fit for purpose" creation?

The critical point is that the atonement focuses on sin as the original cause of human death. Death is the enemy. Christ was born with the same fallen nature so that he could destroy this "enemy" on the cross. The *last enemy that shall be destroyed* (1 Corinthians 15:26) is the problem of human death.

> *"The body is dead because of sin" (Romans 8:10). "The law of sin in my members...the body of this death" (Romans 7:23-24). "This mortal must put on immortality (1 Corinthians 15:53). "...we that are in this tabernacle do groan, being burdened ... that mortality might be swallowed up of life" (2 Corinthians 5:4). "Having the sentence of death in ourselves, that we should not trust in ourselves, but in God who raiseth the dead" (2 Corinthians 1:9).*

The scripturally unsubstantiated objections that animals were killing and eating each other, or that Adam and Eve could tread on a small lizard, are irrelevant to the Apostle Paul's unequivocal teaching in Romans 5 and 1 Corinthians 15 that sin and death entered the world by ONE man – Adam. One man's transgression (the cause) resulted in a state of sin and death reigning over all (the effect). 'What if' questions have no value. **We need to take our cue from what God's inspired word says about human death, not from what it doesn't say.**

- ***many died** (effect) through one man's trespass (cause)* (Romans 5:15, ESV).

- *"...because of one man's trespass (cause), **death reigned** (effect) through that one man (cause)"* (Romans 5:17, ESV).

- *"...one trespass (cause) led to condemnation **for all men** (effect)"* (Romans 5:18, ESV).

- *"For as by a man (cause) **came death** (effect)"* (1 Corinthians 15:21, ESV).

Chapter 10
How Could Adam Name All the Animals?

Typical EC Objection: How could Adam have named all the animals and birds in less than one day?

EC proponents mock a literal reading of Adam naming all the animals and birds before Eve was formed. They do this as part of their overall attempt to prove that the entire creation narrative should not be read in a straightforward manner.

> *"Then the LORD God said, "It is not good that the man should be alone; I will make him a helper fit for him." 19 Now out of the ground the LORD God had formed every beast of the field and every bird of the heavens and brought them to the man to see what he would call them. And whatever the man called every living creature, that was its name. 20 The man gave names to all livestock and to the birds of the heavens and to every beast of the field. But for Adam there was not found a helper fit for him."* (Genesis 2:18-20, ESV)

For example, COD claim that it would have been impossible for Adam to name a total of around 33,000 different species that were paraded past him in less than one day, given that taxonomy experts today tell us that there are more than 5,500 species of mammals, 10,000 species of birds, 10,000 species of reptiles, and 7,000 species of amphibians.[78] Based on this premise, they criticise those who read the Genesis creation record as an accurate historical narrative.

It would be a futile exercise to attempt to determine precisely how many animals and birds God brought before Adam. Nevertheless, there are two salient Biblical reasons why it was not an insurmountable task for Adam to name all the animals and birds in one day.

i) Adam named Biblical "kinds", a much broader classification than today's "species"

Firstly, the creation record in Genesis 1 tells us that God created plants, animals and birds *"after their kind"* (Genesis 1:11, 12, 21, 24, 25). The word *"kind"* is the translation of the Hebrew word *"mîn"*, which occurs ten times in Genesis 1, and God lets us know exactly what He means by defining it as something that can reproduce or bring forth *"after its kind"* (plants 1:11,12; sea creatures 1:21; birds 1:21; animals 1:24-25).

---

[78] John Doe (COD), *Literalist creationists become non-literal when it suits them*, COD Website, November 2018.

Therefore, the Biblical *"kind"* does not always correspond to any given level in the man-made classification system of: Species < Genus < Family < Order < Class < Phylum < Kingdom < Domain.

Moreover, the creation record in Genesis 1 informs us that God created the animals *"after their kind"* and commanded them to *"be fruitful and multiply"*(v22). This contradicts the evolutionary view that animals had already evolved into different kinds and had already spread over the face of the earth in huge numbers. God has plainly told us that He created the various animals *"after their kind"*, so evolution from one kind to another kind was not His revealed method of creation. Having only been created on days 5 and 6, the extent to which each male and female animal *"kind"* had multiplied, by the time Adam began naming them, would have been almost none at all.

Modern scientific taxonomy (the classification of life forms) is different from Biblical taxonomy. The Bible itself only contains about 100 different animal names. The list of 33 animals in Leviticus 11 illustrates that many different species of bats/turtles/grasshoppers according to modern taxonomy can be covered by the one name in Biblical taxonomy.

The *Theological Wordbook of the Old Testament*'s comment on the word "kind" (*min* in Hebrew) makes this point well:

> *Some have argued that when God created mîn, he thereby fixed the "species." This is a gratuitous assumption because a link between the word mîn with the biologist's descriptive term species cannot be substantiated….*

> *In light of the distinctions made in Genesis 1, such as the distinction between herbs and grasses which are, however, members of the same class (Angiosperms), it is possible that in some cases the biblical term mîn may indicate a broader group, such as an order. Elsewhere, in Lev 11:14,15,16,19,22 (four times), 29, mîn appears consistently as equivalent to nothing broader than genus. However, Lev 11:4 "the falcon after its kind," and 11:16 "the hawk after its kind," refer to divisions within the order Falconiformes, yet both have subdivisions called mîn. Likewise, as Payne points out, the locust, bald locust, cricket, and grasshopper all belong to the order Orthoptera and the locust, bald locust, and grasshopper belong to the family Acridiidae, but again each has its subdivisions called mîn (genus?).*

> *God created the basic forms of life called mîn which can be classified according to modern biologists and zoologists as sometimes species, sometimes genus, sometimes family or order. This gives no support to the classical evolutionist view which requires developments across kingdom, phyla, and classes.*

How we might classify the creatures God brought before Adam is irrelevant. It was God's classification that mattered on that day. Adam's task was not to classify them but to name them. Today we stand on solid ground by accepting God's first-hand account of what He did as reliable. God has told us that He brought before Adam every living creature, defined as all livestock, birds of the heavens, and every beast of the field. We can accept this without qualification, and without having to reason based on modern scientific taxonomy, which is very different from Biblical taxonomy. For example, birds and bats are grouped together in Biblical taxonomy (Leviticus 11:13,19) but widely separated in modern taxonomy.

ii) Representatives of "Every Living Creature" were on the Ark and could be observed in less than one day

There is a striking parallel between how all the animals are defined at the time of creation in Genesis 2:19-20 and the time of the flood in Genesis 6, 7 and 9. God brought *"every living creature"* to Adam, just as a single or seven pairs of *"every living creature"* came to Noah *"to preserve their offspring on the face of the **ENTIRE** earth"* (Genesis 7:2-3 NET), at the time when God destroyed *"all flesh in which is the breath of life … everything that is on the earth"* (Genesis 6:17, 21-23). Just as Adam gave names to *"every living creature"* (Genesis 2:19) defined as *"all livestock and to the birds of the heavens and to every beast of the field"* (Genesis 2:20), so *"every living creature that is with you [Noah]"* on the ark was defined as *"the birds, the domestic animals, and every living creature of the earth with you, all those that came out of the ark with you — every living creature of the earth"* (Genesis 9:10, NET).

Immediately after the flood, God made a covenant with Noah's family and all the animals that came out of the Ark, promising that He would never again destroy all life upon the earth via a flood (Genesis 9:9-17). As God destroyed *"all flesh in which is the of breath of life"* during the flood, those animals that came off the Ark with Noah amounted to *"every living creature on the earth"* at the time, and accordingly the progenitors of all such creatures today. It was for the very purpose of *"keeping their offspring alive on the face of **ALL** the earth"* (Genesis 7:3) that God brought them onto the Ark with Noah. We can be certain of this because i) God made a covenant that day with Noah and *"with every living creature that is with you [Noah]"*, even **"as many came out of the ark"** (Genesis 9:9-10,12); and ii) these same animals are further defined as *"all living creatures of all kinds that are on the earth"* (v16) and *"all living things that are on the earth"* (v17).

> **Genesis 9:9-10, 12, 16-17 [NET]**
> "Look! I now confirm my covenant with you and your descendants after you 10 and **with every living creature that is with you, including the birds, the domestic animals, and every living creature of the earth with you, all those that came out of the ark with you – every living creature of the earth.** 12 And God said, "This is the guarantee of the covenant I am making with you and **every living creature with you, a**

> **covenant for all subsequent generations:** 16 When the rainbow is in the clouds, I will notice it and remember the perpetual covenant between God and **all living creatures of all kinds that are on the earth.**" 17 So God said to Noah, "This is the guarantee of the covenant that I am confirming between **me and all living things that are on the earth.**"

If it was possible for Noah to walk around the Ark in a day (which given its dimensions was certainly possible) and observe *"every living creature of the earth"*, then it was also possible for Adam to observe and name every living creature that God created and brought to him in the garden.

None of the created "kinds" was a "helper fit" for Adam

The main reason God brought the various "kinds" before Adam was to make it plain that not one of them was a *"helper fit"* for him. Adam would consider the "kinds" as he named them and realise a complete lack of compatibility between himself and every living creature - all livestock, all birds of the heavens, and every beast of the field – that God had created. This served as an indispensable foundation to prepare Adam for the astonishing event of providing him with the very first *"woman"* who, unlike all the created "kinds", would be *"bone of [his] bones and flesh of [his] flesh"* (Genesis 2:23).

God presented Adam with the woman who would not only be a suitable helper for him, but who would also be distinct from every other animal pair created out of the ground, in that God made the woman out of the man.

But if the hypothetical pre- and co-Adamic race existed, they could have already identified and named the animals. And suppose women from that race already existed outside the Garden of Eden. In that case, God's objective in firstly asking Adam to name the already named animals, and secondly forming the woman from his side and having him name her, is made redundant. He could have brought before Adam one of the multitude of 'evolved' female humans, particularly if they were in exactly the same physical state as Eve and thereby equally qualified to be a "helper fit" for Adam. Yes, the creation of Eve would be a miracle but that, in itself, would not elevate her above the other already existing 'evolved' females who were not *"bone of [Adam's] bone, and flesh of [Adam's] flesh"*. The record is clear - *"for Adam there was **not found** a helper fit for him"* (Genesis 2:20) because none existed.

In the end, Adam gave not one name, as with the animals, but two names to the "helper fit" miraculously created from Adam's side. They were *"woman, because she was taken out of man"* (Genesis 2:23) and later, *"Eve, because she was the mother of all living"* human beings (Genesis 3:20).

Chapter 11
The Old Chestnut:
Whom Did Cain Marry?

Typical EC Objection: As God does not allow incest, doesn't this mean that Cain and Seth could not have married their sisters or other close relatives?

EC promoters reason that Cain and Seth must have married other evolved females living outside the Garden of Eden because: a) Leviticus 18 and 20 forbid marriage between close family members; and b) the context of the moral code in Leviticus 18:24-25 tells us that God was already upset with the Canaanites for committing various abominations before the Law of Moses was given. In their view, this indicates that the prohibitions in Leviticus 18, including relationships between close family members, are eternal principles that applied before the Law of Moses was given. Therefore they argue that for God's "morality" to be consistent, there must have been other humans in existence outside the garden for Adam and Eve's children to marry. Here is an example of their reasoning on this point:

> The Canaanites were judged as defiled and cast out because they committed the things – including incest – considered an abomination by God according to Lev 18:24-25. So God considered incest and the other abominations in Lev18 as a basis for judgement BEFORE the Mosaic code. The Mosaic code was not the start of God hating incest. [79]

With moral outrage, they accuse those who believe that Adam and Eve were the sole progenitors of the human race of teaching that *"God planned on incest as the mechanism of advancing His purpose of filling the earth with His glory."*[80]

There are a number of problems with this EC view, including those listed below, which are addressed in some detail in this chapter:

i. The Bible does not refer to humans outside the line of Adam and Eve

ii. God blessed the marriage relationships of the patriarchs

iii. Eve was more closely related to Adam than a sister

---

[79] John Doe, *Literalists defending incest*, COD Website, October 2019.

[80] John Doe, *Would God use incest to populate the world?*, COD Website, June 2017.

iv. Circumstances that will result in "Godly offspring" is the overriding divine principle in marriage

v. God's laws apply from when He reveals them, and are appropriate to the time and circumstances they govern

vi. Cain feared being killed by members of his own family

vii. Based on the Law of Moses, Cain should have been slain immediately.

i) The Bible does not refer to humans outside the line of Adam and Eve

Not a single book from Genesis to Revelation even hints at the possibility of co- and pre-Adamic humans (whether evolved or not), nor is there mention of Cain and Seth marrying females from outside the line of Adam. If such Biblical evidence did exist, EC proponents would trumpet it. Therefore they have to introduce the incest argument to get their evolved humans in through the back door. At best, this is an inferred argument. At worst, it is fantasy. Do EC advocates really believe that if such creatures existed and interacted with Adam's line, that our Heavenly Father would have neglected to reveal this to readers of Genesis? In fact, God has made it explicit, through the various genealogies and apostolic commentaries, what humans did and did not exist in early Bible history. He is completely silent about supposed multitudes of evolved humans.

As there is no support in scripture for a separate race of evolved humans outside the garden, EC proponents attempt to make a case out of what the Scriptures do *not* say.

For example, Bro Ken Gilmore asserts that Cain's wife was not his sister based on the *absence* of certain details from the Genesis record:

> ' ... When we look at the Bible, nothing is said about Cain's wife other than that she existed. Genesis 4:16-17 ...
>
> Any attempt to postulate the existence of other siblings is hard to reconcile with the first few verses of chapter 4 ...
>
> A straightforward reading of these verses indicates that no other children other than Cain and Abel had been born to Adam and Eve at this moment. Reinforcing this view is Genesis 4:25:
>
>> Adam had relations with his wife again; and she gave birth to a son, and named him Seth, for, *she said*, "God has appointed me another offspring in place of Abel, for Cain killed him." [NASB]

> Eve's concern about replacing Seth [sic] makes no sense if Cain and Abel
> were not her only children at the time.' [81]

The mode of Bro Ken Gilmore's argument, regarding the scriptural text, is inconsistent with its asserted conclusion. When we look at the Bible, nothing is said about humans existing who are not descended from Adam and Eve. A straightforward reading of not just a few verses but the whole of Genesis, and indeed the rest of Scripture, indicates that no other children other than descendants of Adam and Eve were ever born at any time. Any attempt to postulate the existence of other humans is impossible to reconcile with what the Scriptures plainly teach.

ii) *God blessed the marriage relationships of the patriarchs*

The objection on "moral" grounds is refuted by Abraham being married to his half-sister Sarah (cp. Genesis 20:12) and God's blessing on their marriage (Genesis 12:1-5; 13:14-17; 17:19, 21; 18:14; 21:1-2, 12; 22:16-18) contrary to what God later declared in Leviticus 18:9; Deuteronomy 27:22. Also, the Law forbids an Israelite from being married to two sisters simultaneously (Leviticus 18:18), but Jacob was married to both Leah and Rachel, who were sisters. Another case in point is Moses' father and mother, Amram and Jochebed (Numbers 26:59). They were related as nephew and aunt (Exodus 6:20), but this was contrary to the Law God gave Moses in Leviticus 18:12.

EC advocates counter that Abraham married Sarah before God called him, so he married his half-sister in ignorance of God's laws.[82] This is beside the point. At this stage in human history, the incest law was genetically unnecessary and therefore had not been introduced. If it had applied in Abraham's day and it bore the moral weight that EC advocates place on it, Abraham and Sarah's marriage would never have received God's approval, and certainly the promised seed would not have come through this relationship. God could have easily ensured that Sarah remained barren and fulfilled His promises to Abraham through an alternative option such as Hagar or Keturah (Genesis 25:1). In Ezra and Nehemiah's days, when Israel's marriage relationships were opposed to God's principles and laws, the divine solution was the dissolution of those marriages (see point (iv) below).

EC advocates cannot claim that Jacob, at Padanaram, had not been called by God after which he married Laban's two daughters, Leah and Rachel, in apparent contradiction of the law in Leviticus 18:8

---

[81] Gilmore, Ken, *Cain did not marry his sister: correcting Christadelphian misunderstandings on palaeoanthropology*, June 2013, christadelphianevolution.blogspot.com.au.
Re. [sic], Ken obviously meant Abel not Seth.
[82] John Doe, *Would God use incest to populate the world?*, COD Website, June 2017.

which prohibits a man from taking a second wife who is the sister of his first wife.[83] Isaac instructed Jacob not to marry any unbelieving Canaanite women (Genesis 28:1-5). Before arriving at Padanaram, Yahweh appeared to Jacob via the dream of Angels ascending and descending on a ladder, and gave him the same promises made to Abraham and Isaac. This included the promise that Jacob's seed would be like the dust of the earth (Genesis 28:10-15). EC attempts to apply God's prohibitions in Leviticus 18 retrospectively fail in these circumstances because the same laws prohibit a man from marrying two sisters (v18, i.e. like Leah and Rachel). If God found such marriage relationships so morally repugnant in the days of the patriarchs, He would have found other means to further His purpose with mankind. God's destruction of Sodom and Gomorrah in this epoch of history indicates that God is not silent even in the case of non-believers who engage in morally repugnant behaviour.

We have to keep reminding ourselves that these strained EC "incest" arguments are designed to find a way to establish the existence of evolved men that Scripture never mentions.

iii) Eve was more closely related to Adam than a sister

Both EC views A and B accept that Adam and Eve were miraculously created, while at the same time, outside the Garden of Eden, alleged evolved humans were being born, breeding and dying (see Section 4, Question 1). As God used the flesh from Adam's side to create Eve, there could not have been two married people more closely related genetically speaking (like a "clone" today). Just as Adam said, *"this is now…flesh of my flesh"* (Genesis 2:23), Eve was indeed "his flesh" in the fullest possible way – she was "made" or "built", as the Hebrew puts it, out of Adam's rib (Genesis 2:22).

However, in Leviticus 18:6, God's moral laws regarding sexual relations state: *"None of you shall approach to any that is **near of kin** to him"* (Hebrew: *"of his own flesh"*) (Leviticus 18:6). The NET Notes indicate that the original Hebrew reads: *"Man, man shall not draw near to any flesh (שְׁאֵר, shᵉ'er) of his body/flesh (בָּשָׂר, basar)"*. Hence the Law prohibited sexual relations between persons of the same kin or flesh (*basar*), but this same Hebrew word is used twice in Genesis 2:23 when Adam described Eve as – *"flesh of my flesh"*.

Suppose God's moral laws in the Law of Moses applied in Eden as EC proponents insist (despite no record of such until Moses). In that case, they are effectively claiming that God, by creating Eve from Adam's rib and giving her to be his wife, was causing Adam to break His moral laws. The truth of the matter is that Eve was more closely

---

[83] Leah and Rachel were also Jacob's first cousins, but the Law of Moses does not specifically prohibit such a relationship.

related to Adam, before she became his wife, than a sister. And that was by their Creator's own choice and design.

iv) Circumstances that will result in "Godly offspring" is the overriding divine principle in marriage

Scripture prohibits marrying outside the true faith (Genesis 24:3-4; 27:46; 28:1-4; Deuteronomy 7:1-4; 2 Corinthians 6:14; 1 Corinthians 7:39). EC proponents seem to think it was acceptable for this principle to be broken by Cain and Seth marrying females of the ignorant evolved humans, but unacceptable for them to marry a daughter of Adam who would know about God from her parents. But the overriding principle is that God, in making two to be one flesh (Genesis 2:24), seeks a godly seed (Malachi 2:15).

This is evident in the days of Ezra and Nehemiah when Israel intermarried with idolatrous nations. Ezra pleaded with God to show mercy and not consume them for this (Ezra 9). The solution was to put away the strange wives and their children (Ezra 10). We know that this was not just Ezra's personal view that may have been opposed to God's will, because Ezra 10:11 informs us that it was *"God's will/pleasure"* that they do so [84].

However, in the very same historical era, God condemned the people for acting *"treacherously"* by divorcing their Jewish wives in the first place and then marrying *"the daughter(s) of a strange god"* (Malachi 2:11-16). So divorce was God's *"pleasure"* in the case of Ezra, but something He opposed in the case of Malachi.

The context of both Ezra 9 and Malachi 2 provides the key to resolving this seeming conflict. In Ezra 9:1-2, *"the holy race mixing itself with the peoples of the land"* by taking *"some of their daughters to be wives for themselves and their sons"* was declared to be both an *"abomination"* and an act *of "faithlessness"*. Likewise, in Malachi 2:11, marrying *"the daughter of a strange god"* was declared to be both an *"abomination"* and *"faithless"* in God's sight. Accordingly, the faithless abomination was not divorce per se, but intermarrying with foreign nations, who worshipped foreign gods. This is a principle that God does not compromise on. The conflict that can occur when a believer marries a non-believer not only jeopardises their own eternal well-being, but that of their offspring, and it can frustrate God's purpose to take out of the nations a people for His name (Acts 15:14).

---

[84] Ezra 10:11 is not based on Ezra's own imagination or human impulse. Rather Ezra spoke God's words as he was carried along by the Holy Spirit (2 Peter 1:20-21).

v) God's laws apply from when He reveals them, and are appropriate to the time and circumstances they govern

COD claim that God would not have populated the earth via relationships violating his moral code in Leviticus 18 that prohibits marriage between close family members. They argue that the laws in Leviticus 18 are eternal principles that applied before the Law of Moses, given that Leviticus 18:24-25 indicates that God was already angry with the Canaanites for the various sins listed in the chapter:

> "Defile not ye yourselves in any of these things: for in all these the nations are defiled which I cast out before you: And the land is defiled: therefore I do visit the iniquity thereof upon it, and the land itself vomiteth out her inhabitants." (Leviticus 18:24-25, KJV)

The same point is made again in vv27-28, but this time the use of the past tense clarifies that God had already punished the nations inhabiting the land **for these abominations.**

> "For all these abominations **have the men of the land done**, which were before you, and the land is defiled; That the land spue not you out also, when ye defile it, **as it spued out the nations that were before you.**" (Leviticus 18:27-28, KJV)

Therefore divine judgment on the inhabitants of the land had already occurred before God gave Moses the law, and would happen again when Israel entered the land under Joshua. To answer COD's claim, we must ascertain both when and why God intervened to judge individuals and nations prior to the Law of Moses.

Genesis 15 shows iniquity present in Abraham's time, before Israel even existed:

> "And they shall come back here in the fourth generation, **for the iniquity of the Amorites is not yet complete."** (Genesis 15:16, ESV)

We know that in Abraham's day, God judged some inhabitants of the land for their abominations. In particular, God severely punished the inhabitants of Sodom and Gomorrah, and this was a lesson to the nation of Israel before they entered the land, and it is to us today:

> "Now the men of Sodom were wicked, great sinners against the LORD". (Genesis 13:13, ESV)

> 'Then the LORD said, "Because the outcry against Sodom and Gomorrah is great and their sin is very grave,"' (Genesis 18:20, ESV)

> 'And they [the men of Sodom] called to Lot, "Where are the men who came to you tonight? Bring them out to us, that we may know them."' (Genesis 19:5, ESV)

> "… turning the cities of Sodom and Gomorrah to ashes he condemned them to extinction, making them an example of what is going to happen to the ungodly." (2 Peter 2:6, ESV)

> "Just as Sodom and Gomorrah and the surrounding cities, which likewise indulged in sexual immorality and pursued unnatural desire, serve as an example by undergoing a punishment of eternal fire." (Jude 1:7, ESV)

Clearly, God judged Sodom and Gomorrah for acts prohibited in Leviticus 18:22.

But what about all the other sins prohibited in Leviticus 18 (and 20)? Did God enforce all of them from the time of Genesis? It is helpful to consider which of those sins match cases of God intervening before Moses received the Law. What did God already count as "sin", as evidenced by His warnings and judgments upon both individuals and nations? List A below summarises such cases:

LIST A: Cases Where God Did Intervene Before the Law of Moses:

1. **Genesis 4:7** – God warned Cain to worship him correctly (cp. commands to bring offerings, Deuteronomy 12:26-28).

2. **Genesis 4:8** – Cain murdered Abel (violated "*be fruitful and multiply*" in Genesis 1:28; violated Genesis 9:6 and Exodus 20:13).

3. **Genesis 6:5,13** – Noah's flood. Before the flood, the earth was filled with violence (violated "*be fruitful and multiply*" Genesis 1:28 and Genesis 9:6-7).

4. **Genesis 18:20** – Destruction of Sodom and Gomorrah – "*sin is very grievous*" (homosexuality violated "*be fruitful and multiply*" in Genesis 1:28 and God's marriage laws in Genesis 2:18-24. It is also prohibited in Leviticus 18:22 and called an "*abomination*" in 1 Kings 14:24).

5. **Genesis 20:6,9** – God prevented Abimelech from committing adultery which he knew was a "*great sin*" (violates God's marriage laws in Genesis 2:18-24, Leviticus 18:20, and Exodus 20:14,17)

6. **Genesis 38** – God destroyed Judah's son Onan because he refused to raise up seed for his brother (violated "*be fruitful and multiply*" in Genesis 1:28; violated requirement to do this in Deuteronomy 25:5-10).

7. **Genesis 39:9** – Joseph knew that adultery is a great wickedness and sin against God (violates God's marriage laws in Genesis 2:18-24, Leviticus 18:20, Exodus 20:14,17 and it is called an abomination in Ezekiel 22:11).

8. **Exodus 7-14** – God punished Egypt via ten plagues and drowning its army in the Red Sea. In Leviticus 18:3, God states that Israel should not do after the doings of the land of Egypt. Egypt was steeped in the worship of false gods, and it is this sin that is identified explicitly as abhorrent in Ezekiel 20:7-8. God later condemned Israel for doing the same. Idol worship is frequently referred to as an *"abomination"* throughout the Old Testament. It not only violates the first two of the ten commandments in Exodus 20, but it also violates the Genesis record of God as the Creator of heaven and earth. Accordingly, a significant reason for the ten plagues was to condemn each of Egypt's major gods and establish that there is only one true God, the God revealed at Creation.[85]

List A demonstrates that God did intervene to warn or judge individuals or nations who infringed his moral principles on marriage relationships, worship of false gods and other matters. Some of these are stated in Leviticus 18, others in Exodus 22, and at least one other in Deuteronomy 25. But in all cases, they were breaking laws that God had already revealed before the Law of Moses was given.

This is not to negate the probability that many of those destroyed in Noah's flood, the destruction on Sodom and Gomorrah, and the ten plagues in Egypt were also involved in certain sexual relationships that God would later legislate against, in Leviticus 18. But Scripture shows God intervening because people had broken laws they should already know, not laws that God had not yet revealed.

And this holds true for the Canaanites that God would throw out of the land when Israel entered under Joshua (Leviticus 18:24-28). The reason God could justifiably cause the land to spew them was because they had violated the laws for which God held all nations accountable from Genesis. Deuteronomy 12:30-31 refers to this when it identifies the abomination the Canaanites were committing: (i) the worship of false gods and (ii) the sacrificing of their children.

After citing several instances where God did intervene, it is necessary to reconcile List A with the fact that during the same time period, from Genesis to the Law of Moses, God did allow other violations of Leviticus 18 to occur without intervening to warn, condemn or punish. List B contains a non-exhaustive list of such cases.

---

[85] Additionally, Pharaoh murdering all the male Israelite babies violated Genesis 9:6-7. Pharaoh's enslavement of Israel stood in contradiction of what had been known from Genesis 1 – that there is only one true God, the creator of heaven and earth, whom all must serve and obey (cp. Exodus 9:13-17). God also judged Egypt's enslavement of Israel on the basis of His promise to Abraham "I will bless them that bless thee, and curse him that curseth thee." (Genesis 12:3).

LIST B: Cases Where God Did NOT Intervene Before the Law of Moses

1. Adam & Eve - directly arranged by God, *"flesh of my flesh (basar)"*, but later God prohibited relationships between two people of the same kin or flesh (*"basar"*) Leviticus 18:6.

2. Abraham and Sarah (half-sister – prohibited in Leviticus 18:9; Leviticus 20:17)

3. Jacob marrying both Leah and Rachel (two sisters – prohibited in Leviticus 18:18)

4. Amram and Jochebed (nephew and aunt Exodus 6:20 – prohibited in Leviticus 18:12-13; Leviticus 20:19)

5. Lot and his daughters (prohibited in Leviticus 18:6 – note God had just destroyed Sodom for their abominable practices, including homosexuality which is forbidden in Leviticus 18:22)

6. Judah and Tamar (father and daughter in law – prohibited in Leviticus 18:15; Leviticus 20:12 – and note the context in Genesis 38 of God destroying Judah's two sons for their wickedness)

Suppose COD's thesis is correct, that *"God is consistent and doesn't change His moral code depending on circumstances"*, and that *"God considered incest and the other abominations in Leviticus 18 as a basis for judgement BEFORE the Mosaic code"*.[86] In that case, God should have acted to enforce His moral principles consistently during the lives of the patriarchs. But as the contrast between Lists A and B demonstrate, He did not. Faithful men had relationships that would have been in violation of Leviticus 18 had those laws been made known to them, and yet they were not *"abhorred"* by God like the nations God cast out of the land of Israel - *"for they committed all these things, and therefore I abhorred them"* (Leviticus 20:23).

Furthermore, we cannot reason that God just overlooked the events in List B due to the ignorance of those involved. This is because List A presents evidence that God did intervene to judge several sins listed in Leviticus 18 that both believers and non-believers committed. God did intervene to warn against sin, and to condemn and in some cases kill both believers and non-believers who acted wickedly – including all those destroyed in Noah's flood, Abimelech's household, the people of Sodom and Gomorrah, Judah's two sons, and all the Egyptians destroyed during the ten plagues. God did destroy all in Sodom and Gomorrah for homosexuality, but at the very same time God didn't kill Lot's daughters after they made Lot drunk and had sexual relations with him. God did destroy Judah's sons for their

---

[86] John Doe, *Literalists defending incest*, COD Website, October 2019.

wickedness, but he didn't kill Judah or Tamar for their sexual relationship prohibited by Leviticus 18.

Hence, a better explanation is required to harmonise God's justice in enforcing his moral laws in List A but not in List B. A closer look at the cases in List A, where God did intervene, reveals that these "violations" are listed in Leviticus 18 from verse 20 onwards, including adultery, homosexuality, and the passing of children through the fire to Molech. There is also violence and murder more generally speaking, which are not in Leviticus 18 but other parts of the Law including the Ten Commandments. So there appears to be a dividing point of the laws in the chapter, between those up to v19 and those from v20 onwards. God did not intervene for the sins listed vv6-19, but He did for the sins from v20 onwards.

The prohibitions in vv20-23 are all in conflict with God's principles and laws revealed in Genesis 1 and 2 – God as the Creator of heaven and earth and all life therein, His command to be fruitful and multiply and fill the earth, and the importance of the union of male and female in marriage. The sins in vv20-23 are specifically referred to as an "abomination" in the Old Testament: homosexuality in v22, idolatry on numerous occasions (e.g. Deuteronomy 7:25; Isaiah 44:19), giving one's seed to Molech in Leviticus 20:3, and adultery in Ezekiel 22:11. They are abominations because they contravene God's purpose in creation and marriage – to produce a godly seed, to take out of the nations a people for His name.

By comparison, the word "abomination" is never attached in Scripture to the sins listed in Leviticus 18:6-19. This is not to say that those acts prohibited in vv6-19 carried less condemnation after they were made illegal, than those in vv20-23. It is merely to point out that the Bible itself makes a distinction by referring to the sins in vv20-23 as "defiling" and an "abomination". God had already shown His judgments on them, as outlined in List A, because they violated His principles already revealed from Creation.

Therefore, it is more consistent to reason that God judges (both believers and non-believers) based on the laws He has already revealed, and the prohibitions in vv20-23 are all based on laws given in Genesis 1 and 2. Clearly, some of these laws are included in Leviticus 18. However, some of the laws in Leviticus 18 could not be derived from Genesis 1 and 2, so God did not hold men accountable to these unrevealed laws in the period of Genesis and early Exodus.

But then, from the point when God revealed additional moral laws in Leviticus (including the laws in vv6-19 of Leviticus 18), He held the nation of Israel (and by extension, other nations exposed to God's laws) accountable to them.

Under the New Covenant, the laws that we must keep today were modified, so that not all of God's laws under the Law of Moses apply – *"Therefore let no one pass judgment on you in questions of food and drink, or with regard to a festival or a new moon or a Sabbath"* (Colossians 2:16 ESV). However, many moral laws and principles God had revealed in Genesis and in the Law of Moses are to be upheld by believers: *"For you may be sure of this, that everyone who is sexually immoral or impure, or who is covetous (that is, an idolater), has no inheritance in the kingdom of Christ and God"* (Ephesians 5:5, ESV).

List B above presents examples of faithful patriarchs in various ways infringing laws later revealed in Leviticus 18, while upholding the laws of Genesis 1 and 2 that had been revealed to them. All of these people, many of whom appear in the genealogy of Christ, lived according to an understanding of God's laws revealed from creation. They could discern iniquity, discern righteous behaviour, and discern wicked behaviour through the principles taught from creation.

The children of Adam and Eve marrying each other was a special circumstance and one not forbidden in Genesis 1 or 2, and it was the only way they could obey God's command to become fruitful, multiply and fill the earth.

Brothers Mark Allfree and Matthew Davies answer the "incest" objection from page 149 of their book *The Deception of Theistic Evolution*. In addition to scriptural arguments, they also mention the genetic argument – that initially, Adam and Eve's DNA was pure compared to ours, but in subsequent generations larger numbers of genetic errors developed. So the genetic problems common today when brothers and sisters or even first cousins procreate were highly unlikely with Adam and Eve's children. But genetic problems had become an issue by the time of Moses. Therefore, for Israel's benefit, the law against incest was introduced.

vi) Cain feared being killed by members of his own family

Whom did Cain fear was going to kill him (Genesis 4:14)? Why would a Godless, lawless, evolved human group have any interest in avenging the murder of Abel? What law of theirs did Cain break? It is more reasonable to conclude that Cain was in fear of being killed in the first place by Abel's parents Adam and Eve, and secondly by their other children, who had endured the sorrow and pain of their brother Abel's life being unjustly cut short by Cain.

Numbers 35 details the provisions under the Law for cases of either manslaughter or murder, where the person responsible could flee to one of six cities of refuge and find refuge from the *"avenger"* or *"revenger of blood"*, so *"that the manslayer die not until he stand before the congregation in judgment"* (Numbers 35:6,12,19). Those seeking revenge would be the direct family members of the slain, not other people who didn't even know who the slain was. This is confirmed by what Joab instructed the woman of Tekoah to relate to David in 2 Samuel 14, after Absalom murdered Amnon, that the "whole family" was intent on killing Absalom. Likewise, Cain would have been afraid of the vengeance of family members who loved Abel. Cain would have no reason to fear the alleged evolved humans living in the distant areas to which Cain fled. They would have no connection with either Cain or Abel.

vii) Based on the Law of Moses, Cain should have been slain immediately

The appeal to God's moral laws prohibiting marriage between close family members needs to be squared with God's moral laws prohibiting murder, and what actually happened to Cain. Numbers 35 says that murder defiled the land and could only be resolved by the death of the murderer (Numbers 35:31-33). If the Levitical judges determined that the death was not accidental, the person would be delivered to the slain person's avengers.

Therefore, if EC advocates want to insist that God's moral laws about sexual relations, given through Moses, are sufficient to tell us that Cain and Seth could only have married outside the family of Adam and Eve, they must explain why God's moral laws on murder, given at the same time, were not strictly followed through in the case of Cain? Why was Cain not put to death immediately?

Chapter 12
How Could Cain Build a City by Himself?

Typical EC Objection: Where did all the people required to help Cain build a city come from?

EC proponents attempt to prove the existence of evolved humans outside the Garden of Eden, by referring to Cain's departure to the Land of Nod, where he built a city. They reason that he would require the assistance of a large number of people to undertake such a task.[87]

> *"And Cain went out from the presence of the LORD, and dwelt in the land of Nod, on the east of Eden. 17 And Cain knew his wife; and she conceived, and bare Enoch: and he builded a city, and called the name of the city, after the name of his son, Enoch."* (Genesis 4:16-17)

Most English translations state that what Cain built was a "city". Upon first reading, this may suggest that Cain, upon arriving in Nod, immediately embarked on a large construction project that would have required the participation of hundreds, if not thousands, of people. However, a closer look at the context and the Hebrew yield a different conclusion.

Firstly, if Cain was to build and dwell in a great city (one that took much effort and time to build), it implies he was able to defy God's punishment consigning him to be a perpetual wanderer, *"a fugitive and vagabond in the earth"* (v14). He would have received all the fame and recognition from everyone living in the city and nearby. It is highly unlikely that God's "vagabond" sentence only applied to a short period of his life.

Secondly, the Hebrew word for 'city' is *îyr*. In Bible usage, this doesn't automatically mean a city like Sydney or London. 'City' in Scripture can refer to a small, protected encampment. Strong defines it as *"a place guarded by a waking or a watch, in the widest sense (even of a mere encampment or post)"*. Keil and Delitzsch explain that this word *"does not necessarily presuppose a large town, but simply an enclosed space*

---

[87] For example, Bro Ken Gilmore reasons: *"it is hard to see how Cain could build a city by himself; the fact that the narrative does not seek to clarify where Cain obtained his wife, whom he feared would kill him and how he built a city presupposes the existence of people other than Adam, Eve and Cain on the Earth at this time".* Gilmore, Ken, *"Cain did not marry his sister: correcting Christadelphian misunderstandings on palaeoanthropology"*, June 2013, christadelphianevolution.blogspot.com.au.

with fortified dwellings, in contradistinction to the isolated tents of shepherds." In the context of the twelve spies being sent to investigate the land of Canaan, Numbers 13 defines the range of a 'city' *(iyr)* from a camp to a fortified stronghold – *"whether the cities that they dwell in are camps or strongholds"* (Numbers 13:19, ESV). Most of the occurrences of "cities" in the Old Testament describe places that we would more likely call a "village" or "town" rather than a "city".

Thirdly, the Hebrew verb for "built" in v17 is participial, *uayhi boneh.* The same grammatical form occurs twice in v2, used both for Abel keeping a flock and Cain working the ground – which were ongoing activities, not completed actions. So v17 means that Cain was engaged in building a city, not that he finished building it. The NET supports this interpretation: *"Cain was building a city";* and the NIV: *"Cain was then building a city".*

Fourthly, from the outset, only Cain is mentioned as building the city. Unlike Babel's many builders and their great plan – *"let us build for ourselves a city and a tower, whose top reaches to heaven"* (Genesis 11:4), Cain would not require many people to help him construct an enclosed area to dwell in, and no other people are referred to. On his arrival in Nod, Cain could have started building on a small scale, but the perimeter of the enclosed space and the number of dwellings would likely have increased over time in line with the growth of his descendants. We know that later descendants of Cain developed skills in various areas, including brass and ironwork, [88] and eventually there would have been sufficient manpower for extensive building projects.

Putting all of this together, it is reasonable to conclude that Cain began building an enclosed area to dwell in, in contrast to the unprotected and open dwellings of farmers. However, we can be confident that he did not stay permanently in it, based on God's clear sentence that he was to be a fugitive and vagabond. Therefore, it is likely that he entrusted the ongoing task of building to Enoch, his son, after whom the settlement was named (Genesis 4:17).

---

[88] Genesis 4:19-22.

Chapter 13
Did God Make Every Nation From One Man?

Typical EC Objection: Acts 17:26 - Is Paul referring to the origin of the human race or the commonality of all humans?

The apostle Paul's statement in Acts 17:26 that God made all nations from one blood or one man rules out the possibility (i) that an evolved race lived outside the Garden of Eden, (ii) that Adam is not the sole progenitor of humanity and (iii) that Cain or Seth obtained their wives from outside the line of Adam and Eve.

> *"And he made from one man every nation of mankind to live on all the face of the earth, having determined allotted periods and the boundaries of their dwelling place."* (Act 17:26, ESV)

Nevertheless, EC advocates attempt to negate the apostle Paul's plain declaration by reasoning along the following lines:

a. The word "man" (or in some versions "blood") doesn't have much to support it, and hence it should read "God made every nation from one", to which they then append "common humanity";

b. The apostle Paul over vv26-28 is quoting from Greek poets and philosophers, including Epimenides and Aratus, so this section must be understood in terms of how the original audience would have read these poets, as opposed to something that God himself is directly stating via the apostle Paul;

c. Even though Paul himself may have believed that Adam was the father of all nations, he didn't have access to the "wealth of information" that we have today;

d. The purpose of the apostle's speech in Acts 17 is not to inform us about the origin of mankind, but the important spiritual lesson that there is no room for racial or moral superiority before God.

The following quotation from Bro Mike Pearson is one example of EC reasoning on this verse:

Mike Pearson, The Fourth Conversation, pp 122-123 Given his heritage as a Jew, Paul was probably referring to Adam, but this shouldn't be taken for granted as all the Greek says is "he made from [one] every nation of man". (The KJV rendering, "of one blood," is based upon a textual variant which has very little support [Barclay Moon Newman and Eugene Albert Nida, A Handbook on the Acts of the Apostles (UBS Handbook Series; New York: United Bible Societies, 1972), 341.

> ... Therefore, Paul is telling them that all humanity is from 'one stock', and that our purpose in life is not to pursue happiness but to seek God because we are his offspring. [Robert James Utley, Luke the Historian: The Book of Acts (vol. Volume 3B; Study Guide Commentary Series; Marshall, TX: Bible Lessons International, 2003), 208] The emphasis on Paul's message isn't talking about origins specifically, but rather about human commonality before God.
>
> The context of this verse sees Paul preaching a message relevant to the Athenians who viewed themselves as superior beings to all others, and that is the lesson we should be taking out of this. There is no room in God's creation for racial or moral superiority, because we are all 'of one' and our purpose in life is to seek God together.
>
> To be fair, it's reasonable to assume that Paul might well have believed Adam was the father of all. After all, he didn't have access to the wealth of evidence that we have today. But... this is not sufficient evidence to disprove what we know today about human origins. Does the passage conclusively prove all humans are descended from Adam? No, it doesn't, because that is not its purpose. Therefore, once again, we ought not wrest a text out of its context to try and solve a modern problem, because when left in its context, it gives us a far more meaningful spiritual lesson.

This chapter exposes the problems with such EC reasoning on Acts 17 under the following headings:

   i. The translation *"from one man"* is legitimate and scripturally justified

  ii. Paul's speech is based on Scripture, and Paul only quotes Greek poetry where it agrees with Scripture

 iii. Athenian culture – a barrier to belief in the resurrection

 iv. Paul's understanding of Adam as the father of all nations would not change if he were alive today

i) The translation "from one man" is legitimate and scripturally justified

There are two known forms of the Greek text at the start of Acts 17:26, and two corresponding forms of English translation. A longer form found in some manuscripts includes the word αιματος / *aimatos*, "blood", which is followed by the KJV and some other versions. However, EC proponents who discuss the issue (such as Bro Mike Pearson, see above) assume a shorter form lacking that word. We will not pursue the textual question here, but consider only the shorter form. It is shown below, with a range of English renderings:

- επoιησεν τε εξ ενoζ παν εθνoζ ανθρωπων [89]
- And he made from one man every nation of mankind (ESV)
- From one man he made every nation of the human race (NET)
- From one man he made all the nations (NIV)
- He caused to spring from one forefather people of every race (WNT)
- and He made from one *man* every nation of mankind (NASB)

The first point to make is that all the above versions supply the word "man", or in one case "forefather". **So the translators in every case understand that such a word is appropriate.** None inserts a word or phrase such as "stock". This fact alone should give pause to accepting the EC argument.

So we turn to the detail of the Greek. The phrase behind "from one" or "of one" is εξ ενoζ (*ex enos*). Paul told the Athenians that God made from one – *ex enos* – every nation of mankind. But from one *what*? As we saw, English versions here typically insert "man" to give "from one man". Is this a valid translation? Could God actually make every nation from one man? And, is there any other support for this rendering?

Firstly, the Greek word *enos*, "one," is singular, as "man" is. Greek interlinears and dictionaries note it as both masculine and singular in form.[90] [91] It is also in the correct form (spelling) to apply to a masculine object, such as *anthropos*, "man". So grammatically, "one man" is valid, and it fits.

Secondly, it is feasible for God to make every nation of mankind from just "one man". Procreation works exponentially, as the following model shows. If by the age of 30 a typical man produces two sons and two daughters who survive to adulthood and marry in turn, then one man will become over eight billion – more than Earth's current population[92] after only 32 generations, in under 1000 years. In reality, the overall growth rate was lower. The population in Paul's day was much smaller than today, even though mankind had been on the earth for at least 4000 years.

Thirdly, other evidence in the book of Romans supports how the apostle Paul used *ex enos* in Acts 17. In Romans 5:16, he uses the same phrase

---

[89] As in "Nestle-Aland Novum Testamentum Graece (NA27)", 2007, ed. B Aland.

[90] For example, The Lexham Syntactic Greek New Testament defines one (*enos* ἑνὸς) in Acts 17:26 as "Root: εἰς.2, LN: 60.10; adjective, genitive, singular, masculine". Lukaszewski, A. L., Dubis, M., & Blakley, J. T. (2011). The Lexham Syntactic Greek New Testament, SBL Edition: Expansions and Annotations (Ac 17:26). Bellingham, WA: Lexham Press.

[91] Some authorities have 'by one' as neuter in Romans. Fitzmyer has both with a question mark. But the context makes it plain that it applies to 'man' and therefore that is the way it is translated in many leading versions of the Bible.

[92] 7.86 billion in April 2021.

twice, and the English words corresponding to *ex* and *enos* are underlined.

> *"And not as it was <u>by one</u> that sinned, so is the gift: for the judgment was <u>by one</u> to condemnation ..."* (Romans 5:16)

In this context, Paul is comparing Christ the righteous and Adam the sinner. Regarding Adam, Paul says the judgment was *ex enos*, by one, to condemnation. Of course, two parties were involved: God, who made the judgment (Gk. *krima*), and Adam, who was condemned (Gk. *katakrima*, an adverse sentence). How did God bring condemnation by one? God cursed Adam with mortality (a state where "death reigns", Romans 5:17), and this impacted all of Adam's posterity. This was not a legal condemnation, but a physical condemnation. "By one" concerns one man who caused an effect by his own action, but God was active in bringing into effect His judgment.

Paul also teaches that one man's sin affected all men. Death came into the world through the sin of one man, and so death passed upon all men (Romans 5:12); the offence of one man brought condemnation on all men (5:18); by one man's disobedience many were made sinners (5:19). The sense of *ex enos*, "by one", is thus seen to be expansive: by one man, by Adam's sin, judgment to condemnation, and death, came not on him only, but on *all men*.

This last aspect highlights further points of connection between this context and Paul's message in Athens. There, he said that God commands "*all men* everywhere", i.e. "every nation of mankind...on the face of all the earth", to repent (Acts 17:30). He said they must do so because God will in His appointed day judge the world - the same world into which, through one man, sin entered and was judged unto physical condemnation. By the disobedience of one man, Adam, many were made sinners, but God will judge the world by the other one man, Jesus Christ, by whom many will be made righteous.

Another example of *ex enos* is in Romans 9:10:

> *"... when Rebecca also had conceived <u>by one</u>, even by our father Isaac, ..."* (Romans 9:10)

Here *ex enos*, by one, refers to an individual man. However, the effect here was conception in a barren woman, not condemnation. It was by one, namely Isaac, that Rebecca conceived. Genesis 25:21 says that Rebecca was barren, and Isaac appealed to God for her. Hence it was only after 20 years of marriage, through God's response to Isaac's request, that she conceived. Both God and the one man by whom the conception occurred were active in producing their children.

Notably, Paul calls Isaac "*our* father", i.e. the father of himself and other descendants, living long after Isaac died. That is why, even before his sons were born, God termed them "two nations" (Genesis 25:23). By one, that is, by one *father*, Rebecca conceived, and so arose via Jacob and Esau the nations of Israel and Edom. This event ties into Acts 17:26 through both *ex enos*, "by one", and also "nations".

All these cases of Paul using *ex enos* show that the masculine singular *enos* "one" in Acts 17:26 refers to a man, and that God made every nation of mankind by that one *man*. Further, in Paul saying that God made "every *nation* of mankind" by one, he means that the one man is their *father* in the same way that Isaac was the father of the nations of Israel and Edom.

EC interpretations that God created all nations from "one stock", and that Paul is not referring to the origin of the nations from one man, but rather the common humanity shared by all nations, are wide of the mark.

ii) Paul's speech is based on Scripture, and Paul only quotes Greek poetry where it agrees with Scripture

Paul's words stretch back to the very beginning from where all national groups have descended *"when he [God] separated the sons of Adam"* (Deuteronomy 32:8). This becomes obvious when we see that Paul's speech retraces Biblical history from the creation down to the day of judgment.

The numerous parallels with what Paul says in Acts 17 and other parts of Scripture demonstrate that Paul primarily has the teaching of Scripture in mind. For example, the phrase in the latter half of v26 *"on all the face of the earth"* echoes the teaching of Genesis 1:28-29 where, after creating man in His own image, God commanded him to exercise dominion over *"every living thing that moveth upon the earth"*, and gave him every herb bearing seed which is *"upon the face of all the earth"* as food. This identifies the "one", from whom Paul says all are descended, as Adam. There is also a striking parallel between Acts 17:26 and Deuteronomy 32:8 where the nations are defined as having originated from *"the sons of Adam"* - *"When the Most High divided to the nations their inheritance, when he separated the sons of Adam, he set the bounds of the people according to the number of the children of Israel"*. The genealogies in Genesis 4, 5 and 10, as well as 1 Chronicles 1, make it clear that all of the nations on the earth came from Adam via Shem, Ham and Japheth with their respective wives. Adam was miraculously created by God, and called his wife Eve because she was the mother of *"all living"*. This is confirmed by Luke's genealogy, which traces the line of Christ back to *"Adam, which was the son of God"* (Luke 3:38).

The apostle references the third century BC Greek poet Aratus – *"for we are indeed his offspring"* (v28) - to find agreement with a scriptural principle that we are God's offspring – *"Being then God's offspring"* (v29). This is confirmed by the Bible's genealogies which all point back to Adam being the son of God. It is also important not to forget that Paul quoted Aratus to teach that life and death were in the hands of the one true God of the Bible, a God that was completely "unknown" to his Epicurean and Stoic audience. Many of his audience would have seen Aratus in a different light to that of Paul. Albert Barnes' Commentary says, *"The sentiment here quoted was directly at variance with the views of the Epicureans; and it is proof of Paul's address and skill, as well as his acquaintance with his auditors and with the Greek poets, that he was able to adduce a sentiment so directly in point, and that had the concurrent testimony of so many of the Greeks themselves."*

The apostle Paul's speech in Acts 17 forms part of God's inspired word, including the quotation from Aratus because it supports the truth about God's purpose with the earth and mankind. Paul certainly did not quote Greek mythology that conflicts with OT teaching about God's purpose, and then use this as a basis to draw meaningful spiritual lessons. Preaching *"the gospel with the holy spirit sent down from heaven"* (1 Peter 1:12), his entire speech was purposefully designed by God to be understood by all audiences, regardless of time and culture.

iii) Athenian culture – a barrier to belief in the resurrection

The gospel Paul preached clashed with the cultural background of his audience. The Epicurean and Stoic philosophers brought him to the Areopagus because they could not understand his *"new teaching"*. Some of them thought he was a *"babbler"*, and others *"a preacher of foreign divinities"*, but in fact *"he was preaching Jesus and the resurrection"*(vv18-20). Paul declared the *"Unknown God"* (v23), who is soon going to judge the world in righteousness through the man he has appointed (Jesus Christ). The apostle used the resurrection of Christ as "Exhibit A" to provide "assurance" of everything else about the one true God, including His future judgments and their need to repent.

Paul paved the way to his finale by quoting familiar lines from two ancient Greek poets Epimenides and Aratus in v28. But then for his main point in Acts 17:31, Paul quoted the Psalms (Psalms 9:8, 96:13, 98:9) to prove there is a *"man"* whom God has raised from the dead, and this same man is destined to judge *"the world"* in righteousness when he returns. At this point, the Athenians' knowledge of "demons" and of ancient Greek philosophers were of no avail in helping them grasp what Paul was saying. So much so that most *"mocked"* what he was saying. Their cultural background led them to conclude that Paul was preaching *"foolishness"* (1 Corinthians 1:23).

Paul taught the resurrection and the judgment of all nations by the **one man** that God has raised from the dead, in contrast to the **one man** by whom God made all nations. Through **one man** the entire world was populated. Through another **one man** the whole world will be judged in righteousness. No one denies that there are lessons that spring from these first principle teachings, including that we should not consider ourselves superior to any other race or person, and that God is now commanding all men everywhere to repent. But to deny the reality of the two **"one man"** bookends – from **one real man** came all nations, and from **another real man** comes the resurrection - is to remove the very basis upon which these important lessons are grounded.

It is true that Paul does not refer to Adam by name. But he does not refer to Christ by name either. In 1 Corinthians 15:20-22 and 44-49, Paul makes it plain that the two men are Adam and Christ. This is something the Epicurean and Stoic philosophers in Athens had trouble understanding, and it is something with which many of the believers in nearby Corinth grappled as well. The table on the following page illustrates the strong connection between Acts 17 and 1 Corinthians 15, in terms of both the original audience's background and the opposing truth taught by the apostle Paul.

iv) Paul's understanding of Adam as the father of all nations would not change if he were alive today.

The EC assertion that the apostle Paul might well have "believed" that Adam was the father of all nations because he didn't have access to all the "evidence" available to us today, is an alarming claim! To dismiss the apostle by saying that his commentary on Genesis is based on his ignorant opinion, amounts to a belief in the partial inspiration of Scripture and hence is in conflict with the Foundation clause of the BASF. Paul had access to all the inspired words of the Old Testament, including the Genesis record of creation, which is God's first-hand account of how all nations came from one man – Adam. Under inspiration, Paul confirms that the events in Genesis were real historical events, that Adam was the first man whom God made a living creature (1 Corinthians 15:45), that he was created first before Eve (1 Corinthians 11:8-9,11-12; 1 Timothy 2:13), and that Adam was responsible for the entry of sin and death into the world (1 Corinthians 15:21-22; Romans 5:12-21).

The claim that the truth about the origin of the human race, and why we are subject to death, was hidden from Paul due to his inability to access today's scientific information, must be answered by the Bible. Paul's written teachings on these subjects were not his own *"private interpretation"* (2 Peter 1:21) but what God directly inspired him to write. He preached publicly *"with the Holy Spirit sent down from heaven"* (1 Peter 1:12). In Galatians 1, the apostle informs us that the gospel he preached was *"not of human origin"*. He did *"not receive it or learn it from any human source"*, including renowned Hebrew experts such as Gamaliel, Greek philosophers or even the other apostles. Instead, he *"received it by a revelation of Jesus Christ"* (Galatians 1:11-12, NET).[93]

---

[93] The apostle Paul further explains that after Jesus appeared to him on the road to

Acts 17 (ESV)	1 Corinthians 15 (ESV)
The Difficulty Facing the Original Audience: *A wealth of "so-called" knowledge was a barrier to accepting the Resurrection*	
"Some of the Epicurean and Stoic philosophers also conversed with him. And some said, "What does this babbler wish to say?" Others said, "He seems to be a preacher of foreign divinities"—because he was preaching Jesus and the resurrection. And they took him and brought him to the Areopagus, saying, "May we know what this new teaching is that you are presenting?" (vv18-19) "Now when they heard of the resurrection of the dead, some mocked. But others said, "We will hear you again about this." (v32)	"Now if Christ is proclaimed as raised from the dead, how can some of you say that there is no resurrection of the dead?" (v12) "But someone will ask, "How are the dead raised? With what kind of body do they come?" You foolish person!" (vv35-36) "For Jews demand signs and Greeks seek wisdom, but we preach Christ crucified, a stumbling block to Jews and folly to Gentiles," (1Corinthians 1:22-23) "O Timothy, guard the deposit entrusted to you. Avoid the irreverent babble and contradictions of what is falsely called "knowledge," for by professing it some have swerved from the faith" (1Timothy 6:20-21)
Paul's Approach Step 1: *Explain the current death-stricken state of all nations is due to one man God created*	
"And he made **from one man** every nation of mankind to live on all the face of the earth, having determined allotted periods and the boundaries of their dwelling place" (v26)	"The **first man Adam** became a living being…The first man was from the earth, a man of dust" (vv45-47) "For as **by a man came death** … For **as in Adam all die**" (vv21-22)
Paul's Approach Step 2: *Explain that the hope of the resurrection and eternal life is due to one man God raised from the dead*	
"because he has fixed a day on which he will judge the world in righteousness **by a man** whom he has appointed; and of this he has given assurance to all by raising him from the dead." (v31)	"the last Adam became a life-giving spirit … the second man is from heaven." (vv45-47) "But in fact Christ has been raised from the dead, the firstfruits of those who have fallen asleep." (v20) "by a man has come also the resurrection of the dead … so also in Christ shall all be made alive. But each in his own order: Christ the firstfruits, then at his coming those who belong to Christ." (vv21-22) "Then comes the end, when he delivers the kingdom to God the Father after destroying every rule and every authority and power. For he must reign until he has put all his enemies under his feet. The last enemy to be destroyed is death." (vv24-26)

Damascus, he did not seek advice from any human being, nor did he go up to Jerusalem to see the apostles, but he spent three years in Arabia and Damascus, during which time he was taught directly by the "revelation of Jesus Christ" (see Galatians 1:15-18).

There is a parallel between EC beliefs today and the widespread belief in the immortality of the soul that made many unable to accept the resurrection in the first century. Paul had access to the consensus wisdom of the day, which taught that the soul was immortal.[94] Belief in the immortality of the soul, in one form or other, long preceded apostate Christianity's later acceptance of the same belief. In 1 Corinthians 15 the apostle Paul does not state explicitly why some believers in Corinth were saying, *"that there is no resurrection of the dead"*(v12) or why they were asking, *"How are the dead raised? With what kind of body will they come?"*(v35) But it is reasonable to conclude that they were influenced by the belief in the immortality of the soul that pervaded Egyptian, Greek, Roman (deified emperors) and, in part, the Jewish understanding[95] of the afterlife. Given that these believers in Corinth were challenging the whole idea of resurrection, the logical alternative for a future hope after death would be the immortality of the soul.

So when, by the Holy Spirit, the apostle Paul preached the resurrection in Acts 17 and wrote 1 Corinthians 15, he was in direct conflict with the "the wealth of evidence" presented by all his contemporary "credible" experts. But he still instructed Timothy *to "protect what has been entrusted to you"* (the word of God), and to *"avoid the profane chatter and absurdities of so-called knowledge"*, because, by *"professing it some have strayed from the faith"* (1 Timothy 6:20-21, NET).

No man can serve two masters. It is disturbing that EC advocates appear unable to see the contradictory implications of trying to explain God's method of creation through a form of science that denies a Creator. In addition, they reinterpret the Bible to suit their belief in *"what is falsely called knowledge"* (1 Timothy 6:20, ESV). The EC allegiance to the paradigm of non-theistic science as an authority on the subject of origins, makes God's first-hand record of origins in Scripture of none effect.

---

[94] "The belief that the soul continues in existence after the dissolution of the body is … speculation … nowhere expressly taught in Holy Scripture…The belief in the immortality of the soul came to the Jews from contact with Greek thought and chiefly through the philosophy of Plato, its principal exponent, who was led to it through Orphic and Eleusinian mysteries in which Babylonian and Egyptian views were strangely blended." (*Jewish Encyclopedia*, 1941, Vol. 6, "Immortality of the Soul," pp. 564, 566).
The International Standard Bible Encyclopedia comments on ancient Israel's view of the soul: "We are influenced always more or less by the Greek, Platonic idea that the body dies, yet the soul is immortal. Such an idea is utterly contrary to the Israelite consciousness and is nowhere found in the Old Testament (1960, Vol. 2, "Death," p. 812).

[95] The Pharisees believed in both resurrection (Acts 23:8) and the immortality of the soul (Luke 16:19-31) while the Sadducees rejected both (Acts 23:6-8 cp. Luke 20:27). Josephus confirms that the Pharisees believed that *"all souls are incorruptible; but that the souls of good men are only removed into other bodies,—but that the souls of bad men are subject to eternal punishment"* (Josephus, *The Wars of the Jews*, II. viii. 14; see also Josephus, *Antiquities of the Jews.* XVIII. i. 3).

Chapter 14

Don't Demons Illustrate How We Should Read Early Genesis?

Typical EC Objection: The way the NT uses demons illustrates why early Genesis should not be read as a historical narrative.

EC proponents assert that because the Bible sometimes uses unscientific language, including the apparent literal existence of demons, we should be open to the possibility that the language of Genesis 1-3 may also be unscientific and not a historical account.

The following quotation illustrates how they digress to the subject of demons to negate Jesus' clear teaching in Matthew 19 and Mark 10 that the creation of male and female in Genesis 1, and the creation of Adam and Eve in Genesis 2, are parallel historical accounts:

> "Given that Jesus readily accommodated beliefs about demons, any attempt to proof-text this passage [Mark 10:6-8] without keeping in mind the fact Jesus could be accommodating contemporary interpretations and assumptions about a passage for rhetorical purposes is at best risky."[96]

Christadelphians have consistently rejected the literal existence of demons because the Bible itself rules them out. For example, through Isaiah, God declared that there is no god beside Him (Isaiah 45:5-7), so true Israelite Bible students in the time of Christ would know that the popular conception of demons, and Beelzebub as the Lord of demons, was a fallacy. Within the ecclesial world, much evidence in books, magazine articles and lectures has been produced to show why the Bible itself rules out the literal existence of demons. See Chapter 21 for a detailed explanation of demons as various diseases, and that they are a work of the devil or a by-product of fallen human nature.

But EC advocates argue that Jesus did not stop to explain to his audience the truth about demons, as it would be too difficult for many of them to understand. Hence they reason that Jesus accommodated the false belief held by many in the first century in order to teach more important spiritual lessons. The same, they claim, applies to the reading of early Genesis, based on their view that:

---

[96] Gilmore, Ken, *"Appealing to Mark 10:6-8 doesn't mean there aren't two divergent creation accounts"*, January 2019, christadelphianevolution.blogspot.com.au.

- The idea of evolution would be as difficult for ancient readers of Genesis to understand as the truth about demons

- The creation record is therefore couched in terms that the original readers of Genesis could understand – i.e. they claim that much of the material in early Genesis was borrowed from Babylonian mythology to which ancient readers were accustomed.

- This approach was necessary to allow God to undertake the more important task of teaching spiritual lessons, and the truth about Himself as the one true God responsible for all life.

There are at least three reasons to reject this line of reasoning:

1. This is a non sequitur. It does not follow that because Jesus accommodated a false belief in demons that Genesis must be read in the same way. By taking the same approach, we could discount any section of Scripture that did not fit our preconceptions. Any portion of Scripture must be interpreted by its immediate and wider contexts, not by filtering it through a preconceived idea.

2. Christ spoke plainly on creation. His New Testament statements on creation and the creation of Adam and Eve are in perfect harmony with Old Testament teaching, as well as the view of his New Testament contemporaries.

3. If evolution was true, then an inspired Moses could have described it in perfectly understandable terms, just as the ancient Greek philosophers did who first presented the idea to the world[97]. Moreover, the Lord could have easily cited and endorsed Moses' evolutionary description.

EC advocates argue that a natural reading of Genesis 1-3 is not supported by science and should therefore be rejected or reinterpreted to accommodate science. This argument puts them in direct conflict with Scripture.

After all, what is the scientific evidence for the creation of life? What is the scientific evidence for the creation of Adam from dust? What is the scientific evidence for the resurrection of Christ? What is the scientific evidence for Bible miracles? If science declares the creation record to be 'unscientific', then it must rule out these 'unscientific' events as well.

---

[97] For example: 1) Thales of Miletus (640–546 BC) was evidently the first "Greek Philosopher" to advance the idea that life first originated in water [Birdsell, J.B., *Human Evolution*, Rand McNally, p. 22, 1972]; and 2) Aristotle (384–322 BC) claimed that humans are the highest point of one long, continuous 'ascent with modification' of life [Osborn, H.F., *From the Greeks to Darwin*, Charles Scribner's Sons, *p. 54, 1929*].

While taking account of figures of speech, like Abel's blood crying to God from the ground in Genesis 4:10, flashes of poetry such as Genesis 3:15 and the highly structured, prosaic nature of the whole of Genesis, according to Hebrew experts, the book is written as historical narrative[98]. Christ and the Apostles read it that way. We should have the faith to do the same. Otherwise, we effectively accuse our God of being the author of confusion by opening Scripture with a book that has been historically impossible to understand until modern evolutionary science and compromising, liberal theologians arrived to show us the way.

---

[98] See "Genesis is meant to convey real historical events on page 20.

Chapter 15
Why Christadelphians Oppose Walton's "Lost World" Series

EC advocates promote John H. Walton's[99] views

Christadelphian EC advocates regularly present John H. Walton's EC views, even though they do not agree with everything he proposes[100]. One of the main differences is that Walton views Adam and Eve as historical individuals whom God selected from among the existing evolved humans. This is a common EC view held by evangelical advocates. In contrast, many Christadelphian promoters of EC believe that God miraculously created Adam and Eve, but that 'evolved' humans existed before them and contemporary 'evolved' humans lived outside the garden.

Christadelphian EC advocates often repeat Walton's arguments, including:

- Genesis 1 is not about a material creation;

- Genesis 2 is an entirely different creation record from Genesis 1;

- "Unscientific" expressions and figures of speech within the creation record that are not literal, serve as evidence that we cannot take the rest of the creation record to be literal either;

- Adam and Christ are two archetypal heads with whom we identify by our actions, not by our inherited mortal physical state or our prospective immortal physical state;

- Sin is only possible when a human has sufficient knowledge of God's laws.

Is John H. Walton's "Lost World" series[101] compatible with Bible teaching in Genesis 1-4?

In a brief chapter, a comprehensive critique of Walton's series is impossible. However, readers should be able to understand, from the following comments, the general tenor of Walton's views and

---

[99] John H. Walton is "professor of Old Testament at Wheaton College and Graduate School".

[100] For example, Bro Jonathan Burke has made numerous posts on his *"Science and Scripture"* Facebook page where he quotes articles from Biologos.com and excerpts from John H. Walton's books. See https://www.facebook.com/Science-Scripture-1449424052004603/

[101] *The Lost World of Genesis One* (2009); *The Lost world of Scripture* (2013); *The Lost World of Adam and Eve* (2015).

pursue the details for themselves. The best that can be achieved is to make a general comment on the likelihood of his thesis being compatible with Bible and Christadelphian teaching.

The first point to be made is that Walton reads Genesis 1-3 in a way that is not the natural way it has been read in the Christian world, including by Christ and the apostles, for nearly 2,000 years. Moreover, taking into account the Greek words chosen to translate 'created' and 'made' in Genesis, in the New Testament and also by the Septuagint translators (3rd – 2nd centuries B.C.), the Jews have not read it as Walton reads it either.

It is implausible to think that a single Evangelical theologian has finally discovered the 'correct' way to read Genesis after all this time. Many of his Evangelical theological contemporaries reviewing his work (links for five examples, among others, are footnoted) reject his view of Genesis 1-3.[102]

Walton's central thesis is that Genesis should be read in light of the cosmologies of the ancient world. This means that instead of Genesis, as the inspired word of God, being unique, any reading of Genesis must take into account the views of the cosmos and its functions held by people of the Ancient Near East (ANE) at the time Genesis was written. Supposedly, ancient cosmologies or cultures are not so concerned with how the material universe was created but how it functions. The cosmos is regarded as the temple of the gods and how things function in that temple. Therefore, Genesis should be read in that same light. Genesis 1 supposedly describes the origin of the Edenic temple and its functions over six days and how God, on the seventh day, came to rest through occupying His place in that temple. Walton argues that because Genesis 1 is about function, it cannot be taken as a literal description of the material creation any more than the Bible's "…*talk about cognitive processes related to the heart*" can be taken "…*as biblical teaching on physiology*". This being the case, Walton believes that there is no clash between evolution and Genesis 1. Apparently, this is because evolution is a scientific explanation of origins, while Genesis only reveals how order and function were

---

[102] Currid, John D. (2018) *Theistic Evolution Is Incompatible with the Teachings of the Old Testament*. In J.P. Moreland, Stephen C. Myer, et. al, *Theistic Evolution: A Scientific, Philosophical and Theological Critique"*, pp. 839-879. Wheaton, Illinois: Crossway

McFall, L. (2010, January 16), *Critique of John H. Walton's Book*. Retrieved from: lmf12.files.wordpress.com/2012/11/critique_jh_walton.pdf

Ham, S. (2015, July 29), *The Lost World of Adam and Eve: A Response*: Retrieved from: https://answersingenesis.org/reviews/books/lost-world-adam-and-eve-response/

Statham, D. (2010, December), *Dubious and Dangerous Exposition*, Journal of Creation Vol. 24(3), pp. 24-26, Retrieved from: https://creation.com/review-walton-the-lost-world-of-genesis-one

Halley, K. (2015) *John Walton Reimagines Adam and Eve*, Journal of Creation Vol. 29 (2) 2015, pp. 47-51: Retrieved from: https://creation.com/images/pdfs/tj/j29_2/j29_2_47-51.pdf

brought to an already existing material universe and an already existing humanity.

In Genesis 2-3, Walton proposes that Adam and Eve occupy a priestly role in the garden temple as mediators for God. They are also presented as "archetypal" heads of humanity, elected as the first "significant" humans from the previously evolved human race. They are therefore not literally the sole progenitors of our entire human race. Walton also claims that Genesis 1:26-27 is not about the creation of Adam and Eve but describes a group of humans or humanity in general, thus allowing for his view that Genesis 2-3 is later and separate from Genesis 1. The serpent was not a literal beast of the field but, according to Walton, would have been seen by the ancient Hebrews as a "chaos being" who brought disorder. Adam and Eve, after acting on the serpent's lie, brought disorder into the ordered cosmic temple. Therefore, the primary role of Christ should be seen as his work of restoring order to the world, contrary to the Bible's emphasis on his role of conquering, within himself, the problem of sin and death introduced by Adam, and to open the way for our salvation. In an attempt to establish this idea N.T. Wright, in his contribution to Walton's "The Lost World of Adam and Eve", references Paul's comments on the deliverance of creation from the bondage of corruption in Romans 8:18-23.

Reasons for rejecting Walton's thesis

There are many aspects of Walton's work that fail to match the Bible's teaching on creation, the role of Adam and Eve as lone progenitors of our human race, their sin and its effects, the atoning work of our Lord Jesus, and the establishment of God's kingdom on the earth. In the remainder of this chapter, we will limit our discussion to the following topics, summarising Walton's view and providing the Biblical answer.[103]

i. New Testament writers treat Genesis 1-4 as a historical record of real events, including a material creation

ii. The Bible is clear that the need for priests and mediatorship arose after Adam and Eve sinned, not before

iii. The Bible presents Adam's miraculous creation as a literal historical event

iv. The Bible is silent on any pre-Adamic and co-Adamic race of men

v. Being "In Adam" is a physical relationship, not an archetypal relationship

vi. Sin still occurs regardless of any knowledge of God's laws

---

[103] Our comments will centre on *The Lost World of Adam and Eve*, IVP Academic, Intervarsity Press, Downers Grove, Illinois 2015.

    vii. There is no basis for discounting the primary meaning of 'bara' (a material creation) in Genesis 1

    viii. The ancients could distinguish between figurative and literal language

    ix. Walton himself is dreaming when he suggests Eve's creation was just one of Adam's dreams

i) NT writers treat Genesis 1-4 as a historical record of real events, including a material creation

Walton claims that the people of the ANE were more concerned with understanding how roles and functions were established in the cosmos, rather than understanding its material creation. Therefore, Walton claims that Genesis was written with this in mind.

Response: Amazingly, Walton asserts that he understands how the ancient Israelites understood their world. He falsely claims that ancient cosmogonies were more concerned about function than creation, when they are equally concerned about both. Neither the Genesis text nor the inspired New Testament commentators on Genesis 1-4 mention in any direct way the aspects of "function" and order. Although by its very nature aspects of function are involved in the creative acts of Genesis 1, New Testament writers, in explaining both the origin of sin and death and how eventually they will be destroyed, treat Genesis 1-4 as a historical record of real events.[104]

ii) The Bible is clear that the need for priests and mediatorship arose after Adam and Eve sinned, not before

Walton's view is that Eden is a temple and that Adam and Eve had a priestly role as mediators for other contemporary humans. Adam's task to 'dress' and 'keep' the garden (Genesis 2:15) is taken by Walton to refer to his priestly role because these words apply to priestly work elsewhere.

Response: Firstly, the priestly role of Adam and Eve is not indicated by the text. Secondly, Adam's actual role is explained by verse 5 in the same context – *"there was not a man to till the ground"*. Thirdly, because in the text Adam and Eve receive no directives on how to carry out their supposed priestly role, Walton's view is an example of eisegesis[105] rather than exegesis[106]. Fourthly, before they sinned, Adam and Eve enjoyed direct fellowship with God in the garden

---

[104] Acts 14:15; 17:24; Romans 1:19-20; Ephesians 3:9; Revelation 10:6; 14:7 (though symbolic, these last two verses allude to the literal creation); Hebrews 4:4; Matthew 19:4-5; Mark 10:6-8; 1 Corinthians 15:45-47; 1 Timothy 2:13; 1 Corinthians 11:8-9; 6:16; Ephesians 5:31; Revelation 2:7; 2 Corinthians 11: 3; Romans 5:12-21; 1 Corinthians 15:21-22.

[105] Eisegesis (*"to lead into"*) is a subjective method of exposition by introducing one's own opinions into the original text.

[106] Exegesis (*"to lead out of"*) is the exposition of the original text based on a careful, objective analysis. The interpreter is led to his conclusions by closely following the text.

without the requirement for any mediator or animal sacrifice. The first animal death occurred only after their sin when God made them coats of skins. The function of a "temple" and the role of a "priest" as a mediator between God and man are not evident in the garden. Only after God had driven them out, and placed the cherubim to keep the way to the tree of life, were sacrifices brought to him (Genesis 4:3-4). Adam and Eve were not priestly mediators; their sin meant that they needed priestly mediatorship themselves. If, before they sinned, they had a priestly role, on whose behalf was it exercised? The Bible neither states nor implies that other humans besides Adam and Eve even existed.

iii) The Bible presents Adam's miraculous creation as a literal historical event

Given that Genesis 2:7 says that Adam was miraculously created from the dust, Walton has to find an answer to this historical event if, as follows, Adam had parents who belonged to the already existing evolved human population. Walton argues that other men are described as "dust", which he says is a metaphor for their mortality, so Adam's literal creation from "dust" must only be a symbolic reference to his mortality.

Response: Walton's conclusion is not persuasive because Adam's creation is presented as a literal historical event. Walton's argument is the equivalent of saying that as believers are called sons of God, Jesus must only be a son of God in the same limited sense, even though Jesus' Sonship of God through his divine conception is literal. Likewise, the promise to David that his seed would be God's son is applied to Solomon in a figurative sense, but Jesus was God's son literally. The apostle Paul's metaphorical description that all true believers *"have been crucified with Christ"* (Galatians 2:20), only works because it was literally true of Jesus himself. Most importantly, if Adam was already mortal *"dust"* in 2:7, God would not have to condemn him to *"dust"* again in 3:19. Walton is therefore forced to provide this fanciful 'dust' argument that many of his fellow Evangelical exegetes reject.

iv) The Bible is silent on any pre-Adamic and co-Adamic race

Walton's view is that there was a pre-Adamic and co-Adamic race of men from whom Adam and Eve descended. Walton and other promulgators of EC attempt to get around the glaring lack of Biblical evidence for this assertion by raising the old canard, based on Genesis 4:14-17, that (1) Cain was able to find a wife, (2) there were people in existence, outside of Adam and Eve's descendants, that he was afraid would avenge his murder of Abel, and (3) a large number of people were needed to help Cain build a city.

Response: The hypothetical pre- and co-Adamic race idea has absolutely no clear teaching in any Old or New Testament passage to support it. At best, these are inferred arguments; at worst, they are pure invention. See Chapters 11 and 12 for answers to these points that are raised to infer the existence of evolved humans.

v) Being "In Adam" is a physical, not an archetypal, relationship

Walton claims that Adam and Eve were "archetypes" of humanity before and after being selected from among the supposed pre- and co-Adamic humans. "Archetype" comes from the Greek noun ἀρχέτυπον [archetupon], implying an original type or pattern. Therefore, to say that Adam is an archetype is to say that Adam is an example of the original "type" of human. Walton's archetypal view means that the reader should understand the account of Adam and Eve as typical of all other humans before and after them, rather than an account of how those two individuals were uniquely formed.[107] So Adam's sin had no physical impact on humanity. Rather, Adam as an archetype merely displays the human condition. What happened to Adam and Eve as archetypes is a kind of allegory that tells us what happens to every single person. Walton confirms his belief in evolution, states that Adam and Eve may or may not have been the first evolved humans, and proposes that this is theologically viable:

> "Genesis 2 is not making claims about biological origins of humanity, and therefore the Bible should not be viewed as offering competing claims against science about human origins. If this is true, **Adam and Eve also may or may not be the first humans or the parents of the entire human race**. Such an archetypal focus is theologically viable and is well-represented in the ancient Near East."[108]

Response: Walton's view is hardly theologically viable in light of the straightforward commentary on both "Adams" and their critical foundational place in the scheme of salvation, presented in the New Testament and outlined in the BASF.[109] This includes (i) the physical consequences of Adam's sin upon all humanity, including Christ (Romans 5:12-21; 6:9-10; 1 Corinthians 15:20-23; Hebrews 2:9, 14-15), (ii) the physical consequences of Christ's obedience for all who are truly "in Christ" and who will receive grace and the gift of righteousness (Romans 5:17) at his coming (1 Corinthians 15:23). (See Chapter 19 for further discussion on *"in Adam"* and *"in Christ"*).

Walton never explains how a person can be "in" the "archetypal" Christ. For Adam and Christ to be two separate archetypes, what they each separately did cannot be unique to them. What is true for all those who are *"in Adam"* as one archetype, must be true for all those who are *"in Christ"* as the second archetype. EC advocates claim that if we follow Adam's example by sinning, we prove ourselves to be

---

[107] Walton and Wright, *The Lost World of Adam and Eve* (2015), p. 74-75.

[108] Walton and Wright, *The Lost World of Adam and Eve* (2015), p. 89.

[109] Cp. Romans 3-8; BASF Clauses III, IV, V, VIII, IX, X.

"in" the archetypal Adam. But it therefore follows that the only way we can prove to be "in" the archetypal Christ is by following his example and never sinning. As Christ was perfectly obedient and needed no forgiveness, it follows that all those in the archetypal Christ must likewise be perfectly obedient and need no forgiveness. However, the truth is that our state of being *"in Christ"* does require forgiveness of sins, so Christ, who never sinned, cannot be our archetype in the sense that EC advocates believe.

vi) Sin still occurs regardless of any knowledge of God's laws

Walton presents the view, common among his fellow EC believers, that the posited pre-Adamic race was mortal and had the same sinful propensities as our fallen nature. He claims that these supposed pre-Adamic men should not be regarded as sinners because they were not given God's law, were ignorant of it, and therefore could not transgress it. This is based on his reading of Romans 5:12-14, where he likens the proposed race to all those who died between the Law of Eden and the Law of Moses, even though they were not under either law.

Response: Firstly, the Bible, and in particular Paul, is entirely silent about any pre-Adamic race. Secondly, those who died between Adam and Moses were still regarded as sinners, e.g. at the flood.

Thirdly, the period referred to is between Adam and Moses, and has no application whatsoever to the phantom pre-Adamic race.

Fourthly, although Paul says in Romans 4:15, *"…where no law is, there is no transgression"*, this cannot mean that because we are not under the Mosaic Law we cannot sin. Abraham, who lived 400 years before the Law of Moses, and those in Christ by the New Covenant, who are under grace and not under law, are not accountable to the Mosaic Law. However, that does not mean that we do not sin. Abraham certainly did, and so do we. Violations against the Law of Moses are referred to as *"transgressions"*, so where there is no Law, there can be no transgression of that Law. But the apostle informs us that sin is still committed by those not exposed to law: *"For as many as have sinned without law shall also perish without law"* (Romans 2:12). If we commit murder in the country where we are citizens, we cannot be punished a foreign country's penal code. Because the murder took place in our own country, we have not transgressed the foreign country's law, even though its laws also condemn murder. Murder is a sin against God whether or not we are under the penal code of a particular country. Adultery, for example, is a sin against God, and it transgresses the law of some countries, but it does not transgress the law of others.

Fifthly, the Israelites were not called out of Egypt until the iniquity of the Amorites was full.[110] The Amorites were punished for their "iniquity" even though they were not given God's laws like the children of Israel were.

vii) There is no basis for discounting the primary meaning of 'bara' (a material creation) in Genesis 1

Walton claims that the Hebrew word *bara* translated as "create" in Genesis 1 and elsewhere should be understood in the sense of creating functional activity as opposed to creating material things.

Response: *Bara* can be used in the secondary sense[111] of a function or role, but there is no basis in the Genesis 1 text for Walton to insist that bara's secondary usage should override the obvious primary application of the word to the literal creation of the material world. The way *bara* is used elsewhere in Scripture will demonstrate that applying it to 'function' is a far less likely use of the word than applying it to the creation of material things, attitudes of mind etc. Both *bara* (=created) and *asah* (=made) are translated in the Septuagint (LXX) with the same Greek word *epoiēsen* (=made) throughout Genesis 1. So Jewish translators in the 3rd Century BC did not see the concept of 'function' in *bara* that Walton does, even though they had a much closer connection in time with the original Biblical Hebrew language. More importantly, when Jesus referenced the material creation of Adam and Eve to answer the Pharisees' question on divorce in Matthew 19:4 and Mark 10:6, the inspired New Testament record of his words uses the same verb *poieō* as in the LXX of Genesis 1 - "Have ye not read, that he which made (*poiēsas*) them at the beginning made (*epoiēsen*) them male and female".

viii) The ancients could distinguish between figurative and literal

Walton claims that the ancients believed that the centre of thought was found in the heart (and according to Walton, even thought with their intestines, i.e. the 'reins'). This, he claims, is obviously wrong according to modern knowledge because thought is centred in the brain. Walton also claims that the ancients had an inaccurate view of cosmic geography, comprising a flat-earth set on pillars, a solid sky or firmament also set on pillars, and waters above the solid sky. Therefore, he claims that we do not necessarily have to take Biblical words and statements as literal or scientific.

Response: The heart has been used throughout history as a metaphor for our innermost thoughts and emotions. The reason for this is that because our heart reacts strongly to our emotions, it has become a metaphor for our thought processes. Adrenalin pumps extra blood into the heart in 'fight or flight' situations. In love, the

---

[110] Genesis 15:16, 21.

[111] Cp. Jeremiah 31:22.

heart reacts when chemicals are released into the pleasure centre of the brain.

Even today, we talk about having a *'broken heart'* or giving our *'heartfelt thanks'* and so forth. We do not believe that the source of these emotional reactions is in anything other than the mind, and neither did the ancients. For example, Daniel was able to interpret what was troubling the *"mind"* of Nebuchadnezzar. [112] David attacked (with his slingshot) Goliath's head and cut it off with the sword because, as any soldier would know, the brain was the instrument that directed the rest of the body. [113] The ecclesia, the body of Christ, has to grow into Christ, who is its head because the head directs the body. [114]

In one of the oldest books of the Bible, Job refers to the *"pillars of the earth"* shaking (Job 9:6), and he also refers to the *"pillars of heaven"* (Job 26:11). However, in the same book, he also says that God *"hangs the earth on nothing"* (Job 26:7), providing clear evidence that the patriarchs were able to use and understand metaphors that they did not take as being the equivalent of reality. A similar example applies to the Old Testament reference to the *"windows of heaven"* (Genesis 7:11; 8:2; Malachi 3:10). In the days of Elisha, an officer who questioned his claim that the price of flour and barley would dramatically fall within 24 hours stated, *"If the LORD himself should make windows in heaven, could such a thing be?"* (2 Kings 2:19, ESV). Were the ancients so ignorant that they literally believed that there were "windows" in heaven that let the rain through, or is it more reasonable to assume that they were highly familiar with and easily able to distinguish between metaphorical and literal language?

Bible students have long taken care to recognise figurative language and separate it from the literal in historical accounts. To follow Walton's reasoning, we would have to argue that the ancients thought that the earth has a literal mouth that it opened to swallow the blood of Abel and that Abel's blood literally cried from the ground. [115]

ix) Walton himself is dreaming when he suggests Eve's creation was just one of Adam's dreams

Walton claims that the narrative of Eve being miraculously produced from Adam's rib was only a dream that Adam had. He was supposed to have seen half of his body taken from his side. This, according to Walton, represents the female other half of humanity, the counterpart to the male

---

[112] Daniel 2:24-30,36.

[113] 1 Samuel 17:46-51.

[114] Colossians 1:18; Ephesians 1:22-23.

[115] Genesis 4:10-11.

half. For Walton, Adam and Eve were already in existence as descencants of the pre-Adamic race.

Response: The text does not say anything about a dream or a vision. It is one thing to reinterpret the text, but surely we are not entitled to invent what is simply not there. Christ and the Apostles, in referring to these stories provide no hint of Walton's idea and treat the record as a historical narrative. *"...from the beginning of the creation God made them male and female. For this cause shall a man leave his father and mother, and cleave to his wife..."* (Christ's words),[116] *"For Adam was first formed, then Eve."*[117] *"For the man is not of the woman; but the woman of the man. Neither was the man created for the woman; but the woman for the man ... For as the woman is of the man, even so is the man also by the woman."*[118]

Walton's reasoning does not fit the circumstances in the context. Eve was created from Adam's rib because *"...for Adam there was not found an help meet for him"* and *"It is not good that the man should be alone; I will make an help meet for him." "And Adam said, this is now bone of my bones, and flesh of my flesh: she shall be called woman, because she was taken out of man."* The context reveals why there was a need for a woman and the process by which that need was satisfied. It is strange that Eve's creation would even be necessary if, as Walton and others maintain, thousands of females were already in existence from which Adam could choose. After all, as is supposed by some believers in EC, Cain had no problem finding a wife among the 'evolved' co-Adamic population.

God is not the author of confusion

There are other aspects of Walton's thesis with which we could take issue, but enough has been said to demonstrate that his thesis is a long way from Biblical teaching and the Christadelphian Statement of Faith.

Walton interprets Genesis through the filter of ancient Egyptian, Assyrian and Babylonian myths, of which some have loose parallels with Bible history.[119] Despite the uniqueness of the Bible, Walton makes the Bible accounts subservient to the mythical stories. In doing so:

- He overlooks the major differences between the mythical and Genesis accounts;

---

[116] Mark 10:6-7.

[117] 1 Timothy 2:13.

[118] 1 Corinthians 11:8-9, 12.

[119] Readers can easily reference these texts freely online under JB Pritchard *Ancient near Eastern Texts Relating to the Bible.*

- He insists that Moses borrows from these creation myths but demythologizes them to convey a monotheistic perspective and important spiritual lessons. The truth is the other way around. The Genesis account is the source, which all nations would have originally understood from the time of Noah's sons. But it was corrupted among those nations over time and was changed into their various myths;
- He asserts that divine inspiration had no choice but to use Ancient Near Eastern myths as a framework because man's primitive level of understanding meant he would have been incapable of accepting the actual truth of God's material creation, as we moderns are capable of doing today.

So the authority and importance of God's first-hand account of His creation is devalued and derided.

Why has Walton produced this rather bizarre thesis? Is it to provide a way to accommodate evolutionary creation? Why has his theory, which may otherwise have passed unnoticed among the many and various views and articles emanating from Bible colleges, become so popular? Because it is in the interests of institutions like BioLogos to promote it so that they can hold onto Bible teaching (or their warped view of it) and at the same time embrace evolution. Walton's thesis claims that Genesis 1-4 is from God, and is the truth, but he turns Genesis into the supposedly limited, ignorant 'truth' of the Patriarchs, that is no longer 'truth' today. It is beyond credulity to propose that Genesis 1-4 requires knowledge 'hidden' for thousands of years, in order for readers to understand what Genesis 1-4 means. God is not the author of confusion, but if we were to accept Walton's reading of Genesis, confusion would reign, and we would be taken a long way away from saving truth.

SECTION 3

VITAL ASPECTS OF THE ATONEMENT WRESTED BY EC

"For though we walk in the flesh, we are not waging war according to the flesh. For the weapons of our warfare are not of the flesh but have divine power to destroy strongholds. We destroy arguments and every lofty opinion raised against the knowledge of God, and take every thought captive to obey Christ…"
(2 Corinthians 10:3-5, ESV)

Overview of Section 3

Adopting EC necessitates a major re-explanation of core Bible doctrines

EC advocates need to wrest parts of the Bible (cp. 2 Peter 3:15-16) and fundamentally alter the principles of the atonement to accommodate their fixed point of evolution. A perusal of the books and websites of those advocating EC views reveals that they have written quite extensively on these matters, including key passages such as Romans 5:12-21 and 1 Corinthians 15:20-21, arguing that the death that Adam's sin introduced into the world is not the cessation of our mortal existence. In particular, they assert the following:

Four false Evolutionary Creation assertions

1. That God's assessment that everything He created was "very good" in Genesis 1:31 simply means that it was fit for God's purpose. It does not mean that human death, disease and suffering were absent, because the same expression occurs several times in the Old Testament well after Adam and Eve sinned.

2. That God's sentence upon Adam and Eve did not introduce any new kind of physical death because mortality, and the physical death associated with mortality, was already in the world. Instead, God's sentence was a legal sentence labelling one as worthy of "eternal" death.

3. That God's sentence, in consequence of their sin, did not result in any physical change to the condition of human nature. Adam and Eve were just as biased to sin before the fall as they were afterwards. EC advocates assert that this is how God evolved all humans prior to Adam and Eve, and evolved or created Adam and Eve from the outset.

4. That sufficient knowledge of God's laws is required before one can actually sin, and then directly deserve "eternal" death.

The purpose of this section is to address Evolutionary Creationists' arguments on these four subjects.

One of the key symptoms of EC wrong doctrine that relates to these four assertions is their fundamentally different view of the devil in contrast to consistent Christadelphian teaching (see Chapter 21). EC advocates do not write as confidently on this subject as they do on other topics. They are fully aware that they disagree with Christadelphian belief that the devil's origin is coeval or concurrent with the fall, and that it personifies the physical sin-prone and death-stricken condition of human nature that began at the fall. They need to provide clarity on (1) what they believe the devil personifies, (2) when it entered the world, (3) what "death" the devil has power over and (4) whether Christ died the death that the devil has power over (Hebrews 2:14).

Another significant feature of EC wrong doctrine is its inability to explain, in a non-substitutionary way, why Christ had to die in the manner he did. As Christ did not sin and given that, as they believe, he was not subject to the death that Adam's sin introduced, their view appears to be substitutionary. This matter is discussed at some length in Chapters 18, 19, and 21.

The diagram below summarizes the differences between the pre-fall "very good" state and the post-fall corrupted state of God's creation, which are discussed at some length in this section. Importantly, everything before and after the fall was from God, but the transitionary choice was under Adam and Eve's control.

Before and After the Fall

"Very Good" State
(Genesis 1 & 2)

Adam & Eve
- Naked & unashamed (2:25)
- Exercise authority over God's creation (1:28)
- Man – dress and **keep** the garden (2:15)
- Woman – fruitful (1:28), blessed to bear children without intense pain, willingly subject to husband (2:18-22; 1 Cor 11:9; 1 Tim 2:13)
- Direct fellowship with God (3:8)

Serpent thinking in serpent (amoral creature) (3:1)

The tree of the knowledge of good and evil (2:9)

God's laws, including His warning that they would die if they ate from the tree of the knowledge of good and evil (2:16-17, cp. 1:28-30; 2:23-24)

Ground blessed, all other trees pleasant to the sight and good for food (2:9). No thorns and thistles

No shedding of blood associated with worship

The way to the tree of life open – no cherubim

Adam & Eve's choice
- **Adopt serpent thinking**
- **Eat the fruit**

Corrupted State
(Genesis 3)

Adam & Eve
- Serpent thinking **permanently in man** (3:15)
- Death stricken – the consequence of eating from the tree of the knowledge of good and evil (2:17; 3:17-19)
- Eyes opened, ashamed of naked state (3:7)
- Dominion lost, hiding in fear (3:8-10)
- Man – eat bread in painful toil (3:17), in sweat of face (3:19), till the cursed ground (3:23)
- Woman – bear children with intense pain, and *"thy desire shall be to thy husband, and he shall rule over thee"* (3:16)
- Direct fellowship with God lost (3:23-24)

Serpent cursed above all cattle and every beast of the field (3:14)

Ground cursed (3:17), thorns and thistles (3:18)

Shedding of blood necessary to provide a covering (3:21)

Cherubim placed to **keep** the way to the tree of life (3:24)

So when this corruptible shall have put on incorruption, and this mortal shall have put on immortality, then shall be brought to pass the saying that is written, Death is swallowed up in victory. (1Cor 15:54)

Chapter 16
Before and After the Fall

EC advocates insist that the condition of human nature did not change post Adam and Eve's sin

EC proponents reject Christadelphian teaching that a physical change in the condition of human nature to mortality and a bias to sin occurred as part of God's just and necessary sentence upon Adam and Eve. They insist that Genesis 3 does not indicate that a physical change occurred. Note the following two examples of EC reasoning:

> **COD:** *...What consequence did Adam suffer on the day he ate the fruit which resulted in certain death? Exclusion from the tree of life is the only thing recorded in Genesis 3. That is worth repeating. Scripture mentions some specific consequences of their sin, but nothing about a change to mortality, no new genetic rearrangement. Instead of all the things some may wish to read, the clear testimony is Adam was barred from the tree of life which would have brought immortality, and instead doomed to certain death.*[120]

> **Mike Pearson:** *But did this 'fall' actually change Adam's nature at a genetic or cellular level? Well, here we go again trying to read twenty-first century concepts into ancient text, whereas in reality the text doesn't discuss this point at all. Genesis 3 explicitly defines the various consequences of Adam's sin for both him and Eve, and these align to the shame, the defiled conscience and death. The text doesn't specify any change in nature, and to suggest that it does, reads concepts into the text that aren't there. The text simply says, "you are dust, and to dust you will return".*[121]

EC advocates prefer to interpret the Genesis record like this in order to maintain consistency with their firm belief in evolved humans living and dying well before Adam and Eve. This is because, in their view, the condition of evolved human nature is exactly the same as our nature today. If such evolved humans did exist long before the time of Adam and Eve, and they intermarried with Adam and Eve's children, then obviously their nature could not be impacted by Adam and Eve's sin. Therefore they prefer to believe in, and promote a view of the atonement that is completely at odds with the Bible and Christadelphian teaching.

---

[120] John Doe, *Lampstand Magazine 'Death the Last Enemy' Vol 23 (2017) response*, COD Website July 2017.

[121] Pearson, Mike, *The Fourth Conversation*, 2nd Edition, 2017, pp. 113-114.

Genesis 3 informs us that there was a post-sin change in the condition of Adam and Eve's nature

God has not revealed the 'mechanics' of what was involved in the change in the condition of Adam and Eve's nature any more than He has revealed what was involved in the resurrection of our Lord and the change of his mortal body to an immortal body where sin is impossible. Nor has He outlined the 'mechanics' of the change of nature promised to the resurrected faithful at Christ's return. Can science explain this? Or do EC proponents insist on applying science at the fall – by rhetorically asking was Adam and Eve's DNA changed – but accepting that a miraculous resurrection followed by a change to immortality will occur at the return of Christ?

That there was a change in the condition of Adam and Eve's nature is evident in the narration of each of the steps in the process.

1.   God miraculously created Adam and Eve as living souls, or natural bodies of life, which were, from God's perspective, *"very good"* in kind and condition. They had the potential, based on their actions, either of becoming subject to death (mortal) and dying, or being granted immortality and living forever. For further discussion, see Chapter 17.

2.   Adam and Eve had not sinned or even contemplated doing so before the serpent's suggestion. There is no evidence that Eve had any desire to eat from the tree of knowledge of good and evil before the serpent spoke to her. She knew what God had said, that to do so would bring death (Genesis 3:3). The obvious inference from this is that she did not desire it. It was only after hearing the serpent's deceitful reasoning that her mind was corrupted (2 Corinthians 11:3), and the lie begat in her an illegitimate desire to eat the forbidden fruit. This illegitimate desire was not of the Father (1 John 2:15-17). After she had been beguiled and sinned, Eve became a temptress to Adam by persuading him to eat the forbidden fruit (Genesis 3:17; 1 Timothy 2:12-14, cp. Ecclesiastes 8:11). For further discussion, see Chapter 20.

3.   God warned that Adam and Eve would surely die if they disobeyed Him. *After* their sin, not *before*, God's sentence of death was pronounced on them. Specifically, God had warned them that on **the day** they sinned they would surely die. So on **the day** they sinned, He sentenced them to return to the dust. God did not warn Adam and Eve, as some argue, that they would be denied access to the tree of life and die because they were already mortal. Rather, they became mortal, dying

creatures on **the day** they sinned. God had not created them as dying creatures.

4. God's sentence on Adam and Eve involved them returning to the dust *after* they sinned. If Adam and Eve were already mortal, a law warning them of dying would be an empty threat. For further discussion on points 3 and 4, see Chapters 18 and 19.

5. Adam and Eve evidenced a change in the condition of their nature and their relationship with God immediately *after*, and as a result of, their sin, even before God questioned them – "*she took of the fruit thereof, and did eat, and gave also unto her husband with her; and he did eat. And the eyes of them both were opened, and they knew that they were naked*" (Genesis 3:6-7). See below for further discussion on Genesis 3:7.

6. Only *after* their sin did God "*put enmity*" between the serpent and the woman and their respective seeds. This enmity included the internal struggle between their fallen nature and God's righteous ways. If they had been created in the same condition in which we find ourselves in today, the "*enmity*" would have already existed, there would have been no need for them to be tested by external prompting, and God's post-sin pronouncement – "*I will put enmity*" – would have been redundant. For further discussion, see Chapters 20 and 21.

7. Only *after* their sin was a literal talking serpent no longer required to suggest the idea of following a course of action in opposition to God's truth. In Genesis 4 the angel warned Cain, not of the danger of listening to the words of a talking serpent or anyone external but, according to the ESV translation, of "*sin*" that is "*crouching at the door. Its desire is contrary to you, but you must rule over it*" (Genesis 4:7, ESV). The enmity, the conflict, the battle – was now within human nature. As the apostle John states, Cain "*was of that wicked one*" – i.e. the *diabolos* (1 John 3:8,12).

8. Only *after* their sin did God state, "*I will surely multiply your pain in childbearing; in pain you shall bring forth children*" (Genesis 3:16, ESV). This tells us that severe pain in childbirth came as a *result* of Eve's sin, not *before* her sin.

9. Only *after*, and *because of*, their sin, God "*cursed the ground*" with "*thorns and thistles*" and consigned man to eating from this cursed ground "*in sorrow … all the days of thy life*". Consequently, man would toil "*in pain all the days of his life*", and "*by the sweat of his face eat bread, till he [returned] to the ground*" (Genesis 3:17-19). Like the ground, man's physical condition would no longer be as healthy as it was pre-curse. Man would suffer the equivalent of

thorns and thistles in his own body. [122] All creation suffered together in that all things are from the earth, and accordingly all things were corrupted. *"For the creation was subjected to futility – not willingly but because of God who subjected it – in hope that the creation itself will also be set free from the bondage of decay into the glorious freedom of God's children. For we know that the whole creation groans and suffers together until now."* (Romans 8:20-22, NET). For further discussion, see Chapters 17 and 21.

10. Only *after* their sin did God a) sacrifice an animal to cover their literal and spiritual nakedness, and b) place the cherubim at the garden's eastern entrance, to keep the way of the tree of life. The sacrificial way back to the tree of life and fellowship with God in the garden was unnecessary *before* their sin.

The eyes of them both were opened, and they knew that they were naked

Genesis 3:7 informs us that two connected changes occurred immediately after Adam and Eve sinned: (i) the eyes of them both were opened; and (ii) they knew that they were naked.

The fact that Adam and Eve became embarrassed about their naked physical state for the first time, and tried to cover their bodies, is evidence that something had changed at the physical level. In our present state, as adults at least, we are always ashamed of nakedness, whether or not we have just sinned. Moreover, while it is normal for us to experience a deep sense of mental/moral regret over any particular sin we commit, our reaction does not extend to a newfound sense of embarrassment over any part of our physical makeup.

It wasn't merely a change in their awareness. Adam and Eve were fully aware of each other's naked physical state *before* and *after* they sinned. Before sin, they were aware and not ashamed - *"they were both naked, the man and his wife, and were not ashamed"* (Genesis 2:25). They did not seek to cover their nakedness in their "very good" condition. Post sin, they remained aware of each other's naked state, but now for the first time they were deeply ashamed. They immediately resolved to cover themselves by making aprons and tried to hide from God for the very reason that they were naked – *"I*

---

[122] God's curse on Adam and His curse on the ground are connected. In cursing the ground, God cursed the very substance from which He created Adam: *"man of the dust of the ground"* (Genesis 2:7). In the Hebrew this reads *"haadam afar min haadamah"*, making it plain that *"the man (haadam)"* is derived from and connected with *"the ground (haadamah)"*. Therefore, God's sentence on Adam (haadam) to eat of the cursed ground – *"in sorrow shalt thou eat of it (haadamah)"* - negatively impacted him all the days of his now limited life, until he would *"return unto the ground (haadamah); for out of it (hadamah) wast thou taken: for dust thou art, and unto dust shalt thou return"* (Genesis 3:19).

*was afraid, **because I was naked**, and I hid myself"* (Genesis 3:9). Their deep sense of shame and fear over their naked state *afterwards* is evidence that something physically (or physiologically) had changed within them.

The first phrase in Genesis 3:7 confirms that it was much more than a change in their awareness - *"the eyes of them both were opened"*. Literally speaking, their eyes were open before they sinned - they were aware of each other's naked state, but they were not ashamed. Hence, the detail of their eyes being opened post-sin is metaphorical, emphasising that something about their internal condition had changed, and this was causing them to react in a totally new way. It was much more than just knowing in the sense of being aware that they were naked. They were together immediately after they sinned, and each would see not only their own body, but also the other's body from an entirely new perspective. It was not just a *personal* seeing and knowing, but a *mutual* seeing and knowing – *"and **they** knew that **they** were naked"*. It is reasonable to suggest that there was an increased level of sensual awareness between them that was significantly greater than the level that they had experienced before they sinned.

Therefore, the opening of Adam and Eve's eyes to be ashamed of their naked physical state for the first time, is clear scriptural evidence that a fundamental change in their physical condition had taken place. They had known good, but now they also knew evil. It was not merely a new perception that they were both naked and sinners, but a radical alteration in the way their bodies – including their eyes – interacted with their minds.

Jesus Christ fulfilled Genesis 3:15 wearing the crown of thorns

The way back to God for them and for us is through Christ, who daily overcame the promptings of the nature he inherited from our first parents and rendered perfect obedience to his Father's will. He finally destroyed this sin-biased nature in himself by literally crucifying the flesh with its affections and lusts, reconciling believers to God in the body of his flesh.

The promise of Genesis 3:15 was fulfilled when Christ, after a life of complete obedience, put to death the serpent or *diabolos* with which he was born through his own death on the cross (Hebrews 2:14). This enabled his Father to raise him for our justification and bestow upon him a glorious change to immortal spirit nature.

Jesus Christ was crucified with a crown of thorns (John 19:5), confirming the direct link between God's physical sentence on Adam and Eve and the curses He placed on creation in consequence of their sin. The crown of thorns symbolises the sin-cursed state of human nature. It is no longer *"very good"*, but full of thorns and thistles. Thorns, thistles and briars are used figuratively of the human heart and human attitudes (Isaiah 5:4-7; Matthew 13:7-8; Hebrews 6:4-8; Isaiah 55:13). In wearing the crown of thorns, Christ publicly demonstrated God's condemnation of sin in the flesh (Romans 8:3). Ultimately the problems of sin and death will be destroyed, and there will be no more curses on any aspect of God's creation (Psalm 72:16; Revelation 22:3).

Clearly, the Bible teaches, and Christadelphians believe, that there was a change in the condition of human nature after Adam and Eve fell from their "very good" state.

Chapter 17
Was God's "Very Good" Creation, Very Good?

Genesis 1:31 "And God saw everything that he had made, and, behold, it was very good".

Evolutionary Creationist explanation of "very good"

EC advocates agree that "very good" in Genesis 1:31 means that it was a job well done, fit for His purpose, that everything was first-rate. However, at the same time, they insist that there was human death, disease and suffering in the world, and that man was prone to sin long before Adam and Eve sinned.

Reality check – can God call death, the devil and evil "very good"?

Are we expected to accept that God, from His own perspective, regarded a state of death, disease, suffering, and bias to sin, as "very good"? Moreover, since the diabolos personifies human nature, the source of temptation in everyone, including Jesus Christ (Matthew 4:1), this also means that those EC proponents who agree with this definition must view the *diabolos* as *"very good"*, "first-rate", and "fit for God's purpose" as well.

The EC view is inconsistent with what God elsewhere declares is 'evil' or an 'enemy':

1. Can human death, disease and suffering, be called by God *"very good"*, when the Bible says that death is an enemy (1 Corinthians 15:26) that resulted from Adam and Eve's sin (Romans 5)? It was only after Adam and Eve sinned that God subjected His creation to vanity while simultaneously providing hope of a physical redemption from this state (Romans 8:20-23; cp. Genesis 3:15).

2. Can the current condition of human nature be described *as "very good"*, when the apostle Paul states explicitly, *"For I know that in me (that is, in my flesh,) dwelleth **no good** thing ... O **wretched man that I am**! Who shall deliver me from the body of this death?"* (Romans 7:18-24)?

3. Did God create the devil (mortal sin-biased human nature) from the outset and call it *"very good"*? Or was the devil coeval

with the fall and something that God intends to destroy through the work of Christ?

4. Did God create "evil" in the world long before Adam sinned and declare this to be *"very good"*? Or did God bring "evil" in response to man's sin?

A closer look at instances where "me'od" ("very") and "tov" ("good") occur together

All EC adherents need to maintain that the supposedly pre-Adamic evolved natural world was the same as the natural world post Adam and Eve's sin. So, they must establish that God's description of His creation as "very good" applied equally to both the *alleged* pre-Adamic and the *real* post-Adamic worlds. To achieve this, they have to minimise the importance of the description "very good" so they can apply it to sin-biased, diseased and death-stricken pre-Adamic man.

To do this, EC writers often refer to one or more of the ten other places where the words "very" (Heb. *Me'od*) and "good" (Heb. *Tov*) occur in the same verse, and argue that it does not refer to anyone or anything as being more unique than "fit ... to achieve God's purpose". Here are two examples of EC reasoning in this regard:

> *"This phrase 'very good' is used elsewhere in scripture, and there is nothing in the Hebrew to suggest that anything more is meant by the phrase other than to imply something is really good. The two Hebrew words occur together eleven times, ...Therefore, the context of Genesis 1:31, and the subsequent use of the term does not support the suggestion that there is any special significance in the phrase 'very good' in regard to man. It simply means that, like the rest of creation, man was very good in kind and condition."* [123]

> *"My conclusion is that the Hebrew use of the words together through the rest of the Old Testament and the clear reading of Genesis 1 support nothing more or less than a general statement of a work well done and creatures well formed,* **all fit and ready to achieve God's purpose.** *I.e. this expression understood in context neither supports nor denies special creation."* [124]

Therefore they claim that each of these verses uses *"very good"* in the sense of something that is not perfect in every way. Rebekah and Bathsheba were beautiful, but they were still mortal and sinners (Genesis 24:16; 2 Samuel 11:2). The promised land (Numbers 14:7) and the land of Laish/Dan (Judges 18:9) were still full of Canaanites.

---

[123] Pearson, Mike, *The Fourth Conversation*, 2nd Edition, 2017, p. 112.

[124] John Doe, *'Very Good' – What does this phrase mean?*, COD Website, June 2017.

Therefore, they reason that Genesis 1:31 cannot mean perfect in every way either.

However, in seven cases[125] the Hebrew phrase is not the same as in Genesis 1:31 – *"tov me'od"*. Other Hebrew word(s) are inserted between *"tov"* and *"me'od"*, qualifying what is being referred to. In all of these seven cases and the three additional instances[126] where *"tov me'od"* occurs, the context tells us that the character, quality, or appearance of the subject is in contrast to that which is not "very good".

For example, in Genesis 24:16 Rebekah is described as "good appearance very" (Heb. *Tovat mareh me'od*) in contrast to others who were not as fair.

In Numbers 14:7, Caleb's report of the Promised Land as literally "good land very very" (Heb. *Tovah haaretz me'od me'od*), is in contrast to the account of the other spies who did not view the land as good. In Jeremiah 24:2-3 we read of a comparison between two types of figs – in the Hebrew, the good figs are described as *"teenim tovot me'od"*, which literally means *"figs very good"*, and this is in contrast to the *"teenim raot ma'od"*, *"figs very naughty"*. The two types of figs are figuratively contrasting the characters of two different groups of people. In this case, it is actually about morality and not external appearance.

"Tov me'od" can be used to describe external human appearance, as in the cases of Rebekah, Bathsheba and Adonijah (1 Kings 1:6). It can be used to express the appeal of a geographical region in which to live. It can also be used to describe a person's character or actions as in the case of David's soldiers' treatment of Abigail's servants (1 Samuel 25:15), David's treatment of Saul (1 Samuel 19:4), and a good class of people morally speaking (good figs) in contrast to those who were not so good. So, the expression can be used for moral behaviour, not just external characteristics.

But in all cases except for Genesis 1:31, there is a qualification as to what was meant by very good. This qualification occurs either in the Hebrew phrase itself, or based on the context. There is an obvious contrast to something that is not good – whether appearance, actions or behaviour.

However, in Genesis 1:31 God declared His creation to be *"very good"* in all respects – with no qualifications in the Hebrew, and with no contextual contrast of something that was not good. On the contrary, the context of Genesis 1 tells us six times that what God

---

[125] Genesis 24:16; Numbers 14:7; 1 Samuel 19:4; 25:15, 36; 2 Samuel 11:2; 1 Kings 1:6.
[126] Judges 18:9; Jeremiah 24:2; Jeremiah 24:3

crea-ed was *"good"* (Heb. *Tov* – Genesis 1:4, 10, 12, 18, 21, 25) in the lead up to the culmination of declaring everything He had made to be *"very good"*.

Most importantly, these instances of *"good"* and *"very good"* are **God's** evaluation and not **man's** evaluation. It is God's view of the whole of His creation. Not simply very good to look at, very good as a place to dwell, or very good in the sense of morality. It is all that and more. Genesis 1 is different from all the cases above. God is evaluating everything that He had made, including Adam and Eve, and describing it as *"very good"* with no qualifications. The expression not only refers to a creation that was fit for God's purpose, but also stands in sharp contrast to the state it became when God made His creation *"subject to vanity, not willingly"* (Romans 8:20). The post-fall creation became replete with all of God's avowed enemies – sin, disease, suffering and death so it could no longer be described as *"very good"*.

"Very good" vs "pure in heart"

Some EC advocates argue that since mortal, sin-biased, sinful men in other parts of Scripture are referred to as *"good"*, *"pure in heart"*, *"just and perfect"*, the phrase *"very good"* can apply to Adam and Eve before the fall in the same way. This is a form of what exegetes call *"illegitimate totality transfer"*[127] in that parallel expressions to *"very good"* that have a particular meaning in other contexts are imposed on *"very good"* in a context where it has a different and specific application.

As demonstrated above, *"very good"* describes the pre-sin creation in contrast to the cursed post-sin creation. The faithful men of old, such as Noah – *"just and perfect in his generations"* (Genesis 6:9) and Job – *"perfect and upright"* (Job 1:1) are so described because firstly, they were not guilty of the idolatrous practices of the people around them, and secondly, thanks to their faith in God's promises to be accomplished through his Son, they received forgiveness and were counted as righteous.

Likewise, for us today, the only way we can be considered *"pure in heart"*, as our Lord taught in the beatitudes (Matthew 5:8), is by *"obtaining mercy"* (Matthew 5:7) and striving our best to follow all the other aspects of our Lord's description of a true disciple. True *righteousness* is something we cannot achieve by ourselves now. However, it is something we must *"hunger and thirst after"* (Matthew 5:6).

---

[127] Carson, D.A., *Exegetical Fallacies*, Baker Book House, Grand Rapids, 1984 p. 62.

Adam and Eve's position was that God declared everything He had made at the end of the creation week, including them, to be *"very good"*. This was before sin and death entered the world, before God sentenced them, before a lamb was slain as a covering for their sin, and before God placed the cherubim to keep the way to the tree of life.

We need to remind ourselves that EC arguments are specious in that they are produced to bolster the idea of a race of pre- and co-Adamic men. The Bible, from Genesis to Revelation, is not only totally silent on this race but rejects the idea by calling Adam the "first man" and Eve "the mother of all living".

Paul and Jesus knew that the condition of their nature was not *"very good"*

Paul, in Romans 7, confirms man's fallen nature when he says, *"… in me … in my flesh … **dwells no good thing**"* (v18), *"the law of sin which is in my members"* (v23), that human nature is ***"wretched"*** and is a ***"body of death"*** (v24). These descriptions of post-fall man are in sharp contrast to the description of pre-fall man in Genesis 1:31. It cannot be maintained that *"very good"* applies to humans after sin entered the world.

The fallen condition of human nature is something that Christ himself acknowledged when he refused to be called *"good"* during his earthly ministry (Mark 10:17-18; Matthew 19:16-17; Luke 18:18-19). We know that morally, Jesus was *"very good"* – he was the best creation of God since the curses were imposed at the time of the fall, and he was the only man ever to render perfect obedience to his Father's will. So, in what sense was Jesus not "good"?

The answer lies with what he told Nicodemus in John 3, that the Son of Man must be lifted up as the antitype of **the serpent** lifted up by Moses in the wilderness (John 3:14; cp. John 8:28; 12:34). Jesus taught that even he, innocently, came under the physical consequences of Adam's sin, so that he could lead us out of bondage to sin and death. He was born with the problem of the *diabolos* as part of his nature. The *diabolos* is not "good" from God's perspective. Although Jesus was God's son he was born with our identical nature, for the express purpose of destroying the *diabolos* and its works (Hebrews 2:14; 1 John 3:8).

"Very Good" in the BASF

Christadelphians do not believe that God created Adam and Eve in an immortal state whereby it was impossible for them to sin. But their natural body of life was unaffected by sin and death and a cursed creation. As Bro Roberts stated in his article titled "True Principles and Uncertain Details":

> *"Man's state after Creation: He was a living soul or natural body of life, maintained in being by the action of the air through the lungs like us, **but unlike us, a "very good" form of that mode of being, and unsubjected to death.** ... It is sufficient if a man believe that Adam after creation was a very good form of flesh and blood, untainted by curse"*[128]

This is what EC believers deny in asserting that there was no physical change in Adam and Eve. As BASF clause 4 states, *"the first man was Adam, whom God created out of the dust of the ground as a living soul or natural body of life, "very good" in kind and condition, and placed him under a law through which the continuance of life was contingent on obedience"*. Before the fall, creation was *"very good"*, with Adam and Eve enjoying direct fellowship with God and the prospect of being rewarded with immortality without any need for sacrifice.

BASF clause 5 then goes on to state: *"That Adam broke this law, and was adjudged unworthy of immortality, and sentenced to return to the ground from whence he was taken – a sentence which defiled and became a physical law of his being, and was transmitted to all his posterity"*. God's sentence involved physical changes to Adam and Eve. Their nature could no longer be described as *"very good"* in kind and condition.

BASF clause 6 states: *"God, in his kindness, conceived a plan of restoration which, without setting aside His just and necessary law of sin and death, should ultimately rescue the race from destruction, and people the earth with sinless immortals."* God's restoration will be "much more" than a return to the original "very good" state when the progenitors of our human race enjoyed direct fellowship with Him and reigned over all God had created. The restored immortal state of believers will far exceed the state Adam and Eve enjoyed before they sinned.

---

[128] Roberts, Robert, *True Principles & Uncertain Details*, The Christadelphian, volume 35 page 183 (1898).

Fallen Human Nature From Birth – Biased to Sin	
Proverbs 22:15	Foolishness is bound in the heart of a child; but the rod of correction shall drive it far from him.
Psalm 58:3	The wicked are estranged from the womb: they go astray as soon as they be born, speaking lies.
Job 5:7; 14:1	5:7 Yet man is born unto trouble, as the sparks fly upward. 14:1 Man that is born of a woman is of few days, and full of trouble.
Genesis 6:5; 8:21	6:5 And GOD saw that the wickedness of man was great in the earth, and that every imagination of the thoughts of his heart was only evil continually. 8:21 ...for the imagination of man's heart is evil from his youth
Jeremiah 17:9	The heart is deceitful above all things, and desperately wicked: who can know it?
1 Peter 2:11	Dearly beloved, I beseech you as strangers and pilgrims, abstain from fleshly lusts, which war against the soul.
Matt 15:18–20	But those things which proceed out of the mouth come forth from the heart; and they defile the man. 19 For out of the heart proceed evil thoughts, murders, adulteries, fornications, thefts, false witness, blasphemies: 20 These are the things which defile a man
Romans 7	vv16 & 20 Sin that dwelleth in me v18 For I know that in me (that is, in my flesh,) dwelleth no good thing: v21 I find then a law, that, when I would do good, evil is present with me. v23 another law in my members, warring against the law of my mind, and bringing me into captivity to the law of sin which is in my members.
James 4:1-2	1 From whence come wars and fightings among you? Come they not hence, even of your lusts that war in your members? 2 Ye lust, and have not: ye kill, and desire to have, and cannot obtain: ye fight and war, yet ye have not, because ye ask not.
1 John 2:15-16	15 Love not the world, neither the things that are in the world. If any man love the world, the love of the Father is not in him. For all that is in the world, the lust of the flesh, and the lust of the eyes, and the pride of life, is not of the Father, but is of the world.
Conclusion: Fallen human nature is not "very good" from God or even man's perspective	

Chapter 18

What Adam's Sin Introduced: Mortality

Mortality and death are intrinsically related words

EC believers promote the evolutionary view of countless deaths over millions of years before the time of Adam and Eve. They reject the Bible's clear cause and effect teaching that *"by one man sin entered into the world, and death by sin"* (Romans 5:12) and *"by man came death"* (1 Corinthians 15:22). Therefore, they are forced to introduce a new theological concept of death that is either distinct from, or overlays, the natural death resulting from mortality.

They attempt to do this by arguing that "mortal"/"mortality" and "death" are different Greek words in the New Testament, so that it was "spiritual" death or "eternal" death that Adam's sin introduced, not the normal death associated with mortality. They claim confusion will result if "death" and "mortality" are interchanged in the Scriptures.

This EC argument is not convincing because "death" refers to a particular point when our life ceases, whereas mortality refers to the state or condition of our nature that is subject to and ends in death. Replacing the word "death" with "mortality" in a sentence will often confuse the sense. Moreover, in the New Testament, it is always the adjective "mortal" that occurs, not the noun "mortality" [129]. Obviously, interchanging the noun "death" and the adjective "mortal" will be incorrect grammar.

Nevertheless, "mortal", "mortality" and "death" are intrinsically related words. Humans suffer death because they are mortal. In everyday English, mortality refers to a body that is associated with death. Most dictionaries define mortality as the state of being subject to death. The word "mortal" in English is from the Latin *"mors"* or *"mort"* (= death), from which we derive words such as mortuary (or morgue), mortician and mortgage (literally = death pledge). The online etymology dictionary defines "mortal" as follows:

> **mortal (adj.)** mid-14c., "deadly," also "doomed to die," from Old French *mortel* "destined to die; deserving of death," from Latin *mortalis* "subject to death, mortal, of a mortal, human," from *mors* (genitive *mortis*) "death." [130]

---

[129] The single instance of "mortality" in the KJV, 2 Corinthians 5:4, is the adjective "mortal" with the definite article: "the mortal", cf. 1 Corinthians 15:54 "this mortal"; the object is implicit.

[130] www.etymonline.com.

Old Testament usage of "death" refers to the cessation of mortal life

In the Old Testament, the Hebrew word for death (*"muwth"*) occurs around 800 times and always refers to death – the cessation of mortal life. We are reliant on the context as to the manner of physical death the word is referring to – whether natural or violent, whether animal or human, whether from disobeying God's laws or being in ignorance of them.

The word "die" in Genesis 2:17 (*"in the day that thou eatest thereof thou shalt surely **die**"*) marks the first occurrence of the Hebrew word *"muwth"*, and the same word is used when Eve reiterated her understanding of what would happen if they disobeyed God: *"God hath said, Ye shall not eat of it, neither shall ye touch it, lest ye **die**"* (Genesis 3:3); and by the serpent when it claimed *"Ye shall not surely **die**"* (Genesis 3:4). It is fitting, therefore, that the next occurrence of the word in the Old Testament is the actual record of Adam's death *"And all the days that Adam lived were nine hundred and thirty years: and he **died**"* (Genesis 5:5).

"Death" in the New Testament means the death resulting from mortality

In the New Testament, the Greek word for death (*thanatos*) refers to the end result of mortality (Gk. *thneton*) or of being "mortal" (Gk. *thnetos*). Thayer defines *thnetos/thneton* (mortal/mortality) as "liable to death". *Thanatos* occurs 120 times in the New Testament, and the overwhelming majority refer to a physical death.

It is interesting to note that 1 Corinthians 15:54 contains both *"mortal"* and *"death"* in the same verse. This confirms, in a Biblical context, that "death" (Gk. *"thanatos"*) and "mortal" (Gk. *"thnetos"*) are intrinsically related words. Specifically, in this case, they refer to when our **mortal** bodies are changed into an immortal state, when there will be a victory over our enemy, death – *"**death will** be swallowed up in victory"*. Also, in 2 Corinthians 5:4 the phrase *"that **mortality (thneton)** might be swallowed up of life"* is indisputably parallel with the expression *"**death (thanatos)** will be swallowed up in victory"* in 1 Corinthians 15:54.

The few moral applications of "death" do not justify arbitrarily changing the meaning of the numerous physical applications of "death"

There are a handful of occasions where *"thanatos"* refers to our moral status now, anticipating what will happen when Christ returns. For example, in 1 John 3:14 the apostle states, *"…we know that we have passed from death (thanatos) unto life"*. Advocates of EC correctly point out that *"thanatos"* in this verse is not speaking of physically dying but is a description of a believer's spiritual state[131]. But then, they make the mistake of attempting to transfer this meaning to crucial verses in Romans 5 and 1 Corinthians 15, and claim that *"thanatos"* was the legal sentence of "eternal death" (to be pronounced at the judgment seat) that was introduced into the world by one man's sin. *"Thanatos"*, they say, is not the physical death associated with mortality.

They apply the same reasoning to the apostle Paul's description of a believer's status before baptism in Ephesians 2:1 – *"dead in trespasses and sins"*, although in this case the Greek word for "dead" is not the noun *"thanatos"*, but the adjective *"nekros"*. But similarly, *"nekros"* occurs 129 times in the New Testament. The overwhelming majority of cases describe someone who is physically dead, as in the 13 occurrences in 1 Corinthians 15. It can also be used in a moral sense now. For example, Romans 6:11 *"Likewise reckon ye also yourselves to be **dead** indeed unto sin, but **alive** unto God through Jesus Christ our Lord"*.

It is unscriptural to state that a believer who is no longer *"dead in trespasses and sins"*, or *"passed from death (thanatos) to life"* (John 5:24) after baptism, has ceased to be subject to the physical death that Adam's sin introduced. Similarly, a believer's new mental and moral state of being *"alive in Christ"* does not mean that they are already physically *"in Christ"*, in the sense of an actual change of nature to immortality. In Ephesians 2, Paul says that God has *"raised us up with him and seated us with him in the heavenly realms in Christ Jesus"* (Ephesians 2:6, NET). No believer has yet been *"raised up"* literally or is literally sitting with Christ in the 'heavenly realms'.

There is a direct connection between our mental and moral status now and the ultimate physical state in these verses. If we die to the flesh now, and are mentally and morally in Christ, then we won't be subject to a physical death at the judgment seat of Christ. Conversely, if we remain figuratively dead by serving the flesh now, then we will be subject to actual death at the judgment seat. But this does not mean that there is any difference in the physical death that all (both responsible and non-responsible) die before Christ returns, and the second physical death with which the unworthy will be sentenced at the judgment seat after being resurrected. **The difference is not with the "type" or "label" of death, but rather the**

---

[131] COD: *"Death is clearly being used here as a descriptor of the final judgment on an individual or as a label if you will of their spiritual state. It is not speaking of the physical process of dying nor is it speaking of mortality"*. Bro John Doe, *Death in Rom 5:12 is speaking of the permanent fate of the wicked*, COD Website, June 2017.

power of God to firstly resurrect us, and then secondly to change our mortal bodies into glorious immortal bodies.

Adam was not subject to death before sin, for sin was the door through which death entered

Based on (i) the use of the words *"mortal"* and *"death"* in Scripture; (ii) how we understand the word *"mortal"* in everyday usage; and (iii) the etymology of the word itself, the terms *"mortal"* and *"mortality"* describe a body that is subject to *"death"*. But this is not how God first created Adam and Eve. Romans 5:12 states that sin came first, then death. To underline this point, 1 Corinthians 15:21 says, *"…by man came death"*.

In "The Blood of Christ", Bro Roberts makes the same point:

> … we must go back again to Adam in the garden of Eden, and see him condemned to death. The effect of such a sentence upon a creature we see illustrated in Gehazi as he stood before Elisha. "The leprosy of Naaman cleave to thee and to thy seed for ever." That was the sentence, "and he went from his presence a leper as white as snow." The words of Elisha took effect and became leprosy. The word of God to Adam took effect, and made him a death-stricken man; **he was not subject to death before, for sin was the door that death came in by.** "By one man sin entered into the world, and death by sin." "By man came death." "Dust thou art, and unto dust shalt thou return." … **The Word of God against Adam made him a mortal man with a mortal body.** Look at Adam and Eve, mortal; by-and-by, children; what are they? Just the same: they also are mortal. Could a mortal beget an immortal? **Mortal means deathful. The word comes from a Latin word, *"mors"*—death, and is imported into the English language, but in plain Saxon, it is "deathful". Why deathful? Because of Adam's sin.**[132]

The Bible does not refer to two types of physical death – one "death" associated with mortality, and another "eternal" "death" introduced by Adam's sin. Although those responsible to judgment die in hope of the resurrection, the physical death they die, the physical death the unenlightened die and the physical "second" death those rejected at the judgment seat will die, are all the same physical death that is the end result of mortality.

No hint of Adam and Eve being punished with a prospective "eternal" death, or a legal label of eternal death on top of mortality

The EC view is that Adam and Eve, along with the alleged evolved humans, were already mortal. That their sin resulted in the prospect

---

[132] Roberts, Robert, *The Blood of Christ*, 1895 [2006 Edition], pp. 9-10.

of them being sentenced with "eternal" death at the judgment seat, or that legally they became worthy of "eternal" death. If so, we should find evidence of this when God pronounced his punishments upon them in Genesis 3. Yet, neither Genesis 3 nor any other Bible passage mentions that God punished Adam and Eve with a prospective eternal death or a legal label of eternal death. Their punishment was simply a physical death; defined as returning to the dust: *"In the sweat of thy face shalt thou eat bread, till thou return unto the ground; for out of it wast thou taken: for dust thou art, and unto dust shalt thou return"* (Genesis 3:19). This explains that the death threatened in Genesis 2:17 for disobedience (*"thou shalt surely die"*) was the process of dying – a life of labour and continued existence until they returned to the ground.

"Death reigning" is a state of mortality

As shown in the table on page 131, in the letter to the Romans, Paul refers to death as something that "reigns" or has "dominion": *"**death reigned** from Adam to Moses, even over them that had not sinned after the similitude of Adam's transgression"* (Romans 5:14); *"By one man's offence **death reigned** by one"* (Romans 5:17); and *"Christ being raised from the dead dieth no more; **death hath no more dominion** over him"* (Romans 6:9-10). In these verses, the apostle refers to humanity's current mortal state, where death, and fear of death, reigns every day and has dominion over all whether they know God or not.

We are told on at least three occasions in Romans 5 that all humanity is negatively impacted with this state of death, not as a result of our own sins, but because of Adam – *"through the offence of one many be dead"* (v15); *"for the judgment was by one to condemnation"* (v16); *"by the offence of one judgment came upon ALL men to condemnation"* (v18).

Death reigning also means that the death introduced into the world by Adam's sin is ongoing. It cannot be limited to a single event – the judgment – or only apply to the rejected at that time. The apostle makes it clear that death reigns, *"even over them who have not sinned after the similitude of Adam's transgression"*.

Death reigning means that death cannot be restricted to the proposed "eternal" death of the rejected at the judgment seat of Christ. It also rules out the possibility of it being a legal label of "eternal" death that separately applies in addition to the reigning physical death. The death that Adam introduced reigns every single day, has power over all and is an enemy that God will destroy through the work of Jesus Christ at the end of the millennium when God will be *"all in all"* (1 Corinthians 15:26).

"The many" is simply another way of saying "all" in Romans 5

In Romans 5, the apostle Paul varies the way he expresses those impacted by Adam's sin and Christ's obedience, sometimes using the all-inclusive term *"all"* (v12, v18), at other times referring to the impact as *"reigning"*, which implies *"all"* (v14, 17). He also uses the apparently less inclusive *"many"* (v15, v19) in the same context. For example, in verse 15 we read, *"**many** died through one man's trespass"* (ESV), but in verse 18 we read *"one trespass led to condemnation for **all men**"* (ESV).

EC advocates typically reason that as we know that the entire group of those positively impacted by Christ is not all of humanity, it follows that the entire group negatively affected by Adam need not be all of humanity either.

This is where context is important. Paul is contrasting *"the one"* and *"the many"* when referring to both Adam and Christ, to emphasise the different way in which both men affected the rest. In the original Greek, this becomes more obvious. Every time *"many"* and *"one"* occur over verses 15-19, the definite article appears before both words. Young's literal translation makes this apparent:

- *"But, not as the offence so also is the free gift; for if by the offence of **the one the many** did die, much more did the grace of God, and the free gift in grace of **the one** man Jesus Christ, abound to **the many**."* (Romans 5:15, YLT)

- *"So, then, as through one offence to all men it is to condemnation, so also through one declaration of 'Righteous' it is to all men to justification of life; for as through the disobedience of **the one** man, **the many** were constituted sinners: so also through the obedience of **the one**, shall **the many** be constituted righteous."* (Romans 5:18-19, YLT)

The apostle is contrasting *"the many"* - the entire mass of humanity - impacted by *"the one"* man's (Adam) sin to *"the many"* or the entire group of faithful believers who will receive, thanks to *"the one"* man's (Christ's) obedience, the free gift of God – divine nature.

The apostle deploys a similar rhetorical contrast in Romans 12:5 and 1 Corinthians 10:17, when he explains that *"the many"*, not just some, are *"the one bread"* or *"the one body"* of Christ.[133]

Firstly, we noted that the apostle expressed the impact of Adam's sin as a state of "death" reigning over all regardless of actual sin (Romans 5:12, 17), and this state even applied to Christ himself (Romans 6:9-

---

[133] **Romans 12:4-5 (YLT)** "for as in one body we have many members, and all the members have not the same office, so we, **the many**, one body are in Christ, and members each one of one another."
1 Corinthians 10:17 (YLT) "because one bread, one body, are we **the many**—for we all of the one bread do partake."

10). So, Paul means the entire mass of humanity when he refers to *"the many"* who are negatively impacted by Adam's sin. Secondly, regarding the whole group positively affected by Christ, Romans 5:15-17 five times defines this group as those who receive *"the free gift"*. In the immediate context, the *"free gift"* is defined as *"the free gift of righteousness"* that enables us to *"reign in life"* (v17). *"The many"* or the entire group of those who will be positively impacted by Christ are all those who will receive the free gift of eternal life.

Romans 5:17 spells out the difference in the parameters between the two groups.

> *"For if by the transgression of the one, **death reigned through the one**, much more **those who receive the abundance of grace and of the gift of righteousness will reign in life** through the One, Jesus Christ."* (Romans 5:17, NASB)

The result of Adam's trespass unconditionally applies to all of humanity - *"death reigned through the one"*. The result of Christ's righteousness is conditional and only applies to those who respond to the gospel and end up receiving the gift of righteousness and reign in life (immortality).

Bro Carter succinctly summarises this in *Paul's Letter to the Romans*:

> A strictly corresponding statement to the first half of this verse [Romans 5:17] would read, "much more will life reign through the righteousness of the one." But that is not so. **For while the Adamic unity is upon a flesh basis, the individual members being part of it by birth, the Christ unity is upon a different basis altogether. While a person is a part of Adamic unity without any action on his part, he is required to contribute something before he can be included in Christ unity.** Because he has been given freewill and endowed with moral qualities, he must willingly respond to God's invitation to share in the salvation God has made possible. There must be co-operative work with God on the part of man. And because this is so, and because the majority of mankind prove unresponsive, Paul finishes the statement in harmony with the facts of the case—"much more shall they that receive the abundance of the grace ... reign in life."[134]

> The comparison between the two Adams, worked out at length in Romans 5, is briefly referred to in 1 Corinthians 15. Christ is risen and become the firstfruits of them that slept. His resurrection is the pledge of a harvest. And this harvest of resurrection bound up with Christ, but which some in Corinth were denying, is put by Paul as a counterpart to the harvest of death connected with Adam: **"For since by man came death,"** not only for himself, for all his posterity, **"so by man came also the resurrection of the dead." It is by "man" in both cases. The second man must be a descendant of the first man. He must work his way out of the evil into which the first brought all. Only by being in the evil, subject to the effects of sin, can he come out of it. Death can be overcome only by one coming under its**

---

[134] Carter, John, *Paul's Letter to the Romans*, 1931, p. 63.

dominion. And mankind is involved in the consequences of "the fall" of the "man", and of the "rise" of the "man". "For as in Adam all die, even so in Christ shall all be made alive." **In Adam – by physical descent from him, by generation - all die. In Christ – by union with him – by regeneration – shall all be made alive. This defines the "all".** For all universally is not meant. While it is true that all absolutely of Adam's posterity by descent from him die, yet here the apostle's thought is concerned only with those who attain to life and immortality. As in Adam they all inherit death, so in Christ they all obtain eternal life. Both death and life are bound up with a federal head – one head leading along the way to death, the other leading along the way to life.[135]

Christ was subject to and removed the same death that Adam introduced

We know that the reigning *"death"* that Adam introduced into the world is simply the death associated with mortality, because Christ himself was born subject to this same death.

- The first half of Romans 5 tells us that *"Christ **died** (apothnēskō) for the ungodly"* (v6), that he *"**died** (apothnēskō) for us"* (v8), and then in verse 10, the apostle states that *"we have been reconciled to God by the **death (thanatos)** of his son"*. So, two verses before verse 12, where the Apostle explains how one man's sin introduced "death" (*thanatos*) into the world, he makes it plain that Christ suffered physical death (*thanatos*) to reconcile us to God.

- In Romans 6:9, the apostle Paul contrasts Christ's immortal state with his former mortal state: *"**death (thanatos)** hath no more dominion over him"*. Therefore, the physical death that Adam introduced also had physical dominion over Christ during his mortal life.

This is confirmed elsewhere in the New Testament: John 12:31-33; Acts 2:23-24; Hebrews 2:9,14-15; 1 Corinthians 11:26; Revelation 1:18. Christ suffered and abolished the same death that Adam introduced, both for his own benefit and the benefit of all who have faith in him.

Since Christ himself was subject to this death but did not sin, the possibility that death introduced into the world by Adam is anything other than our mortal state, which ends with the cessation of life, oblivion and physical dissolution in the grave, is once again ruled out.

---

[135] Carter, John, *Paul's Letter to the Romans*, 1931, pp. 60-61.

DEATH: CHRIST WAS SUBJECT TO AND REMOVED THE SAME DEATH THAT ADAM INTRODUCED		
	By One Man - Adam	**By One Man - Christ**
Rom 5:12	"**by one man** Sin entered into the world, and death by sin; and so death passed upon all men, for that all have sinned"	
Rom 5:15	"For if through **the offence of one many be dead**...	... much more the grace of God, and the gift by grace, which is **by one man**, Jesus Christ, hath abounded unto many"
Rom 5:16	"And not as it was **by one** that sinned, so is the gift: for the judgment was **by one** to **condemnation** ...	... but the free gift is of many offences unto **justification**."
Rom 5:17	"For if **by one man's** offence **death reigned by one** ...	... much more they which receive abundance of grace and of the gift of righteousness **shall reign in life by one**, Jesus Christ."
Rom 5:18	"Therefore as by the offence **of one** judgment came **upon all men to condemnation** ...	... even so by the righteousness **of one** the free gift came upon all men unto **justification of life**."
Rom 5:19	"For as **by one man's** disobedience **many were made sinners** ...	... so by the obedience **of one** shall **many be made righteous**."
Rom 6:9-10	"For in that he died, **he died unto Sin once**"	"Knowing that Christ being raised from the dead dieth no more; **death hath no more dominion over him** .... But in that he liveth, he liveth unto God".
Rom 7:24-25	"O wretched man that I am! who shall deliver me from **the body of this death?**	... I thank God through Jesus Christ our Lord."

	By One Man - Adam	By One Man - Christ
1 Cor 15:21	"For since **by man** came **death** ...	... **by man** came also the **resurrection of the dead** '
1 Cor 15:22	"For as **in Adam all die** ...	... even so **in Christ shall all be made alive**."
1 Cor 15:25-26	"... The **last enemy** that shall be destroyed **is death**"	"For he must reign until he hath put **all enemies** under his feet ..."
1 Cor 15:49	"And **as we have borne the image of the earthy** ...	... **we shall also bear the image of the heavenly**."
1 Cor 15:50	"Flesh and blood cannot ... Neither doth **corruption** ...	... inherit the Kingdom ... inherit **incorruption**"
1 Cor 15:52	"the **dead**...	... shall be raised incorruptible, and we shall be changed."
1 Cor 15:54	"So when this **corruptible** ... and this **mortal** ... **Death**	... shall have put on **incorruption** ... shall have put on **immortality** ... is swallowed up in **victory**"
2 Cor 5:4	"that **mortality** ...	... might be swallowed up of **life**."
1 Cor 15:55	"O **death** ... O grave ...	... where is thy sting? ... where is thy victory?"
Phi 2:8-9	"**And being found in fashion as a man**, he humbled himself, and **became obedient unto death**, even the death of the cross ...	... Wherefore God also hath **highly exalted him**, and given him a name which is above every name"
2 Tim 1:10		"Jesus Christ, who **hath abolished death**, and hath brought life and immortality to light through the gospel"
Heb 2:9	"But we see Jesus, who was made a little lower than the angels for the **suffering of death** ...	... crowned with glory and honour; that he by the grace of God should **taste death for every man**"
Heb 2:14-15	"Forasmuch then as the children are **partakers of flesh and blood** ... ... **who through fear of death were all their lifetime subject to bondage.**	... he also himself likewise took part of the same; **that through death he might destroy him that had the power of death, that is, the devil**, and deliver them ...."

Chapter 19
All Humans Die *"In Adam"*

"In Adam" is a physical relationship; *"In Christ"* *ultimately* refers to a physical relationship as well

EC advocates reason that, as it is possible to be *"in Christ"* by identification but without actual physical descent from him, being *"in Adam"* must likewise be about identification and not physical descent. EC View B[136] takes this one step further and reasons that all of the supposed evolved humans can legally be regarded as being *"in Adam"*, given that they would have proved themselves to be sinners like Adam if God had revealed His laws to them.

The first problem with this EC view is that (i) the Bible makes no explicit reference to any evolved humans living before and contemporary with Adam, and (ii) it contradicts God's own eyewitness account of history and the Bible's teaching that Adam was the first man.

Evolved humans are, therefore, a figment of human imagination based on man's attempts to construct a historical narrative that deliberately excludes any consideration of God.

Secondly, even if we were to imagine that pre-Adamic humans existed for argument's sake, the EC view would still be invalid. Being *"in Christ"* requires knowledge of God's purpose in Christ, and a faithful response to it by dying to *"the flesh"* and living to God. This applies to all living before Christ and all living after Christ. For example, we know that Abraham living 2,000 years before Christ, *"rejoiced to see my [Christ's] day: and he saw it, and was glad"* (John 8:56).

Being *"in Adam"* must require at least a parallel to being *"in Christ"* by knowing Adam's role in God's purpose. There is, however, no parallel for supposed pre-Adamic humans who did not know, nor had any possible active identification with, Adam and his sin.

Thirdly, what this and other EC views ignore, is that our hope is actually to be physically *"in Christ"* when our vile bodies are made like unto his glorious body. We will then be Christ's descendants, part of a new race of immortal beings of which he is the progenitor.

---

[136] See Section 4 – Questions 2 and 3

Christ is now *"the firstborn of every creature"* (Colossians 1:3), *"the firstborn from the dead, that in all things he might have the pre-eminence"* (Colossians 1:18).

Our hope is to be part of this new immortal race headed up by Christ - *"of his own will begat he us with the word of truth, that we should be a kind of firstfruits of his creatures"* (James 1:18), *"Christ in you, the hope of Glory"* (Colossians 1:27), *"For as in Adam all die, even so **in Christ shall all be made alive.** But every man in his own order: **Christ the firstfruits; afterward they that are Christ's at his coming"***(1 Corinthians 15:22-23). In the Apocalypse, the same point is made when Jesus is styled *"the beginning of the creation of God"* (Revelation 3:14).

Jesus declared to Nicodemus, *"Verily, verily, I say unto thee, Except a man be born of water and of the Spirit, he cannot enter into the kingdom of God"* (John 3:5). Being *"born of water"* occurs at baptism. Being *"born of the Spirit"* can apply in a mental and moral sense this side of the Kingdom. But ultimately, Jesus is referring to a change to spirit nature, without which we *"cannot enter into the Kingdom of God"*. Christ's contextual explanation confirms this, *"that which is born of the flesh is flesh; and that which is born of spirit is spirit"* (John 3:6).

Paul alludes to Christ's words to Nicodemus, when explaining the resurrection and the change to immortality - *"flesh and blood cannot inherit the kingdom of God"*, and appends the supporting phrase *"neither doth corruption inherit incorruption"* (1 Corinthians 15:50). Until this mortal puts on immortality, our nature remains "flesh", not "spirit".

Bro Roberts in Nazareth Revisited identifies being "born of the spirit" as the physical change to immortality:

> Begotten by the Word brought to bear upon their mind, they have, in baptism, been "born of water," **but are not yet finally incorporate in the family of God.** At this stage, they may perish, as Paul recognises (1 Corinthians 8:11). At the return of Christ, ... they become the subject of that change which Paul calls "the adoption, to wit, *the redemption of our body"* (Romans 8:23). **As the result of this physical change, which is effected by the Spirit** "in a moment, in the twinkling of an eye," **they become finally and unalterably sons of God. "They are the children of God, BEING THE CHILDREN OF THE RESURRECTION" (Luke 20:36).** This consummation of their adoption is figuratively compared to a birth, as in the case of baptism. Baptism is not a literal birth, but as it is the act by which a man not a child of God becomes such, it is a natural figure which speaks of it as a birth of water. So the operation of the Spirit of God upon the mortal nature of the accepted saints (Romans 8:11; 1 Corinthians 15:51 52; Philippians 3:21) is not a literal birth, but as **it is the act by which a son of**

the earth becomes a son of heaven (1 Corinthians 15:49), so it is natural to speak of it as a birth—a being born of the Spirit.[137]

This is not to deny that right now we are the children of God by faith in Christ Jesus" (Galatians 3:26), and we need to allow the *"seed"* of the word of God to change us mentally and morally (1 Peter 1:23). But our current status is not the fulfilment of our hope in Christ as *"Abraham's seed, and heirs according to the promise"* (Galatians 3:29). Rather, it anticipates its consummation. When Christ returns, those found worthy will be reborn with divine nature.

From birth, our starting point is *"in Adam"*, and this remains the case until we die. But we have the hope of a change of nature, when we will no longer be *"in Adam"*, in the image of the earthy man, but *"in Christ"*, bearing the image of the heavenly man. Adam's sin resulted in physical consequences for all. Likewise, Christ's obedience will result in physical blessings for all who are truly *"in Christ"*. We start physically *"in Adam"* but end physically *"in Christ"*.

In 1 Corinthians 15, Paul teaches that our ultimate hope *"in Christ"* is far greater than our current "miserable" status:

> *"If in **this life only we have hope in Christ, we are of all men most miserable**. But now is Christ risen from the dead, and **become the firstfruits** of them that slept."* (1 Corinthians 15:19-20)

Being *"in Christ"* physically is the very context of his antithetical comparison of *"in Adam"* and *"in Christ"* in the following two verses:

> *"For since by man came death, by man came also the resurrection of the dead. 22 For as **in Adam** all die, even so **in Christ** shall all be made alive."* (1 Corinthians 15:21–22)

After baptism our status is that of being mentally in Christ (believing the one true gospel), and morally in Christ (trying our best to die to sin, follow Christ's commandments, continuing in fellowship and receiving the forgiveness of sins). This status is our spiritual engagement to Christ (2 Corinthians 11:2) – but not the actual marriage. Our hope is to be finally *"in Christ"* mentally, morally **and physically** when he invests us with divine nature (John 10:28, 17:2).

Bro LB Welch in 1895 expressed this matter clearly:

LB Welch, The Christadelphian, 1895, v32, pp. 219-224

Though saints are "in Christ," it is only in a preliminary sense. Christ is in glorious nature. **No one can be in Christ as he is in Adam till he is of Christ's nature.** This is a self-evident truth. The inference to be drawn from it would clearly be that the phase *"in Christ"* cannot have the same import as the phase *"in Adam"* until a future event takes place. "In Christ shall all be made alive." This is yet in the future. **We must therefore be in Christ as we**

---

[137] Robert Roberts, *Nazareth Revisited*, Chapter 12, 1890, pp 65-66.

are now in Adam (that is by nature) before we are truly alive. It is in Christ we are made alive; that is, by being of his nature. **The nature Christ now has is a life-nature, while Adam's is a death-nature. It is clear that at present we can be made alive in Christ only prospectively.** Our being actually made alive can be only when we are in Christ as we are now in Adam, or of him as we are now of Adam. Surely this ought to be clear to the simplest mind. **At present our being in Christ is, and can be, only a state or condition of relationship.** By baptism into his name we are brought into a relation of reconciliation, or favour, with God, whereby we stand related to a full adoption in Christ by the redemption of our nature and its exaltation to the nature Christ now has.

Until this redemption and perfecting of our nature takes place, we have neither escaped from Adam nor are we in Christ as in Adam. Neither do we have life except as a prospective possession in Christ, and to be realised in our complete escape from Adam and our entrance into Christ. Then are we in Christ and made alive.

Part of the false doctrine Bro JJ Andrew postulated is that a person has to be **legally** *"in Christ"* and not **legally** *"in Adam"* to be raised mortal to receive either everlasting life or everlasting condemnation at the judgment seat (Daniel 12:2). Bro Andrew believed that baptism is the defining moment when a person enters covenant relationship with God and is no longer **legally** *"in Adam"* but **legally** *"in Christ"*. EC View B similarly refers to being *"in Adam"* in a legal sense, as distinct from a mental, moral or physical sense. Specifically, EC View B considers all of the supposed pre-Adamic men to be *"in Adam"* in a **legal** sense. This is because it is impossible for alleged evolved humans living before Adam to be *"in Adam"* mentally and morally, as they knew nothing about Adam or his sin. And they were certainly not *"in Adam"* physically because they were not his descendants. (see Section 4, Questions 3-5). EC View B also regards all of the ignorant since Adam as being legally *"in Adam"*, because they have no knowledge of either Adam or his sin.

Christadelphians reject the idea that anyone can be *"in Adam"* in a **legal** sense.

Christ was subject to and resurrected from the same death that all *"in Adam"* die (1 Cor 15:21; Romans 6:9)

EC advocates assert that the death that Adam introduced is "eternal" death where there is no longer any hope of immortality. They are forced into proposing this definition of death because they believe that natural death associated with mortality evolved long before Adam sinned. They reject Christadelphian teaching that the death God punished Adam with was the cessation of life and a return to the dust. The EC view creates confusion about the work of Christ because Scripture teaches that to save mankind Christ had to die the death, common to all, that came by Adam.

But as a sinless Christ did not and could not die the proposed "eternal" death, the EC view would destroy the Christadelphian understanding of Christ's atoning work.

Christadelphians have always understood that 1 Corinthians 15:21-22 teaches that the death all men die, including believers, is the death Adam introduced. And it is this death from which believers will be raised.

> *For since by man came* **death (thanatos),** *by man came also the resurrection of* **the dead (nekros).***"* (1 Corinthians 15:21)

If the last part of this verse read, *"by man came also eternal life"*, it would be easier for EC advocates to argue their case. However, the second part of the sentence says, *"by man came also the resurrection of* **the dead** *(nekros)"*, leaving no doubt that the death *(nekros)* from which the resurrection will occur is logically linked to the "death" *(thanatos)* that came by man in the first part of the sentence. The two words are different, but they relate to the same physical "death" *(thanatos)*. This is clearly shown in Romans 6:9 concerning Christ himself:

> *"Knowing that Christ being raised from* **the dead (nekros)** *dieth (apothnesko) no more;* **death (thanatos) hath no more dominion over him**.*"* (Romans 6:9)

Paul says that death's *(thanatos)* dominion over Christ has ceased because he was physically raised. Obviously, death *(thanatos)* did have dominion over him prior to this. How did Christ come under the dominion of death *(thanatos)*? Paul already explained this in Romans 5:17, where he says that death *(thanatos)* reigns over all because of Adam's disobedience.

> *"For if by one man's offence* **death (thanatos) reigned by one***; much more they which receive abundance of grace and of the gift of* **righteousness shall reign in life by one***, Jesus Christ."* (Romans 5:17)

Romans 6:9 coupled with 5:17 can only mean that Christ was not exempt from the dominion of death resulting from Adam's transgression.

In 1 Corinthians 15:21, believers who are subject to "death" *(thanatos)* and experience resurrection from the "dead" *(nekros)*, will follow the pattern of Christ. Christ was born subject to the death *(thanatos)* that entered through Adam because "death" had dominion over him during his mortal life, and he died this death *(thanatos)* on the cross. He was then raised from the dead *(nekros)* and rewarded with immortality - a new physical state where "death" *(thanatos)* has no more dominion over him.

The apostle refers to Christ as **"the *firstfruits* of those that sleep"**. "Firstfruits" anticipates the rest of the harvest and highlights Christ as the first of many others who will be delivered from the death state introduced by Adam. Like Christ, those who are *"Christ's at his coming"*, will *"be made alive"* (1 Corinthians 15:20-22). Christ is the progenitor of a new race of immortals. He will grant eternal life (John 10:28; 17:2) to all those who belong to him during their mortal probation. However, in the days of his flesh, Christ was not a part of this new race of immortals; for he was still *"in Adam"*, weak and mortal, bearing *"the image of the earthy"*. The new race will bear *"the image of the heavenly"* immortal state in which Christ now exists.

EC proponents believe *"thanatos"* is a legal sentence of "eternal" death, and that this supposedly was the "death" that Adam's sin introduced into the world. They believe Paul teaches this in Romans 5 and 1 Corinthians 15. But if this were the case, Romans 5:10 could not meaningfully say that we are reconciled to God by the death (*thanatos*) of his son, for Jesus' death was certainly not "eternal". Further, 1 Corinthians 15:21 would be saying that by man (Adam) came "eternal" death at judgment with no hope of resurrection, and by man (Christ) came also the resurrection of the dead (*nekros*), for all those under the dominion of "eternal" death with no hope of resurrection. This would make no sense. A person cannot be under the dominion of "eternal" death with no hope of immortality, but then be raised from this state by Christ and given immortality.

To get around this problem, EC advocates are forced to propose two different kinds of death for different groups of people within the same verse.

Firstly, they maintain that the death that Adam introduced is (i) the "eternal" death of the responsible unworthy at the judgment (both EC View A and B) and (ii) of the ignorant when they die (EC View B only).

Secondly, EC proponents claim that those who die *"in Christ"* before he returns die a "sleep" death, not an "eternal" death, because they are "asleep" in Christ and will be rewarded with immortal life at the judgment seat. Hence, they assert that those *"in Christ"* are not under the dominion of the "eternal" death (*thanatos*) that they claim Adam introduced. They interpret 1 Corinthians 15:21 as in the following paraphrase:

> "by man [Adam] came (**eternal**) death (*thanatos*) (**for the wicked**), by man [Christ] came also the resurrection of the (**sleeping**) dead (*nekros*) (**for those who are 'sleeping in Christ'**)".

Romans 6:9 exposes this EC subterfuge, because Christ himself was under the dominion of death (*thanatos*), and was raised from this dead (*nekros*) state to die no more. Scripture teaches that all men, living and dead (*nekros*), righteous and wicked, are under the dominion of the death (*thanatos*) that came by Adam. All are *"in Adam"*. Death (*thanatos*) had dominion over Christ throughout his life and during his three-day burial. He was *"raised from the dead* (*nekros*), *and dieth (apothnesko) no more; death (thanatos) hath no more dominion over him*". He is now immortal and no longer *"in Adam"* and subject to death (*thanatos*).

It is true that the Apostle portrays those who die with the hope of the resurrection as "having fallen asleep in Christ". However, this is not because they die a different type of death and are no longer *"in Adam"* physically. Rather it is because, based on their faithfulness, they will *"awake"* (Daniel 12:2; Isaiah 26:19) and be given immortality.

The relationship between "death" (*thanatos*) and "dead" (*nekros*), with both words applying to those "in Christ", is confirmed in 2 Corinthians 1:9-10 where we have the same two Greek works in close proximity:

> *"But we had the sentence of **death (thanatos)** in ourselves, that we should not trust in ourselves, but in God which raiseth **the dead (nekros**): 10 Who delivered us from so great a **death (thanatos**), and doth deliver: in whom we trust that he will yet deliver us."* (2 Corinthians 1:9–10)

In v9 Paul refers to the persecutions he suffered where he felt his life could end at any moment. In this same verse, he uses *thanatos* to describe the death he was always in danger of, and *nekros* to explain the dead state from which he would be resurrected. The meaning of *thanatos* does not support the EC's view of "eternal" death for the wicked with no hope of immortality. We know that the apostle Paul will be resurrected and given immortal life. This confirms once again that *thanatos* simply refers to the cessation of our mortal existence, and applies to believers and unbelievers alike.

Moreover, in v10, Paul states that the same "death" (*thanatos*) of which he was always in danger, is something that applied to both himself and other true believers past, present and future – *"who delivered us (**past**) from so great a death (thanatos), and doth deliver (**present**)…and he will yet deliver (**future**)."* An essential part of our faith is in understanding the need for a physical deliverance from the dominion of the *"thanatos"* that came from Adam (cf. 1 Corinthians 15:16-20).

The first man Adam was made a living soul – the last Adam a quickening spirit

> *"And so it is written, **The first man Adam was made a living soul**; the last Adam was made a quickening spirit. 46 Howbeit that was not first which is spiritual, but that which is natural; and afterward that which is spiritual. 47 The first man is of the earth, earthy: the second man is the Lord from heaven. 48 As is the earthy, such are they also that are earthy: and as is the heavenly, such are they also that are heavenly. 49 **And as we have**

> ***borne the image of the earthy, we shall also bear the image of the heavenly."*** (1 Corinthians 15:45-47)

EC advocates attempt to negate a literal reading of Adam as the first human in the apostle Paul's statement *"the first man Adam was made a living soul"*, by pointing out that the immediate context also refers to Jesus Christ as *"the last Adam"* and *"the second man"*. They reason that as Jesus was not literally the last or the second human, Paul cannot be teaching that Adam was the first human that God created. They assert that Paul is teaching that:

a) Adam was the first human to receive knowledge of God's laws and purpose, the first human being in salvation history who brought "eternal" death as a punishment for sin into the world.

b) Christ is the last Adam because salvation history finishes with him – he ended the problem of sin and eternal death when he died on the cross.[138]

Firstly, our understanding of what *"the first man Adam"* and *"the last Adam"* refer to must be governed by what Paul has already established in context. In 1 Corinthians 15:21-23 he has taught that just as a real Adam was responsible for the physical problem of death to all humanity (*"since by man came death"*; *"as in Adam all die"*), so a real Christ will bring deliverance from this death state for all those *"that are Christ's at his coming"*, through *"the resurrection of the dead"* by being *"made alive"* physically in immortality. Paul's exposition in 1 Corinthians 15 is not just about Christ's victory over sin in contrast to Adam's failure and which one we choose to follow in life. The whole context is the resurrection. Paul emphasises that just as the universal state of death originated with one real man, so the resurrection from this state to eternal life originates from another real man.

Secondly, in Hebrews 8:7 and 10:9, the same expressions *"first"* and *"second"* are used to contrast the old and the new covenants. However, from a strict chronological point of view, the Abrahamic/Messianic "second" covenant preceded the Mosaic *"first"* covenant by 430 years (Galatians 3:17), and the Davidic covenant (2 Chronicles 13:5; Psalm 89:3-4; Jeremiah 33:21) lies between them. The application of *"first"* and *"second"* in 1 Corinthians 15:47, in the light of these two examples, should be seen in its local context and not as absolute chronology. While in v45 Adam is literally the first man, in v47 there are two men in view – Adam *"the first"* and Christ *"the second"*.

---

[138] See EC quotes in Section 4, Questions 4-6.

Thirdly, the expressions *"the last Adam"* and *"the second man"* do, in fact, apply to Christ literally. Christ was the *"second man"* that God miraculously created to achieve His purpose with the earth. There are only two men who are literal sons of God - Adam and Christ (Luke 3:38 *"the son of Seth, the son of Adam, the son of God"*; John 3:16; Romans 8:3). We are only sons of God by adoption.

The context of 1 Corinthians 15:45-47 confirms this. The first man or son of God was miraculously created from the dust of the ground - *"the first man became a living soul"* (v45); *"the first man is of the earth"* (v47). This is a direct reference to Genesis 2:7, which says that God created man from the dust of the ground and man became a living soul.

In the case of the second man or son of God, God's power caused Mary to conceive Jesus as *"the only **begotten son** of God"* (John 1:18; 3:16, 18; cp. Hebrews 11:17). Paul states that the *"last Adam was made a quickening spirit"* (v45), and *"the second man is the Lord from heaven"* (v47). Although born of a woman and bearing our physical nature, God was his actual Father. Jesus explained this during his mortal life: *"For I came down from heaven, not to do mine own will, but the will of him that sent me* (John 6:38); *"Ye are from beneath; I am from above: ye are of this world; I am not of this world"* (John 8:23 cp. John 3:13, 31; 6:33; 50). However, in addition to his own divine paternity, Jesus was *"made a quickening spirit"* (v45) and became fully *"the Lord from Heaven"* after God raised him to immortal life (Acts 2:36).

That Christ is called the ***"last** Adam"* indicates that God has no further need for any other miraculously created man to complete His purpose. The dominion of the first man Adam (Genesis 1:26) failed through sin. The second miraculously created man did not fail. Jesus is the *"last Adam"* whom God provided to exercise dominion over the earth, including sin and death that came by the first man Adam. At the end of the millennium, Christ, having removed sin entirely from the earth, will also destroy the last enemy – death, and God will be all in all.

Fourthly, 1 Corinthians 15:45-47 is set in the broader context of the physical reality of the resurrection. The context negates EC views that seek to restrict being *"in Adam"* and *"in Christ"* to a non-physical relationship for the following reasons:

1) We are all "in" the first man Adam by nature and birth. Our progenitor, *"the first man Adam was made a living soul"* (v45). We are all born subject to death because of his sin (v21-22). Although we become mentally and morally *"in Christ"* at baptism, physically we remain in our status as *"living souls"* subject to death. However, ultimately our hope is to be *"in Christ"*, in the same way that *"the last Adam was made a quickening spirit"* (v45) through a change to spirit nature.

2) 1 Corinthians 15:46-49 describes how believers will be transformed from one form of body to another – *"as we have borne the image of the earthy, we shall also bear the image of the heavenly"*. We are *"in Adam"* with a *"natural"* body like his, but afterwards, we will be *"in Christ"* with a *"spiritual"* body like his now glorious body (Philippians 3:20-21).

Paul is not talking about being legally *"in Adam"* or "in Christ." The wider context of verses 39-49 is all about the resurrection and comparing two types of bodies - natural and spiritual. By default, we are all *"in Adam"* with a natural body, but those truly *"in Christ"* will be changed to be united with him in a spiritual body.

All humanity suffers physically from the impact of Adam's sin. All the faithful will experience physically the benefits of Christ's conquest of sin.

Two physical states: all humanity bear "the earthy" but the faithful will also bear "the heavenly"

	In Adam	In Christ
v49	*"as we have borne the image of the earthy, ...*	*... we shall also bear the image of the heavenly"*
v21	Since by man came death	by man came also the resurrection of the dead
v22, 23	As in Adam all die	In Christ shall all be made alive … Christ the firstfruits; afterward they that are Christ's at his coming
v26	death	the last enemy that shall be destroyed is death
v43	dishonour	glory
v43	weakness	power
v44	natural body	spiritual body
v45	first man Adam was made a living soul	last Adam (Christ) a quickening spirit
v46	natural body	spiritual body
v47	of the earth, earthy	from heaven
v50	flesh and blood	kingdom of God
v42,50,53,54	corruption	incorruption
v52	dead	incorruptible
v53,54	mortal	immortality
v56	death	death swallowed up in victory
v56-57	sting of death is sin	God gives the victory through Christ

Chapter 20
What Adam's Sin Introduced:
Our Sin-Biased State

Many Scriptures demonstrate that the condition of our nature is biased to sin

The exact term "sin-prone" or "prone to sin" does not appear in the Bible. However, many similar terms occur frequently. For example, the following is a list of verses in the New Testament based on the ESV translation, where the word "lust" or "desire" (Gk. *epithumea*) occurs, which illustrate the bias to sin that is part and parcel of human nature.

- **Lusts of your father the devil** (John 8:44).
- Let not (King) Sin reign in your mortal body, to make you obey its **passions** (Romans 6:12).
- But Sin … produced in me all kinds of **covetousness** (Romans 7:8).
- Put off your old self … which is corrupt through **deceitful desires** (Ephesians 4:22).
- Put to death … sexual immorality, impurity, passion, **evil desire**" (Colossians 3:5).
- **The passion of lust like the Gentiles**, who do not know God (1 Thessalonians 4:5).
- I urge you … to abstain from the **passions of the flesh**, which wage war against your soul (1 Peter 2:11).
- For all that is in the world – **the desires of the flesh** and the **desires** of the eyes and **pride** of life – **is not from the Father but is from the world** (1 John 2:16).
- See also 1 Timothy 6:9; 2 Timothy 2:22; 3:6; Titus 2:12 1 Peter 1:14; 2 Peter 2:10; 3:3; Jude 1:16,18.

The lusts or desires in the above list are *wrong, evil, sinful, warring against the soul, not from the Father* etc. But Adam and Eve did not have these unGodly desires before they sinned. Genesis 3:6 reveals that it was only after they embraced the serpent's reasoning that their desires became evil. To that point, their God-given natural desires harmonised with God's will. It is vital to differentiate between legitimate desires and evil desires like those listed above. For example, there are three New Testament cases where lust or desire (Gk. "epithumea") is used legitimately.

- I have earnestly **desired** to eat this Passover with you before I suffer (Luke 22:15).

- My **desire** is to depart and be with Christ, for that is far better (Philippians 1:23).

- We endeavoured … with **great desire** to see you face to face (1 Thessalonians 2:17)

Bro Thomas makes the distinction by explaining that one's desires become evil when their attainment is sought by "crossing the limit" (i.e. the meaning of *"diabolos"*) forbidden of God:

> If there had been nothing in the constitution of the original nature of man impressible by the suggestions of the Serpent, there could have been no transgression. Had Eve's nature been "angelic" instead of animal, there would have been no internal response to the external enticement. That internal something was not essentially evil; because, though possessing it, Adam and Eve were pronounced "very good." **It is not evil to admire the beautiful, and to wish to possess it; to desire to gratify the taste, and to aspire to the wisdom of "the gods," or Elohim; but all this becomes evil when its attainment is sought by crossing the limit forbidden of God. The seeking to attain by crossing the line, Paul teaches was the result, not of innate wickedness, but of deception.** The Serpent beguiled Eve. Had she been certain of the consequences she would not have transgressed.[139]

When did the bias to evil begin?

When did the bias to evil in human nature originate? Was it part of God's "very good" creation before Adam and Eve sinned, or was it after their sin? Those who say "before" often attempt to discredit the "after" view with emotive language such as *"it would be ludicrous to suggest that God 'implanted' or 'injected' the bias to sin into their flesh after Adam and Eve sinned"*. But since they acknowledge that sin-bias exists in our nature, and believe it was there before Adam's sin, their view effectively means that God 'injected' or 'implanted' the bias to sin into the flesh of Adam and Eve when He created them.

Emotive terms aside, the fundamental problem with this view is that it undermines the righteousness of God, by making Him directly responsible for the entry into the world of our sin-biased state (King Sin or the devil) well before Adam and Eve sinned. The truth, according to the Scriptures, is that God cursed His whole creation, including the "enmity" in mankind (Genesis 3:15; Romans 8:20), *after* Adam and Eve adopted serpent reasoning and sinned, not before. Although man and creation were cursed, at the same time,

---

[139] Thomas, John, 1852, The Herald of the Kingdom and Age to Come, vol. 2 (1852), pp. 200-201.

our Heavenly Father mercifully provided a way of redemption through His Son.

Scriptural proof that the introduction of the bias to evil was coeval with the fall

God has not revealed the 'mechanics' of what was involved in the change in the condition of Adam and Eve's nature any more than He has revealed the 'mechanics' of what was involved in the resurrection of our Lord and the change of his mortal body to a sinless immortal body. However, based on the following points detailed in Genesis 1-3 and other supporting Scriptures, we know that these changes occurred after Adam and Eve sinned.

- **Genesis 1:31** – God pronounced that creation was *"very good"*, including Adam and Eve. However, post their sin, Scripture teaches that human nature is *"desperately wicked"*[140] and *"the imagination of man's heart is evil from his youth"*[141] (see Chapter 17 and the table of Scriptures on page 122).

- **Genesis 3:6-11** - two connected changes occurred immediately after Adam and Eve sinned: i) the eyes of them both were opened; and ii) they knew that they were naked. This was not merely a new perception that they were sinners, but a radical alteration in the way their bodies – including their eyes – interacted with their minds (see Chapter 16).

- **Genesis 3:14-24; Romans 8:20-23** – Adam's sin led to God's curses with physical consequences. This included *"I will put enmity…"*, which refers to the conflict that would then (post-fall) exist within the fallen serpent-like condition of human nature (Genesis 3:15). We can be sure of this, because God simultaneously promised redemption through Jesus Christ, who would achieve the victory over this same "serpent" problem within himself (cf. John 3:14; 8:28; 12:34; Hebrews 2:14-15). Genesis 3:15 is parallel with the apostle Paul's exposition that God subjected His creation to vanity but at the same time provided hope of a physical redemption from this state (Romans 8:20-23) (see Chapters 17 and 21).

- **Genesis 3:1-6; 4:7** – Prior to sin, God created a literal serpent that tested Adam and Eve's allegiance. Post their sin, the enmity was now within human nature (Genesis 4:7, ESV; Mark 7:21-23). If the bias to evil was already within Adam and Eve when created,

---

[140] Jeremiah 17:9.
[141] Genesis 6:5.

then the serpent's role would have been redundant. In Genesis 4 Cain did not need a talking serpent to tempt him to sin.

- **John 8:38, 44-45; 1 John 3:8** – Jesus and John state that desires contrary to the Father's will derive from another father - the devil, who was *"a murder from the beginning"*, *"the father of lies"*, and *"sinneth from the beginning"*. These references connecting the devil with *the beginning* when sin and death (murder) first occurred, confirm that the entry of the devil into the world, personifying the sin-prone and death-stricken condition of human nature, was coeval with the fall. (see Chapter 21).

- **Romans 5:12** - *"By One Man"* governs every clause in this verse, including the latter phrase *"for that all have sinned"*, which is better rendered in the Greek *"with the result that all have sinned"*. This supports Christadelphian teaching that by one man's transgression, the death-stricken and the sin-biased condition of human nature entered into the world, and then spread to all of Adam's posterity (refer to the detailed explanation of this verse from page 151).

- **Romans 5:19** - *"By one man's disobedience many were made sinners"* – In this short phrase, the apostle Paul explains that as a consequence of Adam's sin, all are born with a physical constitution or state that will inevitably cause us to sin (refer to the detailed explanation of this verse from page 155).

- **Romans 5:21; 6:12** *"Sin reigns unto death"* / *"Sin reigns in our mortal bodies"* are descriptions of our fallen nature. However, these descriptions of "King Sin" exercising dominion over our nature, cannot apply to the *"very good"* condition of Adam and Eve's nature before their sin. The change to a sin-prone and mortal state coincided with their sin.

- **Romans 7:17-25** – In their *"very good"* state, before their sin, Adam and Eve did not have a *"law of sin dwelling in their members"* or *"wretched"* bodies in which *"no good thing dwells"*.

- **2 Corinthians 5:21 and Romans 6:10** - Christ was *"made Sin for us who knew no sin"*, and he *"died unto Sin"*. Christ bore our fallen nature, which is called by metonymy, "Sin". It would therefore be incorrect to call Adam and Eve's unfallen, *"very good"* nature "Sin" (see *"Metonymy in The Bible"* in this chapter).

We can accept that our nature will be changed to immortality by "eating" from the symbolic tree of life (Revelation 2:7) through redemption in Christ. In the same manner, we should be able to accept that the condition of Adam and Eve's nature was changed after eating from the tree of the knowledge of good and evil.

It was a physical sentence that was passed on man, not a legal sentence or legal condemnation. The problem of fallen human nature will be removed by a physical change to immortality, not a legal change at baptism or any other time. However, as Paul explains in Romans 5:17, in Christ, our hope is *"much more"* than merely returning to Adam and Eve's physical state before the fall. The apostle says, *"**much more** they which receive abundance of grace and of the gift of righteousness shall **reign in life**"*.

Consistent Christadelphian teaching on the bias to evil

Christadelphians have consistently taught that the origin of the human bias to evil as a physical trait of human nature was coeval with the fall, as is demonstrated by the following quotations:

John Thomas, Elpis Israel, 1866, p. 90

When [Adam and Eve] adopted the Serpent's reasonings as their own, these being at variance with the truth, caused an "enmity" against it in their thinkings, which is equivalent to "enmity against God". When their sin was perfected, the propensities, or lusts, having been inflamed, became "a law in their members"; and because it was implanted in their flesh by transgression, it is styled, "the law of sin" [Rom 7:23,25]; and death being the wages of sin, it is also termed, "the law of sin and death" [Rom 8:2]; but by philosophy, "the law of nature".

Robert Roberts – Christadelphian 1898, p. 343

Adam was in the 'very good' state before he sinned. He was not in the state his descendants are in. They are heirs of death; he was not. They have the sentence of death 'in themselves' (2 Corinthians 1:9); he had not. Paul had to say, 'sin dwelleth in me'; 'I see a law in my members warring against the law of my mind' (Romans 7:17,23); Adam could not have said this. ...

Sin, as disobedience, arose in their case from a wrong opinion concerning a matter of lawful desire, and not from what Paul calls 'sin in the flesh'. It became sin in the flesh when it bought fourth that sentence of death that made them mortal, and all their children with them: that is, **this sentence, passed because of sin, affected their bodily state and implanted in their flesh a law of dissolution that became the law of their being. As a law of physical weakness and death, it necessarily became a source of moral weakness. That which originated in sin, became a cause of sin in their posterity, and therefore accurately described by Paul as 'sin in the flesh'.**

WF Barling – Redemption in Christ Jesus, 5. Implications Examined, The Christadelphian, vol. 83, 1946, p. 84

Nazarene authors declare that transgression altered only Adam's position in relation to law, and "did not cause his flesh to be changed". They therefore regard man as still "very good", and to be "just what the Creator made him".

... Such reasoning is contrary to Scripture. John explicitly declares the lust of the flesh, the lust of the eyes and the pride of life to be 'not of the father, but of the world' (1 John 2:16). There could be no more emphatic testimony that these 'lusts' are not desires which can be attributed initially to God; but sinful propensities which only came to exist as a result of the first offence. The "lust of the world" and "the will of God" are essentially antagonistic (verse 17). Disciples should therefore "no longer live to the lusts of men, but to the will of God" (1 Peter 4:2), for, far from being "God-implanted", lusts are "of Diabolos" (John 8:44).

… By their voluntary belief in, and consequent obedience to, the first lie, their nature was vitiated so that they hid themselves from God), and their simplicity, or innocence, was corrupted (2 Corinthians 11:3). **Ever since, this moral corruption has persisted as an evil property of human nature, part of the vanity to which God made creation subject until the day of salvation** (Romans 8:20–25).

… There is thus a bias to evil within man which has to be offset by an acquired tendency to do good (Colossians 3:1). **This bias must either have been implanted at Creation or be the direct consequence of Adam's transgression. The first proposition is inconceivable; the second states the facts.**

John Carter – Unity Booklet, 1958

Through Adam's sin **the original very good state was lost, and his posterity inherit a nature with a tendency to sin to which all have succumbed.** *Because this inherited tendency is so evident a characteristic of human nature, and* **because it is the result and cause of sin, Paul by the use of metonymy can describe it as sin:** *"It is no more I but sin that dwelleth in me." He gives it other names as well, such as "a law – evil present with me", the "flesh", "a law in my members" (Romans 7).*[142]

What is it that is within us, that the apostle describes as sin? Clearly there are the impulses that lead to sin. There are impulses there that are the result of sin at the beginning, which we have by inheritance.[143]

… In 1874 (p. 88), Bro. Roberts answered the question, **"What do you mean by "sin in the flesh",** which some speak of as a fixed principle?"

> *"Answer: … There is a principle, element, or peculiarity in our constitution (it matters not how you word it) which leads to the decay of the strongest or the healthiest.* ***Its implantation came by sin, for death came by sin; and the infliction of death and the implantation of this peculiarity are synonymous things."***[144]

Metonymy in the Bible: Fallen human nature is referred to as "sin's flesh" because it is the result of Adam's sin

In Romans 8:3, the apostle Paul's reference to human nature as *"sinful flesh"* or *"sin's flesh"* in itself teaches us that its sin-biased condition is a result of Adam's sin in the beginning. In the excerpt from the Unity Booklet above, Bro Carter explains that the condition of fallen humanity with its tendency to sin is described in the Bible as "sin" by

---

[142] Carter, John – Unity Booklet, 1958, p. 20.

[143] Carter, John – Unity Booklet, 1958, pp. 28-32.

[144] Carter, John – Unity Booklet, 1958, pp. 78 – 81.

way of metonymy because it is the result and cause of sin. Metonymy is a frequently used figure of speech in Hebrew, Greek and English.

"Metonymy" is where something is put for something closely related to it. The Encyclopedia Britannica defines "metonymy" as follows:

> **Metonymy**, (from Greek metōnymia, "change of name," or "misnomer"), figure of speech in which the name of an object or concept is replaced with a word closely related to or suggested by the original, as "crown" to mean "king" ("The power of the crown was mortally weakened") or an author for his works ("I'm studying Shakespeare"). A familiar Shakespearean example is Mark Antony's speech in Julius Caesar in which he asks of his audience: "Lend me your ears."

> Metonymy is closely related to synecdoche, the naming of a part for the whole or a whole for the part, and is a common poetic device. Metonymy has the effect of creating concrete and vivid images in place of generalities, as in the substitution of a specific "grave" for the abstraction "death." Metonymy is standard journalistic and headline practice as in the use of "city hall" to mean "municipal government" and of the "White House" to mean the "president of the United States."[145]

The Bible is full of examples of metonymy, particularly metonymy of cause and metonymy of effect.

Metonymy of cause is when the cause is stated, but the effect is meant. Examples include:

- *"The tongue can no man tame"* (James 3:8) – the tongue is put for the untamed words it is used to produce. There are many other similar Biblical examples of metonymy of cause using the eyes, mouth, lips, voice and throat: John 5:2; Revelation 10:11; 13:7, John 12:30; 1 Corinthians 14:10, Romans 3:13.

- *"Yea, also because the wine transgresseth"* (Habakkuk 2:5), wine itself cannot transgress, but it is put as the cause or reason for people transgressing, that is the effect of drinking it.

- Often sin and its synonyms are put for the effects or punishments of sin. When the angels urged Lot and his family to flee out of Sodom, they warned, *"lest thou be consumed in the iniquity of the city"* (Genesis 19:16). Here, the cause (iniquity) is put instead of the effect (punishment or destruction). See also Deuteronomy 9:21, Jeremiah 14:16 and Zechariah 14:19.

- Similarly, human nature is not "sin", but can be referred to as "Sin" by way of metonymy of cause, because Adam's sin is the reason for the condition of the "flesh" with which we are born.

Metonymy of effect is when the effect is stated, but the cause is meant. Examples include:

---

[145] https://www.britannica.com/art/metonymy, accessed 01 January 2021

- When Simeon took the baby Jesus in his arms and declared, *"mine eyes have seen thy salvation"* (Luke 2:30), he was referring to the cause of God's great work of salvation – *"the Lord's Christ"* (Luke 2:26) whom he was holding.

- When Jesus stated, *"I am not come to send peace, but a sword"* (Matthew 10:34), he was metonymically referring to the sword as what is produced by division or contention.

- When Pilate declared himself to be *"innocent of the blood of this just person"* (Matthew 27:24), he meant the "death" of Christ in which his blood would be spilt.

- For other examples of metonymy of effect, see 2 Kings 4:40; Psalm 49:15; cf. Hosea 13:14; 1 Corinthians 15:55

- Similarly, human nature is not "sin", but can be referred to as "Sin" by way of metonymy of effect, because we are all born with a nature that will inevitably lead to sin.

Bro Carter explained that after Adam and Eve sinned, the condition of human nature can be metonymically described as "Sin" because it is **both the result and cause of sin**. When the Bible refers to the condition of our nature as *"Sin"* or *"Sin's flesh"*, metonymy applies both ways – there is metonymy of cause and metonymy of effect. Bro Roberts similarly states, *"That which **originated in sin**, became a **cause of sin** in their posterity, and therefore accurately described by Paul as 'sin in the flesh'"*[146], Bro CC Walker *"**Sin is both the cause and effect** of the flesh"*[147], and Bro Thomas *"This [human nature] is called "sin," or "Sin's flesh," because it is what it is in consequence of sin, or transgression."*[148]

The top half of the diagram on the following page shows two different examples of one-way metonymy. The bottom half illustrates the two-way metonymical sense, of both cause and effect, by which human nature is referred to as *"Sin"* (King Sin), or *"Sin's flesh"* by the apostle Paul.

As the Encyclopedia Britannica explains, *"metonymy has the effect of creating concrete and vivid images in place of generalities"*. The purpose of the Bible's metonymical references to our nature or flesh as *"Sin"* vividly teaches that our fallen nature came from Adam's sin.

---

[146] Roberts, Robert, *Why Did Adam Sin?*, The Christadelphian, vol. 35, 1898, p. 343.

[147] Walker, CC, The Christadelphian, vol. 50, 1913, pp. 259-261.

[148] Thomas, John, *The Diabolos*, Eureka, 1861, vol. 1, pp. 247-248.

One-way Metonymy

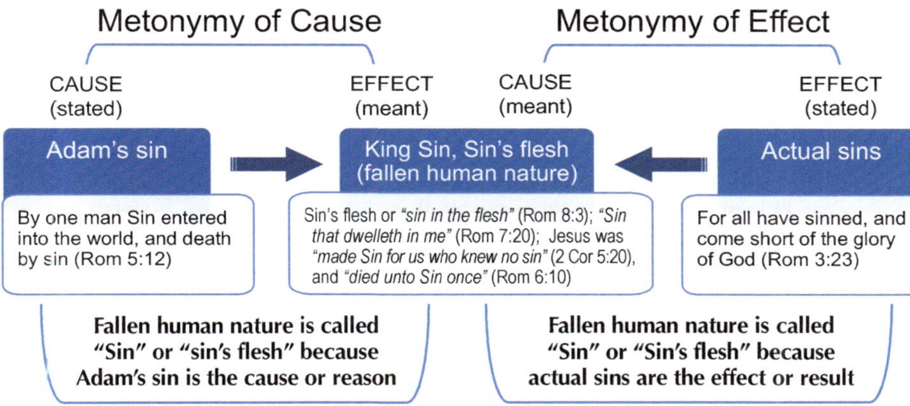

Two-way Metonymy - Sin's Flesh

Romans 5:12 – John Carter: *"By One Man … all sinned as the result of his sin"*

The latter clause of Romans 5:12, *"for that all have sinned"*, supports Christadelphian teaching that by one man's transgression, not only did death spread to all of Adam's posterity, but so did the sin-biased condition of human nature. For clarity, we have divided the four main clauses of Romans 5:12 as follows:

> *[a] Wherefore, as by one man sin entered into the world,*
> *[b] and death by sin;*
> *[c] and so death passed upon all men,*
> *[d] for that all have sinned (Romans 5:12)*

In his book on Romans, Bro Carter points out that *"By one man"* is a phrase that governs every clause in Romans 5:12. He therefore interprets Romans 5:12d as: *"for that, or because, all sinned as a result of his [Adam's] sin"*.

John Carter, Paul's Letter to the Romans, 1931 p. 61

"By one man" is a phrase governing every clause in verse 12. Through one man sin entered the world; through him came death; through him death passed unto all, for that, or because, all sinned as the result of his sin. Thus amplified, some of the difficulty which has occasioned much strife of words is removed. Adam sinned and was punished with death. **His children inherit mortality and also a tendency to sin so inevitable in its sin-producing power that Paul can say that through Adam's sin all sinned, and therefore all die through him.** Paul now turns aside to establish from the universal prevalence of death from Adam to Moses the fact of the unity of the race in its inheritance of a death-stricken nature from a transgressing head...

Romans 5:12 – Joseph A. Fitzmyer: "By One Man . . . with the result that all have sinned"

Supporting Brother Carter's interpretation is a New Testament scholar, Joseph A. Fitzmyer, who, after a detailed review of 11 alternative interpretations of the phrase *"eph' hō"* (KJV: *"for that'"*) in Romans 5:12d, concluded by interpreting the phrase as:

"a conjunction, introducing a result clause" as in "so that" or "with the result that". Hence, he comments that 5:12d should be understood as *"with the result that all have sinned"*, explaining that there is a *"connection between the sin of 'one man' and the death and sins of all human beings. Thus Paul in v. 12 would be ascribing death and human sinfulness to two causes, not unrelated: to Adam and to the conduct of all human beings. Thus the fate of sinful humanity ultimately rests on what its head Adam has done to it; the primary causality for its sinful and mortal condition is ascribed to him, but a secondary resultant causality is attributed to the sinful conduct of all human beings."*; and *"our mortal and sinful condition ... stems from Adam but not without its own resultant responsibility"* [149].

Although stressing the strong connection between Adam's sin, and the sinful condition or sin-biased state with which humanity is born, Fitzmyer goes on to explain regarding the final phrase in 5:12d, *"for all have sinned"*, that:

"The vb. hēmarton should not be understood as "have sinned collectively" or as "have sinned in Adam," because they would be additions to Paul's text. The vb. refers to personal, actual sins of individual human beings, as Pauline usage elsewhere suggests (2: 2; 3:23; 5:14, 16; 6:15; 1 Cor 6:18; 7:28, 36; 8:12; 15:34), as the context demands (vv 16, 20).[150]

---

[149] Fitzmyer, J. (1993). *The Consecutive Meaning of EΦ' Ω in Romans 5.12*, New Testament Studies, 39(3), 321-339.

[150] Fitzmyer, J. A., S. J. *Romans: a new translation with introduction and commentary* (Vol. 33, p. 417). New Haven; London: Yale University Press (2008).

Fitzmyer rejected any notion that the Catholic doctrine of "original sin" is supported by Romans 5:12.

The Christadelphian Origins Discussion (COD) website, which is very forthright in promoting EC View B, quotes Fitzmyer's rejection of Augustine's view that the phrase *"eph' hō"* means "in whom" (in the sense of incorporation)[151]. However, for some reason, they fail to note Fitzmyer's conclusion, where he states:

> *"it would be false to the thrust of the whole Pauline paragraph to interpret 5.12 as though it implied that the sinful human condition before Christ's coming were due solely to **individual personal conduct, as Pelagius advocated, in imitation of Adam**"* [152].

Therefore, Fitzmyer rejects both Augustine's (original sin) and Pelagius' (no change in the condition of Adam's nature) interpretations of Romans 5:12, as do Christadelphians (BASF 3, 5, 6, 8, 9, 10 & 12 and the Australian Unity Agreement). However, COD appears to be interpreting it in line with Pelagius. They (i) deny any causal connection between Adam's sin and the reason why we sin, (ii) state instead that the sin-biased nature with which we are born is just how God created all humans from the outset, and (iii) agree with Pelagius' interpretation of Romans 5:12d that the only link with Adam is that when we sin we imitate what Adam did, and on this basis prove ourselves to be *"in Adam"*.

Romans 5:12 is explained by Paul himself in vv14-21

The remainder of Romans 5 confirms that the human race has physically inherited a death-stricken and sin-biased nature due to its transgressing head. As Fitzmyer states, *"no matter how one understands 5.12d, the universal causality of Adam's sin is presupposed in 5.15a, 16a, 17a, 18a, 19a"*.[153] That is why the apostle Paul goes on to explain that *"many died by one man's trespass"* (V15); that this *"reign of death"* came by *"one"* (v17).

Furthermore, Paul describes the death that came into the world as *"the judgment following ONE trespass that brought condemnation"* (v16). And he further explains that the many who die because of the one man's trespass, including Christ (Romans 6:9), is not limited to those with knowledge of God's laws, but rather is a *"condemnation for ALL men"* (v18).

---

[151] Bro John Doe, *Does a sinner earn death or did Adam earn it for them?*, COD Website, June 2017 – See Appendix 1 Question 3.

[152] Fitzmyer, J. (1993). *The Consecutive Meaning of EΦ' Ω in Romans 5.12*. New Testament Studies, 39(3), 321-339.

[153] Fitzmyer, J. A., S. J. *Romans: a new translation with introduction and commentary* (Vol. 33, p. 417). New Haven; London: Yale University Press (2008).

Romans 5:12 Explained

Romans 5:12			Romans 5:14-21 (ESV)
KJV	Fitzmyer	John Carter	The Apostle Paul's inspired explanation
a. As by one man sin entered the world	Therefore, just as sin entered the world through one man	Through one man sin entered the world	
b. and death by sin;	and death came through sin;	through him came death	
c. and so death passed upon all men,	so death spread to all human beings,	through him death passed unto all	- death reigned from Adam to Moses, even over those whose sinning was not like the transgression of Adam (v14) - many died through one man's trespass (v15) - for the judgment following one trespass brought condemnation (v16) - because of one man's trespass, death reigned through that one man (v17) - one trespass led to condemnation for all men (v18)
d. for that all have sinned	with the result that all have sinned.	for that 'or' because, all sinned as the result of his sin.	- by the one man's disobedience the many were made sinners (v19) - sin reigned in death (v21)

Bro. Carter's explanation: *"By one man" is a phrase governing every clause in verse 12. ...Adam sinned and was punished with death. His children inherit mortality and also a tendency to sin so inevitable in its sin-producing power that Paul can say that through Adam's sin all sinned, and therefore all die through him. Paul now turns aside to establish from the universal prevalence of death from Adam to Moses the fact of the unity of the race in its inheritance of a death-stricken nature from a transgressing head....[154]*

Fitzmyer's explanation: *Thus the fate of sinful humanity ultimately rests on what its head Adam has done to it; the primary causality for its sinful and mortal condition is ascribed to him, but a secondary resultant causality is attributed to the sinful conduct of all human beings...Their mortal and sinful condition, i.e. the upsetting of the normal condition between humanity and God, the strife between the Ego ["I am" – i.e. Yahweh] and the flesh, and humanity's failure to attain its destined goal, stems from Adam but not without its own resultant responsibility. [155]*

---

[154] Carter, John, *Romans*, On Romans 5:12-13 (p. 61).
[155] Fitzmyer, J., The Consecutive Meaning of ΕΦ' Ω in Romans 5.12. New Testament Studies, 39 (3), 321-339 (1993).

In contrast, COD says that Romans 5:12d stands in isolation and refers to those, who like Adam, deliberately and consciously sin. In their view, this is different from vv13-21, where the apostle talks about people who sin in ignorance and are "accounted" as sinners. However, as shown by the table on the previous page, what the apostle Paul sets out in v12 he confirms throughout the remainder of the chapter. He is not talking about different types of sin, or different labels of death, between v12 and the rest of the chapter. The sin (personified as King Sin and *diabolos*) that entered into the world (*kosmos*) through one man (5:12a) is the sin-prone condition of human nature, which has the power of death (5:12b cp. Hebrews 2:14) and results in all of us sinning (5:12d, 5:19a).

Romans 5:19 - *For as by one man's disobedience many were made sinners, so by the obedience of one shall many be made righteous.*

Romans 5:19 explains in cause and effect language that one man's disobedience (the cause) resulted in all inheriting a nature that is biased to sin (the effect). In the Greek, *"made"* is *"kathistēmi"* which means *"set down as"*, *"constituted"*, *"established"*, and hence YLT/Weymouth translate it as: *"constituted sinners"* and the ABP Interlinear Bible translates it as *"established as sinners"*.

COD (EC View B) suggests that the word "made" should be interpreted as "accounted or considered"[156] However, there is an entirely different Greek word for this concept (Gk. *"logizomai"*). The apostle Paul uses this word elsewhere in the book of Romans to explain that it is by our faith in Christ that righteousness is "imputed" unto us. For example, it appears in Romans 4:23 *"**imputed** to him for righteousness"* and Romans 8:36 *"all day long we are **accounted** as sheep for the slaughter"*.

The roots of these two different words explain the difference. The root of *"kathistēmi"* is *"histēmi"*, which means *"to cause or make to stand; to place, put, set"* (Thayer). The root of *"logizomai"* is *"logos"*, which means *"those things which are put together in thought, as of those which, having been thought i.e. gathered together in the mind, are expressed in words"* (Thayer). *"Logizomaias"* is the Greek word used for

---

[156] Bro John Doe, *Paul's argument through Rom 5:14-21*, COD Website, June 2017: "V19 Paul says many are *"made sinners"* is critical here. It should be understood as 'accounted' or 'considered'. We are not sinners because of what Adam did. In the same way, we are not strictly righteous in ourselves because of what Christ did. We are treated as righteous or accounted righteous. This righteousness by association (if I may put it that way) works in reverse with Adam and death coming by sin. Just like in Christ we are considered righteous, so in Adam many are consider/counted as sinners – even those not personally accountable from contact with God's word. They receive the same outcome/punishment in a federal headship sense".

bookkeeping - to take an inventory, count, estimate, compute, calculate, reckon or put to one's account.

"Kathistēmi" occurs 22 times in the NT and is most frequently translated as "made" in the KJV, "set" in the ESV and "put" in the NASB (e.g. compare Matthew 24:25 in all three versions). The Greek-English Lexicon of the New Testament defines *"kathistēm"* as meaning *"to cause a state to be—to cause to be, to make to be, to make, to result in, to bring upon, to bring about."*[157] It always refers to something that literally occurs or comes into existence. Hence it is not referring to a matter that is accounted, considered or rendered to be the case. It is not attaching a meaning to something that, by itself independently, is not the case.

For example, *"kathistēmi"* is used when referring to individuals who are set up or appointed as rulers and judges (Matthew 24:25; 25:21; Luke 12:14; Acts 7:10,27,35), or elders and priests (Acts 6:3; Titus 1:5; Hebrews 5:1; 7:28; 8:3). In all cases, they were actually established as rulers or priests, they were not just "considered" to be rulers or priests.

The two occurrences of *"kathistēmi"* in the book of James are useful comparisons, as in line with Romans 5:19, the word occurs in the passive voice, and the meaning of "to make", "to place", "to set", is correctly conveyed by most translations.

- *"The tongue **is set among our members**, staining the whole body."* (James 3:6, ESV)

- *"whoever wishes to be a friend of the world **makes himself** an enemy of God."* (James 4:4, ESV)

In James 3:6, the tongue is not "accounted" or "considered" to be among our members, but rather is, in reality, a part of our physical makeup. In James 4:4 the apostle is not saying that those who desire to be friends with the world will be "considered" as an enemy of God - such a person "makes himself" an actual enemy of God.

2 Peter 1:8 is another helpful comparison. Here *"kathistēmi"* occurs in the present tense, as it is about the ongoing development of those virtues, which **make** (KJV) or **keep** (ESV) believers productive (not barren nor unfruitful) in the knowledge of Jesus Christ. This is an actual effect occurring in a believer's life, not an "accounted" effect.

- *"For if these things be in you, and abound, they **make** you that ye shall neither be barren nor unfruitful in the knowledge of our Lord Jesus Christ." (2 Peter 1:8, KJV)*

---

[157] Louw, J. P., & Nida, E. A. (1996). Greek-English lexicon of the New Testament: based on semantic domains (electronic ed. of the 2nd edition., Vol. 1, pp. 149–150). New York: United Bible Societies.

In the same way, Romans 5:19 is *not* saying, as COD alleges, that we are only **"accounted"** as sinners because of Adam's sin. Nor is the verse saying, as COD claims, that because of Adam's sin, (i) we all come under the banner of Adam as the federal or representative head of all sinners when we sin and (ii) being under Adam as the federal head means that a person is *"in Adam"* legally, not physically. Instead, the apostle says that we are "established" as sinners because of one man's sin. "By one man's disobedience", we are born with a nature in such a state that it is inevitable that we will sin.

The same Greek word *"kathistēmi"* is used again in the second half of Romans 5:19 to contrast what is achieved by Christ - *"by the obedience of one shall many be **made** righteous."* Once again, the apostle is describing a physical impact on humanity due to one man's actions. In this case, being "made righteous" refers to our ultimate hope of being made immortal. This is evident from the context two verses earlier where the apostle explains that *"they which receive…**the gift of righteousness shall reign in life**"* (v17), and the context two verses later – *"even so might grace reign through righteousness **unto eternal life**"* (v21). The apostle refers to this *"free gift"* of righteousness five times in context *(v15 2x; v16 2x; v17)*, and he defines it again plainly in the next chapter *"**the gift of God is eternal life** through Jesus Christ our Lord"* (Romans 6:23).

The fact that *"kathistēmi"* occurs in the future tense in the second phrase, *"shall many be made righteous"*, confirms that the ultimate goal of being "made", "constituted" or "established" as righteous has yet to occur. In contrast to this, *"kathistēmi"* in the first phrase regarding the result of Adam's disobedience, is written in the aorist tense (a single event in the past): *"many were made sinners"*. We are not made or established as sinners on an ongoing basis. It happened once when we were born, it is our misfortune to inherit a sin-prone death stricken nature, and we can't do anything to change this. Hence, due to Adam's disobedience, each member of humanity is physically constituted as sinners from birth. We are born with a nature that is prone to sin (*diabolos* within). But we are not physically constituted righteous until our sin-prone mortal state is clothed upon with a house from heaven, or swallowed up with eternal life (2 Corinthians 5:1-4).

This is not to deny that we can be mentally and morally accounted (*logizomai*) as righteous now, or justified (*dikaioō*) by our faith now as the apostle Paul resolutely teaches in the early part of Romans 5 and elsewhere using the present and past tenses. However, the Greek word Paul uses in Romans 5:19 for both "many **were made** sinners" and "**shall** many be **made** righteous" is *"kathistēmi"*. The usage of this Greek word is consistent with the immediate context of verses 15 to 21. The apostle is expounding the physical impact of Adam's disobedience upon all from birth, and the future physical impact of Christ's obedience for those who will be reborn with immortality.

As Jesus taught Nicodemus, *"Except a man be born of water and of the spirit, he cannot enter into the kingdom of God"* (John 3:5). This is how we can be constituted righteous. It is a process that starts with baptism, from which point in time a believer has their sins forgiven and is mentally and morally justified. But this is not the end of the process. As the apostle Paul conveyed to those who were denying the hope of the resurrection, *"if in this life only we have hope in Christ, we are of all men most miserable"* (1 Corinthians 15:19). We must be reborn with spirit nature before we can enter the kingdom of God. Jesus further explained to Nicodemus, *"that which is born of the flesh is flesh; and that which is born of the Spirit is spirit"* (John 3:6), and the apostle Paul explained to the Corinthians, *"flesh and blood cannot inherit the kingdom of God; neither doth corruption inherit incorruption"* (1 Corinthians 15:50). Hence the end of the process of being constituted righteous is a physical re-birth, *"for this corruptible must put on incorruption, and this mortal must put on immortality"* (1 Corinthians 15:53).

One man brought the physical state of death and the inevitability of sinning to all of humanity; another man brought the hope of a physical state of righteousness or eternal life for all who are truly in him. In this future immortal state, it's not just that sin will be impossible, but with the devil in each of us destroyed, we will be completely free from the desire to sin in any case.

As shown in the table on the following page, the apostle Paul employs cause and effect logic throughout Romans 5v15-21 to demonstrate that two men were responsible for very different physical outcomes. The physical consequences upon all due to one man's sin are contrasted with the future physical blessings for all those who are truly in Christ, thanks to one man's obedience.

For example, in v17, *"death reigning"* due to Adam's sin is a physical consequence. And in the same verse, we are told that we will receive *"the gift of righteousness"*, which equates to the future physical gift of immortality (cp. Romans 6:23).

God's justice in one sense is balanced. But in another it is not. We did not deserve to be born inheriting the physical consequences of Adam's sin, nor do we deserve the physical blessings promised thanks to Christ's righteousness. But this is where there is imbalance in our favour. The receiving of immortal glory through God's grace will far outweigh the *"in Adam"* state we are born into, and will be *"much more"* than a return to Adam's pre-fall "very good" state.

Romans 5:15-21 – Contrasting Physical Results

Reason 1: By One Man's Disobedience	Reason 2: By One Man's Righteousness	The Result in both cases	The Justice in both cases
15 But not as the offence, so also is the free gift*. For if through the offence of one many be dead,	**much more** the grace of God, and the gift* by grace, which is by one man, Jesus Christ, hath abounded unto many.	PHYSICAL EFFECT ON OTHERS	Not deserved in both cases. Adam's sin resulted in the misfortune of all inheriting a physical nature where:
16 And not as it was by one that sinned, so is the gift*: for the judgment was by one to condemnation,	but the free gift* is of many offences unto justification.	VERDICT WITH PHYSICAL CONSEQUENCES ON OTHERS	1) sin is inevitable; 2) death reigns.
17 For if by one man's offence death reigned by one;	**much more** they which receive abundance of grace and of the gift* of righteousness shall reign in life by one, Jesus Christ.	PHYSICAL EFFECT ON OTHERS	God's provision of His only begotten son, and Christ's obedience resulted in two underserved blessings for others: 1) the abundance of grace (forgiveness of sins);
18 Therefore as by the offence of one judgment came upon all men to condemnation;	even so by the righteousness of one the free gift* came upon all men unto justification of life.	VERDICT WITH PHYSICAL CONSEQUENCES ON OTHERS	2) the free gift of righteousness or eternal life (immortality).
19 For as by one man's disobedience many were made sinners,	so by the obedience of one shall many be made righteous	PHYSICAL EFFECT ON OTHERS	The blessings in Christ far exceed ("much more") the mere reversing of the physical misfortunes that came by Adam's sin.
21 That as sin hath reigned unto death,	even so might grace reign through righteousness unto eternal life by Jesus Christ our Lord	PHYSICAL EFFECT ON OTHERS	

* In context "gift" = eternal life, cp. also Romans 6:23 *"the gift of God is eternal life through Jesus Christ our Lord"*

Made Sinners and Made Righteous

"Made sinners," or "constituted sinners," indicates that men become sharers by birth (the basis of union with Adam) of all the results that come in the train of Adam's transgression. "Made righteous," or "constituted righteous ones," indicates that men share by being born again (the basis of union with Christ), the righteousness and life of which Christ is the possessor.

John Carter, Paul's Letter to the Romans, p. 64,
The Christadelphian, Vol. 66 (1929), p. 453

Summary of Romans 5:19

Based on the meaning of the Greek word *"kathistēmi"* and the context of Romans 5 itself, we can summarise the apostle Paul's teaching in Romans 5:19:

- The apostle firstly describes the physical result of Adam's sin upon all – we are physically made or born with a nature that is prone to sin. This is our misfortune, not our crime. We need forgiveness from our sins and redemption from our present physical state to immortality.

- The apostle then contrasts our present state with the future result for those truly *"in Christ"*. Thanks to Christ's obedience – we will be physically made or constituted with a righteous nature. In this future state of immortality, not only will sin be impossible, but with the devil in each of us destroyed, we won't be burdened by even the desire to sin. Like the angels, we will still have free will (i.e. we won't be robots), but our desires will only ever lead in a righteous direction.

See Section 6 - *Adam's sin resulted in mortality and sin-bias for all mankind* - for further reading on this chapter's subject.[158]

---

[158] In particular the following articles are well expressed, in the opinion of the authors of *By One Man*.

- Page 307: Collyer, Principles & Proverbs, *The Meaning of Sacrifice*, 1938, pp. 94–100.
- Page 317: The Committee of The Christadelphian, *For Whom Christ Died*, The Christadelphian, vol. 108, 1971, pp. 358-363.
- Page 336: Harry Tennant, *The Nature of Christ*, The Testimony, vol. 58, 1988 pp. 234-237.
- Page 341: Tecwyn Morgan, "Studies in the Statement of Faith", 1991, pp. 24-29.

Chapter 21

What Adam's Sin Introduced: The Devil

Christadelphian view of the *diabolos* - a problem for EC advocates

Christadelphians have always understood that the devil (*diabolos*) is the personification of fallen human nature. It came into existence after Adam and Eve adopted the reasoning of the serpent and sinned (John 8:44; 1 John 3:8). God's sentence on the serpent in Genesis 3:15 explains that the problem they had taken on board, i.e. serpent thinking within, would now be a hereditary physical law of human nature – something that they would pass on to their children including, the Lord Jesus Christ as the singular seed of the woman (cp. Romans 7:23,25; 8:2-3; Hebrews 2:14-15). Since then, all are born with the problem of the devil – a nature that is mortal with a predisposition to sin. The table at the end of this chapter lists several important references that demonstrate the connection between the *diabolos* and fallen human nature.

In contrast, EC adherents who claim that the condition of human nature was already subject to death and biased to sin well before Adam and Eve sinned are forced to redefine what the *diabolos* represents and how it entered into the world. There are at least two different explanations of the *diabolos* by those holding EC Views.

> **The Diabolos: EC View A:** Claims that the *diabolos* is not a problem with which we are born, but rather a state of mind that can only arise when we become aware of God's laws and thereby are responsible to judgment; specifically when a person's natural desires come into conflict with those laws. Based on this approach, EC View A teaches that the "death" the *diabolos* holds power over is "eternal" death at the judgment seat of Christ for all who are found unworthy. It is not the ordinary death of returning to the dust associated with mortality (see Section 4, question 8).

This first explanation would mean that every newborn does not have the devil. Only when a boy reaches maturity and can understand God's laws, thereby making him responsible to judgment, does the devil first exists in him. Based on this view, the overwhelming majority of the world's population would not have the devil because they have never reached a mature understanding of God's word.

> **The Diabolos: EC View B:** Appears to claim that the *diabolos* personifies the sin-prone condition of human nature with which all are born, based on what we have been able to ascertain from Bro Mike Pearson and

COD's writings (see Section 4, questions 8). But since they deny that there was any physical change in the condition of Adam and Eve's nature, post their sin, the *diabolos* must refer to Adam and Eve's nature as created by God from the outset. Likewise, it must apply to the posited pre-Adamic human nature supposedly created by God through evolution.

EC View B appears to teach: a) that the devil is something that evolved as humans evolved: b) God created Adam and Eve with the devil from the outset that was on par with the evolved devil; and c) the devil does not have the power over the death that Adam introduced.

In their rebuttal of a *Lampstand Magazine* article (July 2017) that addressed EC View A, COD publicly criticized the Christadelphian view of the devil and the EC View A of the devil (calling EC View A "weird")[159]. Following this, requests were made seeking clarification of COD's understanding of:

(i)   what the devil was that Christ, through his own death, destroyed in Hebrews 2:14-15; and

(ii) what is the "death" that the devil holds power over? Is it mortality, or is it their understanding of "eternal death"?

However, they have not answered these two questions to date and clarified their view of this first-principle subject.

Back to Basics – the meaning of *Diabolos*

The noun *"diabolos"* is a compound of two Greek words: *dia* (through) and *ballo* (to throw), and means that which causes us to cross over or transgress. Bro. Thomas explains the meaning of this word in his detailed exposition on this subject in Eureka, and notes that it is a very *"fit and proper word by which to designate the law of sin and death, or Sin's flesh"*.

> **John Thomas, *The Diabolos*, Eureka, vol. 1, 1861, pp. 246- 251**
> But why doth Paul style Sin *diabolos?* The answer to this question will be found in the definition of the word. *Diabolos* is derived from *diaballo*, which is compounded of *dia*, a preposition, which in composition signifies *across, over*, and answers to the Latin *trans;* and of *ballo* to *throw, cast;* and intransitively, *to fall, tumble*. Hence, *diaballo*, is *to throw over* or *across;* and intransitively, like the Latin *trajicere*, to *pass over*, to *cross*, to *pass*. This being the signification of the parent verb, the noun *diabolos* is the name of *that which crosses*, or *causes to cross over*, or *falls over*.
> **Diabolos is therefore a very fit and proper word by which to designate the law of sin and death, or Sin's flesh.**

---

[159] See Section 4, question 8.

Elsewhere in Eureka, Bro Thomas similarly defines the *diabolos* as *"elements of corruption in our nature, inciting it to transgression, and therefore called "Sin working death in us"—Romans 7:13; Hebrews 2:9,14".*[160]

The vast majority of the 38 times the word *diabolos* occurs in the New Testament, it is in the singular and has the definite article *"ho"* before it. This is the devil *(ho diabolos)* that is the great accuser of humanity or the sin-prone and death-stricken condition of fallen human nature. In a few instances, it is not preceded by *"ho"*, and these include John 6:70 (Judas), and three times in the plural form in 2 Timothy 3:3 (groups of people), 1 Timothy 3:11 and Titus 2:3 (women) where it is translated slanderers or false accusers. By falsely accusing others, these individuals or groups manifested the works of "the devil".

In the case of Christ, he had the problem of the devil *(ho diabolos)* within him, which always needed to be suppressed and ultimately put to death. However, he never manifested the slanderous or false accusative works of the devil. Likewise, all of the 12 disciples had the problem of the accuser *("ho diabolos")* as part and parcel of their nature, but in contrast to Christ, they all often manifested the works of the devil. In the case of Judas, Jesus referred to him as a *diabolos* without the definite article *ho*, because he was about to manifest the works of the devil in betraying Christ.

The devil that tempted Christ and the devil he lifted up on the cross

Three gospel records detail the account of Christ's temptation by the devil or Satan in the wilderness after his baptism (Matthew 4:1-11, Mark 1:12-13, Luke 4:1-13). This was not the only occasion, as shortly before his death he told his disciples, *"Ye are they which have continued with me in my temptations"* (Luke 22:28). Throughout his whole life, Christ was tempted by the devil (his own flesh), and the works of the devil manifested in others, as is the case for every son of Adam. An act of sin is not the devil itself; it is a work of the devil, in line with the distinction the Bible makes between the flesh and the works of the flesh (see page 166). Regardless of whether the tempter in the wilderness is viewed as the personification of Christ's own internal promptings or an external agent, he was *"touched with the feelings of our infirmities"* and *"was in all points tempted like as we are, yet without sin"*(Hebrews 4:15). Ultimately, the devil that tempted him was his own *"flesh and blood"*, with its *"affections and lusts"*, which Christ crucified daily (Galatians 5:24).

---

[160] John Thomas, *Deity Manifested in Spirit*, Eureka, vol. 1, 1861, pp. 106-107.

Hebrews 2:14-17 is one of the most helpful Bible passages because it explains both the representative nature of Jesus' sacrifice and what "the devil" is.

- Firstly, it tells us that Jesus – *"he also himself likewise"* - was born with exactly the same nature as all of us - *"flesh and blood"* - in order to destroy the devil. Therefore, the devil must stand for the nature with which we are born, that tempts us to sin. Christ, having the same nature was, like us, tempted in all points (cp. Hebrews 4:15).

- Secondly, **the devil Christ destroyed** in his own death (*"thanatos"*) **is something that holds the power of death** (*"thanatos"*). The death that Christ died is the end result of the mortality that we all share. This is the same death that the devil has power over because it personifies our mortal nature, and that same nature is the source of our sins styled in Scripture as the "works of the devil".

EC advocates need to explain from Hebrews 2:14 how Christ himself died the same death that the devil has power over, given that the same Greek word for death *"thanatos"* is used in both instances in this verse – *"that through **death** he might destroy him that had the power of **death**, that is, the devil."* It makes perfect sense if *"thanatos"* refers to the end result of the process of mortality. However, if *"thanatos"* relates only to the sentence of "eternal" death to be pronounced at the judgment seat on those deemed **unworthy**, that "eternal" death could not possibly apply to Christ who, by contrast, was without doubt **worthy**. In the context of Hebrews 2:14, their concept of "eternal" death as the "death" that Adam's sin introduced makes no sense because the sinless Christ died the very same death.

Genesis 3:15 confirms that what Christ destroyed or crushed on the head when he obtained the victory was the problem of serpent nature within himself. Importantly, as the serpent was still able to bruise him on the heel in so doing, this means that what he destroyed was not our sins in a substitutionary sense. To propose that the devil did not hold the power of death over Christ would mean that the seed of the woman was able to deliver a fatal blow to the serpent without being bruised on the heel by the serpent.

Christ's own words to Nicodemus state the truth about the serpent or *diabolos* nature with which Christ was born: *"as Moses lifted up the serpent in the wilderness, even so must the Son of man be lifted up"* (John 3:16). He was born with serpent/*diabolos* nature and was subject to all it bestows, including temptation and death, for the very purpose of overcoming and destroying it within himself. His life and death declared God to be righteous and became the basis for the forgiveness of our sins.

In Hebrews 2:15 the apostle Paul goes on to explain that Christ is now able to *"deliver them who through fear of death were all their lifetime subject to bondage."* This means that the *diabolos* has a dominion, and it keeps its subjects, including Christ (Romans 6:9), under bondage throughout their life by its ability to inflict death upon them at any moment.

This was not the position of Adam and Eve when created, for God created *them "to have dominion"* (Genesis 1:28) and as long as they did not eat the forbidden fruit they were not living under "bondage" or in "fear of death". Before they sinned, we are told that *"they were both naked, the man and his wife, and were not ashamed"* (Genesis 2:25), but after they sinned *"they hid themselves from the presence of the LORD God"* (Genesis 3:8) with Adam declaring *"I was afraid, because I was naked; and I hid myself"* (Genesis 3:10). It was only after the fall that they first became afraid and the *diabolos* gained dominion over them.

Consequently, all humans are born into a realm where the *diabolos* or King Sin reigns, and he delivers death to all, including Christ himself. As Paul states in Romans 5:21 – *"Sin reigned unto death"*; and concerning Christ in Romans 6:10 – *"For in that he died, he died unto Sin once"*.

We can summarise what the Bible tells us about the devil in the case of Christ:

1) **It is associated with "flesh and blood" - the body with which we are born**
2) **It is the ultimate source of temptation – the lust of the flesh, the lust of the eyes and the pride of life.**
3) **It holds the power of death regardless of actual sins**
4) **It is something that needs to be destroyed, not forgiven**

The first two points mean that the *diabolos* personifies sin-biased human nature. The third point indicates that the *diabolos* also personifies mortal human nature and the death to which all, including Christ, are subject. The fourth point draws attention to the fact that the *diabolos's* primary meaning is not actual sin but the source of sin and death in all of us.

The devil/flesh, the works of the devil/flesh

This distinction between *"the devil"* and *"the works of the devil"* is no different from the apostle Paul's usage of the expressions *"the flesh"* and *"the works of the flesh"* in Galatians 5:19-21, where these expressions are contrasted to *"the spirit"* and *"the fruits of the spirit"*.

This analogy aids our understanding. We can consider *"the diabolos"*/*"the flesh"* to be like a tree that is corrupt from its roots, and the *"works of the diabolos/works of the flesh"* as the distasteful fruit from this same corrupt tree, including all kinds of sin, disease, suffering and death. Such is the fallen state into which we are born. Serpent or *diabolical* thinking is the natural state of all from birth (Genesis 8:21; Proverbs 22:15; Psalm 58:3; Job 5:7; Jeremiah 17:9).

However, *"the spirit"*, and initially spiritual thinking, is something that needs to be grafted into us mentally and morally by our application to God's spirit word, so that we can produce the fruit of the spirit. As in the case of Christ himself, we won't be free of the problem of *"the flesh"* or *"the diabolos"* until this mortal puts on immortality, when we will be physically changed into *"spirit"* beings.

The Devil and The Works of The Devil

The Devil = Fallen Human Nature = The Flesh

*He also himself likewise took part of the same (**flesh and blood**); that through death he might destroy him that **had the power of death**, that is, **the devil** (Hebrews 2:14)*

The works of the Devil = The works of the Flesh

Sin	Death	Disease & Suffering
The Devil sinneth from the beginning (1 John 3:8)	*The Devil - a murderer from the beginning (John 8:44)*	*"oppressed of the Devil" (Acts 10:38)*
By one man's offense many were made sinners (Rom 5:19) **Individual:** sexual immorality, impurity, strife, jealousy, outbursts of anger, selfish rivalries, envying, murder, drunkenness (Gal 5:19-21) Ye are of your father the devil, and the lusts of your father ye will do (Jn 8:44) **Political/Religious:** the schemes of the devil - rulers, powers, world rulers of this darkness, the spiritual forces of evil in the heavens (Eph 6:11-12)	Sin entered the world through one man and death through sin … Through the offense of one many be dead … By one man's offence death reigned (Rom 5:12,15,17) Since by man came death … as in Adam all die (1 Cor 15:20-21) Christ destroyed *"him that has the power of death, the Devil"*, and can *"deliver those who through fear of death were all their lifetime subject to bondage"* (Heb 2:14-15)	[Jesus] went about …healing all that were oppressed of the devil /*diabolos* (Acts 10:38) "Lord, even the demons submit to us in your name!" So he said to them, "I saw Satan fall like lightning from heaven .. I have given you authority … on the full force of the enemy" (Luke 10:17-19) Creation was subjected to futility – not willingly but because of God who subjected it – in hope … the whole creation groans and suffers together until now (Rom 8:20-23)

*For this purpose the Son of God was manifested, that he might destroy **the works of the devil** (1 John 3:8)*

The devil and its works began at the time of the fall

The apostle John provides a few critical insights on both the meaning and origin of the *diabolos*. 1 John 3:8 states that Christ was manifested to *"destroy the works of the devil"*. The apostle John also explains that the two main works of the devil from the beginning (the time of the fall) are sin and death:

- the devil was a sinner from the beginning (1 John 3:8),
- the devil was a murderer from the beginning (John 8:44).

It is important to grasp the apostle John's emphasis that the *diabolos* produces sin and death, not that sin and death produce the *diabolos*. Just as a bank robber needs to exist for a bank robbery to occur, likewise the devil needs to exist before actual works of sin can occur.

In Adam and Eve's case, the *diabolos* originated when they believed and adopted the serpent's lie – *"ye shall not surely die"*. At that juncture that the *diabolos* was first manifested, and it resulted in sin and death – hence it was both a sinner and murderer from the beginning. The relevance of this is graphically underlined in that the first "death" in the Bible was actually a "murder", committed by Cain, the first-born child of Adam and Eve in their post-sin state.

In Revelation 12:9 and 20:2, the problem of human nature politically empowered in opposition to God's will is described in the comprehensive quadrilateral phrase *"the dragon, that old serpent, which is the Devil, and Satan"*. This expression confirms that the origin of the devil and Satan goes back to "the old serpent" in Genesis. Also, in both occurrences, this power is depicted as a great deceiver (12:9; 20:3,8,10) — a reminder of the role played by the serpent in Eden. The devil is portrayed, not as sin itself, but as the deceiver, that which attracts us to sin.

In Adam and Eve's case, it was initially "that old Serpent" that first enticed them to sin. But once they took on board serpent reasoning and sinned, God's sentence meant that the serpent's way of thinking, which they had embraced, became fixed as a dominant characteristic of their nature. This was then transmitted to all of their posterity.

The Old Serpent, like the Devil and Satan, is a figure of speech for a way of thinking opposed to God. This is precisely what the Old Serpent conveyed when it told the first lie and deceived Eve into sinning. Accordingly, the apostle John confirms that the devil originated from the beginning when Eve, then Adam, sinned. The works of the devil are the sins that our nature produces.

Reality check on EC's explanation of the origin of disease and suffering

According to most EC views, the existence of disease and suffering in the world has nothing to do with the consequences of Adam's sin, including the curses God imposed upon His creation at that time. They argue that disease and suffering are a feature of God's "creation" via evolution for millions of years before Adam and Eve. So the wide range of congenital and viral/bacterial ailments suffered by humanity, is just how God "created" everything from the outset.

However, as shown in the table on page 166, the New Testament informs us that all the suffering and disease in the world is another work of the devil or Satan. This is explained in more detail over the next three pages. Christadelphians have always taught that the reason for all the evil, disease and suffering in the world was Adam's sin. God intends to remove these problems through the work of Christ (Revelation 21:3-4).

The works of the devil include disease and suffering

In Acts 10:38, the devil (*diabolos*) occurs in the context of healing diseases: "*…[Jesus] went about doing good, and **healing all that were oppressed of the devil (diabolos);** for God was with him.*" This verse shows a direct link between the *diabolos* and what the New Testament elsewhere portrays as "demons" or mental illnesses.

Suppose we were to accept EC View A, that the *diabolos* is a state of mind that only exists at the point where human desires conflict with knowledge of God's laws. This would mean that i) there is no relationship between diseases (a physical problem) and the *diabolos* (a mental problem), and ii) diseases afflicting evolved humans existed long before the origin of the *diabolos* (shortly after God revealed his laws to Adam). In that case, we would have difficulty explaining Acts 10:38, which informs us that there is a relationship between the *diabolos* and diseases. Moreover, Acts 10:38 affirms that disease is a work of the *diabolos* and therefore cannot precede the existence of the *diabolos*. Diseases only began when God imposed the curses that *followed* Adam's sin.

The apostle Paul tells us very clearly in Romans 8:20 that "*the creature was made subject to vanity, not willingly, but by reason of him who hath subjected the same in hope*". Therefore, there was a point in time when God, because of sin, cursed his creation, including humanity, so that it was no longer "*very good*". That it was done "not willingly" means that God's creation was not like this from the outset. In so subjecting His creation, God simultaneously provided hope of redemption. This was detailed in Genesis 3:15-19, which is the basis of the apostle's exposition in Romans 8:18-23 where, in contrast to the *"sufferings of this present time"* (v18), he conveys the hope associated with *"the manifestation of the sons of God" (v19)*, or the *"the glorious liberty of the children of God" (v21)*. As part of the consequences of God unwillingly subjecting His creation to vanity, all are under *"the bondage of corruption"(v21)*, *"groaning and travailing in pain"(v22-23)*. Specifically concerning God's curses on man, the vanity[161], bondage of corruption and groaning in pain refers to humanity's fallen state that is biased to sin and subject to death, disease and suffering (cp. Hebrews 2:15; 2 Corinthians 5:1-4). This also includes various congenital disabilities with which many are unfortunately born. The Bible personifies this *"wretched"* state as the *diabolos*.

In contrast to the EC world view of disease and suffering being part of God's evolutionary method of creation, the Bible says that it was only **after** Adam and Eve sinned that God cursed them, their posterity, and the whole creation originally promised to them (Genesis 1:26-28). Christ will regain the dominion over God's creation lost by Adam, and this will coincide with *"the adoption, to wit, the redemption of our body"(Romans 8:23)*, when the *diabolos* in us will be destroyed as well.

Demons are works of the devil or the Satan

That various physical and mental diseases, including "demons", are the works of the devil is also confirmed in Luke 10, when Jesus sent out a group of 72 disciples to *"heal the sick … and say unto them, The kingdom of God is come nigh unto you" (Luke 10:1-11)*. When the 72 returned, they stated *"Lord, even the demons are subject to us in your name"* (Luke 10:17 ESV). The Lord's response to the report of the 72 reinforces the correct understanding of the relationship between the devil/Satan and human disease and suffering - he *"beheld Satan as lightning fall from heaven"* (v18) and his promise to give his disciples power *"over serpents and scorpions, and over all the power of the enemy"* (v19).

Satan is a Hebrew word that has been transliterated into the Greek New Testament, even though several Greek words meaning "adversary" could have been used. Hence, God intentionally chose the Hebrew word Satan for the New Testament. On most occasions in the New Testament, Satan occurs with the definite article – the adversary,[162] and thus refers to a particular adversary in opposition to the will of God.

---

[161] The word "vanity" (Gk mataiotēs) in the context of Romans 8:20 refers to "frailty" (Diaglott), "failing of the results designed" (Vine), "frustration" (NIV), "futility" (ESV, NET, NASB), a state that is "devoid of truth and appropriateness" and "perverseness, depravity" (Thayer). The context of the two other occurrences in the NT demonstrates that the meaning of the word includes the sensual passions of the flesh in opposition to God's will (cp. Ephesians 4:17-19; 2 Peter 2:18-19).

[162] 2 Corinthians 12:7 and when used in direct address, Matthew 4:10; 16:23; Mark 3:23; 8:33; Luke 4:8 and Revelation 20:2 (alt. reading) are examples of exceptions.

"The devil" and "the Satan" are used interchangeably in the New Testament:

- Firstly, we know that Christ was tempted by "the devil" which, in the same context, is also referred to as "the Satan", both in the narrative and in Christ's words (Matthew 4:10; Luke 4:8; Mark 1:13).

- Secondly, the incident of Yahweh rebuking Satan in Zechariah 3:1-2 is quoted in Jude 1:9, where Satan is called the devil.

- Thirdly, in Revelation 12:9 and 20:2, a great deceiving power is described as *"the great dragon, ...that old serpent, called the Devil and Satan"*.

Matthew 12:22-32 and Luke 11:14-23 convey that demons are associated with Satan's kingdom. After Jesus restored sight to someone who was blind and dumb, the Pharisees accused Christ of ***"casting out demons by Beelzebub** the prince of demons"*. In his response, Jesus demonstrated that even by human logic, their proposition was absurd. It doesn't make sense for ***"Satan to cast out Satan"***, or for Beelzebub, the prince of demons, to be casting out demons, for he would be *"divided against himself, and how then shall his kingdom stand?"* (Matthew 12:25-26). Christ's simple point was that if he were one of Satan's agents, he would be engaged in promoting "demon" activity, not destroying it. But Christ was preaching a rival kingdom, the Kingdom of God, and it was by the Spirit of God that Christ was performing these acts that were hostile to the kingdom of Satan. Notably, in this passage, Jesus refers to Satan interchangeably with Beelzebub, who is the prince of the demons, showing that demons constitute part of the kingdom of Satan or the kingdom of the devil.

Having established Satan's correct meaning, we can return to Jesus's exclamation in Luke 10 that he saw *"Satan as lightning fall from heaven"*, after the 72 disciples were able to heal those plagued by demons. This confirms that demons, which are various diseases, are a by-product of fallen human nature. The 72 were successful in dethroning Satan in his own "house" (cf. Matthew 12:26-29), even the house of fallen human nature. Jesus promised his disciples that he would give them power over *"serpents and scorpions"*, which vividly symbolise fallen human nature in hostility to the will of God. Christ clarifies this by promising to give them power *"over all the power of the enemy"*. We will obtain this power when this mortal puts on immortality, when, thanks to Christ's victory over the enemy within himself, the great enemy within us all will be finally vanquished. Christ, therefore, encourages his disciples to rejoice *"because your names are written in heaven"* (Luke 10:20).

A further case in point is Luke 13:10-17 when on the Sabbath day Jesus healed a woman who had *"a **spirit of infirmity** eighteen years and was bowed together, and could in no wise lift up herself."* Jesus described the infirmity as something that *"**Satan hath bound**, lo, these eighteen years"* (v16). So a physical disability is attributed to "Satan", the personification of fallen human nature.

EC advocates will often emphasise how Jesus and the New Testament writers did not correct a contemporary mythical belief in a prince (Beelzebub or Satan) and his demons. They do this in an attempt to "prove" that God's "inspiration" sometimes accommodates the mythical instead of telling the actual truth. EC view holders assert that an ancient society's cultural background would prevent them from accepting the actual truth of a particular matter. However, since God, through Isaiah, declared that there is no god beside Him, true Israelite Bible students would know that Beelzebub, the god of Ekron, did not exist (Isaiah 45:5-7). In this case, Jesus is actually leveraging the common misbelief in a prince and his works, to teach the truth, via an elaborate parable, about the real problem of King Sin and his works, which include suffering and various diseases. Bro Peter Watkins makes this point succinctly:

Peter Watkins, The Devil, the Great Deceiver, 1976, p. 65
Let it be stated categorically that it is not sufficient to say that the New Testament writers were using language that would have reflected current superstitions. It is undoubtedly true that the demon superstition had left its mark upon the language of the day, but this is not the only relevant truth. Nor indeed is it the most important truth. It was not the limitations of language that compelled the Gospel writers to make such elaborate use of demon terminology: it was the Spirit of God. The pagan superstition concerning an evil overlord and his minions provided an admirable basis for a parable concerning the real enemy. Instead of denying the existence of an arch-enemy and his demons, the New Testament writers acknowledge their existence, but regard them in an entirely different way. The real arch-enemy lurks within the heart of man himself.

Christ has the authority to remove all aspects of the devil's works

We also know that Christ healed a person with paralysis who was lowered down through the roof of a house in Galilee, saying *"thy sins are forgiven thee"* (Luke 5:24). He explained his rationale with the words, *"that ye may know that the Son of man hath power upon earth to forgive sins, (he said unto the sick of the palsy), I say unto thee, Arise, and take up thy couch, and go into thine house."* This shows the relationship between actual sins as one work of the devil and physical disabilities as another work of the devil. Clearly the man's disability was not a consequence of his particular sins, as if his sins were so severe that paralysis resulted, and he now required an extra level of forgiveness.

It was simply his misfortune to be so afflicted, because of Adam's sin in the beginning.

Jesus is making the point that if he has the power to heal or remove one work of the devil (physical disabilities), then he has control over the devil itself – the root of the problem. Because the Son of Man was victorious over the devil in himself, all the way to the cross, he was raised by God and now has all power and authority to remove the entire suite of the devil's works from the face of the earth (1 Corinthians 15:24-28).

What Christadelphians have always believed and taught regarding the *diabolos*

Both EC explanations presented in this chapter are very different from the Christadelphians understanding of the *diabolos*. The numerous quotations by Christadelphian authors included in Section 6 on the subject of the devil demonstrate this. Here are just three examples: the first, from Bro Thomas in *Eureka*:

> .. **The Diabolos is something, then, pertaining to flesh and blood**; and the Spirit or Logos became flesh and blood to destroy it. Now, whatever flesh-and-blood thing it may be, Paul says that "it hath the power of death"— that is, it is the power which causes mankind to die. If, then, we can ascertain from Paul what is the power or cause of death, we discover what the thing is he terms the Diabolos; for he tells us that the Diabolos has the power of death.

> ... That the power of death is sin, he illustrates in his argument contained in his letter to the saints in Rome. **In Romans 5:12, he says, "Death by sin." He does not say, "By the Devil sin entered into the world;" if he had, this would have given "the Devil" existence before Sin: but he says, "By one man or Adam, sin entered into the world."** This agrees with Moses, who tells us that there was a time after the creation was finished when there was nothing in the world but what was "very good"—"and Elohim saw all that He (the Spirit) had made, and behold, it was very good"—Genesis 1:31. **Man is, therefore, older than Sin, and, consequently, older than the Diabolos. Man introduced it into the world; and not an immortal devil, nor God. Neither God, then, nor such a devil, was the author of sin; but the authorship was constituted of the sophistry of the serpent believed and experimented by the Man, male and female.**

> ... By this time, I apprehend, the intelligent reader will be able to answer scripturally the question, "What is that which has the power of death?" And he will, doubtless, agree, that it is "the exceedingly great sinner SIN," **in the sense of "the Law of Sin and Death" within all the posterity of Adam, without exception.** This, then, is Paul's Diabolos, which he says "has the power of death;" which "power" he also saith is "sin, the sting of death."[163]

---

[163] Thomas, John, – *Eureka*, vol. 1, 1861, p. 246 – 251 – The Diabolos.

Bro Roberts wrote in *Christendom Astray* and *The Law of Moses:*

> All who are in the first Adam, are "the children of the devil," because **they are the progeny of a serpent-devil contaminated paternity. Their mortality is evidence of this,** whatever be their moral qualities, **because mortality is the fruit of the serpent-devil conceit operating in Adam to disobedience.** [164]

> This is the whole principle: redemption achieved in Christ for us to have, on condition of faith and obedience. It is not only that Israel are saved from the law of Moses on this principle, but it is the principle upon which **we are saved from the law of sin and death, whose operation we inherit in deriving our nature from Adam.** Christ partook of this nature to deliver it from death, as Paul teaches in Hebrews 2:14, and other places: "Forasmuch as the children are partakers of flesh and blood, he also himself likewise took part of the same that through death he might destroy him that had the power of death, that is, the devil". **Understanding by the devil, the hereditary death-power that has reigned among men by Adam through sin, we may understand how Christ, who took part in the death-inheriting nature, destroyed the power of death by dying and rising.** We then understand how "He put away sin by the sacrifice of himself". We may also understand how "our old man is crucified with him, that the body of sin might be destroyed" (Romans 6:6), and how he "died unto sin once", but now liveth unto God, to die no more (verses 9–10). [165]

The *diabolos* in the BASF

The concept of a supernatural devil is rejected in the "Doctrines to be Rejected". But where is the unique Christadelphian view of the Bible devil taught in the positive clauses of the BASF? To answer this, we need to consider those clauses which append Hebrews 2:14, as arguably this is the most important quote Christadelphians cite to explain what the devil is:

> *"Forasmuch then as the children are partakers of flesh and blood, he also himself likewise took part of the same; that through death he might destroy him that had the power of death, that is, the devil."* (Hebrews 2:14)

Hebrews 2:14 is listed under Clauses 8, 9, and 10 of the BASF. These three clauses explain the physical condition of human nature that came by Adam's sin using lexically cohesive expressions: *"the condemned line"; "condemned nature"; "the law of condemnation", "begettal of a human mother"; "enabled to bear our condemnation"; "of like nature with mortal man"; "in the days of his flesh"; "suffering all the effects that came by Adam's transgression, including the death that passed upon all men"; "he shared by partaking of their physical nature".* It is these expressions that convey the Christadelphian understanding of the *diabolos.*

---

[164] Roberts, Robert, *Christendom Astray from the Bible,* 1884, p. 192-203.

[165] Roberts, Robert, – *Law of Moses,* 1898, p. 178-179.

THE REAL BIBLE DEVIL
Fallen Human Nature - Where Both Death and Sin are at Work

The Devil	Subject to death, sin-bias, disease and suffering	Explanation
"The devil sinneth from the beginning" (1 John 3:8)	*"By ONE MAN sin entered into the world, and death by sin" (Rom 5:12)*	Adam and Eve's sin marked the point in time when the devil's way of thinking, which is contrary to God and results in sin, was first exercised.
"The devil … was a murderer from the beginning" (John 8:44)	*"For since by MAN came death" (1 Cor 15:21); "For as IN ADAM all die." (1 Cor 15:22); "By ONE MAN's offence death reigned by one" (Rom 5:17)*	Adam and Eve's sin marked the point in time when the devil was first able to inflict death, and subsequently on all of their posterity without exception.
The devil has the power of death "…him that had the power of death, that is, the devil" (Hebrews 2:14)	*"By ONE MAN's offence death reigned by one" (Rom 5:17); "By the offence of ONE judgment came upon ALL MEN to condemnation" (Rom 5:18); "Death reigned from Adam to Moses, even over them that had not sinned after the similitude of Adam's transgression" (Rom 5:14); "SIN hath reigned unto death" (Rom 5:21); "The wages of SIN is death." (Rom 6:23); "O wretched man that I am! who shall deliver me from the body of this death?" (Rom 7:24); "The sting of death is SIN" (1 Cor 15:56); "SIN, when it is finished, brings forth DEATH." (James 1:15)*	The devil is the Bible's way of personifying *"sin in the flesh"* or fallen human nature in all its forms (individual, aggregate, political), which is prone to sin, death-stricken and subject to disease and suffering. This is the condition of human nature that God imposed as a "physical law" (BASF 5) due to Adam and Eve's sin. Regardless of actual sins, the devil indiscriminately exerts the power of death over all of Adam and Eve's posterity ("death reigns"), including Jesus Christ during his mortal life.
The devil deceives and tempts us to sin "He that committeth sin is of the devil" (1 John 3:8) "the devil, and Satan, which deceiveth the whole world" (Revelation 12:9)	*"Every MAN is tempted, when he is drawn away of his own lust" (James 1:14); "for the imagination of MAN'S HEART is evil from his youth" (Gen 8:21); "And God saw that … every imagination of the thoughts of his heart was only evil continually." (Gen 6:5); "The heart is deceitful above all things, and desperately wicked" (Jer 17:9); "For out of the heart proceed evil thoughts. …" (Matt 15:19); "SIN that dwelleth in me"(Rom 7:17,20); "a law in my members, waring against the law of my mind, and bringing me into captivity to the law of SIN which is in my members" (Rom 7:23); "the law of SIN and death" (Rom 8:2)*	Before Adam and Eve's sin God described everything He had made, including the condition of their natural body of life, as "very good". After Adam and Eve's sin God describes the condition of man's heart or nature as per the scriptures listed adjacent. This is fallen human nature, with its deceitful lusts (Eph 4:22, and is personified in the Bible by the term "devil". By metonymy and personification, fallen human nature is also referred to as "SIN" (or King Sin) because it came in consequence of sin and produces sin.

The Devil	Subject to death, sin bias, disease and suffering	Explanation
Jesus was tempted of the devil "Being forty days tempted of the devil" (Luke 4:2) **By his own death Christ destroyed the devil within himself** "through death he might destroy him that had the power of death, that is, the devil" (Hebrews 2:14) **The purpose of God in Christ is to destroy the works of the devil** 'For this purpose the Son of God was manifested, that he might destroy the works of the devil" (1 John 3:8)	*Jesus partook of "flesh and blood" that "through death he might destroy him that had the power of death, that is, the devil; and deliver them who through fear of death were all their lifetime subject to bondage" (Heb 2:14)* *"in all things it behoved him to be made like unto his brethren…" (Heb 2:17)* *He "was in all points tempted like as we are" (Heb 4:15)* *"Who in the days of his flesh, when he had offered up prayers and supplications with strong crying and tears unto him that was able to save him from DEATH…" (Heb 5:7)* *"For he hath made him to be SIN for us, who knew no sin" (2 Cor 5:21)* *"For in that he died, he died unto SIN once" (Rom 6:10)* *"God sending his own Son in the likeness of sinful flesh, and for SIN, condemned SIN in the flesh." (Rom 8:3)* *"he appeared to put away SIN by the sacrifice of himself … " (Heb 9:26)* *"unto them that look for him shall he appear the second time without SIN unto salvation" (Heb 9:28).* *"Christ being raised from the dead dieth no more; DEATH hath no more dominion over him" (Rom 6:9)* *"Jesus Christ, who hath abolished death" (2 Timothy 1:10)* *"For he must reign, till he hath put all enemies under his feet. The last enemy that shall be destroyed is DEATH." (1 Cor 15:25-26)*	Hebrews 2:14 proves that the devil personifies fallen human nature ("flesh and blood") that is subject to death or mortal ("has the power of death"). Jesus Christ was born with the same nature where the devil or King Sin reigns – prone to sin and death-stricken. When Christ died on the cross, there was a great victory as he destroyed the devil within himself, fulfilling what God promised in Genesis 3:15. This is because he never sinned despite being sorely tempted throughout his whole life. God intends to completely remove the works of the devil (sin, disease and death) from the earth through Christ's future millennial reign. We can be certain that the devil formed no part of God's "very good" creation before Adam and Eve sinned because i) 1 Cor 15:26 plainly states that death is the last enemy that will be destroyed, and ii) Heb 2:14 tells us that the devil "has the power of death". Just as death is God's enemy, it follows that the devil is also an enemy of God, something He only brought about as a consequence of Adam's sin, and something he intends to remove altogether.
Demons (disease and suffering) are also works of the devil	*"… [Jesus] went about … healing all that were oppressed of the devil [diabolos]" (Acts 10:38)* *"Go your way … heal the sick" … "Lord, even the demons are subject to us in your name" … "I beheld Satan as lighting fall from heaven, I have given you authority to tread on serpents and scorpions, and over all the power of the enemy" (Luke 10:3, 9, 17-19)* *"There was a woman which had a spirit of infirmity … and was bowed together, and could in no wise lift up herself." Jesus described this infirmity as something that "Satan hath bound, lo, these eighteen years" (Luke 13:10-17)*	

Chapter 22
All Have Sinned Regardless of Any Knowledge of God's Laws

EC introduces a new theological concept of "sin"

EC believers limit the meaning of "sin" in fundamental passages in the New Testament, including Romans 5:12, to a conscious or deliberate transgression of God's laws. This stems from their need to explain the death introduced by Adam's transgression as something different from the death associated with mortality, which they allege was already in the world thousands of years before Adam's sin. Even though alleged humans living before Adam were doing many wicked works in ignorance, EC advocates need to say this has nothing to do with the "sin" Paul states was introduced into the world "by one man" (Romans 5:12). They reason that the "sin" introduced by Adam refers to a conscious/deliberate transgression of God's laws, which will result in the punishment of "eternal" death for those who do not have their sins forgiven or are deemed unworthy of eternal life.

The following quotation from COD is an example of their reasoning:

> In [Romans 5] v12 it is clear Paul is referencing Adam as the one man who brought sin into the world. Some argue it is impossible for humans to have existed prior to Adam and yet Adam be the first sinner. This assumes a broad definition of sin in Romans 5:12. So it is appropriate to inquire what is "sin" in this context?

> I suggest the definition of 1John 3:4 "sin is the transgression of the law" is appropriate to the context being similar in thought to Romans 4:15. Plus it is clear from Romans 5:13 that we are talking about sin in the context of a law being given (and how these principles are then extended to cover those outside of the law as Paul goes on to explain). Verse 20 also makes clear Paul's use in this pericope is very much sin as conscious transgression.

> Eve 'fell short of God's glory, she was the first to break the commandment. But Paul says the first sin was Adam's. Paul does distinguish between Adam & Eve when he bases teaching on Genesis 2-3 so we can't claim the two were treated as one in his theology. From 1 Tim 2:14 it is evidence Eve was deceived but Adam committed the first deliberate/conscious sin. When people argue for a broad definition of sin (coming short of God's glory) to 'prove' there could not have been people outside the garden (see for example The Lampstand Volume 23, No 3 page 145 – June 2017), they effectively make Paul contradict himself.

> Paul is making a point of the contrasting men – Adam and Christ. His choice

> of Adam provides positive evidence Paul is not using sin in the sense of 'falling short of God's glory' but rather a deliberate transgression, a conscious breaking of the law. This fits the later verses where Paul will deal with men without accountability to law being accounted sinners. If the definition of sin here was a broad one this accounting would be unnecessary.[166]

In short, COD is arguing that even though Eve was the first to break God's command, she did not "sin" like Adam because she was deceived, and hence it was not a deliberate, conscious transgression. EC proponents also try to distinguish between falling short of God's glory and sinning (Romans 3:23). "Sinning" and "falling short of the glory of God", they claim, are not necessarily the same because, as in the case of Eve, one can fall short of the glory of God without *deliberately* transgressing God's commandments.

The Biblical definition of "Sin"

In a bid to support their view, EC advocates often rely on the KJV translation of 1 John 3:4, that "sin is the transgression of the law". However, it should be translated "sin is lawlessness", as in the NIV, ESV, NASB. In the Greek, the word is *"anomia"*, which means "no law". Thayer defines the word as *"the condition of without law a) because ignorant of it, or b) because of violating it"*. Elsewhere in the New Testament, *"anomia"* is mainly translated as "iniquity" in the KJV.

The Biblical definition of sin is when we act without regard to God's laws, whether we know God's laws or not, and whether it is a deliberate conscious act of breaking God's laws or not. Sin is falling short of God's glory (Romans 3:23) or righteousness (1 John 5:17) through acts of omission and commission. This also applies to those who do not know God's laws (1 Kings 8:46; Psalm 130:3; Ecclesiastes 7:20; Romans 2:12; 3:23; 5:13-14; 14:23; Galatians 3:22). Even under the Law of Moses, a sin offering was required for sins of ignorance (Leviticus 4:2-3).

John affirms his definition of sin as "lawlessness" by adding that *"all unrighteousness is sin"* (1 John 5:17). He confirms the universal prevalence of sin irrespective of any knowledge of God's laws when he states that Jesus *"is the propitiation for our sins, and not for ours only but also for the sins of the whole world"* (1 John 2:2). The apostle distinguishes between believers who know God (**"our** sins") and all those who are ignorant of God and Jesus ("the sins of the **whole world**"). But importantly, both groups are classified as having "sins" for which Jesus died. The "sins of the world" describes the state of all humanity living in ignorance. They are still sinning despite not knowing the truth. However, after belief, repentance and baptism, their sins can be forgiven through Jesus Christ.

---

[166] Bro John Doe, *In what sense was Adam the first sinner?*, COD Website, June 2017.

All have sinned (missed the mark) AND fallen short of God's glory

The two phrases in Paul's statement *"For all have sinned, and fallen short of the Glory of God"* (Romans 3:23), are parallel and complementary. They do not describe two separate ways of displeasing God – the one by sinning and the other by falling short, as EC advocates propose. There is a direct connection between "sinning" and "falling short". The Greek word for sin is *"harmartano"*, which means to "miss the mark". It is not saying that "sinning" is just one aspect of falling short of the Glory of God. It allows for people without knowledge of God's laws to still fall short of the glory of God. We know this because the verse plainly tells us that ALL have sinned. It does not say, *"for MANY have sinned, but ALL have fallen short of the glory of God."*

Wuest's *Word Studies* explains the original Greek in this phrase as follows: *"Have sinned" is constative aorist, presenting a panoramic view of the human race as doing nothing except committing sin. The word is hamartanō, "to miss the mark," thus, "to fail in obeying the law." "Come short" is present tense, "right now come short." The verb is hustereō, "to be left behind in the race and so fail to reach the goal, to fall short of the end, to lack." Wuest then translates the phrase as: "for all sinned and are falling short of the glory of God".*[167]

The context of Romans 3 itself tells us that the "all" who have sinned includes Jew and Gentile, not just the Jews who knew God's laws:

> *1 "What advantage then hath the Jew? or what profit is there of circumcision? 9 What then? Are we [Jews] better than they [Gentiles]? No, in no wise: for we have before proved both Jews and Gentiles, that they are all under sin; 10 As it is written, There is none righteous, no, not one."* (Romans 3:1, 9-10)

For Paul, salvation for the Gentiles from their state of sin while in ignorance was an essential part of the Gospel message he preached. On the road to Damascus, the Lord Jesus Christ directly told him *"I am Jesus whom thou persecutest…But rise, and stand upon thy feet: for I have appeared unto thee for this purpose, to make thee a minister…[to* **the Gentiles,** *unto whom now I send thee, To open their eyes, and to* **turn them from darkness to light,** *and* **from the power of Satan unto God, that they may receive forgiveness of sins,** *and inheritance among them which are sanctified by faith that is in me"* (Acts 26:15-18 cp. Acts 10:42-43; 17:30).

---

[167] Wuest, K. S., *Wuest's Word Studies from the Greek New Testament: for the English reader*, 1997, vol. 2, p. 59. Grand Rapids: Eerdmans.

Sin indeed was in the world before the Law

In Romans 5:13, the apostle Paul confirms that "Sin" existed for all of humanity, even when God's laws were not known, by plainly stating that *"sin indeed was in the world before the law was given"*.

> *"for sin indeed was in the world before the law was given, but sin is not counted where there is no law."* (Romans 5:13, ESV)

"Before the law" refers to the period from Adam to when the Law of Moses was given (cp. v14). Paul divides human history into two periods, from Adam to Moses, and from Moses to his day. The latter phrase, *"but sin is not counted where there is no law"*, confirms that people still sin and fall short of God's glory, even though they do not know God's laws. Sin still occurs; it is just not counted.

The apostle is stressing that it is not just "death" that all inherit from Adam, but the natural tendency to sin. The wickedness of those destroyed by the Flood (Genesis 6:5), the iniquity of the Amorites in the days of Abraham (Genesis 15:16), and those consumed in Sodom and Gomorrah whose *"sin was very grievous"* (Genesis 18:20), are examples of "sin" being in the world well before the Law of Moses.

When stating that *"sin is not **counted** where there is no law"*, the apostle uses the Greek bookkeeping verb *ellogeitai*, which means "to charge to someone's account." The only other NT occurrence of *ellogeitai* is in Paul's letter to Philemon: *"If he has wronged you at all, or owes you anything, **charge** that to my account"* (Philemon 1:18). Paul was prepared to shoulder the responsibility for any wrong Onesimus may have done by counting it as his own. In Romans 5:13, *ellogeitai* is used in the negative sense, *"sin is **not counted** where there is no law"*.

Millions of people living in ignorance were all still sinning before the Law of Moses was written – *"sin indeed was in the world before the law"* - but their sins were not counted against them. God does not account those without knowledge of God's law as responsible to a specific law and judgment. In most cases, God did not intervene to judge them. However, two apparent exceptions include the time of the Flood and the destruction of Sodom and Gomorrah. In these cases, God did hold people accountable, not based on the Law of Moses, but based on the laws He had revealed since creation (see pages 74 to 76 for further discussion on this point).

Paul makes a difference between sin (hamartia) and transgression (parabasis):

In Romans 5:14 the apostle continues his explanation of the first period of human history from Adam to Moses by stating that the "death" that Adam introduced in v12 reigns over all regardless of the type or magnitude of one's sin.

> *"Yet **death reigned** from Adam to Moses, even over those whose sinning was not like the **transgression** of Adam, who was a type of the one who was to come."* (Romans 5:14, ESV)

All of humanity suffered the death introduced by Adam, and all sinned whether their sins were a conscious transgression of God's laws or in complete ignorance of them.

In v14 the apostle refers to Adam's sin as a transgression and thereby makes a distinction between "sin" (*hamartia*) and "transgression" (*parabasis*). Transgression always refers to disobedience of a specific commandment, as in the case of Adam and Eve. The apostle refers to the consequences of Adam's "trespass" (*paraptōma*) in vv15, 17, 18 and Adam's "disobedience" (*parakoē*) in v19, and these two words indicate a violation of a specific commandment. The apostle explains that between Adam and Moses, people were still sinning, even though their *"sinning was not like the transgression of Adam"*. His point is that humanity is subject to the same death that Adam's sin introduced even though the sins committed by a significant proportion of humanity cannot be classified as a transgression of God's law.

Suppose that the sin Adam introduced is the narrow definition of a conscious transgression of God's laws, as COD asserts. In that case, their argument could only be sustained if Paul had stated in v12 that "By one man 'transgression'" (*parabasis*) entered into the world, and death by "transgression" (*parabasis*). But v14 confirms that the "sin" that Adam introduced in v12, by his specific transgression (v14), refers to sin in the broader sense and covers both those whose sin is like Adam's transgression (*parabasis*) and those whose sin is not like Adam's transgression because they sin in ignorance of God's laws.

The Law served to multiply trespasses (parabasis) or bring the knowledge of sin

Throughout Romans, Paul informs us that the Law brought the knowledge of sin, made personal sins obvious, and revealed the degree of natural enmity between man and God. Law is not the cause of sin; our fallen nature is (James 1:13-15). Although EC advocates believe that sin is only possible with awareness of God's laws, this is refuted when Paul states that *"all who have sinned without law shall perish without law"* (Romans 2:12).

- *"For as many as **have sinned without law** shall also perish without law"* (Romans 2:12)
- *"For by the law is **the knowledge** of sin."* (Roman 3:20)
- *"For until the law **sin was in the world**: but sin is not imputed when there is no law."* (Romans 5:13)

- *"Moreover the law entered, **that the offence might abound.**"* (Romans 5:20)

- *"Did then a thing which is good become death to me? No, indeed, but sin did; so that through its bringing about death by means of what was good, **it might be seen in its true light as sin**, in order that by means of the Commandment **the unspeakable sinfulness of sin might be plainly shown.**"* (Romans 7:13, WNT)

The law multiplies trespasses (*parabasis*) because it provides "knowledge of sin" (3:20; cp. 7:13). Those living in ignorance of God's laws are still sinning; they just don't have the "knowledge of sin" that the law provides.[168]

The apostle's statement in Romans 4:15 *"where there is no law there is no transgression (parabasis)"*, which EC believers often quote in support of their view, does not mean that a knowledge of God's laws is a pre-requisite for sin. Paul deliberately used the word *"parabasis"*, and not the·broader *"hamartia"*, to define the type of sin that occurs when God's laws are known. Knowledge of God's laws makes a sinner a "transgressor", but without that knowledge a person falls under the broader definition of a "sinner".

This is confirmed when Paul declares that humanity is a prisoner of sin:

*"But Scripture has shown that **all mankind are the prisoners of sin**, in order that the promised blessing, which depends on faith in Jesus Christ, may be given to those who believe."* (Galatians 3:22, WNT)

All who have faith in Jesus Christ can be justified. The law brought the realisation, to those under it, that law could not justify them and that they would have to look elsewhere for salvation.

Eve transgressed (*parabasis*) God's law; Adam transgressed (*parabasis*) God's law

COD attempt to support their view on the specific type of sin that Adam introduced into the world (deliberate and conscious transgression of the law) by highlighting that:

1) Eve sinned before Adam, yet Paul says it was "by one man"; and

2) Eve was deceived (1 Timothy 2:14), whereas Adam deliberately and consciously transgressed.

---

[168] As per the apostle's usage of "Sin" (*hamartia*) and "death" (*thanatos*) in Romans 5, the "law" (*nomos*) is also personified and treated as an actor on the stage of human history. The apostle is explaining that instead of being a source of life for the Jews (cp. Leviticus 18:5), the law was actually an informer against them as it accused them and made it plain that they were worthy of death. Hence the law "came in" to increase the trespass, to make it obvious that man is a sinner.

COD assert that Romans 5:12 only applies to those who, like Adam, sin by consciously transgressing God's laws, and then from v13-21 the apostle includes all who live in ignorance of God's laws as well. In their view, people living in ignorance are not actual sinners but are only "considered" or "accounted" as sinners, based on the false premise of COD's incorrect translation of "made" (Gk. *kathestēmi*) in verse 19 (see Chapter 20 page 155, where we specifically address this). The truth is what the apostle plainly states in Romans 5:13-14, as discussed earlier in this chapter. People living in ignorance of God's laws are sinning when they murder, steal, etc., but God doesn't "account" them as sinners due to their ignorance of His laws. COD theory is actually teaching the opposite to Paul – that those living in ignorance are not actual sinners, but then God "accounts" them as sinners.

What type of sin did Eve commit? The COD argument is that because she was deceived, hers was not a deliberate, conscious sin like the case of Adam. Did God pronounce His sentence upon Eve in Genesis 3:16, which included increased pain in childbirth because she was merely "accounted" as a sinner or because she was an actual sinner? Moreover, was Eve condemned with the same "death" with which Adam was condemned or not (Genesis 3:19)?

Although Eve was deceived, she knew what God's commandment was, as is evidenced by her response to the serpent – *"God hath said, Ye shall not eat of it…"* (Genesis 3:2-3). After she sinned, God didn't let her off lightly because she was deceived – He pronounced punishments appropriate to her gender and others in common with Adam (Genesis 3:15-19).

In 1 Timothy 2, Paul points out that even though she was deceived, she still "transgressed" (*parabasis*). He used the same Greek word for Adam's sin in Romans 5.

> *"For Adam was formed first, then Eve; and Adam was not deceived, but the woman was deceived and became a **transgressor**."* (1 Timothy 2:13-14, ESV)

So Eve was still a transgressor of God's laws even though she was deceived. She was fully cognisant of God's laws, and her lapse in discounting God's law due to the serpent's beguiling influence does not make her any less a "transgressor" in God's sight. This would be no different to sins we commit that we know are wrong, but in the pressure of the moment we are deceived into sinning.

COD makes an unnecessary distinction between the way Adam and Eve sinned, to single out Adam's sin as the particular type of sin that results in "eternal death" in their theory. However, Adam and Eve were fully cognisant of God's law, both of them "transgressed" (*parabasis*), and both were sentenced to death.

When Paul states that *"**By one man** sin entered into the world"*, and *"since **by man** came death"*, he refers to Adam as the head of humanity who God first created. Adam is held responsible for sin and death entering the world because he could have prevented sin from going beyond Eve. Instead, he "hearkened unto the voice" of his wife.

To claim that Paul is only referring to the specific type of sin committed by Adam when he states *"By one **man** sin entered into the world"*, as distinct from Eve's sin, would be equivalent to reading Genesis 3:22-24 and concluding that only Adam came to "know good and evil" and God only drove Adam out of the garden, because only "the man" is mentioned. It would be ludicrous to argue that because Genesis 3:22-24 only refers to "the man" sinning and being sent from the garden, that "the man's" punishment did not apply to Eve as well. It is not just Paul in Romans who incorporates both Adam and Eve in the term "man"; this pattern can be seen throughout the Bible.

What is the "sin" the apostle Paul is referring to in Romans 5:12?

We agree with COD that "it **is appropriate to inquire what is "sin" in this context?"** However, we disagree with their conclusion that it was sin in the sense of "a deliberate transgression, a conscious breaking of the law". Based on the context of Romans 5, the wider context of the book of Romans, and other verses in the Bible, we have seen that sin (*hamartia*) is used in the broad sense of falling short of God's glory. It applies to all, regardless of any knowledge of God's laws. When the apostle becomes specific on the exact nature of Adam's sin, he refers to it as a "transgression" (*parabasis*). He contrasts this with those who are still sinning in ignorance but not transgressing like Adam.

How is Paul using "sin" in this context? Firstly, it is important to note the apostle's double usage of cause and effect language in Romans 5:12ab[169]. It could be said that one man's transgression (*parabasis*) brought death into the world. But that is not what the apostle is saying in Romans 5:12ab. He states that *"By one man sin entered into the world, and death by sin"*. There is a cause and effect relationship between "one man" (i) and "sin" (ii), and then there is a second cause and effect relationship between "sin" (ii) and "death" (iii):

    i.   by one man (cause 1)

    ii.   sin (result 1 and cause 2) entered into the world,

    iii.   and death (result 2) by sin (cause 2).

---

[169] the first two clauses of Romans 5:12.

It is helpful to read a few different translations of Romans 5:12a & b and note that the word "by" or "through" occurs twice, confirming the double usage of cause and effect language. There are two causes: 1) *by or through one man*; and 2) *by or through sin*, and both have results.

> "**through** one man THE SIN did enter into the world, and **through** THE SIN THE DEATH" (YLT)
>
> "just as sin came into the world **through** one man, and death **through** sin" (ESV)
>
> "just as sin entered the world **through** one man and death **through** sin" (NET)

Secondly, the first two occurrences of "sin" in Romans 5:12 have the definite article *"hē"/"tes"*, indicating that something hostile to God is personified as Sin or King Sin. Young's Literal translation makes this plain, by translating the first two occasions of sin, which are nouns, in Romans 5:12ab as "THE SIN", whereas "sin" or "sinned" in 5:12d (the last clause) is a verb and is referring to actual transgressions.

In verse 13, the two occurrences of the noun "sin" do not have the definite article, and therefore refer to actual sins. In vv14 and 16, sin appears in the verb form ("having sinned", "did sin") and in v19 as an adjective ("sinners"). But in vv20 and 21, the noun sin is once again personified as *"THE SIN did abound"* and *"THE SIN did reign"*. Note that "death" also has the definite article in vv12, 14, and 21, so it is also personified.

> **Romans 5:12-14, 16, 19-21 (YLT)**
>
> 12 because of this, even as through one man **THE SIN** did enter into the world, and through **THE SIN THE DEATH**; and thus to all men THE DEATH did pass through, for that all did **sin**;
>
> 13 for till law **sin** was in the world: and **sin** is not reckoned when there is not law;
>
> 14 but **THE DEATH** did reign from Adam till Moses, even upon those not having **sinned** in the likeness of Adam's transgression, who is a type of him who is coming. ...
>
> 16 and not as through one who did **sin** [is] the free gift, for the judgment indeed [is] of one to condemnation, but the gift [is] of many offences to a declaration of 'Righteous,' ...
>
> 19 for as through the disobedience of the one man, the many were constituted **sinners**: so also through the obedience of the one, shall the many be constituted righteous.
>
> 20 And law came in, that the offence might abound, and where **THE SIN** did abound, the grace did overabound,
>
> 21 that even as **THE SIN** did reign in **THE DEATH**, so also the grace may reign, through righteousness, to life age-during, through Jesus Christ our Lord.

So, this rules out COD's explanation that "sin" in Romans 5:12a and b refers to conscious transgression of God's laws. The cause of sin (our sin-prone nature) is metonymically called sin or is being personified as

King Sin in Romans 5:12a and b. But actual sin is being referred to in v13-14. Even a cursory reading of Romans 5 to 8 reveals that in the vast majority of cases where the word "sin" occurs, the pattern of personification and use of metonymy for sin continues. Refer to the list of quotes over Romans 5 to 8 included in the table at the end of this chapter, where we highlight the personification of King Sin by using capital letters for SIN. We could interchange all of these instances of SIN with "the *diabolos*", and the meaning would be the same.

Everyone who commits sin is a servant of "the sin" or "the devil"

Perhaps the apostle is taking his cue from Jesus himself, who in John 8 distinguishes between actual sins and the personification of our sin-prone nature when he stated: *"Every one who is committing sin, is a servant of **the sin**"* (Gk *tes hamartias*) (John 8:34, YLT). Later in this chapter, Jesus gives another name to this same King Sin, whom the Jews were obeying by sinning: *"Ye are of a father -- the devil, and the desires of your father ye will to do"* (John 8:44, YLT). This helps establish that King Sin and the *diabolos* are one and the same.

By one man "the devil" or "the constitution of sin" entered into the world

So we can summarise by returning to COD's original question regarding Romans 5:12: *"So it is appropriate to inquire what is "sin" in this context?"* – Answer: The *diabolos*.

The apostle Paul is stating that King Sin (the *diabolos*) obtained its status of indiscriminately reigning over all humans because of one man's transgression. "By one man (King) Sin entered into the world (*kosmos*), and death by (King) Sin". The *diabolos* wields the power of death to all born under his domain or *kosmos*, including Jesus Christ. We know this because "the serpent" was still able to *"bruise him on the heel"* (Genesis 3:15; Hebrews 2:14) even though he lived a sinless life.

Another way to respond to COD's question regarding the sense of "sin" in Romans 5:12 is to refer to *Elpis Israel*, where Bro Thomas devotes an entire chapter to this subject and calls it "The Constitution of Sin".

John Thomas, *The Constitution of Sin*, Elpis Israel, 1866, pp. 126-131
The introduction of *sin* into the world necessitated the constitution of things as they were laid in the beginning. ... It is the constitution of the world; and as the world is sin's dominion, or the kingdom of the adversary, it is the constitution of the kingdom of sin. ... it represents that physical principle of the animal nature, which is the cause of all its diseases, death, and resolution into dust. It is that in the flesh *"which has the power of death;"* and it is called *sin*, because the development, or fixation, of this *evil* in the flesh, was the result of transgression.

Finally, EC insistence that exposure to God's laws is a prerequisite for sin to exist implies that the more we learn of God's word and laws, the greater our sins will be. Yes, it is undoubtedly true that a deeper knowledge of God's laws makes us more conscious of our sins. However, this needs to be counterbalanced with the overall exhortation of the Bible, that those who ruminate upon His word are more likely to do His will (cp. Ephesian 4:17-24). A deeper knowledge of God should motivate a believer to follow the way of "the spirit" and deny our fallen nature's unGodly tendencies. We can't do this perfectly, but Christ, our exemplar, knew his Father's laws like no other and delighted to do His will.

God's laws do not make a person a sinner. They shine the spotlight on the problem of sin and motivate us to overcome. It is the *diabolos* within that came by one man that makes us sinners.

Occurrences of King Sin or the *diabolos* throughout Romans 5 to 8

Rom.	Greek	NET	YLT
5:12	1. "ἡ ἁμαρτία" hē - hamartia the - sin 2. "τῆς ἁμαρτίας" tes - hamartias of the – sin	So then, just as SIN entered the world through one man and death through SIN, and so death spread to all people because all sinned	because of this, even as through one man THE SIN did enter into the world, and through THE SIN the death; and thus to all men the death did pass through, for that all did sin
5:20	"ἡ ἁμαρτία" hē - hamartia the - sin	Now the law came in so that the transgression may increase, but where SIN increased, grace multiplied all the more,	And law came in, that the offence might abound, and where THE SIN did abound, the grace did over abound
5:21	"ἡ ἁμαρτία" hē - hamartia the - sin	so that just as SIN reigned in death	that even as THE SIN did reign in the death,
6:1	"τῇ ἁμαρτίᾳ" te hamartia to the - sin	What shall we say then? Are we to remain in SIN so that grace may increase?	What, then, shall we say? shall we continue in THE SIN that the grace may abound?
6:2	"τῇ ἁμαρτίᾳ" te hamartia to the - sin	Absolutely not! How can we who died to SIN still live in it?	let it not be! we who died to THE SIN — how shall we still live in it?
6:6	1. τῆς ἁμαρτίας" tes - hamartias of the - sin 2. "τῇ ἁμαρτίᾳ" te hamartia to the - sin	We know that our old man was crucified with him so that the body of SIN would no longer dominate us, so that we would no longer be enslaved to SIN.	this knowing, that our old man was crucified with [him], that the body of THE SIN may be made useless, for our no longer serving THE SIN;
6:7	τῆς ἁμαρτίας" tes - hamartias of the - sin	For someone who has died has been freed from SIN	for he who hath died hath been set free from THE SIN.
6:10	"τῇ ἁμαρτίᾳ" te hamartia to the - sin	For the death he died, he died to SIN once for all, but the life he lives, he lives to God.	for in that he died, to THE SIN he died once, and in that he liveth, he liveth to God

Rom.	Greek	NET	YLT
6:11	"τῇ ἁμαρτίᾳ" tē hamartia to the - sin	So you too consider yourselves dead to SIN, but alive to God in Christ Jesus.	so also ye, reckon yourselves to be dead indeed to THE SIN, and living to God in Jesus Christ our Lord
6:12	"ἡ ἁμαρτία" hē - hamartia the - sin	Therefore do not let SIN reign in your mortal body so that you obey its desires,	Let not then THE SIN reign in your mortal body, to obey it in its desires
6:13	"τῇ ἁμαρτίᾳ" tē hamartia to the - sin	and do not present your members to SIN as instruments to be used for unrighteousness	neither present ye your members instruments of unrighteousness to THE SIN
6:14	No definite article in Greek. But sin is being personified as a master.	For SIN will have no mastery over you, because you are not under law but under grace.	for SIN over you shall not have lordship, for ye are not under law, but under grace
6:17	τῆς ἁμαρτίας" tes - hamartias of the - sin	But thanks be to God that though you were slaves to SIN, you obeyed from the heart that pattern of teaching you were entrusted to,	and thanks to God, that ye were servants of THE SIN, and – were obedient from the heart to the form of teaching to which ye were delivered up
6:18	τῆς ἁμαρτίας" tes - hamartias of the - sin	and having been freed from SIN, you became enslaved to righteousness.	and having been freed from THE SIN, ye became servants to the righteousness.
6:20	τῆς ἁμαρτίας" tes - hamartias of the - sin	For when you were slaves of SIN, you were free with regard to righteousness.	for when ye were servants of THE SIN, ye were free from the righteousness
6:22	τῆς ἁμαρτίας" tes - hamartias of the - sin	But now, freed from SIN and enslaved to God, you have your benefit leading to sanctification, and the end is eternal life.	And now, having been freed from THE SIN, and having become servants to God, ye have your fruit – to sanctification, and the end life age-during
6:23	τῆς ἁμαρτίας" tes - hamartias of the - sin	For the payoff of SIN is death, but the gift of God is eternal life in Christ Jesus our Lord.	for the wages of THE SIN [is] death, and the gift of God [is] life age-during in Christ Jesus our Lord.
7:5	τῶν ἁμαρτιῶν tōn hamartiōn of the - sins	For when we were in the flesh, the SINFUL desires, aroused by the law, were active in the members of our body to bear fruit for death.	for when we were in the flesh, the passions of THE SINS, that [are] through the law, were working in our members, to bear fruit to the death;
7:7	τὴν ἁμαρτίαν tēn hamartian the - sin	What shall we say then? Is the law sin? Absolutely not! Certainly, I would not have known SIN except through the law.	What, then, shall we say? the law [is] sin? let it not be! but THE SIN I did not know except through law,
7:8	"ἡ ἁμαρτία" hē - hamartia the - sin	But SIN, seizing the opportunity through the commandment, produced in me all kinds of wrong desires. For apart from the law, SIN is dead.	and THE SIN having received an opportunity, through the command, did work in me all covetousness – for apart from law sin is dead.

Rom.	Greek	NET	YLT
7:9	"ἡ ἁμαρτία" hē - hamartia the - sin	And I was once alive apart from the law, but with the coming of the commandment SIN became alive	And I was alive apart from law once, and the command having come, THE SIN revived, and I died
7:11	"ἡ γὰρ ἁμαρτία" hē - gar - hamartia the-for-sin	For SIN, seizing the opportunity through the commandment, deceived me and through it I died.	for THE SIN, having received an opportunity, through the command, did deceive me, and through it did slay me];
7:13	1. "ἡ ἁμαρτία" hē - hamartia the - sin 3. "ἡ ἁμαρτία" hē - hamartia the - sin	Did that which is good, then, become death to me? Absolutely not! But SIN, so that it would be shown to be sin, produced death in me through what is good, so that through the commandment SIN would become utterly sinful.	That which is good then to me hath it become death? let it not be! but THE SIN, that it might appear sin, through the good, working death to me, that THE SIN might become exceeding sinful through the command,
7:14	τὴν ἁμαρτίαν tēn hamartian the - sin	For we know that the law is spiritual – but I am unspiritual, sold into slavery to SIN.	for we have known that the law is spiritual, and I am fleshy, sold by THE SIN
7:17	η οικουσα εν εμοι αμαρτια He oikousa en emoi hamartia the-dwells-in-me-sin	But now it is no longer me doing it, but SIN that lives in me.	and now it is no longer I that work it, but THE SIN dwelling in me,
7:20	η οικουσα εν εμοι αμαρτια He oikousa en emoi hamartia the-dwells-in-me-sin	Now if I do what I do not want, it is no longer me doing it but SIN that lives in me.	And if what I do not will, this I do, it is no longer I that work it, but THE SIN that is dwelling in me
7:23	τῆς ἁμαρτίας" tes - hamartias of the - sin	But I see a different law in my members waging war against the law of my mind and making me captive to the law of SIN that is in my members.	and I behold another law in my members, warring against the law of my mind, and bringing me into captivity to the law of THE SIN that [is] in my members
7:25	τῆς ἁμαρτίας" tes - hamartias of the - sin	Thanks be to God through Jesus Christ our Lord! So then, I myself serve the law of God with my mind, but with my flesh I serve the law of SIN.	I thank God — through Jesus Christ our Lord; so then, I myself indeed with the mind do serve the law of God, and with the flesh, the law of SIN.
8:2	τῆς ἁμαρτίας" tes - hamartias of the - sin	For the law of the life-giving Spirit in Christ Jesus has set you free from the law of SIN and death	for the law of the Spirit of the life in Christ Jesus did set me free from the law of THE SIN and of the death
8:3	τὴν ἁμαρτίαν tēn hamartian the - sin	For God achieved what the law could not do because it was weakened through the flesh. By sending his own Son in the likeness of sinful flesh and concerning sin, he condemned SIN in the flesh,	for what the law was not able to do, in that it was weak through the flesh, God, His own Son having sent in the likeness of sinful flesh, and for sin, did condemn THE SIN in the flesh,

SECTION 4

THE DOCTRINES OF TWO EC VIEWS COMPARED

"But examine everything carefully; hold fast to that which is good." (1 Thessalonians 5:21, NASB)

Overview of Section 4:
Different EC Views

Many Evolutionary Creation advocates publicly present their views via the Internet and social media forums. In doing so, they sharply criticise what Christadelphians have always believed. Based on what they have written, Section 4 collates relevant quotations from four specific EC advocates and arranges the quotations under the headings of the following eight questions.

Key Doctrinal Questions for EC Adherents

1. **Were Adam and Eve miraculously created, and were they the sole progenitors of our human race?**

2. **What death did Adam introduce?**

3. **How did Adam's sin impact the whole human race?**

4. **Were all the alleged evolved humans *"in Adam"* before Adam existed?**

5. **Are all humans *"in Adam"* after Adam was created?**

6. **Do worthy believers remain and die *"in Adam"* while they are mortal?**

7. **Was Christ *"in Adam"*? Did Christ die the death that Adam introduced?**

8. **The devil – meaning, origin and what is its *"power of death"*?**

It is crucial that EC advocates, and those willing to accommodate EC views, explain how EC teachings can be harmonised with Christadelphian core doctrines. The eight questions were chosen specifically with this in mind. This section shows how the EC believers quoted would answer most of these questions based on their writings.

The quotations from EC writers in this section confirm (a) the extent to which EC views conflict with core Christadelphian teachings and (b) that *By One Man* is not arguing against a "straw man". The reason we have cited their writings and named each author is to make it plain what each writer is publicly preaching. Our desire is to play the ball, not the man. The only personal aspect of this section of *By One Man* is our hope that they will return to saving truth.

The quotations by the four EC views are arranged under two main groups, as follows:

EC View A	EC View B
• Bro Ken Gilmore • Bro Jonathan Burke	• Bro "John Doe"[170] (COD – Christadelphian Origins Discussion) • Bro Mike Pearson

Both groups agree that Adam did not introduce the death associated with mortality, as they believe that countless humans were already mortal and dying before Adam. They both agree that the death Adam introduced is "eternal death". However, the main difference is that EC View A believes that a person can only be *"in Adam"* and subject to the supposed "eternal" death at the judgment seat that Adam introduced by being exposed to God's laws and breaking them.

By contrast, EC View B group assert that Adam's sin meant that all men living in ignorance of God's laws (both before and after Adam) are accounted as sinners, accounted as being *"in Adam"*, and legally condemned to death forever. This applies retrospectively to all the alleged evolved humans before Adam, and can only be a legal condemnation because they are already dead. In addition to the ignorant class, they also agree with EC View A that all those who know God's laws and sin by transgressing them will be potentially subject to "eternal death" at the judgment seat. Regarding the class responsible to judgment, both EC views agree that the judgment seat will reveal whether one is *"in Adam"* and hence worthy of eternal death, or *"in Christ"* and therefore worthy of eternal life.

We acknowledge that within EC View A, Bro Ken Gilmore and Bro Jonathan Burke may not entirely agree on the way they would answer all of the questions presented in this section. Likewise for EC View B, COD and Bro Mike Pearson may not exactly agree on all matters presented. This disharmony between EC advocates is a reflection of their struggle to harmonise what the Bible plainly teaches with their firm acceptance of evolution.

The tables at the start of each question contain summaries of EC View A and EC View B's teachings by the authors of *By One Man* relating to the particular question covered. They are drawn from what EC believers have written and can be confirmed by reading through the EC quotations included. We could not find appropriate quotations to clarify some aspects of their teachings, particularly on

---

[170] "John Doe" is the common pseudonym applied to COD's anonymous contributors by the authors of *By One Man*.

(i) whether or not Christ himself was *"in Adam"* (ii) whether he was born subject to and died the same death Adam introduced, and (iii) certain critical questions on the devil. We have left these as questions, hoping that EC advocates will clarify.

EC adherents have written extensively on Questions 1 to 7, as they insist that Adam was not the first human of our race, and have expounded Romans 5:12-21 and 1 Corinthians 15 to explain their view that:

(i)   There was no physical impact on the human race as a consequence of Adam's sin

(ii)   That the death Adam introduced was the legal condemnation or the label of "eternal death"

(iii)   That being *"in Adam"* or *"in Christ"* is through imitation and not the **physical** relationship to Adam now and the promised **physical** relationship to Christ, post the resurrection in which Christadelphians believe.

Question 8 focuses on the devil, about which EC believers have not written extensively. The likely reason is that this subject exposes the extent to which EC beliefs conflict with core Christadelphian doctrines.

EC View A proposes that the devil is a state of mind that arises when one's natural desires conflict with one's knowledge of God's laws. Therefore, it does not exist in the ignorant or any of the alleged humans before Adam.

In the case of EC View B, COD stated that they regard EC View A as "weird" in a rebuttal to a *Lampstand* article[171] that addressed EC View A's view of the devil. At the same time, COD criticised the Christadelphian view that the origin of the devil was coeval with the fall[172] (see Christadelphian writers on the devil in Section 6 of *By One Man*), but did not explain their own view of this subject. COD only responded to certain questions on the devil when asked directly. While confirming that the devil includes the personification of human nature (*"what you see when you look in the mirror"*), COD has not explained the death that the devil holds power over and how did Christ destroy the devil through his own death?

EC advocates need to reveal their view of this first-principle subject and show how their ideas can harmonise with what Christadelphians have always taught.

---

[171] Larsen and Jamieson, *Death the Last Enemy, Parts 1,2 & 3*, The Lampstand Magazine, vol. 23, 2017, March, May, July.
[172] See Question 8 page 229.

Chapter 23
Key Doctrinal Questions for EC Adherents

Question 1: Were Adam and Eve miraculously created, and were they the sole progenitors of our human race?

Question 1	a) Were Adam and Eve miraculously created? b) Were Adam and Eve the sole progenitors of our human race?
Relevant Bible Verses	Genesis 1:27; 2:7; 2:21-23; 3:20; 1 Corinthians 15:45; Luke 3:38; Matthew 19:4-6; John 3:16; 2 Peter 3:9
Summary EC View A*	*a) Yes.* *b) No. Adam was the first human in a covenant relationship with God, and he was the first person to break that covenant and "sin". People before Adam could not sin as they had no knowledge.*
Summary EC View B*	*a) Yes.* *b) No. Adam was the first human in a covenant relationship with God, and he was the first person to break that covenant and "sin". People before Adam could not sin as they had no knowledge.*
Christadelphian Beliefs	**Yes**. Adam was literally the first man, Eve the first woman, miraculously created from his side, and they were the progenitors of our whole human race. BASF 3,4,6,12 **CBM Baptism Guidelines 3.2** *"Does the Bible support the theory that man evolved from animals? Answer: The Bible condemns the theory of evolution by revealing that God created the first man, Adam, and the first woman, Eve; and that all other men and women are descended from them. See Genesis 1:27; Genesis 3:20; Matthew 19:4; Romans 5:12"*

* Based on the Christadelphian EC writers quoted over the next three pages, there appears to be little difference on their views to both parts of this question. However, it is important to note that other Christadelphian EC view holders, and most if not all of the leading evangelic promoters of EC quoted on BioLogos.org, do not believe that Adam and Eve were miraculously created.

Key Bible Verses

- 1 Corinthians 15:45...***The first man Adam***

- Luke 3:38 *Which was the son of Enos, which was the son of Seth, which was the son of **Adam**, **which was the son of God.***

- Genesis 1:27 *So God created man in his own image, in the image of God created he him; **male and female created he them.***

- Genesis 2:7 *And the LORD God formed man of the dust of the ground, and breathed into his nostrils the breath of life; and man became a living soul.*

- Genesis 2:21-23 *And the LORD God caused a deep sleep to fall upon Adam, and he slept: and he took one of his ribs, and closed up the flesh instead thereof; 22 And the rib, which the LORD God had taken from man, made he a woman, and brought her unto the man. 23 And Adam said, **This is now bone of my bones, and flesh of my flesh**: she shall be called Woman, because she was taken out of Man.*

- Matthew 19:4-6 *...he which **made them at the beginning** made **them male and female,** 5 And said, **For this cause shall a man leave father and mother, and shall cleave to his wife: and they twain shall be one flesh**? 6 **Wherefore they are no more twain, but one flesh.** What therefore God hath joined together, let not man put asunder.*

- Genesis 3:20 *And Adam called his wife's name Eve; because **she was the mother of all living.***

- John 3:16 *For God so loved the world, that he gave his only begotten Son, **that whosoever believeth in him should not perish, but have everlasting life.***

- 2 Peter 3:9 *The Lord is not slack concerning his promise, as some men count slackness; but is longsuffering to us-ward, not willing that any should perish, **but that all should come to repentance.***

EC View A: Bro Ken Gilmore (KG) / Bro Jonathan Burke (JB)

KG: ... we don't reject the special creation of Adam. What we do reject is the mistaken belief that he was the sole ancestor of the entire human race. Adam was not only a special creation, but the first person to whom God revealed himself. Prior to this, the concept of sin was meaningless and pre-Adamic humans lived and died as the beasts that perish. Genesis 1, while not a literal account of creation (clearly shown by its allusion to a pre-scientific cosmogeography in its reference to a solid firmament, a view denied only by a tiny, irrelevant, fundamentalist rump of modern scholarship) nonetheless alludes strongly to more than two people in verses 26-28, whereas Genesis 2 clearly refers to the creation of two people. In other words, the creation accounts are sequential, rather than concurrent.[1]

KG: Adam and Eve would not be the first members of the species Homo sapiens to walk the earth, but rather the first people with whom God entered into a covenant relationship. While human beings had been living and dying well before Adam and Eve were created, the concept of sin – as transgression of the divine law – was simply meaningless as God had not revealed Himself prior to then. They died simply "as the beasts that perish" and returned to the dust of the ground. It is trivially true to say that Adam introduced death to the covenant community as it consisted at that time of two people specially created who had never seen human death.[2]

KG: Those who reject evolution...are obliged to show how Paul's theology is contingent on Adam being the first human being who ever existed, rather than just the first human being to whom God revealed Himself, the first human being to sin, and the first human being to fall under the dominion of death as a punishment for sin, rather than the simple dissolution of the organic body when it reaches its use-by date.[3]

KG: The dogmatic assertion that human death was unknown prior to Adam's sin is cf course incorrect. The fossil record shows that Homo sapiens have been living and dying on this planet for at least 300,000 years, with the genus Homo stretching back at least two million years ago. Add to that the fact that the human genetic evidence confirms the human race has never been smaller than a few thousand, and the belief that the entire human race descended exclusively from two people living six thousand years ago is one that can only be maintained in defiance of the overwhelming evidence against it.[4]

KG: I regard Adam and Eve as historical figures, but not the ancestors of the entire human race. The evidence from human genetics shows without doubt that it is impossible for the entire human race to have descended exclusively from two people living a few thousand years ago.[5]

KG: The other claim made by evolution denialists is that Adam was the first human being who ever lived, and that he was the sole ancestor of the human race. The scientific evidence rules this out, so it does not matter how many times a special creationist appeals to Romans 5:12, it will not make the fossil evidence and genomic record of human-ape common ancestry vanish. The question we need to ask is what does it mean for Adam to be the first Man? While it is quite likely that Paul believed Adam was the first human being to exist (Paul of course not being privy to the palaeoanthropological data), does Paul's theology depend on it? [6]

JB: [interpretation of BASF 3] As a result of Adam's sin a unique opportunity for life offered in Eden to this **representative of the** human race was lost.[7]

JB: [interpretation of BASF 4] Adam was the first man with whom God entered into a covenant relationship. [*footnote: this view was known and rejected by our pioneers, due to their rejection of evolution: "Observe! The first man "made", not the first man whom God took into covenant-relationship", Roberts, 'The First Man', The Christadelphian, 1888]* This clause describes Adam as a mortal being, someone who will die unless kept alive by God as a reward for obedience.[8]

EC View B: Christadelphian Origins Discussion (COD) / Bro Mike Pearson (MP)

COD: I believe that God did make Adam as a special creation. ... Adam was the son of God in the sense he was directly created (Luke 3:38). He was the first to whom God was revealed and stands as the beginning of God's revealed purpose.[9]

MP: ... the idea of God miraculously creating Adam is not that unrealistic in the grand scheme of things. The Bible is full of miracles - and by "miracles" we are talking about singular events that are especially notable because they happened in spite of God's natural laws. ... The creation of Adam is a miraculous event, and God - who exists beyond the natural realm - is perfectly capable of operating outside that realm if it serves to establish a suitable purpose or principle in his plan. However, just because God chose to act outside the boundaries of his natural laws in a given situation, doesn't mean this singular act invalidates the evidence of other actions that are in accordance with his natural laws.

So, if God chose to create a human being as a special creation alongside the others that existed - rather than using that singular event to try and invalidate the evidence that he created other humans over a longer period and allowing the how debate to dominate our sensibilities, we should be asking ourselves why, and looking for the spiritual lessons.[10]

MP: On occasion God does operate outside the realms of natural law to establish certain milestones - the most notable being the resurrection of Christ. If God was able to resurrect Christ, then creating Adam from dust is not outside the realm of possibilities.[11]

MP: Adam bought [sic] sin into the world, because Adam was the first human in a covenant relationship with God, and he was **technically** the first person to break that covenant and, **well**, "sin".[12]

MP: The proposition put forward in this book is that creation has been a single, continuous, evolutionary one. If this is true, then it follows that there must have been other humans contemporary with Adam and Eve...there are at least three biblical hints that there were other human beings in existence at the time of Adam and Eve. 1. Cain - Driven Out and Afraid... 2. The wives of Cain and Seth... 3. People Began to Worship God...This is a critically important point to acknowledge because one of the main sources of angst in the creation debate is the thought that the Genesis narrative describes Adam and Eve as the sole progenitors of the entire human race. This is what most of us have grown up believing, but the references that we have looked at above show the text in Genesis does not force us into this interpretation.[13]

MP: The evidence for continuous habitation is not limited to archaeology. The fields of genomics and genetics also provide robust proof that the races of people contemporary with Adam and Eve were part of a continuous, evolutionary creation...[14]

Bible truth believed by Christadelphians

Adam was literally the first man, Eve the first woman, miraculously created from his side, and they were the progenitors of our whole human race (Genesis 1:27; 2:21-23, Matthew 19:4-5; Luke 3:38; 1 Corinthians 15:45).

> **BASF 3** — That the appearance of Jesus of Nazareth on the earth was necessitated by the position and state into which **the human race had been brought by the circumstances connected with the first man.**

> **BASF 4 — That the first man was Adam**, whom God created out of the dust of the ground…

Paul's "theology" in the New Testament is contingent upon Adam being the first human. Because of Adam's sin, God sentenced him to death and subsequently *"death reigns"* (Romans 5:14,17) over all humanity because we have all descended from him, including Christ (Romans 6:9). Paul's "theology" depends upon Christ suffering the physical effects of Adam's sin, including death, in order to deliver us from death (Hebrews 2:14-15). Christ became the *"firstfruits"* of deliverance from death (1 Corinthians 15:20-23), which is *"the position and state into which the human race had been brought by the circumstances connected with the first man."*

EC proponents reject Paul's "theology" and accept as true "theology" that vast numbers of evolved humans, that Scripture never mentions, were already pro-creating, subject to disease, suffering and death, long before Adam and Eve's creation and sin. Therefore they insist that Adam's sin had no physical impact on the condition of human nature, and the death he introduced is not the death associated with mortality. Rejection of Paul's "theology", as though it was Paul's "theology" and not God's, forces EC advocates to propose that Adam introduced a legal condemnation to "eternal death" for all those who knowingly sin against God's laws or, alternatively, those who are "accounted" as sinners.

This would also mean that Christ was not born subject to the death that Adam introduced. Nor, as a sinless man, could he die the "eternal death" allegedly introduced by Adam. If this EC view is true, Christ could not have been included in his work of delivering humanity from the death that came by Adam. This is a denial of God's "theology" (and Christadelphian theology), which insists that Christ had to bear our fallen nature so that he could overcome it in himself and be *"the firstfruits of them that slept"*, even *"the firstborn from the dead"*.

The EC proponents quoted in this book know Christadelphian beliefs. So they are either urging us to adopt their beliefs and reject ours, or tolerate their beliefs alongside ours even though the two beliefs are irreconcilable.

As Bro Roberts succinctly stated regarding the death that Christ died, it was *"for himself, that it might be for us" (see page 278)*. And in the following article, Bro Carter points out the substitutionary error of those who propose that Christ was not born subject to and died the death introduced by Adam's sin.

John Carter, *The Reign of Death*, The Christadelphian, vol. 75, 1938, pp. 173-174

The theory is being put forward that death belongs inevitably to the body of man as he was created; that Adam in course of time would have died apart from having disobeyed the law of God; and that the sentence of death imposed for sin is "the second death." We die, according to this view, because it is a law of our nature, and not because of any sentence which has been passed by God upon Adam, and which has involved all his descendants. ...

No one disputes, whatever explanation of it may be believed that Jesus had to die as a part of his work. "He was obedient unto death," as Paul says. If Jesus was a member of the race, sharing the nature which is subject to death because of sin, then we can see in his voluntary submission to it a declaration of God's righteousness, which Paul says was necessary that God might be righteous while bestowing righteousness by the forgiveness of sins on those who believe (Romans 3:21–26). We see the grace of God in providing Jesus, but we see the triumph of that grace reached through righteousness.

But if Jesus and all others inherit a nature which is mortal quite independent of Adam's sin, why did Jesus have to die? If it be answered that he died for us, then we can only conclude that **the innocent suffered for the guilty upon the basis of substitution**; and he should not have been raised while those for whom he died should not die. Further, in that case, it was not necessary that he should have to die for himself in any sense, for how can a nature undefiled by sin need a cleansing sacrifice? It could not, and Jesus would not then be a partaker of the benefits of his own work. But this is contrary to the teaching of Scripture. He was "saved out of death" (Hebrews 5:7); "by his own blood he entered in once into the holy place, having obtained eternal redemption" (Hebrews 9:12). The Mosaic patterns were purified with animal sacrifices, but "the heavenly things themselves with better sacrifices than these. For Christ is not entered the holy places made with hands . . . nor yet that he should offer himself often . . . For then must he often have suffered since the foundation of the world: but now once in the end of the world hath he appeared to put away sin by the sacrifice of himself" (Hebrews 9:23–28). "Now the God of peace, that brought again from the dead our Lord Jesus Christ, that great shepherd of the sheep, *through the blood of the everlasting covenant,* make you perfect" (Hebrews 13:20).

The Bible tells us that God is willing to have every human saved (John 3:16; 2 Peter 3:9). With this governing "theology" in mind, it does not make sense to believe that there were many humans evolved by God, living and dying hundreds of thousands of years before Adam and Eve, yet God did nothing to reveal himself to even one of them.

Further explanation

Chapter 25 - No Humans have Evolved: Adam - the Progenitor of All Humanity

---

[1] Gilmore, Ken, *A Christadelphian special creationist gets himself into a bind on the question of Adam and genomics,* June 2015, christadelphianevolution.blogspot.com.au.

[2] Gilmore, Ken, *Understanding God's Word Through His Creation - 9,* June 2013, christadelphianevolution.blogspot.com.au.

[3] Gilmore, Ken, *The Faith of an Evolutionary Creationist -2*, January 2018, christadelphianevolution.blogspot.com.au.

[4] Gilmore, Ken, *Adam in Innocence,* February 2018, christadelphianevolution.blogspot.com.au.

[5] Gilmore, Ken, *New Testament references to Adam and Eve by Paul and Jesus do not disprove evolution,* November 2013, christadelphianevolution.blogspot.com.au.

[6] Gilmore, Ken, *Evolution does not threaten fundamental theology,* September 2013, christadelphianevolution.blogspot.com.au.

[7] Burke, Jonathan, *Bro. Jonathan Burke's Interpretation of the BASF*, November 2013, See Taipei Christadelphian Ecclesia Timeline, October 2016, Appendix 3.

[8] Ibid.

[9] John Doe, *The first and last Adams,* COD Website, June 2017 **"John Doe" is the common pseudonym applied by the authors of *By One Man* to COD's anonymous contributors.**

[10] Pearson, Mike, *The Fourth Conversation*, 2nd Edition, 2017, p. 74.

[11] Ibid., p. 108.

[12] Ibid., pp. 113-117.

[13] Ibid., pp. 46-48.

[14] Ibid., p. 56.

Question 2: What death did Adam introduce?

Question 2	What death did Adam introduce?
Relevant Bible Verses	Genesis 2:17; 3:17-19; 5:5; Romans 5:12-19; 7:24; 1 Corinthians 15:20-22,26; Hebrews 2:14-15
Summary EC View A	*Adam was created mortal. Men outside the garden were mortal long before Adam. Adam did not introduce the death that is a result of mortality. The death Adam introduced was the death that is a consequence of sin. This is "eternal" death at the judgment seat.*
Summary EC View B	*Adam was created mortal. Men outside the garden were mortal long before Adam. Adam did not introduce the death that is a result of mortality. The death that Adam introduced is the label or description that one is worthy of eternal death, a morally deserved death, and this is the final outcome of the unrighteous/those not in Christ.*
Christadelphian Beliefs	Adam was created with a natural body of life, very good in kind and condition, that was neither mortal (subject to death) nor immortal (incapable of death). Adam introduced the death that is part and parcel of mortality (being subject to death) as this was God's punishment for his sin. BASF 4,5,10, CCA.

Key Bible Verses

- Genesis 2:17 *But of the tree of the knowledge of good and evil, thou shalt not eat of it:* **for in the day that thou eatest thereof thou shalt surely die.**

- Genesis 3:17-19 *Because thou hast...eaten of the tree, of which I commanded thee, saying, Thou shalt not eat of it: cursed is the ground for thy sake; in sorrow shalt thou eat of it all the days of thy life; 18 Thorns also and thistles shall it bring forth to thee; and thou shalt eat the herb of the field; 19 In the sweat of thy face shalt thou eat bread,* **till thou return unto the ground; for out of it wast thou taken: for dust thou art, and unto dust shalt thou return.**

- Genesis 5:5 *And all the days that Adam lived were nine hundred and thirty years:* **and he died.**

- Romans 5:12 *Wherefore, as* **by one man sin entered** *into the world and* **death by sin***; and so* **death passed upon all men,** *for that all have sinned:*

- Romans 5:14 *...* **death reigned from Adam** *...*

- Romans 5:15 *... through* **the offence of one many be dead,** *...*

- Romans 5:17 *For if by* **one man's offence death reigned by one**

- Romans 5:18 *...* **by the offence of one** *judgment came upon* **all men to condemnation** *...*

- Romans 7:24 *O wretched man that I am! who shall deliver me from **the body of this death?***

- 1 Corinthians 15:21 *For since **by man came death,** by man came also **the resurrection of the dead.***

- 1 Corinthians 15:22 *For as **in Adam all die,** even so in Christ shall all be made alive*

- 1 Corinthians 15:26 *The **last enemy** that shall be destroyed is **death***

- Hebrews 2:14-15 *Forasmuch then as the children are partakers of flesh and blood he also himself likewise took part of the same; that **through death** he might **destroy him that had the power of death, that is, the devil**. 15 And deliver them who through **fear of death** were **all their lifetime subject to bondage.***

EC View A: Bro Ken Gilmore (KG) / Bro Jonathan Burke (JB)

KG: One of the fundamental errors made by opponents of evolution in our community…[is] their failure to differentiate between death as a punishment for sin and mortality. Death is not the same thing as mortality. Humans die because they are corruptible creatures, made from the 'dust of the ground', not because of their sins. They remain dead after they die if they reject Christ.[15]

KG: What the verse [Romans 6:23] does not say is "the wages of sin is mortality". I die because I am an organic creature with a finite lifespan. If I sin and knowingly spurn the offer of salvation, then I will be judged and sentenced to eternal death. [16]

KG: What came through human action was the introduction of eternal death as a punishment for sin, which is effected by letting people die, and not raising them from the dead.[17]

KG: The terms 'death' and 'mortality' are expressed by two different Greek words (thanatos, and thnētos, respectively) and theological confusion results if these terms are confused. Paul meant death, not mortality when he used thanatos (Romans 5:21; 6:16, 21, 23 and 1 Corinthians 15:21) and these verses show that death, and not mortality, is the inevitable consequence of sin.[18]

KG: I'm already mortal, not because of Adam's sin, not because of my own but because I am a flesh and blood creature. However, if I sin and remain unrepentant, then I will suffer eternal death as a punishment for that sin.[19]

KG: In short, Adam introduced death as a punishment for sin. He never introduced mortality into the human race because **Adam was created mortal…Adam's physical nature was the same before and after the fall. What changed was his relationship with God.**[20]

JB: [Interpretation of BASF 5] As a result of sin Adam was deemed unworthy of immortality; his sentence was exile from Eden and being left to suffer the natural consequences of his mortal body (death and decay), which was inherited by all his descendants.

JB: The Bible never says mortality is the result of sin. It says Adam was created mortal, and death is the wages of sin, not mortality. And that death is **the second death.**[21]

JB: "There is a difference between mortality, and death. As I demonstrate, they are two different words in Greek, representing two different concepts (as in English), and Paul does not equate them; he uses them in distinctively different ways…The death we experience as a result of being mortal, is not the death which is the wages of sin…the death which is the wages of sin is a punishment for sin which we receive at the seat of judgment."[22]

JB: We believe that humans are only sentenced to eternal death at the judgment seat of Christ, and that this only happens to the "enlightened rejector"; those who know and are responsible to God's laws, but who wilfully reject them without repentance. Thus there is no delinking of "the causal connection between sin and death as outlined in the Scriptures"; the wages of sin is death, just as the Scriptures say. It is true that Evolutionary Creationists believe that all humans (not just those descended from Adam) die because they are mortal; they "just wear out". This obviously has nothing to do with Paul's description of the "law of sin and death", because Paul's description of the "law of sin and death" is that death is the wages of sin. The "law of sin and death" is simply Paul's way of explaining that death is the penalty God has appointed for sin; the wages of sin is death.[23]

EC View B: Christadelphian Origins Discussion (COD) / Bro Mike Pearson (MP)

COD: The passage [Romans 5:12-21] does not say mortality started with Adam. It says sin (as in deliberate transgression of the law) commenced with Adam and **death as a punishment for sin started with Adam**. The passage sees **Adam as a federal head** similar to Christ. In one we are accounted sinners and worthy of death (as **punishment for sin despite individual circumstances**), in the other we are accounted worthy of eternal life and mortality's impact on us is temporary[24]

COD: …with Adam came morally deserved death, death as the wages of sin, a moral judgment[25]

COD: **Death in the context of 1 Corinthians 15 is not mortality** …This use in 1 Corinthians 15 is **the same meaning of death Paul uses in Ephesians 2 and** clearly in Romans 6:23, where **death as the wages of sin** is contrasted to the gift of eternal life in Christ.[26]

COD: [Ephesians 2:1-5] Death is used as descriptive of our position in relation to judgment.[27]

COD: [1 John 3:14] Death is clearly being used here as a descriptor of the final judgment on an individual or as a label if you will of their spiritual state. It is not speaking of the physical process of dying nor is it speaking of mortality.[28]

COD: [Romans 5:21] Clearly this is not death as mortality but something more permanent, death as the final outcome/reward of the sinner.[29]

COD: [Romans 5:16-17] **Mortality is not the judgment against men.** Saved, unfaithful, wicked and ignorant all die due to mortality, but the wicked, unfaithful and ignorant will stay dead (albeit some rise temporarily to receive their final judgment and then return to death). **Condemnation is judgment – a final decision**

COD: when we read "by man (Adam) came death", do we have to believe this is the first death of any sort? Such a reading is not consistent. The context should govern our interpretation. Paul draws a direct link between "as in Adam all die even so in Christ shall all be made alive". Others were made alive before Christ and before the still future judgment seat in a limited sense. **Can we rule out others dying before being "in Adam? No.**[30]

COD: ...Death is used of the cessation of life. ...death is ALSO used as shorthand for the spiritual state/fate of an individual. I.e. will they receive death as the wages for sin or will they receive the gift of life (despite being mortal and possibly falling asleep in the Lord).[31]

MP: Some might look to verses such as Romans 5:12 to suggest that it's Adam's fault that there is death in the world. It is true that Paul consistently regarded sin as a responsible act and death as its consequence, but let's explore this further. In the New Testament death is seen more as a *theological problem* than as a personal event. New Testament authors knew that we die; their problem was to find words to explain the difference between a believer's death, and those who do not belong to Christ and therefore might suffer a final and total separation from God. Paul was very careful to differentiate between 'death' in the natural sense of mortality as opposed to 'the death' that is a consequence of sin. He mostly uses two terms: Thnetos, which refers to the mortal natural life that is subject to both physical and spiritual death; and thanatos, which designates the spiritual - physical condition of humanity in Adam, and through which Paul shows sin and death operating closely together...

...Thus, in a spiritual context, we can see from the use of the different Greek words that *being subject to death through sin* is not the same as being *mortal by nature*. If these were inter-changeable concepts, then the question begs asking as to what sin should be imputed on pre-Adamic beings and animals who were not under a covenant with God in the way Adam was. This is what Paul is referring to when he says that Adam bought sin into the world, because Adam was the first human in a covenant relationship with God, and he was technically the first person to break that covenant and, well, "sin".[32]

MP: Whilst death (mortality) is our final *physical* destination, it doesn't have to be our final *spiritual* destination. Because we are mortal, we are also imperfect just as Adam was (thnetos - mortal). Because of this imperfection, we will fall short of God's standards (sin) and the wages of sin is death (thanatos - death), however, life in Christ means that this death (thanatos) does not have to be permanent, and this is the basis for our hope in a resurrection to a new spiritual life.[33]

Bible truth believed by Christadelphians

Adam was created neither mortal (subject to death) nor immortal (incapable of death). Adam's sin introduced the mortality that ends in the death with which God punished him.

Adam's sentence was to return to the ground. In Genesis 3 there is no mention of "eternal" or "spiritual death" as something distinct from, or laid upon, the death connected with mortality. Instead, we are simply informed of God's declaration that Adam and Eve would return to the dust as the punishment for sin (Genesis 3:19). From the beginning, the punishment for sin was a physical death, as Genesis 5:5 and 1 Corinthians 15:21 "...*by man came death*" demonstrate. This sentence became a physical law of Adam's being which was transmitted to all his posterity. The result is that all are born with a mortal and sin-prone nature.

> **BASF 4** — That the first man was Adam, whom God created out of the dust of the ground **as a living soul, or natural body of life, "very good" in kind and condition,** and placed him under a law through which the continuance of life was contingent on obedience.

> **BASF 5** — That Adam broke this law, and was adjudged unworthy of immortality, **and was sentenced to return to the ground from whence he was taken - a sentence which defiled and became a physical law of his being, and was transmitted to all his posterity.**

> **BASF 10** — ... [Jesus] was, during his natural life, **of like nature with mortal man,** being made of a woman of the house and lineage of David, and **therefore a sufferer, in the days of his flesh, from all the effects that came by Adam's transgression including the death that passed upon all men, which he shared by partaking of their physical nature.**

> **Australian Unity Agreement (CCA):** We believe that Adam was made of the earth, and declared to be very good; because of disobedience to God's Law, he was sentenced to return to the dust. He fell from his very good state, and **suffered the consequences of sin** - shame, a defiled conscience **and mortality. As his descendants, we partake of that mortality that came by sin, and** inherit a nature, prone to sin.

Further explanation

Chapter 18 - What Adam's Sin Introduced: Mortality

Chapter 26 - Adam's Sin Resulted in Mortality and Sin-proneness for all Mankind

---

[15] Gilmore, Ken, *4. Death and mortality are not the same thing*, December 2015, christadelphianevolution.blogspot.com.au.

[16] Ibid.

[17] Gilmore, Ken, *5. Romans 5:12 does not demand monogenesis*, December 2015, christadelphianevolution.blogspot.com.au.

[18] Gilmore, Ken, *New Testament references to Adam and Eve by Paul and Jesus do not disprove evolution*, November 2013, christadelphianevolution.blogspot.com.au.

[19] Gilmore, Ken, *Evolution does not threaten fundamental theology,* September 2013, christadelphianevolution.blogspot.com.au.

[20] Ibid.

[21] Burke, Jonathan, June 2015, *"Science & Scripture"* Facebook Page, www.facebook.com/Science-Scripture-1449424052004603.

[22] Burke, Jonathan, - as quoted in the Taipei Christadelphian Ecclesia Timeline [distributed to all ACBM Regional Committees and the ecclesias they represent], 25 October 2016, pp.35 and 38.

[23] Burke, Jonathan, – *Review: "Death – The Last Enemy (Part One)" (6)*, April 2017, www.facebook.com/The-Lampstand-reviewed-500484383419073/

[24] John Doe, *Paul's argument through Rom 5:14-21*, COD Website, June 2017.

[25] John Doe, *The first and last Adams*, COD Website, June 2017.

[26] John Doe, *Death in Rom 5 is not "mortality" but the fate of the wicked*, COD Website, June 2017.

[27] Ibid.

[28] Ibid.

[29] Ibid.

[30] John Doe, *The first and last Adams*, COD Website, August 2017.

[31] John Doe, *Lampstand Magazine 'Death the Last Enemy' Vol 23 (2017) response*, July 2017.

[32] Pearson, Mike, *The Fourth Conversation*, 2nd Edition, 2017, pp. 115-116.

[33] Ibid., p. 117.

Question 3: How did Adam's sin impact the whole human race?

Question 3	How did Adam's sin impact the whole human race?
Relevant Bible Verses	Romans 5:12-19; 1 Corinthians 15:21-22; Hebrews 2:14-15
Summary EC View A	*No physical impact, as there was no physical change in the condition of Adam's nature when he sinned. Adam was cast out of the garden and taught the knowledge of God to those outside the garden and to his posterity. As a consequence, "all men" became potentially accountable to judgment and potentially subject to "eternal death".*
Summary EC View B	*No physical impact, as there was no physical change in the condition of Adam's nature when he sinned. However, all men either: a) imitate Adam by sinning with the knowledge of the law and deserve death or b) are ignorant but nevertheless legally "accounted" as sinners, "in Adam" and worthy of eternal death, because Adam demonstrated that all men will sin if exposed to God's laws.*
Christadelphian Beliefs	**All men** are physically in Adam by physical descent. They are born mortal (subject to death) and prone to sin as a consequence of Adam's sin. BASF 5,6,8,9,10,12,30 and CCA. **CBM Baptism Guidelines: 3.3** *How does the Bible explain the fact that all men die? Answer: Adam rebelled against God. As his punishment he was sentenced to death by God. This curse of death has been passed down from Adam to us, because we are descendants of Adam, and through him, we are naturally rebellious against God. See Genesis 3:1-19; Romans 3:9-10; Jeremiah 17:9; Mark 7:21-23; Romans 5:12.*

Key Bible Verses

- Romans 5:12 *Wherefore, as **by one man sin entered** into the world and **death by sin**; and so **death passed upon all men**, for that all have sinned:*

- Romans 5:14 *...**death reigned from Adam***

- Romans 5:15 *...through **the offence of one many be dead**, ...*

- Romans 5:17 *For if by **one man's offence death reigned by one***

- Romans 5:18 **by the offence of one** *judgment came upon* **all men to condemnation** *...*

- Romans 5:19 **by one man's disobedience many were made sinners**

- 1 Corinthians 15:21 *For since **by man came death,** by man came also **the resurrection of the dead.***

- 1 Corinthians 15:22 *For as **in Adam all die,** even so in Christ shall all be made alive*

- Hebrews 2:14-15 *that **through death** he [Jesus] might **destroy him that had the power of death, that is, the devil**; and deliver them who through **fear of death** were **all their lifetime subject to bondage.***

EC View A: Bro Ken Gilmore (KG) / Bro Jonathan Burke (JB)

KG: Far from Adam's sin being the cause of human death, it is the universality of human sin which causes death, and that negates the need for us to be physically descended from Adam in order to inherit any 'genetic' consequence of that sin.[34]

KG: "...The first point that needs to be stressed is that death, not mortality is the consequence of Adam's sin. I do not die because I sin. I die because I am made of corruptible material. I remain dead as a punishment for sin if I choose to reject the offer of salvation, and that is the point Paul is making here – death as a punishment for sin was introduced into the world when the first sin was committed. Prior to Adam's sin, humans lived and died as the 'beasts that perish' but as God's law was unknown, sin as a concept did not exist and therefore death as a punishment for sin simply did not apply."[35]

KG: What Paul is arguing in Romans 5 is that because all human beings sin, they will all die, assuming they do not repent and seek God. Paul is not arguing that the guilt and physical consequence of Adam's sin were genetically inherited by his descendants. [36]

KG: Differentiating between death as the inevitable end-point of organic, corruptible creatures, and eternal death as a punishment for sin is crucial...Death as a punishment for sin is not something that one inherits. Irrespective of whether we all descended exclusively from Adam, or have common ancestry with apes, we will remain dead forever if we sin, and do not seek repentance.[37]

JB: [interpretation of BASF 6 and 8] Though eternal death remained the punishment for sin, the opportunity of eternal life was offered by God to all humans who become part of His plan through Christ, who bore exactly the same mortal and sin-prone nature as all other humans who have ever lived.[38]

JB: [interpretation of BASF 10] As a human being descended from Adam and therefore identical to those he came to save, Christ shared the same mortal and sin-prone nature as every other human being who has ever lived, which all of Adam's descendants inherit as an inevitable consequence of his sin, and was uniquely used by God for his plan of salvation.[39]

JB: The "law of sin and death" is simply Paul's way of explaining that death is the penalty God has appointed for sin; the wages of sin is death. ...The "law of sin and death" is not a kind of physical law like gravity, or some kind of special substance or activity within the human body which makes them die. Humans die because they are mortal, not because they are being punished for their sins before they ever stand at the judgment seat of Christ. [40]

EC View B: Christadelphian Origins Discussion (COD) / Bro Mike Pearson (MP)

COD: ...What consequence did Adam suffer on the day he ate the fruit which resulted in certain death? Exclusion from the tree of life is the only thing recorded in Genesis 3. That is worth repeating. Scripture mentions some specific consequences of their sin, but nothing about a change to mortality, no new genetic rearrangement. Instead of all the things some may wish to read, the clear testimony is Adam was barred from the tree of life which would have brought immortality, and instead doomed to certain death (i.e. he suffered mortality because of sin)...consequently, when sin entered the world through Adam, death came by sin as the appropriate response to sin. The path was set. Rather than the opportunity to receive immortality then and there, Adam would now indeed die.[41]

COD: The record of Genesis 3 is very clear about the consequences of sin for Adam: He was aware of and shamed of his nakedness Gen 3:7; He appears to have a guilty conscience manifesting itself in fear of God Gen 3:8; He is condemned to a life of toil to produce food Gen 3:18; He will die Gen 3:19; He gained a knowledge of good & evil like the angels Gen3:22; He is expelled from the garden and cut off from the tree of life Gen 3:23-24.

... Insisting that the single most important consequence of Adam's failure was the introduction of an inheritable change in his nature and proneness to sin requires acceptance of a reality where the angel communicating to Adam forgot to mention it. Such a suggestion is bordering on blasphemy, but I make the point to underline the reality – of all the consequences ascribed to Adam's sin, the single most debated point on which people condemn EC believers is absent from the record. This should inform our interpretation of later passages.[42]

COD: "...and so death passed upon all men, for that all have sinned" Romans 5:12b KJV. Misunderstanding of this phrase, along with much of Genesis 3, led the Catholic doctrine of Original Sin. ... the debate over the meaning of this last phrase has a long history. Championed by Augustine among others, the Catholic church has tended to favour reading the verse 'death passed upon all men, in whom (Adam) all have sinned'. Yet this reading fails as Fitmyer [sic] notes:

> "if Paul had meant "in whom" (in the sense of incorporation), he would have written en hō, as he does in 1 Corinthians 15:22; cf. Hebrews7:9-10. Moreover, Adam as the personal antecedent of the rel pron [relative pronoun] is too far removed in the sentence from the pronoun."

Cranfield also rejects the Augustinian position on grammatical grounds. The NET notes make mention of three options without commending or rejecting any. However, the translation (along with the ESV) follow the lead of the KJV in seemingly pointing to individual responsibility rather than inherited/origin sin. While Cranfield prefers a reading of the phrase which accords to his doctrinal position, he acknowledges that grammatically the phrase can validly mean *"men's sinning in their own persons quite independently of Adam, though after his example"*. The Hermenia commentary also acknowledges the complexity of translation and concludes *"While certainty about Paul's theory is hardly possible, this line of interpretation would imply that each person in v. 12d replicates Adam's fall because of his or her own free will."*

What is this all saying? Simply the grammar in Romans 5:12 does not say we all sinned in Adam or any other version of original sin. The simple clear reading, which is consistent with the rest of Scripture, is that our sins separate us from our God (as per Isaiah 59:2). Adam was the first to receive a law, he consciously transgressed it and was punished with death. He (like Christ) is a representative figure and we inevitably sin ourselves and demonstrate death is our appropriate reward also. Because Paul has used 'sin' in the sense of transgressing the law, he then proceeds to qualify and explain his remarks and comparison of Adam and Christ from v 13-17.[43]

COD: By default we are all in Adam – a **representative man**.[44]

COD: Because **all men** are **naturally in Adam** and **Adam proved when there is a law we will sin/break it**. Like Christ, **Adam was a federal head**, a **representative individual** who demonstrated the righteousness of God (in Adam's case in the **death of all men**). [45]

COD: Even though men didn't commit the precise sin of Adam, those who lived prior to the Law of Moses are still considered sinners (*"made sinners"* v19 which is better understood as '*accounted*'), in the same way that through Christ's righteousness many can be accounted as righteous. Paul explicitly says they had no law but they experience death as sinners i.e. they die and will end up/stay dead (v eternal life which comes through being in Christ). The passage in v12 must be understood in the context of the contrast which forms Paul's point.[46]

COD: One man's sin has many – who never had the same access to law/opportunity for failure – accounted as sinners and dead without hope.[47]

COD: [Romans 5:19] in Adam many are consider[sic]/counted as sinners – even those not personally accountable from contact with God's word. They receive the same outcome/punishment in a federal headship sense.[48]

COD: [Romans 5:21] The verse stands against those who read death as mortality...Paul is talking about the two ultimate ends of man. Eternal death or eternal life. **Sinners (actual and accounted as such) get eternal death.** Those accounted righteous (through the grace of God) get eternal life.[49]

COD: Paul notes that while there was sin in the world from Adam to Moses (clearly a broad use of the word sin) people were not personally accountable, "sin was not imputed when there is no law" (Romans 5:13). On what basis can Paul then say "by the offense of one judgment came upon all men to condemnation" Romans 5:18? They are **treated as legally condemned**, as if they were sinners, despite sin not being imputed due to their ignorance. How is this so? Paul reconciles the apparent anomaly by simple fact of Adam being a **representative man**, like Christ who Adam is being contrasted with. As Paul goes on to say "by one man's disobedience many were made [or 'accounted as'] sinners, so by the obedience of one shall many be made righteous" Romans 5:19. The article by contrast argues the judgment of death is applied "and rightly so, because even in ignorance they were still sinning or falling short of God's glory". Paul says they were accounted as sinners but sin was NOT imputed to them, the basis of judgment is being accounted sinners based on Adam **(their representative)**.[50]

COD: Paul's argument demonstrates why all either sin with knowledge of the law and deserve death (Romans 5:12) or are ignorant but **accounted as sinners**[173] based on Adam their representative (Romans 5:18-19). The ignorant are not personally accountable (no imputing of sin – Romans 5:13) but them suffering the same end as the wicked is not unjust. Adam comprehensively demonstrated that all men will inevitably break God's law no matter how all good their circumstances if they have exposure to His word.[51]

MP: But did this 'fall' actually change Adam's nature at a genetic or cellular level? Well, here we go again trying to read twenty-first century concepts into ancient text, whereas in reality the text doesn't discuss this point at all. Genesis 3 explicitly defines the various consequences of Adam's sin for both him and Eve, and these align to the shame, the defiled conscience and death. The text doesn't specify any change in nature, and to suggest that it does, reads concepts into the text that aren't there. The text simply says, *"you are dust, and to dust you will return".*

… animals have the same nature of man - they both die. But they don't have mortality as a result of a transgression, they have it as consequence of the natural cycle of life. Humans on the other hand have to deal with mortality as a result of natural cycle of life, and with death as a punishment for sin.[52]

MP: [See other quotations that relate to this question included under Question 1]

Bible truth believed by Christadelphians

All humans are in Adam by physical descent. In consequence of Adam's sin (*"by one man's offense"*) all are born mortal (subject to death – *"death reigned by one"*) and prone to sin (*"by one man's disobedience many were made sinners"*).

---

[173] Note: In Romans 5:19 Paul does not say by one man's disobedience many are "accounted as sinners", but rather "made sinners" or "constituted sinners". See Chapter 20, page 155 for a detailed discussion on Romans 5:19.

Christadelphians reject both Augustine's view of original sin, and Pelagius' view that there was no change in the condition of Adam's nature and that the only link with Adam is when we merely imitate his sin. The Australian Unity Agreement (CCA), and BASF clauses 3, 5, 6, 8, 9, 10 and 12 state what Christadelphians believe. EC views A and B are widely opposed to the Apostles' teachings.

Further explanation

BASF Clauses 5, 6, 8, 9, 10, 12, CCA

Chapter 18 - What Adam's Sin Introduced: Mortality

Chapter 19 - All humans die *"in Adam"*

Chapter 20 - What Adam's Sin Introduced: Our Sin-Biased State

Chapter 26 - Adam's Sin Resulted in Mortality and Sin-proneness for all Mankind

---

[34] Gilmore, Ken, *The Faith of an Evolutionary Creationist -2*, January 2018, christadelphianevolution.blogspot.com.au.

[35] Gilmore, Ken, *4. Death and mortality are not the same thing*, December 2015, christadelphianevolution.blogspot.com.au.

[36] Gilmore, Ken, *The Faith of an Evolutionary Creationist -2*, January 2018, christadelphianevolution.blogspot.com.au.

[37] Gilmore, Ken, *4. Death and mortality are not the same thing*, December 2015, christadelphianevolution.blogspot.com.au.

[38] Burke, Jonathan, *Bro. Jonathan Burke's Interpretation of the BASF*, November 2013, See Taipei Christadelphian Ecclesia Timeline, October 2016, Appendix 3.

[39] Ibid.

[40] Burke, Jonathan, – *Review: 'Death – The Last Enemy (Part One)' (6)*, April 2017, www.facebook.com/The-Lampstand-reviewed-500484383419073/.

[41] John Doe, *Lampstand Magazine 'Death the Last Enemy' Vol 23 (2017) response*, COD Website July 2017.

[42] John Doe, *The consequences of sin for Adam detailed and limited*, COD Website June 2017.

[43] John Doe, Does a sinner earn death or did Adam earn it for them?, COD Website, June 2017.

[44] John Doe, *The first and last Adams*, COD website, June 2017.

[45] John Doe, *Rom 5:12 – an overview*, COD Website, June 2017.

[46] Ibid.

[47] John Doe, *Paul's argument through Rom 5:14-21*, COD Website, June 2017.

[48] Ibid.

[49] Ibid.

[50] John Doe, *Lampstand Magazine 'Death the Last Enemy' Vol 23 (2017) response*, COD Website July 2017.

[51] Ibid.

[52] Pearson, Mike, *The Fourth Conversation*, 2nd Edition, 2017, pp. 113-114.

Question 4: Were all the alleged evolved humans *"in Adam"* before Adam existed?

Question 4	Were all the alleged evolved humans *"in Adam"* before Adam existed?
Relevant Bible Verses	Romans 5:12, 14-17; 3:23; 1 Corinthians 15:22
Summary EC View A	*No. None were. They were not in Adam as they were not accountable to "eternal" death at the judgment seat as they had no knowledge of God's law.*
Summary EC View B	*Yes. All these men were "in Adam". Adam is a "Federal head" to them. All these men were **legally** accounted as sinners and died (eternal death) "in Adam" as their "Federal head". Adam proved that if they had been given a law they would have broken it. None of these had opportunity to be "in Christ". They have all "died in Adam". They will not be at the judgment seat.*
Christadelphian Beliefs	**Not applicable**, as there were no members of our human race living before Adam. BASF 3,4

Key Bible Verses

- Romans 5:12 *Wherefore, as **by one man sin entered** into the world, and **death by sin**; and so **death passed upon all men,** for that **all have sinned:***
- Romans 5:14 *... **death reigned from Adam***
- Romans 5:15 *… through **the offence of one many be dead**, …*
- Romans 5:17 *For if by **one man's offence death reigned by one***
- Romans 3:23 For **all have sinned**, and come short of the glory of God;
- 1 Corinthians 15:21 *For since **by man came death,** by man came also **the resurrection of the dead.***
- 1 Corinthians 15:22 *For as **in Adam all die,** even so in Christ shall all be made alive*

EC View A: Bro Ken Gilmore (KG)

KG: The first Adam brought death as a punishment for sin into the world. The last Adam showed how one could escape eternal death. The existence of human beings prior to Adam, or the fact that human ancestry stretches back millions of years into the past is simply irrelevant from the point of view of Paul's theology as we are talking about the introduction of eternal death as a punishment for sin. Prior to Adam, those who lived did so as the 'beasts that perish'.[53]

KG: Prior to Adam, countless millions lived and died and passed into oblivion. However, none of them were sinners, because God's law had not been revealed to them. Where there is no law, there is no sin, and where there is no sin, death as a punishment for sin had no meaning. Salvation history began when God revealed himself to Adam and placed him under the law of sin and death. Adam failed, and we have been swift to follow his example since then.[54]

EC View B: Christadelphian Origins Discussion (COD) / Bro Mike Pearson (MP)

COD: EC doesn't limit in Adam to those responsible personally to judgment. Plainly Paul includes those without knowledge of the law as falling into the class *"in Adam"* in Romans 5:14 and 19[55]

COD: ...when we read "by man (Adam) came death", do we have to believe this is the first death of any sort? Such a reading is not consistent. The context should govern our interpretation. Paul draws a direct link between "as in Adam all die even so in Christ shall all be made alive". Others were made alive before Christ and before the still future judgment seat in a limited sense. **Can we rule out others dying before being *"in Adam"*? No.**[56]

COD: [Romans 5] v19 Paul says many are "made sinners" is critical here. It should be understood as 'accounted' or 'considered'. We are not sinners because of what Adam did. In the same way, we are not strictly righteous in ourselves because of what Christ did. We are treated as righteous or accounted righteous. **This righteousness by association (if I may put it that way) works in reverse with Adam and death coming by sin.** Just like in Christ we are considered righteous, **so in Adam many are considered/counted as sinners – even those not personally accountable from contact with God's word.** They receive the same outcome/punishment in a federal headship sense. As Paul has already established – all men are incapable of showing God's glory (Romans 3:23). Adam demonstrated once and for all that all men everywhere will transgress God's law if given opportunity...**Sinners (actual and accounted as such) get eternal death.** Those accounted righteous (through the grace of God) get eternal life.[57]

MP: It's no accident that the first man was named Adam ("man"), because although he was a single person, he still represented the entire human race. [58]

MP: Adam and Eve are representatives whose actions and experiences demonstrate God's purpose with all humans. Hence Adam is a representative, or collective head if you like, similar to Christ (e.g. Romans 5:14); and in this sense Eve can be viewed as the mother of the living in the same way that holy women are daughters of Sarah (1 Peter 3:6), and we are all children of Abraham (Galatians 3:29). [59]

Bible truth believed by Christadelphians

Not applicable, as there were no members of our human race living before Adam.

It is impossible for any humans of our race to have died before Adam, as none existed before Adam.

The Bible is silent on members of our human race living before Adam. If such men had existed for aeons and were all *"in Adam"*, where does the Bible explicitly state this? Paul, an inspired apostle, must be ignorant of this? If such humans existed and, as is claimed, are related or connected with Adam, it would be relevant for the Bible to mention this. But the claim that "Paul's theology" allows for such pre-Adamic men, in the absence of even a single didactic Bible passage alerting us to this great hidden "truth" is, in effect, laying at our Heavenly Father's feet a charge of serious neglect. The level of neglect is compounded in that, according to EC advocates, God never revealed His will and plan of salvation to any of these countless millions living before Adam. However, the Bible tells us that God wants every human to be saved, and He is not willing that any should perish (John 3:16; 2 Peter 3:9).

Furthermore, to talk of "Paul's theology" as though it is, in some sense, not God's theology strongly suggests that Paul is less than an inspired Apostle. This has serious ramifications for the Christadelphian doctrine of inspiration presented concisely in the Foundation clause of the BASF.

---

[53] Gilmore, Ken, *The Faith of an Evolutionary Creationist -2*, January 2018, christadelphianevolution.blogspot.com.au.

[54] Gilmore, Ken, *Evolution does not threaten fundamental theology*, September 2013, christadelphianevolution.blogspot.com.au.

[55] John Doe, *Lampstand Magazine 'Death the Last Enemy' Vol 23 (2017) response,* COD Website, July 2017.

[56] John Doe, *The first and last Adams*, COD Website, June 2017.

[57] John Doe, *Paul's argument through Rom 5:14-21*, COD Website, June 2017.

[58] Pearson, Mike, *The Fourth Conversation*, 2nd Edition, 2017, p. 115.

[59] Ibid., p. 122.

Question 5: Are all humans *"in Adam"* after Adam was created?

Question 5	Are all humans *"in Adam"* after Adam was created?
Relevant Bible Verses	1 Corinthians 15:21-22, 44-49; Romans 5:12, 17-18; 3:23;
Summary EC View A	*No. Only some are "in Adam" if they are accountable to "eternal" death at the judgment seat. Not all people are "in Adam." Men ignorant of the knowledge of God are not "in Adam".*
Summary EC View B	*No. Those "in Christ" are not "in Adam". Adam and Christ are federal heads of two classes of people, and one is either "in Adam" or "in Christ" by association, not physical descent. By default, all men are in Adam either because a) they know God's laws and do sin, or b) they are ignorant but are legally accounted as sinners and worthy of death. However, those "in Christ" are accounted as worthy of eternal life.*
Christadelphian Beliefs	**Yes**. "All men" are in Adam by physical descent, including Christ. *"In Adam"* means that as a result of his sin ("by one man's offence") all men inherit mortality and a bias to sin. BASF 3,4,5,10,12, CCA.

Key Bible Verses

- 1 Corinthians 15:21 *For since **by man came death,** by man came also **the resurrection of the dead.***

- 1 Corinthians 15:22 *For as **in Adam all die,** even so in Christ shall all be made alive*

- 1 Corinthians 15:44-49 … **There is a natural body, and there is a spiritual body.** *45 And so it is written,* **The first man Adam was made a living soul; the last Adam was made a quickening spirit.** *46 Howbeit that was not first which is spiritual, but that which is natural; and afterward that which is spiritual. 47* **The first man is of the earth,** *earthy:* **the second man is the Lord from heaven.** *48* **As is the earthy, such are they also that are earthy**: *and as is the heavenly, such are they also that are heavenly. 49* **And as we have borne the image of the earthy, we shall also bear the image of the heavenly.**

- Romans 5:12 *Wherefore, as **by one man sin entered** into the world, and **death by sin**; and so **death passed upon all men,** for that **all have sinned:***

- Romans 3:23 *For **all have sinned**, and come short of the glory of God*

- Romans 5:17 *For if by **one man's offence death reigned by one***

- Romans 5:18 **by the offence of one** *judgment came upon **all men to condemnation***

EC View A: Bro Ken Gilmore (KG)

KG: The other proof text used by those who insist that monogenism - the belief that the entire human race descends from two people - is 1 Corinthians 15:45-49...Those[174] who reject evolution and cite these verses as evidence are obliged to show how Paul's theology is contingent on Adam being the first human being who ever existed, rather than just the first human being to whom God revealed Himself, the first human being to sin, and the first human being to fall under the dominion of death as a punishment for sin, rather than the simple dissolution of the organic body when it reaches its use-by date...Jesus is obviously not the last Adam in a chronological sense, as 2000 years have passed since he was born. Rather, Jesus was the last Adam in the sense that Adam was the first - each being the end and beginning, respectively, of the narrative historical stream which began when Adam first sinned, and ended at the Cross, when Jesus ended the unchallenged reign of sin and death by showing how one can finally overcome. The first Adam brought death as a punishment for sin into the world. The last Adam showed how one could escape eternal death.[60]

KG: The reference in verse 22 [1 Corinthians 15] to dying 'in Adam' needs to be read in parallel to being made alive 'in Christ'. Being 'in Adam' has nothing to do with being physically descended from Adam, and remember, the genomic data rules out universal human descent from Adam, so this interpretation is impossible. Rather, being in Adam refers to following his example of disobedience. The way in which we are made alive in Christ gives us the context to properly interpret the reference to being in Adam. Put simply, we are dealing with two different paths to follow. One leads to eternal death. The other leads to eternal life.[61]

KG: Paul refers to Christ as the Last Adam, which gives us the context in which we can work out how Adam was the first Adam. Christ most certainly was not the last human being to exist, and therefore one can argue that from Paul's perspective, Adam did not have to be the first Homo sapiens to walk the earth, but the first human being in salvation history. ...Christ is the Last Adam because salvation history finishes with him. He followed God's way perfectly, and has given us a perfect example to follow. What Adam failed to do, Christ completed.[62]

KG: Of note here is the question of what it means to 'die in Adam'. The argument that we have solidarity in Adam through physical descent from him does not follow, as the reference here [1 Corinthians 15:21-22] is more to participating in two examples – Adam's failure to trust God, and Christ's ability to follow

---

[174] **"Those" just happen to be the vast majority of Christadelphians upholding Bible teaching, the standard view held from Bro Thomas to the present and the BASF. Let's keep well in mind whom KG is criticizing here - Christadelphians. KG's criticism and completely novel view of these passages, that speak to Christadelphians very differently, reveal that he is clearly stepping outside our community's doctrinal and fellowship bounds. In effect Christadelphians are being asked to overturn our birthright of long-established beliefs for a mess of pre-Adamic evolutionary pottage.**

God's way. It is by participating in either of these two examples that we are either in Adam or in Christ, with physical descent having nothing to do with it.[63]

EC View B: Christadelphian Origins Discussion (COD) / Bro Mike Pearson (MP)

COD: By default we are all in Adam – a representative man. Christ is THE son of God and perfect manifestation of God's purpose. **We are in Christ by association** (not literal descent). Paul's point is not about literal numbers. Rather Paul is using the numbers as contrasting federal heads – two classes of people.[64]

COD: Paul's point through the passage to [Romans 5] v21 is to demonstrate that in Adam (the wording is not 'descended from') all are accounted as sinners who die, but in Christ (again literal genealogical descent is not in view) grace leads to eternal life. Paul is explaining too that God's righteousness isn't compromised by the death of a man who never was accountable to God (never had the law) – why? Because all men are naturally in Adam and Adam proved when there is a law we will sin/break it. Like Christ, Adam was a **federal head, a representative individual** who demonstrated the righteousness of God (in Adam's case in the death of all men).[65]

COD: The passage [Romans 5:12-21] …sees Adam as a federal head similar to Christ. In one **we** are accounted sinners and worthy of death (as punishment for sin despite individual circumstances), in the other we are accounted worthy of eternal life and mortality's impact on us is temporary. The passage doesn't say death by sin comes through descent in Adam. This may be implied but is not explicit. As with life in Christ, the issue is identification not strictly descent.[66]

MP: It's no accident that the first man was named Adam ("man"), because although he was a single person, he still represented the entire human race. Twenty-first century thinking emphasises the individual, whereas the Hebrews and other Near Eastern peoples often saw an individual as **representative** of an entire body, and the actions of an individual were often transferred upon a social group such as a family or tribe (e.g. Jeremiah 31:29 and Ezekiel 18:1-4). Hopefully, this little detour explains why in scriptural terms (i.e. **adoption and group representation**), **we should consider ourselves to be Adam's descendants**, and included within the same family or covenant group as Adam. Therefore, even though we are mortal by virtue of the fact that we are biological creatures, the rules of a punitive death that applied to Adam apply to us as well.[67]

MP: So, death in the New Testament is can now [sic] viewed in the light of the resurrection of Jesus. As in *Adam* all died (because **we are adopted into that broader family**), so in Christ shall all be made alive (1 Corinthians 15:22), and those who have not yet encountered Christ are dead in sin (Ephesians 2:1). [68]

Bible truth believed by Christadelphians

"In Adam" means that all humans are physical descendants of Adam, including Christ. In consequence of Adam's sin (*"by one man's offence"*), all are born with a nature that is mortal (subject to death - *"death reigned by one"*) and prone to sin (*"by one man's disobedience many were made sinners"*).

"As in Adam all die" means that all humans of our race, including the Lord Jesus, have either died in the past or will die in the future as *"death passed upon all men"* and *"by man came death"*.

"In Christ" primarily expresses our hope of being physically transformed to become part of a new immortal race of which Christ is the firstborn (Colossians 1:15; 18, 27-28). However, right now, it also indicates the mental and moral relationship we have by faith and obedience, with our sins (works of the devil) forgiven. Nevertheless, as long as we are mortal, we remain physically *"in Adam"* as his descendants. Now we are mentally and morally *"in Christ"*. As such, we are 'betrothed' to him; our hope is *"in him"*. But when we are *"made alive"* - given immortality, we will be physically *"in Christ"* and no longer *"in Adam"*. In other words, the devil in us, which is a physical problem with which we are born, will be destroyed when this *"corruptible shall have put on incorruption, and this mortal shall have put on immortality"* (1 Corinthians 15:54).

Further explanation

BASF 3, 4, 5, 10, 12

Chapter 19 - All humans die *"in Adam"*

Chapter 26 - Adam's Sin Resulted in Mortality and Sin-proneness for all Mankind

---

[60] Gilmore, Ken, *The Faith of an Evolutionary Creationist -2*, January 2018, christadelphianevolution.blogspot.com.au.

[61] Gilmore, Ken, *New Testament references to Adam and Eve by Paul and Jesus do not disprove evolution*, November 2013, christadelphianevolution.blogspot.com.au.

[62] Gilmore, Ken, *Evolution does not threaten fundamental theology*, September 2013, christadelphianevolution.blogspot.com.au.

[63] Ibid.

[64] John Doe, *The first and last Adams*, COD Website, June 2017.

[65] John Doe, *Rom 5:12 – an overview*, COD Website, June 2017.

[66] John Doe, *Paul's argument through Rom 5:14-21*, COD Website, June 2017.

[67] Pearson, Mike, *The Fourth Conversation*, 2nd Edition, 2017, p. 115.

[68] Ibid., p. 116.

Question 6: Do worthy believers remain and die *"in Adam"* while they are mortal?

Question 6	Do worthy believers remain and die *"in Adam"* while they are mortal?
Relevant Bible Verses	Romans 5:12; 3:23; 1 Corinthians 15:19-23,44-49; Revelation 2:11; 20:14; Psalm 49:12,20; Hebrews 9:27
Summary EC View A	*No. A worthy believer cannot be "in Adam", because to be "in Adam" means you will be condemned to "eternal" death at the judgment seat.*
Summary EC View B	*No. Because worthy believers won't be forever/eternally dead. They don't experience the death in Adam, because scripturally believers who die are not "in Adam" – they sleep "in the Lord".*
Christadelphian Beliefs	Yes. Physically they remain *"in Adam"*, being mortal (subject to death) and prone to sin. However, they are *"in Christ"* mentally and morally, with the prospect of being *"in Christ"* physically (and hence no longer *"in Adam"*) once they are "made alive" when Christ returns.

Key Bible Verses

- Romans 5:12 *Wherefore, as **by one man sin entered** into the world, and **death by sin**; and so **death passed upon all men,** for that **all have sinned:***

- Romans 3:23 *For **all have sinned**, and come short of the glory of God*

- 1 Corinthians 15:19-20 ***If in this life only we have hope in Christ**, we are of all men **most miserable.** 20 But now is Christ risen from the dead, and **become the firstfruits of them that slept.***

- 1 Corinthians. 15:21-23 *For since by man came **death**, by man came also the resurrection of **the dead**. 22 **For as in Adam all die**, even so **in Christ shall all be made alive**. 23 But every man in his own order: **Christ the firstfruits**; afterward **they that are Christ's at his coming.***

- 1 Corinthians 15:44-49 *… **There is a natural body, and there is a spiritual body.** 45 And so it is written, **The first man Adam was made a living soul; the last Adam was made a quickening spirit.** 46 Howbeit that was not first which is spiritual, but that which is natural; and afterward that which is spiritual. 47 **The first man is of the earth**, earthy: **the second man is the Lord from heaven.** 48 **As is the earthy, such are they also that are earthy**: and as is the heavenly, such are they also that are heavenly. 49 **And as we have borne the image of the earthy, we shall also bear the image of the heavenly.***

- Psalms 49:20 *Man that is in honour, and understandeth not, is like the beasts that perish.*

- Revelation 2:11 *…he that overcometh shall not be hurt **of the second death.***

- Hebrews 9:27 *And as it is appointed unto men **once to die**, but after this the judgment:*

EC View A: Bro Ken Gilmore (KG)

KG: Being in Adam refers to following his example of disobedience. The way in which we are made alive in Christ gives us the context to properly interpret the reference to being in Adam. Put simply, we are dealing with two different paths to follow. One leads to eternal death. The other leads to eternal life.[69]

EC View B: Christadelphian Origins Discussion (CCD) / Bro Mike Pearson (MP)

COD: Are we all "physically in Adam from birth to death"? This is not the witness of Scripture. Paul is emphatic as he develops his argument into Romans 6 that we were the servants of sin but are now servants of God. We used to serve sin, now we serve righteousness. This is all past tense. To speak of us as remaining in Adam in any sense is foreign to Paul, so it ought to be foreign to us. It is certainly true that we fail to live according to our new allegiance to righteousness as Paul bemoans in Romans 7. Mentally he (and hopefully we) wanted to serve righteousness but the proneness to sin inevitably led to failure. Does this mean he was still in Adam and prospectively in Christ? No, this failure to live perfectly does not exclude us from being in Christ. On the contrary Paul says "there is therefore NOW no condemnation to those who are in Christ Jesus" Romans 8:1.[70]

COD: Because his believers won't be forever/eternally dead. I suggest they don't experience the death in Adam, scripturally believers are not 'in Adam' – it is clearly sleep in the Lord.[71]

MP: Death (mortality) is our final *physical* destination, it doesn't have to be our final *spiritual* destination.[72]

Bible truth believed by Christadelphians

Worthy believers are physically in Adam, being prone to sin and unable to avoid dying the same death that Adam introduced into the world. However, they are in Christ mentally (belief) and morally (keeping his commandments and being forgiven when they fail), with the prospect of being *"in Christ"* physically, by being "made alive" when Christ returns.

Worthy believers experience the "first death" in Adam as did Christ, but not the **second death** *"in Adam"*, which responsible but unworthy believers will face at the judgment seat.

Worthy believers remain physically *"in Adam"* until this mortal puts on immortality after the judgment seat at the return of Christ. At that time, they will be physically *"made alive"* *"in Christ"*. As the apostle Paul plainly states when contrasting the two physical states of worthy believers before and after Christ returns, *"The first man (Adam) is of the earth, earthy: the second man (Christ) is the Lord from* *heaven, ... **as we have borne the image of the earthy we shall also bear the image of the heavenly**"* (1 Corinthians 15:47-49).

Further explanation

Chapter 19 - All humans die *"in Adam"*

Chapter 26 - Adam's Sin Resulted in Mortality and Sin-proneness for all Mankind

---

[69] Gilmore, Ken, *New Testament references to Adam and Eve by Paul and Jesus do not disprove evolution*, christadelphianevolution.blogspot.com.au, November 2013.

[70] John Doe, *Lampstand Magazine 'Death the Last Enemy' Vol 23 (2017) response*, COD Website, July 2017.

[71] John Doe, *Death in Rom 5 is not 'mortality' but the fate of the wicked*, COD Website, June 2017.

[72] Pearson, Mike, *The Fourth Conversation*, 2nd Edition, 2017, pp. 113-117.

Question 7: Was Christ *"in Adam"*? Did Christ die the death that Adam introduced?

Question 7	Was Christ *"in Adam"*? Did Christ die the death that Adam introduced?
Relevant Bible Verses	John 12:31-33; Acts 2:24; Hebrews2:9,14-15; Romans 6:9-10
Summary EC View A	*Need to clarify. We were unable to find an answer to this very important question. It is likely that they would answer no, as they believe that Adam only introduced "eternal" death at the judgment seat.*
Summary EC View B	*Need to clarify. We were unable to find an answer to this very important question. It is likely that they would answer no, based on their view that Adam's sin only introduced eternal death/spiritual death as the final outcome of the unrighteous/those not in Christ.*
Christadelphian Beliefs	Yes. Jesus was a sufferer, in the days of his flesh, from all the effects that came by Adam's transgression including the death that passed upon all men, which he shared by partaking of their physical nature. BASF 10

Key Bible Verses

- John 12:31-33 *Now is the judgment of this world: now shall the prince of this world be cast out. 32 And I, if I be lifted up from the earth, will draw all [men] unto me. 33* **This he said, signifying what death he should die.**

- Acts 2:24 *Whom God hath raised up, having loosed the pains of* **death***: because it was not possible that he should be holden of it.*

- Hebrews 2:9 *But we see Jesus, who was made a little lower than the angels* **for the suffering of death,** *crowned with glory and honour; that he by the grace of God* **should taste death (thanatos) for every man.**

- **Hebrews 2:14-15** *Forasmuch then as the children are partakers of flesh and blood, he also himself likewise took part of the same;* **that through death he [Jesus] might destroy him that had the power of death, that is, the devil, and deliver them who through fear of death were all their lifetime subject to bondage.**

- Romans 6:9-10 *Knowing that Christ being raised from the dead dieth no more;* **death hath no more dominion over him.** *10 For in that he died,* **he died unto sin once***: but in that he liveth, he liveth unto God.*

Bible truth believed by Christadelphians

Yes. This is the way he destroyed the devil (Hebrews 2:14).

Jesus was born *"in Adam"* and inherited Adam's fallen nature. He died *"in Adam"* but is no longer *"in Adam"* because he is immortal. He destroyed the devil when, after a life of perfect obedience, he submitted to the public crucifixion of his flesh, and his Father delivered him from death (Hebrews 2:15; Romans 7:24; 2 Corinthians 1:10) by raising and rewarding him with immortality. Christ then was no longer *"in Adam"*. Hence *"through death"* (Hebrews 2:14), he simultaneously was bruised on the heel and crushed the serpent on the head.

> **BASF 10 —** … Jesus was…**a sufferer, in the days of his flesh, from all the effects that came by Adam's transgression including the death that passed upon all men, which he shared by partaking of their physical nature**. Matthew 1:23; 1 Timothy 3:16; Hebrews 2:14; Galatians 4:4; Hebrews 2:17

Further explanation

Chapter 18 - What Adam's Sin Introduced: Mortality

Chapter 19 - All humans die *"in Adam"*

Chapter 26 - Adam's Sin Resulted in Mortality and Sin-proneness for all Mankind

Question 8: The devil – meaning, origin and what is its power of death?

EC advocates need to clarify their understanding of the devil. This is crucial given their insistence that there was no change in the condition of human nature in consequence of Adam and Eve's sin.

- Is the devil part and parcel of the "evolved" human nature that God allegedly created from the outset? Hence, did God evolve the devil?
- What is the power of death that the devil holds (Hebrews 2:14)? Is it the mortality with which we are born as Christadelphians teach? Or is it their view of God's legal condemnation to "eternal" death?
- How did Christ, by partaking of flesh and blood, destroy the devil through his own death?

EC View A proposes a new theory that attempts to harmonise the devil with their view of "eternal death". They believe that the devil is not something you are born with but rather a state of mind that only exists at the point when our natural impulses come into conflict with God's laws. They believe that the power of death held by the devil is the divine condemnation to "eternal death" at the judgment seat for those who are responsible but unworthy.

EC View B - Neither COD nor Bro Mike Pearson have provided a direct explanation of this subject. However, in a rebuttal of a *Lampstand* article[175] that addressed EC View A's view of the devil, COD stated that EC View A's teaching was "weird". At the same time, they rejected the Christadelphian view (see Christadelphian writings on the devil in Section 6 of *By One Man*) that the devil's origin was coeval with the fall[176], but then did not explain their own understanding of this subject.

Subsequent requests to COD to further explain their view of the devil have only been partially answered. What is clear is that COD (i) rejects EC View A and (ii) believes that proneness to sin is part and parcel of mortality. This strongly suggests that they believe that the devil evolved as part of God's supposed evolutionary creation.

This question follows a slightly different format from the previous questions. It is divided into seven sub-questions presented in the table across the following two pages, where two EC Views are contrasted with the Christadelphian view.

---

[175] Larsen and Jamieson, *Death the Last Enemy*, Parts 1,2 & 3, The Lampstand Magazine, vol. 23, 2017, March, May, July.
[176] See page 229.

For questions where we have been unable to obtain a direct answer from EC writings, we have noted either that (i) the answer presented is based on **indirect** EC comments or (ii) the EC writers have **not clarified** their view.

After the table, relevant Bible verses are grouped according to each of the questions, followed by quotations obtained from EC writers on this subject. The more detailed *"Bible Truth believed by Christadelphians"* section is not included for this question, but instead refer readers to the summary comments in the table below, and the detailed discussion in Chapters 21 and 27.

Questions on the devil for EC view holders

EC View A	EC View B	Christadelphian View
A) What is the devil and when did it first exist?		
A state of mind that only exists when our natural impulses conflict with God's laws. Sufficient knowledge of God's laws is first required before the devil can exist.	[Indirect] "Prone to sin" is part of our imperfect mortal state, the life-cycle that God designed. The world is controlled by and filled with unrestrained lust.	*The devil personifies fallen human nature that is prone to sin and subject to death. It came into existence after Adam and Eve embraced serpent reasoning and sinned (John 8:44; 1 John 3:8), and it became a law in their members (Genesis 3:15; Romans 7:23, 25; 8:2). Since then, all are born with the problem of the devil.*
B) Did all the alleged humans before Adam have the devil?		
No. Only those responsible to judgment can have the devil. These humans had no knowledge of God's laws.	[Indirect] Yes, being prone to sin is part of mortality.	*Not applicable. No such humans existed. They are never mentioned in the Bible.*
C) Do all people after Adam have the devil?		
No, not all. Only those responsible to judgment by a knowledge of God's laws have the devil.	[Indirect] Yes, being prone to sin is part of mortality.	*Yes. All people are "In Adam" by physical descent and therefore inherit the same condition of human nature that the devil personifies.*

EC View A	EC View B	Christadelphian View
D) Does the devil have power over the death that Adam introduced?		
Yes. Adam introduced "eternal" death that will be carried out at the judgment seat, on those who are both responsible and unworthy. This is the death that the devil has power over	Clarification Required	*Yes. Adam's sin introduced our state of being both subject to death (mortality) and biased to sin. As the devil personifies this condition of fallen human nature, it has power over the death that Adam introduced. BASF 8,9,10*
E) Was Christ born with the devil in him?		
No (based on Question a)	[Indirect] Yes (based on question a)	*Yes. Jesus was born with the same mortal, sin-biased nature: "he also himself likewise took part of the same; that through death he might destroy ... the devil" (Hebrews 2:14)*
F) Did Christ die the death that the devil has power over?		
No. A sinless Christ could not die an "eternal death" at the judgment seat	Clarification Required	*Yes. Hebrews 2:9, 14-15 makes it plain that the death Christ died is the same death that the devil has power over. It was only by dying this death that Christ was able to fulfil Genesis 3:15 (wounded on the heel by the serpent as he fatally destroyed its head) and be the anti-type of the brazen serpent that Moses lifted up (John 3:14). BASF 8,9,10*
G) How did Christ destroy the devil when he died?		
He destroyed the state of mind that exists at the point when there is conflict between human nature and God's law	Clarification Required	*Jesus was born with fallen human nature (i.e. the devil) so that he could destroy the devil within himself through his own death. Throughout his whole life, he never yielded to the temptations of the devil (whether internal or external) and rendered perfect obedience to his Father's will (Hebrews 2:14-15; Mark 3:27). Hence, in his life and victoriously in his death, Jesus destroyed the problem of sin in the place where it resided. He condemned or destroyed sin in the flesh (Romans 8:3), which is synonymous with the devil.*

Key Bible verses on the devil

A) What is the devil and when did it first exist?

- Hebrews 2:14 *Forasmuch then as the children are* **partakers of flesh and blood**, *he also himself likewise took part of the same; that* **through death** *he might* **destroy him that had the power of death, that is, the devil**.

- 1 John 3:8 **He that committeth sin is of the devil; for the devil sinneth from the beginning.** *For this purpose the Son of God was manifested, that* **he might destroy the works of the devil.**

- Genesis 3:15 *And I will put* **enmity** *between thee and the woman, and between* **thy seed** *and her seed; it shall bruise thy head, and thou shalt bruise his heel.*

B) Did all the alleged humans before Adam have the devil?

- Romans 5:12 *Wherefore, as* **by one man sin entered into the world, and death by sin; and so death passed upon all men,** *for that all have sinned.*

- Luke 3:38 *Which was the son of Enos, which was the son of Seth, which was the son of* **Adam, which was the son of God.**

C) Do all people after Adam have the devil?

- Ephesians 4:26-27 *…let not the sun go down upon your wrath:* **neither give place to the devil**.

- Genesis 6:5 *And GOD saw that the wickedness of man was great in the earth, and* **that every imagination of the thoughts of his heart was only evil continually.**

- Matthew 4:1 *Then was Jesus led up of the Spirit into the wilderness to be tempted of the* **devil**.

- 1John 3:10-12 *In this* **the children of God** *are manifest, and the* **children of the devil: whosoever doeth not righteousness is not of God,** *neither he that loveth not his brother.*

- Matthew 15:18-19 *But* **those things which proceed out of the mouth come forth from the heart; and they defile the man.** *19* **For out of the heart proceed evil thoughts, murders, adulteries, fornications, thefts, false witness, blasphemies:**

- Hebrews 9:26 *he [Jesus] appeared* **to put away sin** *by the sacrifice of himself.*

- Romans 8:3 *For what the law could not do, in that it was* **weak through the flesh**, *God sending his own Son in the* **likeness of sinful flesh**, *and for sin,* **condemned sin in the flesh**

- Jeremiah 17:9 *The* **heart is deceitful above all things**, *and desperately wicked: who can know it?*

D) Does the devil have power over the death that Adam introduced?

- Hebrews 2:14-15 *Forasmuch then as the children are partakers of flesh and blood, he also himself likewise took part of the same; that* **through death** *he might* **destroy him that had the power of death, that is, the devil**. *And*

- *deliver them who through **fear of death** were **all their lifetime subject to bondage.***

- John 8:44 *Ye are of your father **the devil, and the lusts of your father ye will do. He was a murderer from the beginning**, and abode not in the truth, because there is no truth in him. When he speaketh a lie, he speaketh of his own: for he is a liar, and the father of it.*

- Romans 5:12 *Wherefore, as **by one man sin entered into the word, and death by sin; and so death passed upon all men,** for that all have sinned.*

- Romans 5:17 *For if by **one man's offence death reigned by one***

- Romans 5:18 ***by the offence of one** judgment came upon **all men to condemnation**…by the **righteousness of one** the free gift came upon all men to the **justification** of life*

E) Was Christ born with the devil in him?

- Matthew 4:1 *Then was Jesus led up of the Spirit into the wilderness to be **tempted of the devil.***

- Hebrews 4:15 *For we have not an high priest which cannot be touched with the feeling of our infirmities; but was **in all points tempted like as we are,** yet without sin*

F) Did Christ die the death that the devil has power over?

- Hebrews 2:14-15 *Forasmuch then as the children are partakers of flesh and blood, he also himself likewise took part of the same; that **through death** he might **destroy him that had the power of death, that is, the devil**.*

- Genesis 3:15 *And I will put **enmity** between thee and the woman, and between thy seed and **her seed; it** shall bruise thy head, and thou shalt bruise **his** heel.*

- John 3:14 *And as Moses **lifted up the serpent in the wilderness,** even so must **the Son of man be lifted up.***

G) How did Christ destroy the devil when he died?

- 1 John 3:8 ***He that committeth sin is of the devil; for the devil sinneth from the beginning.** For this purpose the Son of God was manifested, that **he might destroy the works of the devil.***

- Hebrews 9:26-28 *he [Jesus] appeared **to put away sin** by the sacrifice of himself … 28 So Christ was once offered to bear the sins of many; and unto them that look for him shall **he appear the second time without sin** unto salvation.*

- Romans 8:3 *For what the law could not do, in that it was **weak through the flesh,** God sending his own Son in the **likeness of sinful flesh,** and for sin, **condemned sin in the flesh.***

- Hebrews 2:9 *But we see Jesus, who was made a little lower than the angels **for the suffering of death,** crowned with glory and honour; that he by the grace of God should **taste death for every man.***

- Philippians 2:8 *[Christ] became **obedient unto death,** even the death of the cross. Wherefore **God hath also highly exalted him**…*

- John 12:31-33 *Now is the judgment of this world: now shall **the prince of this world be cast out**. 32 And I, if I be lifted up from the earth, will draw all men unto me. 33 This he said, signifying what **death he should die**.*

- Ephesians 2:2 *Wherein in time past ye walked according to the course of this world, according to **the prince of the power of the air,** the spirit that now worketh in the children of disobedience:*

EC View A: Bro Jonathan Burke (JB)

JB: "the diabolos is the state of mind which arises when our natural impulses come into conflict with divinely revealed law, …You can't sin without the diabolos being there in the first place, and the diabolos can only be there in the first place if you are enlightened by divine law; before that, none of your natural impulses can be described as the diabolos, nor can any of your actions be described as sin"[73]

JB: The evolved humans had the same natural desires in them as Adam did, before they met Adam. They did not yet have the diabolos, any more than an animal has the diabolos, because the diabolos is the state of mind which arises when our natural impulses come into conflict with divinely revealed law, and they were completely ignorant of divine law (as animals are). As soon as such law was revealed to them, they would experience the struggle with the diabolos described in Romans 7.[74]

JB: "The diabolos has the power of eternal death, not mortality. We do not die because we have impulses to sin. We die because we are mortal. Christ destroyed the diabolos which has the power of eternal death as punishment for sin; that is the death which is the wages of sin…the death which is the wages of sin is a punishment for sin which we receive at the seat of judgment."[75]

EC View B: Christadelphian Origins Discussion (COD) / Bro Mike Pearson (MP)

COD: We know a few people were scratching their heads on the final part of the *Lampstand's* insert on EC wondering what was up. The table moved on to discuss the devil. Honestly the representation of the EC position[177] is so weird it is hardly worth comment.[76]

> EC Position[178]: The Devil is a state of mind that arises when our natural desires (God created proneness to sin) comes into conflict with God's law. This conflict produces sin and if unforgiven results in eternal death after the judgement. Hence sufficient knowledge of God's laws is first required before the Devil can exist. Only those responsible to judgement have the Devil. The Devil has the power over eternal death only.

---

[177] Ibid.

[178] i.e. EC View A. *The Lampstand* article and Bible insert, which COD is criticising, directly quotes Bro Jonathan Burke's view, as quoted immediately above in this same Question 8. See Larsen and Jamieson, *Death the Last Enemy*, Parts 1,2 and 3, *The Lampstand Magazine*, vol. 23, 2017, March, May, and July.

COD: We don't believe in a supernatural devil who has a single particular and personal identity, so what "the devil" means depends on context. If we ask "who is/was the devil?" the answer is sometimes "what you see when you look in a mirror" and other times it's personified suffering and at other times it's even some nasty person in the ecclesia who causes trouble by talking about others (1 Tim 3:11). …

We definitely can't be so precise as to say that the devil (let alone the Devil) "personifies the physical condition of human nature from birth, part of our mortal condition" – that's going way too far into specifics, and not merely because it leaves out mental illnesses which were surely part of the oppression that Jesus relieved. … We have clearly and repeatedly stated that humans have all been the same for a considerable period, the lusts which existed in Eve prior to eating the fruit were/are right enough kept in control. That we, Adam and our ancestors – who clearly predate Adam – were the same is evident in archaeology and genetics.[77]

COD: Does Paul's description of the evil in his mind preclude Adam and Eve having our proneness? No – I suggest the passage neither supports nor denies the proposition. The passage simply reinforces the reality that law brings knowledge of lust/sin/evil and the frustration that the sons and daughters of God feel in their current state.[78]

COD: Cain was born of the same parents as Abel and Seth but his **thirking spiritually was of the serpent.** None of us are created by God or born by Him literally, but spiritually we have our origin in Him. So too the lusts weren't magically created by the world, rather the world is full of them and hence they "come from" the world just as the righteous come from God. Simply that the world is controlled by and filled with **unrestrained lust**.[79]

MP: Mortality is simply part of the life-cycle that God designed, and it has been this way for millennia. **Therefore, man is "imperfect" and has a nature that is mortal. As a result of our imperfection, we are also prone to sin.**[80]

MP: *very good* doesn't imply any special attributes to humans that shouldn't be applied to any other part of creation; and secondly, that as biological organisms, mortality is simply part of the life-cycle that God designed, and it has been this way for millennia. Therefore, man is "imperfect" and has a nature that is mortal. As a result of our imperfection, we are also prone to sin.[81]

For a full Christadelphian explanation of the devil:

> **Chapter 21** - What Adam's Sin Introduced: The Devil
>
> **Chapter 27** - The Devil – Personification of Fallen Human Nature
>
> **BASF** Clauses 3, 5, 8, 9, 10, 12, 26, 28 & 30

---

[73] Burke, Jonathan, December 2013, as quoted in the Taipei Christadelphian Ecclesia Timeline [distributed to all ACBM Regional Committees and the ecclesias they represent], 25 October 2016, p. 35.

[74] Ibid.

[75] Burke, Jonathan - as quoted in the Taipei Christadelphian Ecclesia Timeline [distributed to all ACBM Regional Committees and the ecclesias they represent], 25 October 2016, pp.35 & 38.

[76] John Doe, *Response to the Lampstand July 2017 on the Devil*, COD Website, July 2017.

[77] Ibid.

[78] John Doe, *Our evil mind, interaction with law and the struggle to obey – Rom 7*, COD Website, June 2017.

[79] John Doe, *Do the 3 lusts come from the world not God (1Jn 2:16)?*, COD Website, June 2017.

[80] Pearson, Mike, *The Fourth Conversation,* 2nd Edition, 2017, pp. 113-117.

[81] Ibid.

SECTION 5

EC BREAKS MANY LINKS IN THE BASF CHAIN

*"Examine yourselves, whether ye be in the faith;
prove your own selves"* (2 Corinthians 13:5, KJV)

Chapter 24
EC Views in Conflict With the BASF

EC views conflict with 13 clauses in our statement of faith, specifically the Foundation clause and clauses 3, 4, 5, 6, 7, 8, 9, 10, 12, 26, 28, 29 and 30.

It is impossible for EC proponents to harmonise their views consistently across all clauses of the BASF. They can only attempt to interpret the BASF by ignoring the logical flow and lexical cohesion that occurs from one clause to the next on the critical subjects of the human race, God's physical sentence on Adam as a consequence of sin, and God's plan of restoration. They can only interpret these clauses contrary to the intended meaning of the original authors.

The BASF clauses above all refer to at least one of the following three passages: Romans 5:12-21, 1 Corinthians 15:21-28, 46-49 and Hebrews 2:14-17. These three Bible passages concern the origins of the human race, how sin and death entered into the world and God's method of reconciling the human race back into fellowship with Himself. Therefore, these three passages represent important anchors of Christadelphian doctrinal understanding, which the BASF adequately defines. However, EC advocates are driven to explain these three important Bible passages in a substantially different way from their original meaning and purpose. This is due to their firm belief in evolution that, of necessity, sets adrift their reading of the BASF.

EC advocates deny the Christadelphian doctrine of the atonement in that they deny that Christ was subject to the law of sin and death introduced by Adam into the world. From clause to clause in the BASF, there is a direct link showing that Christ did die the death that the *diabolos* has power over (Hebrews 2:14), the same death that Adam introduced. They deny that there was any physical change in the condition of Adam's nature. This denial requires them to constantly change their definition of key terms, depending on which particular clause of the BASF they are attempting to harmonise their beliefs with.

Promulgating or accommodating false EC doctrines makes shipwreck of the BASF as the positive, unifying document that has enabled worldwide fellowship for the past 130 years (1 Timothy 1:19; Hebrews 6:19).

Christadelphian Doctrines Negatively Impacted by EC Teaching

Core Christadelphian Doctrines	EC Views in Conflict
BASF 3,4 The origin of the human race – Adam & Eve as the sole progenitors.	Adam and Eve were not the sole progenitors of the human race. A race of evolved humans already existed before Adam and Eve.
BASF 4 Before sin, Adam & Eve were created with natural bodies of life that were *"very good in kind and condition"*, and their life in this state would continue so long as they remained obedient to God's law. Hence, they were not subject to a state of death. **BASF 5, 6, 8, 9, 10, 12** After sin, God's just and necessary sentence on Adam and Eve involved a physical change in the condition of their nature, which impacted all of their progeny. Specifically, a state of being subject to death (mortal) and prone to sin. Adam died this death when he was 930 years old. It is the misfortune of all humans to be born with this same physical state that came by Adam's sin. BASF 5 states that Adam was *"sentenced to return to the ground ... a sentence which defiled and **became a physical law of his being**, and was transmitted to all his posterity"* (BASF 5). This fallen condition of human nature is lexically cohesive with other phrases in the BASF including: *"the law of sin and death"*, *"the condemned line"*, *"condemned nature"*, *"the law of condemnation"*, *"bear our condemnation"*, *"all the effects that came by Adam's transgression including the death that passed upon all men"*, *"sin in the flesh"*, *"Adam's disobedient race"*.	No change in the condition of human nature due to Adam and Eve's sin. All humans, whether evolved or created miraculously (in the case of Adam and Eve), were in a state that was mortal and prone to sin from the outset. Adam and Eve's children intermarried with evolved humans, who had exactly the same condition of human nature. Adam's sin did not introduce the death associated with mortality. Adam introduced "eternal death" as the consequence of transgressing God's laws. "Eternal death" is distinct from or overlays as a legal or judicial condemnation the normal death associated with mortality. For the unworthy responsible, this condemnation to "eternal death" will be pronounced at the judgment seat.
BASF 3, 8, 9, 10, 12, 28, 30 It was necessary for Jesus Christ, as our representative saviour, to be born with exactly the same fallen condition of human nature that was introduced by Adam's sin (in one word – the *diabolos*). This enabled Christ's life, death and resurrection to declare the righteousness of God as He provided the propitiation (the means) by which our sins can be forgiven, we can walk in fellowship and ultimately be granted immortal life. The purpose of his millennial reign will be to subdue all enemies, including death, and completely restore the human race to the friendship of the Deity.	The condition of human nature that Christ was born with and died to had nothing to do with Adam and Eve's sin, but rather just the way God created all humans from the outset. There was no historical point when the entire human race was in friendship with the Deity. Therefore the human race can only be brought to a position of friendship with God, not restored to such a state.

Error undermines the BASF

The current attempt to persuade the ecclesial world to accept pre- and co-Adamic humans, who were the product of an evolutionary creation, has serious ramifications that should be apparent to all Christadelphians.

Whenever the obvious conflict with the BASF is pointed out to those promoting error, there are generally two responses, both of which seek to undermine or minimise the importance of the BASF.

1. They point out that the BASF is a man-made document.

2. They portray the BASF's development in a negative light. They argue that changes occurred to the wording from its initial form to its final form, and that it has an unbalanced focus on controversies that were prevalent in the late 19th century. Accordingly, they reason that the BASF is no longer a reliable or truly representative document. It should be either revised or Christadelphians should be allowed greater freedom to interpret it as they see fit.

In response to point 1, the BASF is of course a man-made document. It is designed to set out what Christadelphians believe are the fundamental teachings of Scripture for salvation in contrast to the teachings of the churches and sects of the Christian world. As such, it also sets out the basis of our fellowship and marks out fellowship boundaries. It was necessary from the beginning of the Christadelphian movement to separate us from the many teachings that had corrupted the true gospel of Christ, the apostles and the early first century Christians.

Brother John Carter expresses this point succinctly in the Australian Unity Agreement Booklet:

> "What are the essentials of saving truth? We have generally recognised that the essentials are formulated in the Birmingham Amended Statement of Faith. Not that other Statements may not also give a true outline but the Birmingham Statement is the one most widely known ....
>
> A Statement of the Faith is essential for any community of believers to define their beliefs to ensure harmonious working together and consistent testimony to those without. To decry a Statement as man-made and to speak of the Bible as alone sufficient reveals a marked failure to perceive the problems of ecclesial life and its duties. All the sects of Christendom claim to base their beliefs on the Bible, a fact which in itself demonstrates the need for a Statement of what we understand to be the teaching of the Bible."[179]

---

[179] Carter, John – Unity Book, p. 9.

Brother Robert Roberts similarly stated in the Ecclesial Guide:

> "It is necessary to have the truth defined. It is not enough for an applicant (for baptism or fellowship) to say he believes the Bible or the testimony of the apostles. Multitudes would profess belief in this form who we know are ignorant or unbelieving of the truth, and, therefore, unqualified for union with the brethren of Christ. The question for applicants is, do they believe what the Scriptures teach? To test this, the teaching requires definition. This definition agreed to forms the basis of fellowship among believers, whether expressed in written or spoken words."[180]

Point 2 represents a jaundiced view of the development of the BASF. Yes, in the late 1800s, there were changes in wording, additions, and amendments before the final form of the BASF that we still use was adopted in 1898. Subsequently, various ecclesias and wide groups of ecclesias have produced explanations in harmony with the BASF, such as the Australian Unity Agreement in 1958. But these were all to provide clarity and help resolve differences in a manner that upheld the BASF as our basis of fellowship. It was challenges to core Christadelphian beliefs that lay behind the need for this clarity.

As Brother CC Walker points out in his response to the "Amity" movement during his time as editor of the Christadelphian[181], if strong stands had not been made against past errors, the truth that we hold would have been lost. After listing all the major false doctrines the Christadelphian movement had to deal with from 1866 to 1902, he then comments on who exactly was causing the trouble or division in our community:

> "It is quite true that there are "evils of division"; but who are the sinners in the case? The majority above referred to [200 odd ecclesias in England in central fellowship]? No, but the introducers and espousers of the heresies before alluded to. We are exhorted to "mark" and "avoid" these. Surely, you do not want to exhort us to do otherwise.
>
> The present position, though not ideal, is quite tolerable. Those who are not prepared to "mark" and "avoid" heresies and heretics, can find society with the tolerationists; but if they try to bring about "amity" (friendship amounting to recognition in fellowship) between the "avoiders" and the "avoided," they will only precipitate more "division." The thing has been tried over and over again, always with this inevitable result."[182]

As the Christadelphian Committee in 1972 stated, it is dishonourable to enjoy fellowship based on the truths we hold as expressed in the

---

[180] Roberts, R., *The Ecclesial Guide* (34. Basis of Fellowship). Birmingham: The Christadelphian, 1989 edition, p. 23.

[181] Walker, C.C. – The Christadelphian, 1938, vol. 75, pp. 324-326.

[182] Ibid.

BASF while at the same time not believing them and actively working against them (see article quoted on page 28).

Christadelphians have historically used the BASF as an apt summary of those core doctrines essential for our salvation, our basis for baptism and fellowship. The positive and negative clauses are our agreed basis of how, as a worldwide community with autonomous ecclesias, we can:

a. separate ourselves from false doctrines such as the Trinity, the immortality of the soul, the substitutionary death of Christ, a supernatural devil; and

b. immediately fellowship brothers and sisters from other ecclesias we have never met before.

Discounting the importance of the BASF as our basis of fellowship will only serve to erode these wonderful benefits.

A strong stand against the false teachings that *By One Man* opposes, guided by the principles stated above by CC Walker and *The Christadelphian*, is necessary. This is because EC advocates are asking Christadelphians to accommodate their belief in a pre- and co-Adamic evolved race of humans that not one inspired writer of the Bible even begins to mention. On the contrary, their view contradicts what the Bible plainly tells us. Moreover, if we were to incorporate their beliefs, it would require us to dismantle the Bible and Christadelphian teaching on the fallen condition of human nature (the physical consequences of Adam's sin) and the atoning work of Christ, and to rewrite approximately a third of the BASF's clauses.

The great strength of the BASF is that it has been tried and refined in the fire of doctrinal controversy, and is all the stronger for having been through that process.

All past errorists thought they were 'saving' Christadelphians from ignorance by calling on them to adopt or accommodate the particular brand of error they were propagating. In reality, they were breaking a link in the BASF chain of belief and undermining the cohesive set of doctrines that form the basis of our worldwide faith and fellowship. History is, at present, repeating itself.

The BASF is a logical progression of related ideas.

To fully appreciate the extent to which EC beliefs contradict the BASF, it is essential to understand that the BASF is not a sequence of unrelated clauses but, in fact, a logical progression of related ideas. The meaning of words and expressions in any particular clause is based on what has been clearly defined in previous clauses and what is elaborated upon further in subsequent clauses.

The logical progression becomes self-evident when reading through the BASF:

- **Clause 1** introduces the only true God
- **Clause 2** flows from this by explaining that Jesus was the Son of God
- **Clause 3** flows from this by stating that the appearance of Jesus was necessitated by the position and state the human race had been brought by circumstances connected with the first man
- **Clause 4** flows from this by explaining that the first man was Adam created by God from the dust of the ground with a natural body of life that was very good in kind and condition, and the continuance of his life was contingent on obedience to God's laws
- **Clause 5** flows from this by explaining that Adam broke this law, was sentenced to return to the dust, and God's sentence became a physical law of his being which was transmitted to all of his posterity
- **Clause 6** flows from this by explaining that God in his kindness conceived a plan of restoration to rescue the race from destruction
- **Clause 7** flows from this by stating that God announced this plan via the promises he made to Adam, Abraham and David
- … and we could continue through every clause of the Statement of Faith in this manner.

Clause 3 states that the appearance of Jesus was necessitated by the position and state into which the human race had been brought due to circumstances connected with the first man. Clause 30 ends with the human race being completely restored to the friendship of the Deity.

The same point about the BASF being a logical progression of Bible truths is made in *"Studies in the Statement of Faith"*:

> "From the Foundation Clause which emphasises the need for implicit belief in the inspiration of the Scriptures to Clause XXX which looks forward to the day when "God will be all and in all" **there is set forth a logical progression of Divine teaching** which finds the honest assent of Christadelphians throughout the world who meet in a fellowship based upon belief in all these doctrines"[183]

It is imperative that each clause, or even a particular phrase in that clause, is not read in isolation. It needs to be read in the wider context of all the clauses, to ensure that the meaning is consistent and in harmony with the logical flow of the entire BASF.

---

[183] Ashton, Michael, *Studies in the Statement of Faith,* The Christadelphian Magazine and Publishing Association, 1991, p. 91.

SECTION 6

CHRISTADELPHIAN WRITERS ON CREATION AND THE ATONEMENT

"Remember those who led you, who spoke the word of God to you; and considering the result of their conduct, imitate their faith." (Hebrews 13:7, NASB)

Authors' Preface to Section 6

Christadelphian writers on the creation and the atonement

This section brings together eighteen Christadelphian writers from the 1840s to the 1990s on the critical subjects addressed throughout *By One Man*. Their comments also provide an overview of each writer's teachings relating to clauses 3-6, 8-10 and 12 of the BASF.

The three chapter titles in this section correspond to the three main headings at the top of the *Summary Table: Christadelphian Authors – Creation and the Atonement* presented in Section 1 on page 44. The main conclusion from this table, and the following 137 pages of quotations, is that none of these authors could agree with EC views that conflict with the BASF.

Chapter 25

No humans have evolved. Adam - the progenitor of all humanity

- *Our human race did not evolve from lower animal forms*
- *Adam was miraculously created and is the progenitor of our entire human race*

Chapter 26

Adam's sin resulted in mortality and sin-bias for all mankind

- *By one man's offence death reigns (mortality) over the human race (Romans 5:15-18)*
- *By one man's disobedience all are born with a nature that is prone to sin (Romans 5:19)*

Chapter 27

The devil - personification of fallen human nature

For the larger context of each quotation, along with additional relevant quotations by each author, please refer to the accompanying document: *By One Man: Supplementary Material*. The *Supplementary Material* is available in pdf format from either of the following websites:

cbmresources.org/forums/index.php?/topic/1156-by-one-man/

lulu.com

The authors hope that *By One Man* will serve as a valuable resource for current and future generations of Christadelphians. In this regard, the extent of Christadelphian writings presented, in both this section and the *Supplementary Material*, will significantly reduce the time and effort required for readers to search through standard books and past magazines to find sound exposition specific to these critical topics.

For Christadelphian commentary since the year 2000, a "Further Reading" bibliography is included at the end of this book.

The quotations in Chapter 26 (mortality and sin-bias) and Chapter 27 (the devil) emphasise Christ's human nature. However, often the context they are drawn from also highlights the divine side of Christ, and the paramount importance of the divine begettal in enabling Christ to be a sinless bearer of our sin-prone nature (BASF 9). Regrettably, in order to keep the number of pages of *By One Man* down, this important balance has been lost. The balance, however, can be seen in the full context provided by the *Supplementary Material*.

Chapter 25

No Humans have Evolved
Adam - the Progenitor of All Humanity

Our human race did not evolve from lower animal forms.

Adam was miraculously created and is the progenitor of our entire human race.

John Thomas

John Thomas, *The Creation of Earth and Man*, Elpis Israel, 1866, p. 11
… the earth became "without form and empty; and darkness overspread the deep waters"(Genesis 1:2). Its mountains, hills, valleys, plains, seas, rivers, and fountains of waters, which gave diversity of "form" to the surface of our globe, all disappeared; and it became "void", or empty, no living creatures, angels, quadrupeds, birds, or fishes, being found any more upon it.

John Thomas, *The Creation of Earth and Man*, Elpis Israel, 1866 pp. 11-12
Geologists have endeavoured to extend the six days into six thousand years. … The six days of Genesis were unquestionably six diurnal revolutions of the earth upon its axis. This is clear from the tenor of the sabbath law. "Six days shalt thou labour (O Israel) and do all thy work; but the seventh day is the sabbath of the Lord thy God: in it thou shalt not do any work: for in six days the Lord made heaven and earth, the sea, and all that in them is, and rested the seventh day: wherefore the Lord blessed the sabbath day, and hallowed it" (Exodus 20:9-11). … Would any Israelite or Gentile, unspoiled by vain philosophy, come to the conclusion of the geologists by reading the sabbath law? We believe not. Six days of ordinary length were ample time for Omnipotence, with all the power of the universe at command, to re-form the earth, and to place the few animals upon it necessary for the beginning of a new order of things upon the globe.

John Thomas, *Made in the Image and Likeness of Elohim*, Elpis Israel, 1866, p. 38
Man, however, differs from other creatures in having been modelled after a divine type, or pattern. In *form* and *capacity* he was made like to the angels, though in nature inferior to them. This appears from the testimony that he was made "in their image, after their likeness" (Genesis 1:26-27), and "a *little lower* than the *angels*", or Elohim (Psalm 8:5). I say, he was made in the image of the angels, as the interpretation of the co-operative imperative. "Let *us* make man in *our* image, after *our* likeness". The work of the six days, though elaborated by the power of Him "who dwelleth in the light", was executed by "his angels, that excel in strength, and do his commandments,

hearkening unto the voice of his word" (Psalm 103:20). … Man, then, was made after the image and likeness of Elohim, but for a while inferior in nature.

John Thomas, *The Formation of Woman*, Elpis Israel, 1866, pp. 47-49

Adam, having been formed in the image, after the likeness of the Elohim on the sixth day, remained for a short time alone in the midst of the earthborns of the field. He had no companion who could reciprocate his intelligence; none who could minister to his wants, or rejoice with him in the delights of creation; and reflect the glory of his nature. … Well aware of this, Yahweh Elohim said, "It is not good that the man should be alone. It will make a help fit for him" (Genesis 2:18).

But previous to the formation of this help, God caused "every living soul" (*kol nephesh chayiah*) to pass in review before Adam, that he might name them. He saw that each one had its mate; "but for him there was not found a suitable companion" (Genesis 2:20). It was necessary, therefore, to form one, the last and fairest of His handiworks. The Lord had created man in His own "image and glory"; but He had yet to subdivide him into two; a negative and a positive division; an active and a passive half; male and female, yet one flesh.

… the Lord Elohim made woman in the likeness of the man, out of his substance. … The most wonderful part of the work had yet to be performed. The quivering rib, with its nerves and vessels, had to be increased in magnitude, and formed into a human figure, capable of reflecting the glory of the man. This was soon accomplished; for, on the sixth day, "male and female created he them" (Genesis 1:27): and "the rib which the Lord God had taken from man, he made a woman, and brought her unto the man" (Genesis 2:22). … Believing this portion of the testimony of God, need our faith be staggered at the resurrection of the body from the little dust that remains after its entire reduction?

John Thomas, *The Old Serpent*, Eureka, vol. 4, 1866, pp. 66-76

In the beginning, the Serpent-World consisted of no more than two sinners—Adam and his wife; yet small as was its extent, all the evil that has since manifested itself, was latent in them.

… Genesis 3:15-19. The specifications in these sentences upon the serpent, the woman, and the man form THE CONSTITUTION of the Serpent-World, or KINGDOM OF SIN; and termed in Scripture "the Kingdom of Men"— dominion hostile to the Divine law administered by the Serpent's seed. It matters not what form the dominion assumes, whether imperial, regal, republican, or papal, its basis is one and the same; and most appropriately symbolized by the serpent which was in the beginning—*ho ophis, ho archaios*.

In after times, far distant from the beginning, the serpent-world acquired an immense development. From two persons it had increased to myriads of millions …

Robert Roberts

Robert Roberts – A Statement of the "One Faith", 1877

II. Nature of Man. - That God created Adam, the progenitor of the human race, out of the dust of the ground, as a living soul, or natural body of life; "very good" in kind and condition,[1] and placed him under a law through which the continuance of life was contingent on obedience.[2]

> [1] Genesis 2:7; Genesis 18:27; Job 4:19; Job 33:6; I Corinthians 15:46, 49.
> [2] Genesis 2:17.

Robert Roberts –The Christadelphian, vol. 15, 1878, p. 495

The evolution theories of Darwin, Huxley and Spencer, are with a small substratum of fact, mere guesses, and hideous at that, with quite as much of mystery at their roots as may ever be felt to attach to the idea of a Creator. A primary, eternal, intelligent, and, therefore, personal force, with a located nucleus of form, power and glory, is, in reality, more in harmony with the facts of the universe as we find them, than the notion of impassive force, which is only a name for something nobody can conceive.

Robert Roberts –The Christadelphian, vol. 25, 1888, p. 14

It is one of the many melancholy spectacles of the age in which we live, to find men (including numerous so-called "clergymen" and "ministers" and some Jews, alas), holding the Darwinian doctrine of evolution and yet professing to believe that the holding of that doctrine is not inconsistent with belief in God and acceptance of the Bible.

Robert Roberts, *The First Man*, The Christadelphian, vol. 25, 1888, pp 618-619, 679-681

That there was a first man, from whom the whole race of mankind extant upon the face of the earth have been derived, is among the earliest things revealed in the Scriptures, as it is also among the things subsequently confirmed by the whole tenor of Bible history. To begin with, take the situation at the period that the six days' work was commenced, and we have before us a dark waste of waters, that everywhere overspread the solid earth; and which at this point was as manifestly "void" of human life as it was of the creature existences that in due course were developed in earth, air, and sea, preliminary to the introduction of man upon the scene. Then, before the earth was fit habitation for either man or animals, it had to be clothed with verdure and planted with trees, and nature's productions of every imaginable kind (Genesis 1:11-12; 2:5). Then, again, until Adam was created it is expressly said that "there was not a man to till the ground" (Genesis 2:5). Then the fact that Adam was formed directly from the dust of the ground shows that he was an original creation, and the first of his kind, as Paul afterwards calls him in the words "the first man Adam was made a living soul" (1 Corinthians 15:45). Observe! the first man "made,' not the first man whom God took into covenant-relation. This last idea is at variance with all the essentials of the account. That this creation referred to the one particular man, afterwards called Adam, and not to "mankind" in the general sense claimed by some, admits of no question, for, says the writing, "the Lord God planted a garden eastward in Eden;

and there he put the man whom he had formed:" yes, "the man" that is definite enough for anything.

Putting Genesis and Corinthians together, we get the simple fact that "God formed the first man Adam out of the dust of the ground." To say that Adam was not the only man then existing on the face of the earth is to introduce confusion into a matter that left alone is simplicity itself; more than that, it is to introduce an element that is entirely excluded by all the facts of the case. To ask the question, "Where did Cain get his wife from?" is of no avail against such an all-excluding account. ...

To suggest that in the first instance wives were obtained from another race, altogether outside Adam and his descendants, is to seek to account for the posterity of Cain and Seth on principles that take the bottom out of the whole record, and that give the human race a start inconsistent with the unity of the race, on which the work of Christ on behalf of both Jew and Gentile is based; and which will at last include results "out of every kindred, tongue, people, and nation" (Revelation 5:9). Paul establishes the matter beyond all controversy in his address to the Gentile Athenians in saying so expressly that "God who made the world hath made of one blood all nations of men for to dwell on all the face of the earth" (Acts 17:24) and determined both "the times and bounds of their habitation." Added to this, he quotes and applies the words of Aratus, a Greek poet, that "we are also his offspring." Forasmuch, then, says he, that it is an admitted thing with the Gentiles that we are the offspring of God, we ought not, says he, to regard the Godhead as like unto gold and silver. Jew and Gentile then are equally the offspring of "Adam, who was the son of God" (Luke 3:38).

Turning back again to the beginning of things, we find that in course of time the Sethite "sons of God" (Genesis 4:26), and the Cainite "daughters of men" began to intermarry, with the results before us at the crisis of the deluge (Genesis 6:1-7), in which the whole of Cain's descendants manifestly perished; the only human souls that survived being the "eight souls saved by water" (1 Peter 3:20), consisting of Noah and his wife, and his three sons and their wives. From these the world received, as it were, a new start, with no more possibility of any outside themselves than in the watery chaos that preceded creation's dawn. Upon this point the inspired record is very express, for we read that "all flesh died that moved upon the earth, both of fowl, cattle, beast, and creeping thing, *and every man*." Then repeating the "all," it goes on to say that "all in whose nostrils was the breath of life, of all that was in the dry land died;" and that every living substance was destroyed which was upon the face of the ground; both man, cattle, creeping things, and the fowl of heaven; repeating it again, that "they were destroyed from the earth;" and that as the result of this, "Noah only remained alive, and they that were with him in the ark" (Genesis 7:21-23). This again leaves no room for any other race on the earth, than such as have descended from Noah and his three sons, and, speaking in general terms, the well-known progenitors of the people inhabiting Europe (Japhet), Asia (Shem), and Africa (Ham), and of course America, which, excepting the small percentage of its probably Hamite aboriginals, is for the most part made up of settlers from Europe. Added to this, the languages of the various nations are all manifestly but the variations of the "one language," at first common to all mankind (Genesis 11:1); but eventually diversified in connection with the postdiluvian building of Babel (Genesis 11:7–9) as at this day.

Then, the genealogies of the scriptures all confirm the fact that universal man had a common origin in one parent: take first the antediluvian genealogies; then the postdiluvian; then such as were subsequently incorporated with the history of Israel (1 Chronicles to wit, which begins with Adam); then the New Testament genealogies, which in one case begin with Abraham; and in the other run backwards up to Adam again. …

Robert Roberts, The Blood of Christ, 1895 [2006 edition], pp. 23-24
The final triumph will show us at the end a generation of Adam's race brought from the grave, belonging to different ages, having lived in different circumstances, but all related to the same hereditary evil, and who all in their several days overcame by the same power, the power of the truth testified to them, and the power of God's will declared to them and submitted to by them.

LB Welch

LB Welch, The Christadelphian, vol. 28, 1891, pp. 416-418
It was "In the Beginning" that God created the earth, or gave it material existence as the earth. Beyond that statement He has vouchsafed us no information respecting the earth's primary creation, or even an antecedent creation of living organisms upon the earth. We are next informed that the earth is in a certain state, "without form and void" (Genesis 1:1-2) This would be beautifully illustrated by assuming that the entire surface of the earth in all its parts was covered and hidden by an overwhelming flood. It would thus appear "without form and void (empty)." How long the earth had been in this condition is not stated. It may have been for many years or ages for aught we know. The next thing in order was to prepare it for new inhabitants, vegetable and animal and man. This was the work of the six creation days of Genesis. … God, as before stated, has not condescended to tell us anything about His creative work upon the earth in the preceding ages, its vegetable and its animal organic forms and the man (angel) organisms. Why should He? We do not belong to their age. Ours is the Adamic, with its vegetable, and animal, and man organisms and life.

LB Welch, The Christadelphian, vol. 32, 1895, pp. 219-224
No one can understand who Christ is until he first understands God's purpose with Adam's race, and how He proposes to carry out His purpose. The Bible tells us how the race has its origin in Adam, and how it has been condemned to death and dust in him. …

CC Walker

CC Walker, *In the Beginning*, The Christadelphian, vol. 45, 1908, pp. 5-8
We know that the popularly received doctrine of evolution scorns a literal interpretation of the Genesis account; but philosophical speculation is of little weight as against the divine revelation attested by the facts of history. It has been supposed that life came at the first by spontaneous generation, but more careful study and more refined experiment have altogether discredited this philosophy, and left us with the idea expressed in Christ's own doctrine, that the Father "hath life in Himself," and that out of Him has all life come. The divine manipulation of human affairs is altogether opposed to the doctrine of evolution. The "survival of the fittest," as men reckon fitness, is no part of God's plan, as may be seen plainly in the cases of Esau and Saul, who were rejected in favour of the comparatively undesirable Jacob and David, undesirable that is, from a merely human notion of fitness.

The creation of Adam and Eve was God's beginning of the race. There the direct divine work ceased, and the beginning of the human family was upon a different principle, namely, that of natural reproduction. Here is a sad beginning, the multiplication of sin's flesh through sorrow, which is continued in such vastly increasing proportions down to our own day, and which presents a problem which appeals to merely natural thinkers. Not so, however, with those who are enlightened by the word of God. They know the Father's purpose, and the end that He proposes in Christ.

CC Walker, The Christadelphian, vol. 46, 1909, pp. 400-405
Take, then, the Bible view, and begin at the very beginning—the account of the creation. We are fully aware that this is scoffed at by Mr. Blatchford, in common with many thousands of others, who have espoused the contradictory doctrine of evolution. He puts it exceedingly bluntly, and even offensively, talking of "our ancestors the beasts." We are well aware that that doctrine has become current, and has been widely received almost as gospel, but we nevertheless attach no weight to it, and many first-class minds are expressing their dissatisfaction with the doctrine now, even apart from the scriptures, so we need not be considered so ignorant or "behind the times" when we prefer Christ and the Bible.

... "In the beginning, God created the heaven and the earth"(Genesis 1:1); and it goes on to record the various stages of the creation of day and night, firmament, sea, and vegetation, and animal life. But this creation does not so particularly concern us now. We want to come down to the creation of man, for that is where the conflict between the Bible and modern philosophy comes in upon this particular question. "God said, Let us make man in our image, after our likeness, and let them have dominion. . . . So God created man in his own image, in the image of God created he him, male and female created he them" (Genesis 1:26-27).

... Thus Eve, together with Adam, was, indeed, *the direct creation of God*, and here it may be remarked that we have the first *allegorical* intimation of "the will of God in Christ." We take this record as Christ himself took it, as divine, and worthy of all acceptance. ... Under these circumstances, then, the first human pair, *the direct creation of God*, were placed under probation by reason of God's command contained in Genesis 2:17 …

CC Walker, The Christadelphian, vol. 77, 1940, p. 109
… Likewise, the Apostle Paul says: "The first man Adam was made a living soul" (1 Corinthians 15:45), eliminating that same doctrine, which says there never was such a being, but he evolved from the anthropoid apes; and you cannot put your finger on anyone, and say, This is the first man. Paul, like Christ, worked miracles. He was a real man of God, to whom we should listen. And Jesus says: "He that made them at the beginning" (Matthew 19:4-5).

Henry Sulley

Henry Sulley, The Christadelphian, vol. 45, 1908, p. 519
"… Mr. Sulley deprecates the theory of evolution, and thus opposes himself at the start to the main hypothesis on which men of science build their biological and geological data. His sturdy stand by the letter of Christian law must command respect even from those who are unable to regard it with sympathy."

Henry Sulley, The Christadelphian, vol. 58, 1921, p. 437
Sin having entered into the world, and death having passed upon all men (Romans 5:12), deliverance from death must be according to the Divine prerogative. Just as one born a slave under State law is only liberated upon the condition which the supreme authority imposes, so deliverance from the state or constitution of Sin which passed upon the human race from Adam, can only come on the condition, or conditions, prescribed by the Father.

Henry Sulley, *The Atonement (10)*, The Christadelphian, vol. 59, 1922, pp. 435-441
… In thus voicing the obvious change which occurred in creation after the introduction of sin in the world I know that I am in opposition to scientists with their foolish imaginings against God, but "there are more things in heaven and earth than are dreamt of in their philosophy." So it is written that "the wisdom of this world is foolishness with God. For . . . He taketh the wise in their own craftiness" (1 Corinthians 3:19). Continually the inferences of the scientists are shown to be wrong, and a new generation abandons the conclusions of their fathers. Not so with the Bible, its simple truths are constantly receiving verification. Written and unwritten changes have occurred in the past, others lie ahead of which we have definite information in the word of God.

John Carter

John Carter, *Evolution Or Creation*, The Christadelphian, vol. 72, 1935, pp. 444-448
DESIGN - … Many eminent scientists have not hesitated to avow their conviction that the world bespeaks a Creator. In the words of Lord Kelvin: "Overpowering proofs of intelligent design lie around us"; and of Agassiz: "The phenomena of organic life have all the wealth and intricacy of the

highest manifestations of mind." The very character of some features of design are a powerful argument against evolution. Holes in bones for arteries and sinews to pass through them, pulleywise, could not be a development; they could not come gradually, for they are only of use when complete.

The case is well put by Paul when he says that God has not left Himself without witness, in that He did good, and gave us rain from heaven and fruitful seasons (Acts 14:15). Again: "The invisible things of God, from the creation of the world are clearly seen, being understood by the things that are made, even his everlasting power and divinity" (Romans 1:20).

CHRIST AND GENESIS - ... The divine origin of the Old Testament being proved by the endorsement of the risen Lord, its testimony to the facts of creation is the testimony of God. Bible teaching excludes evolution. "God created the heavens and the earth." "After its kind" is a recurring description of the separation that exists between the different kinds of creatures (Genesis 1:11, 12, 21, 24, 25). And, "God created man in his own image" (Genesis 1:26-27).

John Carter, *The Reign of Death*, The Christadelphian, vol. 75, 1938, pp. 173-174

In apostolic language, Death reigns. A child is born—it may die during its earliest days before it has known either good or evil, or it may grow to adult life. But we know that in time death will come. Why? Is it for the same reason that other forms of life come to an end? The insect, which is a creature of few days, and the animal whose natural span of life exceeds that of man, alike die. Is there no other cause for man's death than for that of the insect or the animal? We might so conclude if we had no revelation; we should so conclude if we accepted the theory of man's descent from animal origin as set forth by the teachers of evolution. But with revelation to guide us, another conclusion is reached.

John Carter – Prophets After the Exile, 1945, pp. 66-67, 80 (1962 Edition)

We are all mortal independently of personal sin; and that mortality is an inherited one, and its ultimate cause is the sin at the beginning of human history. All Adam's posterity are involved in the consequences of his transgression, Jesus being no exception.

John Carter, *Marriage – The Divine Ideal*, The Christadelphian, vol. 86, 1949, p. 168

Theories of origins of human life influence thought, and slowly but surely are reflected in the customs of men and women. If evolution provides the correct explanation of life on earth, and therefore has proved the idea of God to be baseless, then men are free to devise such marriage relationships as they choose, trial and error showing what is best for the individual and for society.

... When the Bible is accepted as a divine record of man's origin and of his history, the subject of marriage relationships is lifted on to the highest level. Speculations concerning origins of various customs can be forgotten; the subject is seen in the context of divine aims and purposes with man.

Islip Collyer

Islip Collyer, The Vegetable in the Witness Box, 1922, pp. 93-94

... the [Evolution] development theory does not and cannot, throw any light upon the origin of Nature's wonders; it is not in any way the complete explanation of life that some people have supposed; it is, nevertheless, a serious challenge to religion in that it tends to remove God so far from His creatures.

Islip Collyer, Conviction & Conduct, 1944, pp. 33-34

An exponent of an evolution theory once rather sneeringly remarked that Christians were continually trying to find gaps in the doctrine of development that they might fill them up with God. The truth lies exactly the other way. The atheistic theorists say in effect, "Grant us a world of matter with certain forces and properties which make it fall into proper order. Grant us creatures with life, and able to reproduce their kind; creatures with nerves sensitive to light in a world where there is light, with nerves sensitive to sound and surrounded by a medium which will convey sound. Grant also that these creatures are liable to produce chance variations covering in the aggregate the whole range of Nature's equipment; and we can fill in the gaps without the aid of God." The answer is that there are no gaps to fill in.

Islip Collyer, Conviction & Conduct, 1944, pp. 62-63

The sceptical deist moves a step farther back. He says God did not make these creatures, but that they are the products of a natural evolution. ... To our limited perceptions, it may seem terrible that God should curse man for his sins, and that so many tragedies should be enacted during this period of selection and probation; but surely it would be vastly more terrible if God has started life on earth, and then without a care for any of His creatures and without any final object in view, had left the earth to a million years of purposeless suffering.

WF Barling

WF Barling, Law and Grace, 1952, p.24

God again declared, "Let us make man in our image, after our likeness" (Genesis 1:26-27). This similarly expressed both His decision to create man and also His motive in doing so; that is, it defined both the nature and the destiny of man at once. The decision became fact like the others before it— "So God created man in his own image, in the image of God created he him"—yet not in the full sense intended. As far as Adam was concerned it became true of him physically and mentally when he was formed of the dust of the ground; but through his failure under trial it was prevented from becoming true of him morally and spiritually as well. Moreover, as subsequent events so sadly confirmed, his lapse involved all his progeny so that in his one failure the whole of mankind fell short of its ideal destiny.

WF Barling, Law and Grace, 1952, p.81
Yet she and other men and women like her did God's work by preserving from generation to generation the knowledge of the promises to Abraham; and not only of the promises, but also of Abraham's call, and of all that that bespoke—the dividing of the nations; before that, the Flood; and backwards, eventually, to the events of Creation with their tragic sequel in the sin of Adam, the father of us all.

AD Norris

AD Norris, *Where Science and Religion Meet, 1. What Does the Plain Man Do?*, The Christadelphian, vol. 101, 1964, pp. 437-439
The Lord and the Genesis Record - In setting out his teaching on the permanence of marriage, the Lord answers his critics in terms of Genesis 1 and 2 (Matthew 19:1–8, etc.). God made them in the beginning male and female (Genesis 1), and said, "Therefore shall a man leave his father and mother and cleave unto his wife" (Genesis 2). Both the "creation records" are included in one statement, and made the basis of the true teaching on marriage. …

Though outside the record of the Creation, other aspects of the Genesis story also receive the Lord's confirmation, including the assassination of Abel (Matthew 23:35), the historicity of the Flood (Luke 17:26–27), of the destruction of Sodom and Gomorrah (Luke 17:28–32), and of the life of Abraham in general. In all these cases, his confirmation of the record is bound up with the lesson which he draws from it, and the one would fall without the other.

The Apostles and the Genesis Record - The evidence is more specific here. As the apostles settle down to write for us the meaning of the work of the Lord, they draw in the historical basis and interpret it for us; and so, when Paul says that "by one man sin entered into the world, and death by sin, and so death passed upon all men, for that all have sinned" (Romans 5:12), it is impossible to understand this without the assurance that Paul was satisfied of the existence and the uniqueness of that "one man" to whom he refers. When he adds, "Since by man came death, by man came also the resurrection of the dead" and "As in Adam all die, even so in Christ shall all be made alive" (1 Corinthians 15:21–22), he bases the work of the Lord Jesus in overcoming sin and death, on the fact that sin and death are owed by all of us to our descent from this Adam. Adam and Christ are equally real to Paul: the one man is from the earth, earthy (a very evident quotation of Genesis 2), while the second is "the Lord from heaven".

Paul seems, in fact, to have indicated something of the kind in his address to the Athenians, saying that "God hath made of one all nations of men for to dwell on the face of the earth" (Acts 17:24–26). For this, too, has the Genesis record as its basis.

AD Norris, *Where Science and Religion Meet: 7. The Creation and Fall of Man*, The Christadelphian, vol. 102, 1965, pp. 148-150
If these man-like creatures were on the earth long before a few thousand years B.C., then the conception of Adam as the first man is obviously not as

simple as used to be thought before these discoveries were made. If they should be accepted as the "ancestors", or as related to the ancestors, of civilized man, then our ideas of Adam's origin and uniqueness, if we felt able to form any at all, would need radical readjustment.

At this point, particularly, we must refresh ourselves with the confidence we have expressed throughout this series: whatever conclusions we may come to, and whatever matters are left inconclusive, the foundation of God standeth sure. The Genesis record is divine by its own marks, and it is divine and authoritative on the testimony of the Son of God himself. We are troubled, if we are troubled at all, by the tangled surface of things, and not by any doubts as to the solid foundation for faith we possess in the records.

… Whatever the unsolved problems we have left, the risen Lord vindicates the Scriptures; their own sublimity in their creation records marks them out as from God, in contrast to the views held by the nations around at the time when they were written; the nature of our thinking demands that God, as supreme Thinker, lies behind our being; the nature of the scientific evidence available does nothing to militate against this; the facts of our moral nature both testify to the truth of the Fall as recorded in Genesis, and provide the reason for the coming of the Son of God—the Son of God whose resurrection irresistibly assures us that this fabric of revelation comes from his Father in heaven.

AD Norris, *The Universal Consequences of the Sin of Adam*, Acts and Epistles, pp. 425-427
Romans 5:12: First of all we have the plain fact that we are all descended from the first created man, Adam, and that it was his sin that involved us in the situation in which we find ourselves.

LG Sargent

LG Sargent, *The Origin of Man*, The Christadelphian, vol. 102, 1965, pp. 340-346
Bro. Lovelock's solution is that Adam was "a selected and divinely modified member of a race already numerous in the earth", that he was selected by God to be His witness to this race, and given such extra powers as marked him out as a leader and assured the successful spread of his way of life. Adam, like Christ, was a "representative man", and this did not exclude the incorporation among his descendants of those who were not physically of his race.

Against this we have the words of Paul at Athens: "He made of one every nation of men for to dwell on all the face of the earth" (Acts 17:26, R.V.); and as was recently pointed out, while this can mean "of one man" or "of one race", it cannot mean anything else. Nor can there be any doubt that Paul was referring to the Biblical account of man's creation in Genesis 2, and it is not enough to say that the whole race is from one pre-Adamic interbreeding stock.

Against this bro. Lovelock would stress the representative character he attributes to Adam, and would appeal to 1 Corinthians 15:45–49. But Paul's contrast of the first Adam and the last surely only strengthens the case against his view: "For as in Adam all die, so in Christ shall all be made alive" (1 Corinthians 15:22). Can there be any doubt that Paul means we are "in" Adam as mortal sinners because we inherit our nature from him, but we are "in" Christ on the spiritual basis of faith and obedience in baptism, so that in him "there is neither Jew nor Greek, bond nor free, male nor female: for ye are all one in Christ Jesus"? Paul's argument is "first the natural, then the spiritual", and the very point of his teaching is that in the spiritual relationship the bounds of race and even of sex are transcended. It is simply not relevant to argue back from this to the natural, and suggest (as bro. Lovelock does) that because "aliens" may be incorporated into Christ "aliens" from the Adamic race might be assimilated into Adam's descendants. And only with a wrench from anything which Paul could conceivably have meant himself can it be reconciled with Paul's teaching on the coming of sin and death into human life, and the consequences for the whole race which followed from Adam's transgression. "By one man sin entered into the world, and death by sin, and so death has passed upon all men, for that all have sinned" (Romans 5:12). What happened to any pre-Adamic race, we cannot know; that there may have been such beings has never been denied; what we cannot admit is that they could have had any part in the Gospel of salvation as preached to the race of Adam.

The point which has been discussed is another example of the fallacies which pervade this work—arguing back from antitype to type; confusing the symbol with the thing symbolized; depriving the symbol of its literal basis (which must be different in kind from the thing symbolized) and then confusing the symbol with its object. To describe Christ, who comes within the Adamic race and represents it in sacrifice, as a "representative man" expresses a truth; to apply the same term to the one whom all scripture presents as the progenitor of the race is not a true comparison; it rests on a theory which is against the whole tenor of the scripture message which so clearly portrays the first pair as unique and alone, and their acts as governing the condition of the whole succeeding race.

.... The further development of bro. Lovelock's study is dependent on the line of argument so far surveyed. ... That archaeology presents problems, we must admit; but it is the supposed intermingling of the Adamic strain with contemporary races outside Adam which is so intractable to reconcile with the Biblical revelation; and Genesis 6:1–2 is a wholly inadequate basis for the structure of speculation offered here.

... Now, it is true that there are devout Christians such as Professor C. A. Coulson who take a strictly uniformitarian view of the universe and believe that evolution can be regarded as God's method in creation. The objection to this does not rest only, or even mainly, on the early chapters of Genesis. It is that an evolutionary view does not fit in with essential elements of the Faith; where it is adopted there must sooner or later be changes in the Biblical conceptions of the Fall and Atonement, in the nature of revelation, in the literal fact of resurrection, and in the character of the Kingdom of God. Of this there is abundant example in the teaching of the churches around us where an evolutionary philosophy has come to be accepted. If adopted among us I am convinced that it would in time pervade the whole of our belief and change it as the doctrine of the Immortality of the Soul changed the belief of the early church.

LG Sargent, The Christadelphian, vol. 102, 1965, p. 401
As to Acts 17:26, in my view "of one man" or "of one race" included all that could be meant by the reading "of one blood". Bro. Lovelock has made me imply that "a large portion of mankind is cut off from salvation". Of course I meant no such thing. Such an idea could only arise where it is first accepted that they are not of Adamic descent. The fact remains that throughout revelation the only race dealt with in creation, fall and redemption is the race of Adam; and there is no indication of the existence of any other race unless it be in a few vague hints of doubtful interpretation such as Genesis 6:1. The conclusion must be that any beings of a creation prior to Adam indicated by archaeological remains could have no place in redemption in Christ Jesus.

LG Sargent, *Our Faith and our Body*, The Christadelphian, vol. 103, 1966, p.124
I believe that the early chapters of Genesis mean that the first man and woman came into being by a special act of Divine creation, and that they are the progenitors of the race who are the subjects of God's redemptive work. I believe that on this fact the Bible teaching on God's redemptive purpose is based, and that the revelation through psalmists, prophets, Christ and the apostles rests upon it. It is therefore involved in later Bible teaching, and does not stand only upon our own reading of Genesis.

Edward Whittaker

Whittaker, E, *The Genesis Record of Creation*, The Testimony, vol. 39, 1969, pp. 127-134
As may be expected, some Christians, especially among the young, have been profoundly disturbed by the apparent conflict between science and Genesis, and many anxious attempts have been made to resolve the differences. Unfortunately, it has to be said without fear of contradiction that this problem has done more than any other to divide the Brotherhood into "intellectuals" and "non-intellectuals".

... Evolution, whether Darwinian or Theistic, requires an imperceptibly slow progress of all forms of life over millions of years. By contrast, Genesis describes creative acts performed instantaneously, at the fiat of God's will. No amount of mental or verbal jugglery can harmonise the two viewpoints. "And God said . . . and it was so" (the first phrase nine times, the second phrase seven times). "He spake and it was done: He commanded and it stood fast" (Psalm 33:9). Such a rapid execution of "the good pleasure of His will" would need no more than twenty-four hours for each stage of creation, especially when the case for a very limited scope of creation advanced later is agreed on.

... The living species seem to have been made according to one general pattern of procedure. Man was first formed of the dust of the ground and then made to live (2:7), as also were "every beast of the field and every fowl of the air" (2:19). The plants were first formed and then planted in the soil to "bring forth, each yielding seed" (Genesis 2:5; 1:11-12). Which came first, the hen or the egg? Scripture supplies the answer.

… Scripture teaches repeatedly that all the human race has descended from one pair. "The first man Adam was made a living soul… the first man is of the earth" (1 Corinthians 15:45, 47). "By one man sin entered into the world… death reigned from Adam to Moses… if by one man's offence death reigned by one… by the offence of one judgement came upon all men to condemnation" (Romans 5:12-18). God "hath made of one every nation of men for to dwell on all the face of the earth" (Acts 17:26 R.V.). "There was not a help meet found for man" (Genesis 2:20).

If, therefore, it is scientifically proved that the fossils that have been discovered are actual remains of races living hundreds of thousands of years ago—and many still are not satisfied with the evidence—such pre-Adamic men must have become completely extinct before God founded our present race.

Peter Watkins

Peter Watkins, *Some Difficult Passages, Book 1*, The Christadelphian Isolation League, p. 9
Next, we take note of the description of the Lord Jesus as "the image of the invisible God, the firstborn of all creation" (Colossians 1:15,R.V). These words are an echo of Genesis 1:26: "And, God said, Let us make man in our image, after our likeness". Although the Lord Jesus was doubtless in the mind of God when this intention was expressed, there was obviously an immediate application to Adam. In a limited sense, he was created in God's image, as Genesis 1:27 states; and he was the firstborn of the human creation — all others descending from him. Adam failed, and the image was shattered. The natural descendants of Adam were doomed to failure. A new creation was necessary. Accordingly the Lord Jesus was created in the image of God, and it was God's intention that he should be the beginning — the firstborn — of the new creation.

Alfred Nicholls

Alfred Nicholls, *The Spirit of God*, The Christadelphian, vol. 111, 1974, pp. 315-318
In Genesis 2:7 we read of the formation of man from the dust of the ground to await the quickening breath which made him "a living soul". The Spirit of God had made him, and the breath of the Almighty had given him life. So God "who only hath immortality" is He "who quickeneth all things" (1 Timothy 6:13–16), and we are once again taught that the study of the Spirit of God is the study of God Himself in action and in the revelation of Himself. His purpose and activity, however, extend far beyond the natural creation, and beyond the gentle sustaining of what He has made, and His life is fuller than the existence of man with whom His spirit strives, "for that (man) also is flesh" (Genesis 6:3). God therefore sent His Son, that men "might have life, and that they might have it more abundantly". He who made the first man Adam a living soul, made the last Adam "a quickening spirit" (1 Corinthians 15:45).

The Committee of the Christadelphian (Alfred Nicholls), *In Adam or In Christ,* **The Christadelphian, vol. 112, 1975, pp. 390-403**
… Adam was not merely an individual man, but the progenitor of the human race of which he and his wife were then the sole representatives.

Alfred Nicholls, *The Legacy of Darwinism,* **The Christadelphian, vol. 119, 1982, pp. 146-148**
… Surely, then, evolution is a sign of the times, an indication of what Peter foresaw: "There shall come in the last days scoffers, walking after their own lusts, and saying, Where is the promise of his coming? for since the fathers fell asleep, *all things continue as they were from the beginning* of creation" (2 Peter 3:4). No words could better describe current uniformitarian and evolutionary thought—the belief that all that we see around us has come about of its own accord through aeons of gradual change.

In God's dealings with this planet, and most particularly in the outworking of His purpose with man, all things do *not* "continue as they were", steered only by some law of chance towards an unknown and uncertain goal. God, though He gave man freewill, has intervened; He has "determined the times before appointed, and the bounds of their habitation" (Acts 17:26). We believe in catastrophism—the opposite of evolution—for God has worked, and will fulfil His works in acts of revelation, in miracles, in deeds of judgement and of grace. The day of the Lord will come, not by slow processes of change and improvement (in any case the present trend of civilisation is downward not upward), but suddenly and cataclysmically, "as a thief; in the which the heavens shall pass away with a great noise, and the elements shall be dissolved with fervent heat … Seeing that these things are thus all to be dissolved, what manner of persons ought ye to be in all holy living and godliness" (2 Peter 3:10–11).

Alan Hayward

Alan Hayward, God's Truth, 1973, *Chapter 23 – How the Human Race Began*
One thing we dare not do. We must not take the easy way out and say, "Adam was just a myth." That way lies disaster. I have tried to show throughout this book that we must let the Bible speak for itself. We must not twist it, to make it mean what we think it ought to have said. We must let it make its own message clear to us.

… So we have to begin with the question: what does the New Testament say about Adam? The answer is sharply defined, clear and unmistakable. Adam was a real person. He and his wife, Eve, were the ancestors of the whole human race. Several lines of evidence lead to this conclusion. There are the words quoted from Luke's Gospel in the first paragraph of this chapter 1. There is the way that Jesus referred to Adam and Eve. He spoke of them in the same literal way as the other historical characters of the Old Testament. Above all, there is the teaching of Paul. As was shown in Chapter 14, his whole teaching about sin and death and salvation had two foundation stones. One was a historical Adam, whose sin started a pattern of sinfulness that has affected all his descendants. The other was a historical Jesus, who came to save some of the sons of Adam from sin and death, and give them everlasting life. Remove one of those twin foundations and the whole structure of Christianity collapses. If Adams sin was a myth, then Christ's righteousness might have been a myth, too.

One thing is certain: Christianity - that is, real Christianity, Biblical Christianity, the Christianity of Christ and His apostles - starts with the sad, true story of events in the Garden of Eden. This is our starting point. Within this framework we must look for a solution to our problem.

.... The Bible's teaching about the origin of mankind is beautiful in its simplicity. By a special creative act God made the first man and woman, after He had made all the rest of creation. From these two the whole human race is descended. This explanation satisfied men and women three thousand years ago. It is still eminently sensible today. It can stand up to the critical scrutiny of our scientific age.

How can this be? Every other ancient account of creation and the origin of life reads like childish nonsense in the modern world. Why is the Bible so different? There is an obvious answer. The Bible is the inspired Word of God.

Alan Hayward, God's Truth, 1973, *Chapter 25 – The Real Problems*
… Chapter 23 showed that the shakiest part of this shaky theory is that which deals with the evolution of man. We saw that Adam and Eve were real people; that they were specially created by God as the ancestors of the whole human race; and that we are not told how long ago they lived.

Alan Hayward, *The Real Devil*, Christadelphian Bible Mission, 1975
The first three chapters of the first book, Genesis, tell us how God created this world and the first human beings, Adam and Eve. He gave them a law to keep, but they disobeyed Him. (page 3)

Alan Hayward, Creation and Evolution, 1985, pp. 198–199
Conservatives quite rightly take their lead from the New Testament and insist that the Fall was a real historical event, and not just a myth or an allegory. Yet they always seem to gloss over the Biblical details of the Fall, which are exceedingly difficult to fit into any sort of evolutionary picture.

HP Mansfield

HP Mansfield, The Christadelphian Expositor, Genesis, 1972, p.44
"After their kind" (Genesis 1:11, 12, 21, 24, 25) — This is a very important statement and disposes at once with all variation of evolutionary theories. There was no provision of transition from one specie to another, but all brought forth "after their kind." This statement provides no room for divergence as mutants from a common ancestor, but shows that each form of life was independently created. However there is scope for development within a species, so that it is possible, by breeding, to improve the quality of a particular species of animal, but a horse remains a horse, a sheep remains a sheep, a dog remains a dog, even in spite of cross-breeding.

HP Mansfield, The Christadelphian Expositor, Genesis, 1972, p.48
"So God created" — This is the third and last time that this word, bara, occurs in this chapter (see Genesis 1:1, 21). In each case it implies something different from that stated before, and certainly does not suggest continuity with that which previously existed, as evolutionists suggest. On the contrary, its emphasis is on a new departure caused by creation. In Numbers 16:30, the words, "Make a new thing" represent in literal Hebrew, "Create a creation." There is no room for evolutionary development from the lower animals in the declaration of Genesis 1:27. Any such theory whether Theistic evolution or otherwise is at variance with the Word of God.

HP Mansfield, The Christadelphian Expositor, Genesis, 1972, p.109
Genesis 5:5 *"And all the days that Adam lived were nine hundred and thirty years: and he died"* — Adam did not live a millennium; even Methuselah failed to do that in contrast to the hope set before the faithful who will, exceed that period of time (Revelation 20:6). It must have been a dramatic moment for the human race when its progenitor Adam, finally died, and the Divine decree (Genesis 3:19) was evident in his decease. The stark statement, and he died occurs with monotonous regularity throughout this chapter (Genesis 5:5, 8, 11, 14, 17, 20, 27, 31), emphasising the hopelessness of flesh in spite of the long lives lived by the antediluvians. Inevitably the same end awaits even a Methuselah, so that the reoccurring statement he died becomes the theme of a life related to the flesh.

HP Mansfield, The Christadelphian Expositor, Genesis, 1972, p.112
Genesis 5:23 *"And all the days of Enoch were three hundred sixty and five years"* — Like the shining Sun of Righteousness (Malachi 4:2), he completed his course: a prophetical solar year. Two notable yet contrasting events occurred during this period, within sixty years of each other. In the year 930 A.C. Adam, the father of the human race, died; and in the year 987 A.C., Enoch was "translated that he should not see death" (Hebrews 11:5). The death of so notable a man as Adam must have caused a sensation, and would have united both branches of the human race (sons of God and sons of Cain) in a common mourning.

Harry Whittaker

Harry Whittaker, Genesis 1-2-3-4, Biblia, 1986
The Creation versus Evolution controversy has gone almost without mention. This present author protests that he has not the vivid imagination (nor the gullibility) to take modern evolution theory seriously. On the other hand, he has tremendous confidence in the commentary on Genesis 1-4 which has been provided, more copiously than is usually believed, by the Lord Jesus Christ and the writers of the New Testament. (p. vi)

These creatures, like all the rest, are to multiply, but only "after their kind" (Genesis 1:11, 12, 21, 24, 25). Here is laid down the continuing law of life on earth - the permanence of the species. Here are boundaries which no amount of scientific research and contrivance can overpass. All cross-breeds go sterile or revert to type. So evolution is an impossibility. (p.30

The words "image" and "likeness" have a variety of very suggestive associations, especially in the New Testament:

(a) "Verily every man at his best state is altogether vanity. Surely every man walketh in a vain shew" (Psalm 39:6; literally: "in an image", of his own devising? or in an image not of his Creator but of his fallen forefather? "Adam begat a son in *his own* likeness, after *his* image" (Genesis 5:3). Likeness to Elohim must not be over-stressed at the expense of man's kinship with the beasts. He was made out of dust on the same day as they; like theirs, his "multiplying" was blessed; and he was appointed the same food (v. 29, 30). At the same time, "in our image"(Genesis 1:26-27) utterly denies man's evolution from a lower state. (p.32)

Harry Tennant

Harry Tennant, *Living to Die*, The Christadelphian, 1963, vol. 100, pp. 56-57
Let us take very careful note. There is witness here to creation as well as death. When the dust returns to the earth and the spirit to God this is the complete undoing of that first work when the Lord God formed man from the dust of the ground, breathed into his nostrils the breath of life and man became a living soul. He came from unconsciousness—and we all bear witness to that—and he goes back into it.

Harry Tennant, *One*, The Christadelphian, vol. 100, 1963 pp. 314-316
ONE is a beginning. Indeed, it was the beginning, for all things spring from the one God. Such, too, was the beginning of the human race. Paul gave emphasis to this on Mars Hill when he declared: "God . . . made of one every nation of men for to dwell on all the face of the earth" (Acts 17:26, R.V.). From one man all men have come, and all share the one's blessings and cursings. And so with the new creation. There was one new man when Christ our Lord was glorified in immortality. He remains the unique, the first, the one Lord who still awaits the day of meeting with his brethren. The black heavens hold one star, the Star of Jacob, and we wait in faith for the day when he shall be joined by a numberless host of radiant orbs whose eternal light will show forth the praises of the Father of lights and His Son, the light of the world.

Harry Tennant, The Christadelphians – What They Believe And Preach, 1986 pp. 6-9
The crown of creation was man. Man was unique. He was made from the lowest of materials, but was wonderfully fashioned and given life by God:

"The Lord God formed man of the dust of the ground, and breathed into his nostrils the breath of life; and man became a living soul." (Genesis 2:7)

"IN THE IMAGE OF GOD"
The Bible tells us something more about man, something which accounts for the uniqueness which differentiates him from the other parts of creation. Man was related directly to his Maker:

"God created man in his own image, in the image of God created he him; male and female created he them." (Genesis 1:27)

The expressions, "in the image of God" and "after our likeness" (see verse 26 also) are used only about man. At this stage the Bible does not develop all that lies behind these intriguing words, but it is preparing us for the accounts which follow.

Michael Ashton

Michael Ashton, *The Beginning*, The Christadelphian, vol. 136, 1999, p.104
The opening chapters of Genesis contain information which records the Creative work of God by His Spirit, but they do not explain precisely how long ago it occurred, nor in modern scientific terms how it was accomplished: "Through faith we understand that the worlds were framed by the word of God, so that things which are seen were not made of things which do appear" (Hebrews 11:3). We are told about the introduction of human life and the test to which it was put; and the consequences of failure, both for our first parents and for all their descendants.

… Apart from the revelation in Genesis itself, what do the scriptures reveal about the beginning of life? Some words of the Apostle Paul to the philosophers of his day form a useful introduction:

> "God that made the world and all things therein … is Lord of heaven and earth … he giveth to all life, and breath, and all things; and hath made of one blood all nations of men for to dwell on all the face of the earth … they should seek the Lord … For in him we live, and move, and have our being … we are the offspring of God." (Acts 17:24–29)

There are some important statements here which confirm the message of Genesis. Paul told the Athenians that:

- all the material world was made by God
- He is the author and sustainer of life
- He peopled the world with a race of individuals who all descended from one original source
- Men and women should "seek the Lord", who intends to fill the earth with His glory.

It is therefore of no surprise to find the same Apostle writing to believers in Corinth and referring to, "*The first man* Adam (who) was made a living soul" (1 Corinthians 15:45). Jesus himself commented on these early events in human history and, as we would expect, he confirmed what we have already discovered: "He which made them at the beginning (i.e., from the beginning of the creation, Mark 10:6) made them male and female" (Matthew 19:4).

… This common heritage of the human race is explained in Genesis when we are told that Adam at the age of 130 years, "begat a son in his own likeness, after his image" (Genesis 5:3). And the New Testament comment continues the idea when we read, "That which is born of the flesh is flesh" (John 3:6). Like begets like. Adam's new condition was shared by all his descendants, without exception.

Chapter 26
Adam's Sin Resulted in Mortality and Sin-Bias for All Mankind

By one man's offence death reigns (mortality) over the entire human race (Romans 5:12, 15-18)

By one man's disobedience all are born with a nature that is prone to sin (Romans 5:12, 19, 21; 6:6, 12).

John Thomas

John Thomas, The Herald of the Future Age, vol. 2, 1846, p. 80.
When born into the existing world, we come under the curse and a sentence of death; or, as the Apostle saith, we are *"made subject to* vanity (*mataiotes,* all that pertain to the state of good and evil and which ends in dissolution,) *not willingly"*[Romans 8:20]. It is in this sense, that the world of mankind is said to be *"condemned already"*—"he that believeth not," whether the faithlessness be predicated on physical or circumstantial disability matters not, all unbelievers are "condemned already." John 3:18. Because of this congenital condemnation it is that we suffer evil from our birth, die and return to the ground from which we originally came; but, well would it be for multitudes, if the condemnation which rests upon them did not transcend this. The sentence under which we are involuntarily born has no reference to the Second Death; it subjects mortals only to present evil and to a return to the dust, which is final and eternal, to those who die in "times of ignorance." Were there no other sentence than this pronounced upon mankind there would be no Second Death, which is the penalty, not of the Eden Law, but for the transgression of subsequent ones.

John Thomas, Clerical Theology Unscriptural, 1850, pp. 9–10
BOANERGES: O fie, Heresian; I thought you had more sense than to talk thus. You do not seem to know what *sin* is. If I did not know otherwise, I should have concluded that you had been studying tractarianism in the dark and mystic groves of Isis, among the Puseys and the Newmans of its cloistered halls. You ought to know that the primitive sense of the word is *"the transgression of law;"* and the derived sense that of *evil in the flesh.* Transgression is to this evil as cause to an effect; which effect re-acts in the posterity of the original transgressors as a cause, which, uncontrolled by belief of the truth, evolves transgression in addition to those natural ills, disease, death, and corruption, which are inherent in flesh and blood. Because he transgressed the Eden-law, Adam is said to have sinned. *Evil* was then evolved in his flesh as the punishment of his *sin;* and because the evil was the punishment of the sin, it is also styled sin. "Flesh and blood"

is naturally and hereditarily full of this evil. It is, therefore, called "sinful flesh," or flesh full of sin. Hence, an apostle saith, "in me, that is, in my flesh, dwelleth no good thing" (Romans 7:18). The absence of goodness in our physical nature is the reason of flesh and blood being termed *"sin."* "The Word was made flesh;" a saying which Paul synonymizes by the expression, "God hath made Jesus *sin* for us who knew no sin" (2 Corinthians 5:21): and Peter by the words, "He made his own self bear our sins *in his own body*" (1 Peter 2:24). "God made Jesus sin," in the sense of "making him of a woman" (Galatians 4:4), or of flesh and blood; so that having the same nature, its evil was condemned in his flesh, and consequently the sins of those who believe the gospel of the Kingdom were then borne away, if they have faith also in the breaking of his body for sin (Romans 8:3; Luke 22:19). Besides this, John says, that "all unrighteousness is sin;" and another apostle, that "whatsoever is not of faith is sin." Now, Heresian, I should like you, or some of your spiritual lords, to inform me what sins, actual or original, are remitted to an infant in the "baptismal regeneration" they talk so much about?

HERESIAN: Really, I must confess that in view of the premises you have laid down, I am at a loss to say. They cannot be actual, because they have transgressed no law. May it not, however, be the original sin? They committed that sin when in the loins of Adam. Their souls then contracted a liability to the pains of hell for ever; but by regeneration they are freed from that liability, and become "heirs of the grace of life."

BOANGERES: Who told you that men, women, and babes became liable to eternal torments in hell-fire because Adam transgressed the Eden-law? There is no such absurdity in the Bible; it is but a fiction of the schools. Adam's offence entailed upon us *subjection to vanity* (Romans 8:20), or to the ills that flesh inherits in the present state, which are terminated in death and corruption. If after the Lord God had sentenced man to this (Genesis 3:17–19), he had interposed between him and his destiny no more his race, by the operation of natural causes, would have become as extinct as though it had never existed. But God's philanthropy is preparing a better state for man, to which they of this and past generations stand related *by faith in the truth concerning it*. Infants die because they are born of mortal flesh, and not because they have committed sin, or are responsible for Adam's sin. If this were remitted in baptism *they ought not to die*; for when God remits sin He also remits the punishment, or consequences, it entails.

John Thomas, The Herald of the Kingdom and Age to Come, vol. 2, 1852, p. 182
The word *sin* is used in two senses; first, to represent that combination of principles within us which in excitation is manifested in passion, evil affections of the mind, diseases, death and corruption. They are called sin, because their manifestation was permitted as the consequence of transgression. And this is the second sense of the word; as it is written, "sin is the transgression of law." Transgression was the effect of *the unbridled inworking of humanity*; and when the transgression was complete, or "finished," that inworking and its result were both styled *sin*.

John Thomas, The Herald of the Kingdom and Age to Come, vol. 2, 1852, pp. 200-201
If there had been nothing in the constitution of the original nature of man impressible by the suggestions of the Serpent, there could have been no transgression. Had Eve's nature been "insangelic" instead of animal, there would have been no internal response to the external enticement. That internal something was not essentially evil; because, though possessing it, Adam and Eve were pronounced "very good." It is not evil to admire the beautiful, and to wish to possess it; to desire to gratify the taste, and to aspire to the wisdom of "the gods," or Elohim; but all this becomes evil when its attainment is sought by crossing the limit forbidden of God. The seeking to attain by crossing the line, Paul teaches was the result, not of innate wickedness, but of deception. The Serpent beguiled Eve. ... "Weakness," mental and physical, is an original element of animal nature; as "power" is of the angelic. Adam's nature was "very good" as an animal nature; but still weak, and therefore, deceivable and terminable. ...When Adam's weak nature began to think and act, independently of the divine law, its weakness, before an undefiled weakness, became evil in its workings, and deteriorating in its effects, and acquired the name of Sin from its having brought forth sin, or TRANSGRESSION of the Law.

John Thomas, The Tree of Knowledge of Good and Evil, Elpis Israel, 1866, pp. 66-67
Adam and Eve were permitted to take freely of all the other trees in the garden, "but of the tree of knowledge of good and evil", said the Lord God, "thou shalt not eat of it, neither shall ye touch it: for in the day that thou eatest thereof thou shalt surely die" (Genesis 2:17; 3:3). Naturally, it was as good for food as any other tree; but, as soon as the Lord God laid His interdict upon it, its fruit became death to the eater; not instant death, however, for their eyes were to be opened (Genesis 3:5, 7), and they were to become as the gods, or Elohim, being acquainted with good and evil even as they (Genesis 3:22). The final consequence of eating of this tree being death, it may be styled the Tree of Death in contradistinction to the Tree of Life. Decay of body, and consequent termination of life, ending in corruption, or mortality, was the attribute which this fatal tree was prepared to bestow upon the individual who should presume to touch it.

John Thomas, The Tree of Knowledge of Good and Evil, Elpis Israel, 1866, pp. 68-69
The sentence *"Thou shalt surely die"*, is proof that the phrase *"in the day"* relates to a longer period than the day of the natural eating. This was not a sentence to be consummated in a moment, as when a man is shot or guillotined. It required time; for the death threatened was the result, or finishing, of a certain process; which is very clearly indicated in the original Hebrew. In this language the phrase is *muth temuth*, which literally rendered is, dying thou shalt die. The sentence, then, as a whole reads thus – 'in the day of thy eating from it dying thou shalt die'. From this reading, it is evident, that Adam was to be subjected to a process, but not to an endless process; but to one which should commence with the transgression, and end with his extinction. The process is expressed by *muth, dying*; and the last stage of the process by *temuth*, thou shalt die.

..."Thou shalt return unto the ground", and "Unto dust shalt thou return" [Genesis 3:19], are phrases equivalent to "Dying thou shalt die". Hence, the divine interpretation of the sentence, "In the day thou eatest thereof thou shalt surely die", is, "In the day of thy eating all the days of thy life of sorrow, returning thou shalt return unto the dust of the ground whence thou wast taken". Thus, *"dying"*, in the meaning of the text, is to be the subject of *a sorrowful*, painful, and *laborious* existence, which wears a man *out*, and brings him down to the brink of the grave; and, by *"die"*, is signified the end, or last stage of corporeal existence, which is marked by *a ceasing to breathe, and decomposition into dust.*

John Thomas, *Man in his Novitiate*, Elpis Israel, 1866, pp. 71-72
"God made man upright" [Ecclesiastes 7:29]

When the work of the six days was completed, the Lord God reviewed all that He had made, and pronounced it "very good" [Genesis 1:31]. This quality pertained to everything terrestrial. The beasts of the field, the fowls of the air, reptiles, and man, were all "very good"; and all made up a natural system of things, or world, as perfect as the nature of things required. Its excellence, however, had relation solely to its physical quality. Man, though "very good", was so only as a piece of divine workmanship. He was made different from what he afterwards became. Being made in the image, after the likeness of the Elohim, he was "made upright." He had no conscience of evil; for he did not know what it was. He was neither virtuous, nor vicious; holy, nor unholy; but in his beginning simply innocent of good or evil deeds. Being without a history, he was without character. This had to be developed; and could only be formed for good or evil, by his own independent action under the divine law. In short, when Adam and Eve came forth from the hand of their potter, they were morally in a similar condition to a new-born babe; excepting that a babe is born under the constitution of sin, and *involuntarily* subjected to "vanity" (Romans 8:20); while they first beheld the light in a state of things where evil had as yet no place. They were created in the stature of a perfect man and woman; but with their sexual feelings undeveloped; in ignorance, and without experience.

The interval between their formation and their transgression was the period of their novitiate. The Spirit of God had made them; and during this time, "the inspiration of the Almighty was giving them understanding" (Job 33:4; 32:8).

Guided by the precepts of the Lord God, his conscience continued good, and his heart courageous. "They were naked, both the man and his wife, and were not ashamed" (Genesis 2:25) They were no more abashed than children in their nudity; for, though adults in stature, yet, being in the infancy of nature, they stood before the Elohim, and in the face of one another, without embarrassment. This fact was not accidentally recorded. As we shall see hereafter, it is a clue, as it were, given to enable us to understand the nature of the transgression.

John Thomas, *Man in his Novitiate*, Elpis Israel, 1866, pp. 72-73
In this sense, therefore, I say, that in their novitiate, Adam and his betrothed had a nature *capable* of corruption, but were not subject to death, or mortal. The penalty was "dying thou shalt die"; that is, "You shall not be permitted to eat of the Tree of Life in arrest of dissolution; but the inherent tendency of your animal nature shall take its course, and return you to the dust whence you originally came". Mortality was in disobedience as the wages of sin, and not a necessity.

But, if they were not mortal in their novitiate, it is also true that they were not immortal. To say that immortals were expelled from the garden of Eden, that they might live forever by eating of the tree, is absurd. The truth is in few words, man was created with a nature endued with certain susceptibilities. He was capable of death; and capable of endless life; but, whether he should merge into mortality; or, by a physical change be clothed with immortality, was predicated on his choosing to do good or evil. Capacity must not be confounded with impletion. A vessel may be capable of holding a pint of fluid; but it does not therefore follow that there is a pint in it, or any at all. In the Paradise of Eden, mortality and immortality were set before the man and his companion. They were external to them. They were to avoid the former, and seek after the latter, by obedience to the law of God. They were capable of being filled with either; but with which depended upon their actions; for immortality is the end of holiness (Romans 6:22), without which no man can see the Lord.

John Thomas, *The Carnal Mind*, Elpis Israel, 1866, pp. 90-91

Now, the law of God is given, that the thinking of the flesh, instead of being excited by the propensities within and the world without, may be conducted according to its direction. So long as Adam and Eve yielded to its guidance, they were happy and contented. Their thoughts were the result of right thinking, and obedience was the consequence. But when they adopted the Serpent's reasonings as their own, these being at variance with the truth, caused an "enmity" against it in their thinkings, which is equivalent to "enmity against God". When their sin was perfected, the propensities, or lusts, having been inflamed, became "a law in their members; and because it was implanted in their flesh by transgression, it is styled, "the law of sin" [Romans 7:23,25]; and death being the wages of sin, it is also termed, "the law of sin and death" [Romans 8:2]; but by philosophy, "the law of nature". …

Such is the carnal mind, or thinking of the flesh, as illustrated by the works of the flesh: a hideous deformity, whose conception is referable to the infidelity and disobedience of our first parents: by whom 'sin entered into the world, and death by sin' (Romans 5:12). It is the serpent mind; because it was through his untruthful reasonings believed, that a like mode of thinking to his was generated in the heart of Eve and her husband. The seed sown there by the serpent was corruptible seed. Hence the carnal mind, or thinking of the flesh, unenlightened by the truth, is the serpent in the flesh. It was for this reason that Jesus styled his enemies 'serpents, and a generation of vipers' (Matthew 23:33).

John Thomas, *The Carnal Mind*, Elpis Israel, 1866, pp. 93-94

As I have remarked before, *sin* is personified by Paul as "preeminently *a sinner*"; and by another apostle, as "the Wicked One" (1 John 3:12). In this text, he says, "Cain was of that Wicked One, and slew his brother." There is precision in this language which is not to be disregarded in the interpretation. Cain was of the Wicked One; that is, he was *a son of sin*—of the serpent-sin, or original transgression. … When therefore, in the "set time" afterwards, "Eve bare Cain", though procreated by Adam, he was of the Serpent, seeing that he suggested the transgression which ended in the conception of Cain. In this way, sin in the flesh being put for the Serpent,

Cain was of that Wicked One, the pre-eminent sinner, and the first-born of the Serpent's seed.

… "Ye are of your father the devil, and the lusts of your father ye are willing to do. He was a murderer from the beginning, and stood not in the truth, because there is no truth in him" (John 8:44). We have seen in what sense this is affirmed of the Serpent, the unaccountable and irresponsible author of sin. Every son of Adam is "conceived in sin and shapen in iniquity" [Psalm 51:5], and therefore "sinful flesh"; on the principle that "what is born of the flesh is flesh" [John 3:6]. If he obey the impulses of his flesh, he is like Cain, "of the Wicked One"; but if he believe the "exceeding great and precious promises of God" [2 Peter 1:4], obey the law of faith, and put to death unlawful obedience to his propensities, he becomes a son of the living God, and a brother and a joint-heir of the Lord Jesus Christ of the glory to be revealed in the last time.

But serpent-sin, being a constituent of human nature, is treated of in the scripture in the aggregate, as well as in its individual manifestations. The "lust of the flesh, the lust of the eyes, and the pride of life" [1 John 2:16], generated in our nature by sin, and displayed in all the children of sin, taken in the aggregate constitute "the world", which stands opposed to God. Serpent-sin in the flesh is the god of the world, who possesses the glory of it. Hence, to overcome the world is to overcome the Wicked One; because sin finds its expression in the things of the world.

John Thomas, Elpis Israel, 1866, p. 110 – Genesis 3:15

The allegorical reading of the text founded upon these particulars is as follows: *"I will put the enmity of that mode of thinking thou hast elicited in Eve and her husband against My law, between the powers that shall be hereafter, in consequence of what thou hast done, and the faithful and unblemished corporation I shall constitute: and I will put this enmity of the spirit against the flesh, and of the flesh against the spirit, between all who obey the lusts of the flesh which thou hast excited, and those of My institution who shall serve me: their Chief shall bear away the world's sin which thou hast originated, and shall destroy all the works that have grown out of it: and the sin-power shall wound him to death; but he shall recover it, and accomplish the work I now pre-ordain him to do."*

John Thomas, *The Foundation of The World*, Elpis Israel, 1866, pp. 123-126

These three sentences; and the New Law, constitute *the foundation of the world*. … At this crisis, there appeared a natural system of things, with two transgressors, in whom sin had enthroned itself; and who were endued with the power of multiplying such as themselves to an unlimited extent.

… in "the Rudiments of the World" are traceable the things of the future Kingdom of God. These rudiments, or elements, are exhibited in the sentences upon the serpent, the woman, and the man; and in that institution styled, "The Way of the Tree of Life". …

The things laid, or fixed, in the rudimental constitution of the world, may be summarily stated in the following particulars:—

1. Sin in the flesh, the enemy of God, contending for the dominion of the world.

2. Mankind in a state of nature, subject to the propensities; and to pain, trouble and death.
3. Labour and toil the condition of existence in the present state.
4. The subjection of woman to the lordship of man.

John Thomas, *The Constitution of Sin*, Elpis Israel, 1866, pp. 126-131

The introduction of *sin* into the world necessitated the constitution of things as they were laid in the beginning. If there had been no sin there would have been no "*enmity*" between God and man; and consequently no antagonism by which to educe good out of evil. Sin and evil are as cause and effect. God is the author of evil, but not of sin; for the evil is the punishment of sin. "I form the light, and create darkness: I make peace, and *create evil:* I the Lord do all these things" (Isaiah 45:7). "Shall there be evil in a city, and the Lord hath not done it?" (Amos 3:6). The evil then to which man is subjected is the Lord's doing. …

This is the constituted order of things. It is the constitution of the world; and as the world is sin's dominion, or the kingdom of the adversary, it is the constitution of the kingdom of sin.

The word *sin* is used in two principal acceptations in the scripture. It signifies in the first place, "*the transgression of law*"; and in the next, it represents that physical principle of the animal nature, which is the cause of all its diseases, death, and resolution into dust. It is that in the flesh "*which has the power of death*" [Hebrews 2:14]; and it is called *sin*, because the development, or fixation, of this *evil* in the flesh, was the result of transgression. Inasmuch as this evil principle pervades every part of the flesh, the animal nature is styled "sinful flesh," that is, *flesh full of sin;* so that *sin*, in the sacred style, came to stand for the substance called *man*. In human flesh "dwells no good thing" (Romans 7:17-18); and all the evil a man does is the result of this principle dwelling in him. …

Sin, I say, is a synonym for human nature. Hence the flesh is invariably regarded as unclean. It is therefore written, 'How can he be clean who is born of woman?' (Job 25:4). 'Who can bring a clean thing out of an unclean? Not one' (Job 14:4). 'What is man that he should be clean? And which is born of a woman that he should be righteous? Behold, God putteth no trust in His saints; yea, the heavens are not clean in His sight. How much more abominable and filthy is man, who drinketh iniquity like water?' (Job 15:14–16). This view of sin in the flesh is enlightening in the things concerning Jesus. The apostle says, 'God made him sin for us, who knew no sin' (2 Corinthians 5:21); and this he explains in another place by saying that, 'He sent His own Son in the likeness of sinful flesh, and for sin, condemned sin in the flesh (Romans 8:3) in the offering of this body once (Hebrews 10:10, 12, 14). Sin could not have been condemned in the body of Jesus, if it had not existed there. His body was as unclean as the bodies of those he died for; for he was born of a woman, and 'not one' can bring a clean body out of a defiled body; for 'that' says Jesus himself, 'which is born of the flesh is flesh.' (John 3:6)

… Sinful flesh being the hereditary nature of the Lord Jesus, he was a fit and proper sacrifice for sin; especially as he was himself 'innocent of the great transgression', having been obedient in all things. Appearing in the nature of the seed of Abraham (Hebrews 2:16-18), he was subject to all the emotions by which we are troubled; so that he was enabled to sympathise with our infirmities, being 'made in all things like unto his brethren'. But, when he was "born of the spirit" in the quickening of his mortal body by the spirit (Romans 8:11), he became a spirit; for "that which is born of the spirit is spirit." Hence, he is "the Lord the Spirit," incorruptible flesh and bones.

Sin in the flesh is hereditary; and entailed upon mankind as the consequence of Adam's violation of Eden's law. The "original sin" was such as I have shown in previous pages. Adam and Eve committed it; and their posterity are suffering the consequences of it. … Mankind being born of the flesh, and of the will of man, are born into the world under the constitution of sin. That is, they are the natural born citizens of Satan's kingdom. By their fleshly birth, they are entitled to all that *sin* can impart. …

It is absurd to say that children are born holy, except in the sense of being legitimate. None are born holy, but such as are born of the Spirit into the Kingdom of God. Children are born sinners or unclean, because they are born of sinful flesh; and 'that which is born of the flesh is flesh' or sin. This is a misfortune, not a crime. They did not will to be born sinners. They have no choice in the case; for, it is written, 'The creature was made subject to the evil, not willingly, but by reason of him who subjected it in hope' (Romans 8:20). Hence, the Apostle says, 'By Adam's disobedience the many were made sinners' (Romans 5:19); that is, they were endowed with a nature like his, which had become unclean, as a result of disobedience; and by the constitution of the economy into which they were introduced by the will of the flesh, they were constituted transgressors before they were able to discern between right and wrong.

… But men are not only made, or constituted, sinners by the disobedience of Adam, but they become sinners even as he, *by actual transgression*. … Thus men are sinners in a twofold sense; first, by natural birth; and next, by transgression. In the former sense, it is manifest they could not help themselves. They will not be condemned to the Second Death because they were born sinners; nor to any other pains and penalties than those which are the common lot of humanity in the present life. They are simply under that provision of the constitution of sin which says, "Dust thou art, and unto dust thou shalt return". Now, if the Lord God had made no other arrangement than that expressed in the sentence upon the woman and the man, they and all their posterity in all their generations would have incessantly gone to dust and there have remained for ever. "The wages of sin is death." Sinful flesh confers no good thing upon its offspring; for holiness, righteousness, incorruptibility, and life for ever are not hereditary. None of these are inherent in animal flesh. Sinners *can only acquire* them by a conformity to the law of God; who offers them freely to all who thirst after the water of life eternal (Revelation 22:17).

John Thomas, *The Way of the Tree of Life*, Elpis Israel, 1866, pp. 155-167
Religion is not coeval with the formation of man; neither had it any existence during his novitiate. Though it was instituted in the paradise, it was not for his observance there; for while he continued the *sinless* tenant of the garden, he stood in no need of the *healing* consolations it affords. Until he ate of the forbidden fruit, there was no *breach* of friendship, no misunderstanding, no alienation, between him and the Lord God; there

needed not, therefore, any means, or system of means, for the *reconciliation* of estranged parties. But, as soon as the good understanding was interrupted by disobedience to the Eden law, sentence of condemnation to the dust was pronounced upon the offenders; and *means were instituted* to put them *at one again* with the Lord, that He might bring them back from the ground, no longer naked and ashamed of their condition; but clothed with glory and honour, incorruptibility and life, as a crown of righteousness that should never fade away.

… Man having been made subject to evil, and consigned to the bondage of a perishing state, the Lord God repudiated their fig-leaf invention, and "appointed coats of skins" [Genesis 3:21] for their covering. In this testimony there is much expressed in few words. To appoint coats of skins implies a command for the sacrifice of animals whose skins were converted to this purpose. It also implies that Adam was the priest on the occasion, who presented himself before the Lord with the mediatorial blood. When the sacrifice was accepted, the offence was *provisionally* remitted; for the scripture saith, that it is not possible for the blood of animals to take away sins (Hebrews 10:4). It was impossible, because sin was to be condemned in sinful flesh. This required the death of a man; for the animals had not sinned. …

… When sin is eradicated from the world there will be no more death; for death and sin are boon companions; as it is written, "The wages of sin is death" [Romans 6:23]. The abolition of death presupposes the extinction of sin in the flesh; and consequently that the *animal nature* of man has been transformed (not evaporated, but changed) into the *spiritual nature* of the Elohim. Man will then be no longer subject to evil. His race will have passed through its 7,000 years of probation; and all of its individuals, who have been the faithful subjects of God's religion, will become the incorruptible and perpetual inhabitants of the earth, emancipated from every curse. …

Religion begins in the third chapter of Genesis, and finds the record of its end in the last two chapters of the Revelation. Its abolition is expressed in these words: "Behold, the tabernacle of God is with men, and he will dwell with them, and they shall be his people, and God himself shall be with them as their God. And he shall wipe away all tears from their eyes: and *there shall be* NO MORE DEATH, neither sorrow, nor crying, neither shall there be any more pain: for the former things are passed away. And he that sat upon the throne said, Behold, *I make all things new.* And *there shall be* NO MORE CURSE" (Revelation 21:3-5, 22:3). Then will the victory be complete. *The Sin-power and all its works will be finally abolished; and an eternal jubilee gladden the hearts of men, in whom God will be all and in all* (1 Corinthians 15:28).

SUMMARY OF PRINCIPLES.
1. Religion is that *system of means* by which the *breach* made by sin between God and man is repaired; and the wound inflicted upon the latter is healed.

2. Man's defilement was first a matter of conscience; and then corporeal[184]. For this cause, his purification is first a cleansing of his

---

[184] Corporeal = physical, relating to a person's body.

understanding, sentiments, and affections; and afterwards, the perfecting of his body by spiritualizing it at the resurrection. ...

13. The elementary doctrinal principles of religion are few and simple ... They may be thus stated:—

   a. No sinner can by any means redeem his brother, nor give to God a ransom for him, that he should still live for ever, and not see corruption (Psalm 49:7-9).

   b. Sin cannot be covered, or remitted, without the shedding of blood.

   c. The blood of animals cannot take away sin.

   d. Sin must be condemned in sinful flesh innocent of transgression.

   e. Sins must be covered by a garment derived from the purification-sacrifice made living by a resurrection.

John Thomas, *Who are the Servants of God,* Eureka, vol. 1, 1861, pp. 19-20
"Know ye not," says Paul, "that to whom ye yield yourselves *servants* to obey, his servants ye are to whom ye obey; whether of SIN unto death, or of OBEDIENCE unto righteousness?" [Romans 6:16] **Here are two masters**; the first, the Lord of the world, the last, the ruling principle of Jehovah's people. "Sin is the transgression of law;" and because this is the natural tendency of our nature, "sin" is sometimes used for "the flesh." He, therefore, that serves his own lusts, "the lust of the flesh, the lust of the eye, and the pride of life" [1 John 2:16], which not only constitute the man, but the world, or aggregate of such, is Sin's servant or slave.

John Thomas, *Deity Manifested in Spirit*, Eureka, vol. 1, 1861, pp. 106-107
However perfect and complete the moral manifestation of the Deity was in Jesus of Nazareth, the divine manifestation was nevertheless imperfect as concerning the substance, or body, of Jesus. This was what we are familiar with as the flesh. It was not angel-flesh, or nature; but that common to the seed of Abraham, styled by Paul *sarx hamartias, flesh of sin;* "in which," he says, "dwells no good thing"—Romans 7:18; 8:3. The anointing spirit-dove, which, as the Divine Form, descended from heaven upon Jesus at his sealing, was holy and complete in all things; the *character* of Jesus was holy, harmless, undefiled, without spot, or blemish, or any such thing; but *his flesh* was like our flesh, in all its points,—weak, emotional, and unclean. Had his flesh been like that of Angel-Elohim, which is consubstantial with the Eternal Spirit, it would have been unfit for the purpose of the Deity in his manifestation. Sin, whose wages is death, had to be condemned in the nature that had transgressed; a necessity that could only be accomplished by the Word becoming Adamic-Flesh, and not Elohistic. ...

Another reason why the Word assumed a lower nature than the Elohistic was, that a basis of future perfection might be laid in obedience under trial. Jesus has been appointed Captain of Salvation in the bringing of many sons to glory. Now these sons in the accident of birth are all "subject to vanity" [Romans 8:20] with inveterate propensities and relative enticements, inciting and tempting them to sin. A captain, therefore, whose nature was primarily consubstantial with the Deity, could not be touched with the feeling of their infirmities. ...

John Thomas, *The Diabolos*, Eureka, vol. 1, 1861, pp. 247-248

Man, then, having introduced Sin, "death entered into the world by Sin; and so death passed upon all men to condemnation; for by one man's disobedience the many were constituted sinners; and the wages of sin is death to those who obey it" - Romans 5:12, 18, 19; 6:23, 16. But though constituted sinners in Adam, if no law had been given after his transgression, his posterity would not have known when they did right or wrong; for Paul says, "I had not known sin, but by the law." The law is, therefore, "the strength of Sin." Sin reigns by "the holy, just, and good law," through the "weakness of the flesh" - Romans 7:7, 12; 8:3. Where there is no law there is no sin; for "sin is the transgression of law:" so that "without the law sin is dead" - Romans 7:8; 1 John 3:4. This shows how inherently bad flesh is in its thoughts and actions, that a good thing should stir it up to wickedness. Its lusts and affections are impatient of control. Paul therefore said, "in me, that is, in my flesh, dwells no good thing." When this, which is utterly destitute of any good thing, is placed under a good law, scope is afforded it to display itself in all its natural deformity; and to prove that "the law of its nature" is not the law of God, but "the law of sin and death." Thus, the introduction of a good law, demanding obedience of that which has nothing good in it, is the occasion of sin abounding in the world (Romans 5:20), and thereby evinces its enormity, and shows that "SIN *is an exceedingly great sinner"—kath, hyperbolen amartolos* - Romans 7:13. In this expression Paul personifies Sin; and says that it deceived him, slew him, and worked death in him.

"SIN" is a word in Paul's argument, which stands for "human nature," with its affections and desires. Hence, to become sin, or for one to be *"made sin"* for others, (2 Corinthians 5:21) is to become flesh and blood. This is called *"sin,"* or *"Sin's flesh,"* because it is *what it is* in consequence of sin, or transgression. When the dust of the ground was formed into a body of life, or living soul, or as Paul terms it, a *psychical or natural body*, it was a very good *animal* creation. It was not a pneumatic, or spirit-body, indeed, for it would then have been immortal and incorruptible, and could neither have sinned nor have become subject to death; but for an animal or natural body, it was "very good," and capable of an existence free from evil, as long as its probationary *aion*, or period might continue. If that period had been fixed for a thousand years, and man had continued obedient to law all that time, his flesh and blood nature would have experienced no evil; and at the end of that long day, he might have been permitted to eat of the Tree of the Lives, by which eating he would have been changed in the twinkling of an eye into a spirit-body, which is incorruptible, glorious, and powerful; and he would have been living at this day. But man transgressed.

… This perishing body is "sin," and left to perish because of "sin." *Sin*, in its application to the body, stands for all its constituents and laws. The power of death is in its very constitution, so that the law of its nature is styled "the law of Sin and Death" [Romans 8:2]. In the combination of the elements of the law, the power of death resides, so that "to destroy that having the power of death" [Hebrews 2:14], is to abolish this physical law of sin and death, and instead thereof, to substitute the physical "law of the spirit of life" [Romans 8:2], by which the same body would be changed in its constitution, and live for ever.

John Thomas, *The Old Serpent*, Eureka, vol. 4, 1866, pp. 66-76
Thus was the mother of all living "drawn away of her own lusts, and enticed." She was attracted by "the lust of the flesh, the lust of the eyes, and the pride of life" [1 John 2:16]. These instincts of the flesh predisposed her to believe the serpent and to follow his suggestion, regardless of the divine law. Lust conceived within her. The doctrine of the serpent sown in her heart inflamed her desires, and stirred them up into rebellious exercise. Faith in the word was obliterated; her mind was darkened by false teaching; she was beguiled and corrupted from the simplicity of the truth; her thinking was serpentized, and she "brought forth sin," or the transgression of the law; and when the sin was perfected, contrary to the serpent's theory and her own expectation, "it brought forth death" (James 1:14-15).

... The serpent was the progenitor of the whole transaction. Animal intellectuality, or the thinking of flesh in accordance with its own lusts, emanating from the serpent in discourse, was the spirit that worked in the disobedient, and caused them to stumble at the word. ... The intellectualism of the serpent had been transferred to the man. The serpent-system of ideas and mode of thinking had become characteristic of the man, whose lustful nature, inflamed to rebellion by the serpent's reasoning, came to occupy the same relation to the word of the Deity in all after ages, that the original speaking beast did before the fall of man. ...

The serpent, then, is the reasoning of the flesh, which is inseparable from it, and tends only to death. This is human nature, and styled by Paul in Romans 8:3, *sarx hamartias*, SIN'S FLESH, in which, in Romans 7:18, he says, "dwelleth no good thing." ... Thus, the serpent's reasoning which she adopted as her own, worked death in her by the good and just and holy law, by which, when the reasoning was perfected in transgression, Human Nature displayed itself as an exceedingly great sinner—*kath' huperbolen hamartolos*.

... After the death of the particular serpent that beguiled Eve, the only speaking serpent was within man. His own lusts are the internal serpent by which he is drawn away and enticed. Thus, mankind in whom the truth is not, being the Seed of the Serpent, the flesh of sin, is their natural parent. This is "their father the Devil, whose lusts they do" [John 8:44]. ...

In the beginning, the Serpent-World consisted of no more than two sinners— Adam and his wife; yet small as was its extent, all the evil that has since manifested itself, was latent in them. Their symbol was the Serpent, or Dragon, and *represented falsehood, unbelief, and rebellion against the Deity.* ...

Now, after Adam had brought sin into being by transgression of the law, the Deity proceeded to organize the *"evil"* to which man had subjected himself by his rebellion. He had come to know it elohistically, as the serpent had said; but he was not also to be like the *Elohim* in abiding for ever. He had sinned, and the law he had violated was now to take its course. YAHWEH *Elohim* therefore proceeded to expound the penalty of the law, and to teach him the practical import of the phrase, *"Dying thou shalt die."* ... (Genesis 3:15–19). The specifications in these sentences upon the serpent, the woman, and the man form THE CONSTITUTION of the Serpent-World, or KINGDOM OF SIN; and termed in Scripture "the Kingdom of Men"— dominion hostile to the Divine law administered by the Serpent's Seed. It matters not what form the dominion assumes, whether imperial, regal, republican, or papal, its basis is one and the same; and most appropriately symbolized by the serpent which was in the beginning.

In after times, far distant from the beginning, the serpent-world acquired an immense development. From two persons it had increased to myriads of millions.

John Thomas, *No More Sea*, Eureka, vol. 5, 1866, pp. 339-340

But flesh and blood, or Sin's flesh, is radically bad. When Paul subjected the nature he possessed in common with all the race of men, to an enlightened scrutiny, he declared that "in his flesh dwelt no good thing". He felt that he bore about a loathsome, leprous, nature, which he styled "a vile body;" so that it caused him to exclaim, "O wretched man that I am! who shall deliver me from this body of death?" (Romans 7:18, 24; Philippians 3:21). Such a nature is incurable. It is essentially turbulent, rebellious, and prone to evil; and can only be controlled by the power of Divine principles, or an iron despotism.

John Thomas, *No More Curse*, Eureka, vol. 5, 1866, pp. 362-363

… The occasion of the curse was the transgression of the divine law by the 'very good' nature formed in and of the dust of the ground … [Genesis 3:17-19]. So long, then, as the Sin-Nature continues to inhabit the earth, there must be sorrow, toil, and death; for the sentence pronounced upon the sinning nature, declares the continuance of the curse to be in all the days of its life.

To abolish the curse, then, is equivalent to the abolition of the nature cursed with sorrow, toil, disease, and death. This abolition was the consummation of all things, by which is introduced an entirely new creation; the basis of which is a nature that neither has nor can transgress – that is, the Divine Nature. All that comes out of the ground is cursed, and unclean; so that even the body of Jesus, and the bodies of the approved saints, in resurrection, required to be justified, rectified, purged, or perfected, by all – absorbing spirit; which makes every atom of their substance instinct within corruption and life; in other words, transforms it into spirit.   … When they are transformed into the New-Jerusalem by the *energeia* (Philippians 3:21) or inworking power, that "descends from the Deity out of heaven" [Revelation 21:2] there is to them entire freedom from everything pertaining to the curse.

John Thomas – Catechesis, 1869, pp. 11 –12

37. *What relation did the first man sustain to mortality and immortality?*
    Ans. That of *a candidate* for the one or the other. If obedient to the law, he would obtain *the right* to eat of the tree of life and live for ever (Genesis 3:22; Revelation 22:14); if disobedient, he would incur *the penalty* of the law, which consigned him to the dust from which he was taken (Genesis 2:17; 3:19).

38. *Having come under the penalty of the law, when did it begin to take effect?*
    Ans. After he had given account of himself at the judgment which sat upon his case, and sentence of *death* was pronounced upon him.

39. *What is Death?*
    Ans. The cessation of the life of an earthy body.

40. *What is Corruption?*
    Ans. The returning of a lifeless earthy body to its primeval dust.

John Thomas, The Christadelphian, vol. 11, 1874, pp. 156-160[185]
EVIL: Seven attested propositions on the origin and the operation of evil in relation to the human race.

Proposition III
Sin entered into the world by man, and not by the serpent.
ROMANS 5:12. — By one man, sin entered into the world.

Proposition IV
Sin is the transgression of law; therefore, the transgressor, and not he that occasions the transgression, is the sinner in the case before us.

This is manifest from Moses' account. The law was given to Adam and not to the serpent. Adam, and not the serpent, ate of the fruit of the forbidden tree; the serpent spoke according to the subtlety of his nature, which was uncontrolled by moral sentiment or law. Adam was the sinner, and by disobedience became the subject of a corrupting principle, which, because it is the consequence of his transgression, is termed "SIN IN THE FLESH" [Romans 8:3]. Hence, as human nature is full of it, it is styled *"sinful flesh,"* and "sin that dwelleth in me" [Romans 7:17,20], or "lust which bringeth forth sin."

The case of Adam differs from that of his descendants in this, namely: the *"deceivableness"* which enticed him to transgress resided in the serpent, whereas, every man that is *beguiled* since, "is drawn away of his own lust and enticed; then when lust hath conceived it bringeth forth sin, and sin, when it is finished, bringeth forth death."—(James 1:14.)

"Lust" and *"sin"* bear the relation of cause and effect; and are often put one for another. Hence *"sin"* taking occasion by the commandment, *deceived me* (not the serpent, nor the devil) and by it (the law) *slew* me."—(Romans 7:11.) Here the deceivableness is placed in "sin," though really inherent in the "lust," which reviving under law "brings forth sin." "Sin," however, is generally used by Paul as expressive of *the inherent evil principle of human nature.*

This EVIL PRINCIPLE in man, Paul represents as *reigning* and having dominion over all natural men. Hence it may be personified as KING SIN— for they are kings who reign and have dominion (Romans 6:12,13,20; 5:14,12; 7:13).

Corollary
There was in Adam, after he sinned, as there is in all his descendants hereditarily from him, a physical principle, which reigns in the whole man, causes pain and sorrow, and finally brings him to the dust of death. It is, therefore, a principle of corruption, which superinduces a desire to gratify all the propensities of our nature without restraint. It is selfish stimulating to seek only our own gratification. It is styled *"the law of sin"* [Romans 7:23,25] or the ELEMENTAL PRINCIPLE OF EVIL, the excessive depravity of which can only be known by an attempt to subject it to a holy, just, and good commandment. This develops all the latent virulence which belongs to it; and proves it to be "ENMITY" to everything that is *"holy, just and good, "* and

---

[185] Published by Bro Roberts with the comment: *"Found in an old MS. of Dr. Thomas, which, so far as we know, has never been published."*

everything which is excellent is "ENMITY" to it. It is "enmity against God; it is not subject to the law of God; neither, indeed, can it be"—(Romans 8:7).

Proposition V

This elemental principle of evil diffused itself through man's nature as the property or the poisonous quality of the evil fruit disobediently eaten.

GENESIS 3:15.—I will put enmity between thee and the woman, and between thy seed and her seed; HE shall bruise thy head, and thou shalt bruise his heel.

Robert Roberts

A Declaration Of The First Principles Of The Oracles Of The Deity, 1867 [186]

XXI - JESUS AS THE SECOND ADAM

That, with the exception of the mode of his conception and his anointing with the Holy Spirit, Jesus was essentially A MAN, raised up as a SECOND ADAM (constituted of flesh and blood as we are, and tempted in all points like unto us, yet without sin), to remove by obedience, death and resurrection, the evil consequences resulting from the disobedience of the first Adam.

1 Timothy 2:5; Romans 8:3; Hebrews 2:14; Galatians 4:4; 2 Corinthians 5:21; 1 Corinthians 15:21, 45; Romans 5:15, 19; Hebrews 5:7, 8; Hebrews 2:17; Hebrews 4:15.

XXII – THE OBJECT OF HIS DEATH

The object of his death was not to appease the wrath of offended Deity, but to express the love of the Deity, by abrogating the law of sin and death through a full discharge of its claims in a temporary surrender to its power; and developing immortality by resurrection to a legally-acquired possession of it, in trust of the obedient of Adam's race.

John 1:20; Hebrews 9:26; John 3:16; Galatians 1:4; Titus 2:14; 2 Corinthians 5:21; Acts 10:43; Romans 3:25; Acts 4:12.

XXIV – HUMAN NATURE – WHAT IS IT

A. That man is a creature of dust formation, whose individuality and faculties are the attributes of his bodily organization.

   Genesis 2:7; 3:19, 23; 5:2; 28:27; Job 4:19; 10:9; 14:10; 33:6; Psalm 103:14; 104:29; Isaiah 64:8; John 3:6, 31; 1 Corinthians 15:47-49; 1 Peter 1:24; James 1:10-11; Ecclesiastes 3:19-20; 12:7.

B. That Man, thus constituted, is mortal (that is, subject to the law of death or dissolution of being) in consequence of the disobedience of Adam, which brought death as the penalty of sin.

   Job 14:17; Romans 5:12; Genesis 2:17; 3:19, 22, 23; 7:22; 1 Corinthians 15:22; Psalm 30:3; 86:13; 89:48; Job 33:22; Isaiah 2:22; 1 Timothy 6:16-17.

---

[186] Bro R.C. Bingley was the author of this document published by Bro Roberts. Importantly, since this first edition in 1867, it has served as a standard Christadelphian pamphlet outlining essential first principles of the Bible, even the one true faith as taught by the apostles in the first century, which Christadelphians consider as essential for salvation.

Robert Roberts – The Christadelphian, vol. 11, 1874, p. 526

1.—Do you think that Adam was created mortal?
Answer.—No; he was created neither mortal nor immortal, but capable of becoming either.

2.—Was there any difference in nature between Adam when created and [Jesus] before baptism?
Answer.—Yes. Adam was "very good;" Jesus, who refused the application of the term "good" to himself (Matthew 19:17) was Adam's nature the worse for a four thousand years' sin-wear.

Robert Roberts, *For Himself, That It Might Be For Us*, The Christadelphian, vol. 12, 1875, pp. 139-140

The statement of Paul in Hebrews 7:27 is, that Christ did "once" in his death what the high priests under the law did daily, viz., offered "first for his own sins and then for the people's." But there is all the difference between the two cases that there always is between shadow and substance. Christ's "own sins" were not like the sins of the priests; they were not sins of his own committing. He was without sin, so far as his own actions were concerned. Yet as the bearer of the sins of his people—whether "in Adam" or otherwise, he stood in the position of having these as "his own," from the effects of which he had himself first to be delivered. Consequently, he offered first for himself; he was the first delivered. He is "Christ the first fruits." He obtained eternal redemption in and for himself, as the middle voice of the Greek verb *euramenoz* (Hebrews 9:12) implies. (The "for us" is not in the original.) He was brought again from the dead *"through the blood of the everlasting covenant."*—(Hebrews 13:20.) But this offering for himself was also the offering for his people. The two aspects of the double typical offering were combined in one act. He had not twice to offer for himself. "By one offering he hath perfected forever them that are sanctified." Yet, though combined, the two relations of the act are visibly separate. Christ was the first saved from death (Hebrews 5:9); "afterwards, they that are Christ's at his coming."—(1 Cor 15:23.) In this way the Mosaic type has its counterpart.

There is no inconsistency whatever between these facts and the constant declaration that "Christ died for us." All that Christ was and did was "for us."

Robert Roberts – Christadelphian, vol. 14, 1877, p. 471

The article in the Christadelphian for March 1869, continues to represent our convictions on the subject of which it treats, viz., the relation of Jesus to the condemnation which we all inherit from Adam. On some details, however, of that general subject, we should, if we were writing it again, express ourselves more explicitly, in view of the searching controversy which has arisen on the subject of sin in the flesh. We should guard ourselves against forms of expression which seem to favour the false ideas that have come to be advocated. In asserting, for instance, that there was no change in the nature of Adam in the crisis of his condemnation, we should add, that though his nature continued of the order expressed in the phrase "living soul," a change occurred in the condition of that nature through the implantation of death, as recognised in the article in question on page 83, col. 2, line 15, in the statement that death ran in the blood of Mary. And on the subject of sin in the flesh, while retaining the declarations on page 83, as regards the operation of our moral powers, we should add that the effect of the curse was as defiling to Adam's nature as it was to the ground which thenceforth brought forth briars and thorns: and that therefore, after transgression, there was a bias in the wrong direction, which he had not to contend with before transgression. Our mind has not changed on the general subject, but some of its details have been more clearly forced on our recognition by the movements and arguments of heresy.

Robert Roberts – A Statement of the "One Faith", 1877

III. Disobedience of Adam. - That Adam broke the law, and was adjudged unworthy of immortality, and sentenced to return to the ground from whence he was taken[1] - a sentence carried into execution by the implantation of a physical law of decay, which works out dissolution and death,[2] and while a man is yet alive, gives him, where it is left to its uncontrolled operation, a tendency in the direction of sin.[3] This is the law of sin in the members, spoken of by Paul, which the new law established by the truth brings into subjection.[4] In Adam's sentence, all mankind are involved, in consequence of their being physically derived from his physically-affected and unclean being.[5]

[1] Genesis 3:15-19; 22-23.

[2] 2 Corinthians 1:9; Romans 7:24; 2 Corinthians 5:2-4.

[3] Romans 7:18-23.

[4] Galatians 5:16-17; Romans 6:12; 7:21.

[5] John 3:6; Romans 5:12; 1 Corinthians 15:22; Psalm 51:5; Job 14:4.

VI. The Last Adam. - That these promises had reference to a second (or last) Adam,[1] to be raised up in the condemned line of Abraham and David,[2] who should purchase life by perfect obedience,[3] and by dying, abrogate the law of condemnation for those who were under condemnation,[4] and, therefore, for himself,[5] who was made in all points like them;[6] that having thus died unto sin once,[7] he should afterwards be raised to immortality;[8] in which (death having no more dominion over him) he should be permitted to extend a participation in his life and inheritance[9] to all who should believe and obey him;[10] and that he should afterwards become the head and ruler of the whole world.[11]

[1] 1 Corinthians 15:45.

[2] Hebrews 2:14,16; Romans 1:3.

[3] Hebrews 5:8-9; 1:9; Romans 5:19-21.

[4] Galatians 4:4-5; Romans 8:3-4; Hebrews 2:15; 9:26; Galatians 1:4.

[5] Hebrews 7:27; 5:3-7; 2:17.

[6] Hebrews 2:17.

[7] Romans 6:10.

[8] Romans 6:9; Acts 3:34, 37; Revelation 1:18.

[9] John 5:21, 22, 26, 27; 14:3; Revelation 2:7; Revelation 3:21; Matthew 25:21.

[10] Hebrews 5:9; Mark 16:16; Acts 8:38-39; Romans 3:22.

[11] Psalm 2:6-9; Daniel 7:13-14; Revelation 11:15; Jeremiah 23:5; Zechariah 14:9; Ephesians 1:9-10

VII. Jesus the Christ, the Son of the Living God. - That this second Adam was God with us,[1] manifested in the flesh[2] and known as Jesus of Nazareth,[3] being begotten of the Holy Spirit, without the intervention of man,[4] and afterwards anointed with the same Spirit, without measure, at his baptism,[5] to speak the words of his Father,[6] yet of like nature with mortal man, being born of the Virgin Mary (of the house and lineage of David), and, therefore, a sufferer, in the days of his flesh, from all the effects that came by Adam's transgressions, including the death that passed upon all men, which he shared by partaking of their physical nature.[7]

[1] Matthew 1:23.

[2] 1 Timothy 3:16.

[3] Acts 2:22, 24, 36.

[4] Matthew 1:18-25; Luke 1:26,35; Galatians 4:4; Isaiah 7:14.

[5] Matthew 3:16-17; Isaiah 11:2; 42:1; 61:1; John 3:34.

[6] John 7:16; 8:26-28; 14:10-24.

[7] Romans 1:3-4; 8:3; Galatians 4:4; 2 Corinthians 5:21; Hebrews 2:17; 4:15.

Robert Roberts, The Visible Hand of God, pp. 30–34[187]

The whole incident of the entrance of death into the world by Adam's disobedience, may be considered as the next exhibition of the visible hand of God in human affairs – an exhibition reaching down to our own day in the continuance and propagation of the death constitution then miraculously established. It has become quite unfashionable to suppose that death entered into the world at that time. It is universally accepted in learned circles that death has always been in the world.

… The question is—the mortality of Adam's race; how did it come? Was the race created subject to death? or did death come as a specific divine super-addition for a reason that came into play after Adam was made? … The Adamic race is a new start; and our enquiry relates to it. Did it commence mortal, or was it brought down to a mortal state after it appeared?

It is impossible to get any light on this question from geology or any other natural source. Speculation on this subject on scientific premises is only pretentious maundering. There is a short and satisfactory way to the root of the matter. As on many other subjects, so in this, the resurrection of Christ is the key of the whole position. If Christ rose from the dead, Paul, his specially selected apostle, is an inspired declarer of truth. Consequently, his dogmatic assertion that, "by one man (Adam) sin entered into the (human) world and death by sin" is a settlement of the question. Paul's dogmatic assertion does not stand alone. It is founded on and endorses the Mosaic account, which is itself commended to our confidence as divine on separate and independent grounds.

… However unfashionable it may have become, therefore, and however un-scientific and far behind it may seem, the man stands on logically unassailable ground who holds that death did not come into the world with Adam, but by him after he came; that at the first, he was free from the action of death in his organisation; that though not absolutely immortal in the sense of being indestructible in nature, he was in that state with respect to

---

[187] Originally published in *The Christadelphian*, vol. 18, 1881, pp. 250-257.

the working and tendency of his organisation, that death did not wait him in the natural path, but had to be introduced as a law of his being before he could become mortal. His was an animal nature that would not die left to itself – a natural body free from death.

… But this immortality Adam did not attain. Nay, he lost the good natural state which was his by creation. He had to confess to having eaten of the tree which he was commanded not to eat; and he had to suffer the dread sentence which doomed him, after a life of toil, to return to the ground from which he had been taken. In the execution of this sentence, we have the visible hand of God. Left to himself as God had made him, he would not have returned to the ground; left to itself, too, the ground would have brought forth beneficially and plentifully. It required what men call a miracle to depress to the level of the beasts that perish, the noble creature formed in the image of the Elohim, and to cause the earth to yield spontaneously 'thorns also and thistles'. 'Cursed is the ground for thy sake' (Genesis 3:17-18). It was not cursed before. 'Thou shalt die' (Genesis 2:17); this was not the prospect apart from disobedience. How were the two results effectuated? By the interposition of the Divine will causing the one and the other. The Divine power that made man and the ground 'very good' at the beginning easily modified the constitution of things for evil.

… Death is written in our present nature. It was written in Eden. It is the writing of God; no man can blot it out. God can, and will in the cases He chooses. He began the work at Nazareth, in harmony with his own greatness. He sent forth his son in the death-written nature that in him it might be cleansed, redeemed and perfected. "Since by man came death, by man came also the resurrection of the dead." (1 Corinthians 15:21). …

Robert Roberts – The Christadelphian Instructor, 1886 [Logos Ed., 1969]
35.—Why is man in his present mortal and evil state?

Answer: Man is mortal because of sin. It is God's law that sinners must die. Adam, our first father, sinned, and was sentenced to death before he had any children. Death began with him, and came to us through him. We receive the nature that he had after he was condemned to die. We thus inherit his sentence of death. Besides this, we are all sinners ourselves.

Proof: *"The wages of sin is death" (Romans 6:23). "By one man sin entered into the world, and death by sin, and so death passed upon all men" (Romans 5:12). "Because thou hast eaten of the tree of which I commanded thee not to eat … dust thou art, and unto dust shalt thou return" (Genesis 3:17–19). "In Adam all die" (1 Corinthians 15:22). "By the offence of one judgment came upon all men to condemnation" (Romans 5:18). "All have sinned, and come short of the glory of God" (Romans 3:23). "We had the sentence of death in ourselves" (2 Cor 1:9). "This mortal (that is, "deathful")" (1 Cor 15:53). "This body of death" (Rom 7:24). "Our mortal flesh" (2 Cor 4:11).*

54. What has been accomplished in the death of Christ?

Answer: Sin has been condemned in his death on the cross, and the righteousness of God has been declared and exhibited to all the world in the shedding of his blood.

Proof: *For in that he died, he died unto sin once: but in that he liveth, he liveth unto God. (Romans 6:10). Who his own self bare our sins in his own body on the tree, that we, being dead to sins, should live unto righteousness: by whose stripes ye were healed. (1 Peter 2:24). For what the law could not do, in that it was weak through the flesh, God sending his own Son in the likeness of sinful flesh, and for sin, condemned sin in the flesh: (Romans 8:3). Whom God hath set forth to be a propitiation through faith in his blood, to declare his righteousness for the remission of sins that are past, through the forbearance of God; To declare, I say, at this time his righteousness: that he might be just, and the justifier of him which believeth in Jesus. (Romans 3:25-26).*

55. How could sin be condemned in Christ who was sinless? and how could the righteousness of God be declared in the blood-shedding of a righteous man?

Answer: Because being born of Adam's condemned race, and partaking of their condemned nature, Christ was made subject, equally with them, to the consequences of Adam's transgression. Therefore his public execution was a public exhibition of what was due to man from God. It pleased God to require this before inviting man to reconciliation through the man in whom this vindication should take place.

Proof: *Forasmuch then as the children are partakers of flesh and blood, he also himself likewise took part of the same; that through death he might destroy him that had the power of death, that is, the devil; (Hebrews 2:14). For then must he often have suffered since the foundation of the world: but now once in the end of the world hath he appeared to put away sin by the sacrifice of himself. (Hebrews 9:26).Concerning his Son Jesus Christ our Lord, which was made of the seed of David according to the flesh; (Romans 1:3). Knowing that Christ being raised from the dead dieth no more; death hath no more dominion over him. For in that he died, he died unto sin once: but in that he liveth, he liveth unto God. (Romans 6:9-10).*

QUESTIONS FOR CHILDREN UNDER EIGHT

24.—What was the consequence of their disobedience?

Answer: *They were sentenced to die, and they were driven out of the beautiful garden, to get their living by labour.*

25.—Are we under the sentence?

Answer: *Yes, because we are their children. We have come from them. It was a sentence that cursed their bodies, and we have the same bodies.*

28.—Is it true what people say that God breathed into Adam an immortal soul that cannot die?

Answer: *No; that is not true. Man is mortal because of sin.*

Robert Roberts, The Christadelphian, vol. 25, 1888, pp. 407-408

… Now is the time for evil. God has a purpose in the earth, and the realization of that purpose requires at present that evil should be the rule. It is what Paul says in Romans 8, "The creature was made subject to vanity, not willingly, but *by reason of Him who hath subjected the same in hope.*" God has subjected us to misery *in hope*. That is the explanation, the full explanation, the perfectly satisfactory explanation of the presence of evil and death in the earth. God has done it; *and there is hope in connection with it.*

Robert Roberts, *The First Man*, The Christadelphian, vol. 25, 1888, pp. 618-619, 679-681

To say that the Gentiles whom we see every day in the street are the members of a race derived altogether outside of Adam, is to make void the entire genealogy of revelation, and to make of none effect the most express testimony to the contrary; and indeed to overthrow completely the doctrine that "by *one* man sin entered into the world, and death by sin" [Romans 5:12] and that "through the offence of *one* many be dead;" that "death reigned by *one*; " that "by the offence of *one* judgment came upon all;" and that "by *one man's* disobedience many were made sinners" [Romans 5:19]. Then, overthrowing this fact with regard to the first Adam, it logically disestablishes the parallel that Paul institutes between him and the "last Adam" as the "one man by whom grace hath abounded to many;" the one by whom they shall reign in life; the one righteousness by which comes justification of life, and the "obedience of one by which many are made righteous" (Romans 5). They are both cases of "many" in "one," and therefore equally cases, illustrating the federal principle upon which God has dealt with the human race; first with regard to sin and death (many being made sinners by the transgression of one); and second, with respect to righteousness and life (many being made righteous by the obedience of one). Had there been two Adams in the beginning (or two parents of mankind), then there must needs have been two Christs, else one race must have been left out of account altogether with respect to the redemptory institution. This, however, is wholly impossible in every particular, for as the phrase "in Adam" covers all who die, so the phrase "in Christ" covers all who like him shall be made "alive for evermore."

The doctrine that Adam was only the "first man" of a covenant, and not literally the first man of the whole race, with which the earth is peopled, is a mistaken interpretation that requires the application of the same kind of unwarrantable treatment to the whole line of route from Adam to Moses, and from Moses to Christ. This is only natural to a wrong start. As illustrating this, it is claimed that the death pronounced against Adam was the "second death", and that the historic comparison that Paul institutes between Adam and Christ, in the words "as in Adam all die" [1 Corinthians 15:22] is referable to the resurrection; and further, that men only get into Adam by being baptised into Christ. This is certainly the climax of absurdity if ever there was one. It is the case of a simple matter treated in a way that obscures its true features, and gives us the elements of chaos and confusion, in the place of light, and "sound speech"; and this is increased by remarks to the effect that they are not all of Adam's race that we see in the street; thus giving the thing at once a past, present, and future bearing upon the work of the truth; and so stumbling the judgment and embarrassing and limiting the operations of faith and duty, at every step of the way; with equally crippling results upon the house within, and the world without.

… In all this Adam was but "the figure of him that was to come" (Romans 5:14), who is "Lord of all" he surveys, in both a higher and more permanent sense than anything present in the actualities of the typical Adam.

Nevertheless the parallel and contrastive resemblances are many; here's another, "For since by man came death, by man came also the resurrection of the dead;" "for," says Paul (illustrating what he means by the two men), "as in Adam all die, even so in Christ shall all be made alive" (1 Cor 15:21–22). This is only another way of saying what he says in Romans, viz., that sin and death entered the world by one man; and that in the outworking of this, "death hath passed upon all men;' therefore in Adam all die, for all men, naturally speaking, are but the offspring of a man with the sentence of death in him. In Christ all this has been reversed; for, says Jesus, "because I live, ye shall live also." But the facts and logic of this are all sent flying to the four winds by the doctrine which plants men "in Adam" (for the first time) as the result of their being baptised into Christ.

Robert Roberts – The Christadelphian, vol. 29, 1892, p. 24

Those who deny that any physical change was produced in Adam's sentence of death, forget the physical power of the curse of God. Its power was seen in the effect produced on Gehazi and Elisha's simple sentence (2 Kings 5:27). It was seen in the thorn and thistle yielding tendency of the ground after the curse pronounced (Genesis 3:17-18). It was seen in the land of Israel under the law, in blight and sterility, and pest and physical derangements of various kinds (Deuteronomy 28:18-22). And it is seen in our corruptible and mortal state which we inherit from Adam in whom it came by sin (Romans 5:12; 2 Corinthians 1:9). Before transgression, he was 'very good' in nature, for so the record declares. After transgression he was no longer in the very good state, but in the evil state ensuing on sentence of death.

Robert Roberts, The Blood of Christ, 1895 [2006 Edition]

… we must go back again to Adam in the garden of Eden, and see him condemned to death. The effect of such a sentence upon a creature we see illustrated in Gehazi as he stood before Elisha. "The leprosy of Naaman cleave to thee and to thy seed for ever" [2 Kings 5:27]. That was the sentence, "and he went from his presence a leper as white as snow." The words of Elisha took effect and became leprosy. The word of God to Adam took effect, and made him a death-stricken man; he was not subject to death before, for sin was the door that death came in by. "By one man sin entered into the world, and death by sin." "By man came death." "Dust thou art, and unto dust shalt thou return." Not to be killed straightway—"Thou *shalt*". God's purpose with man required a slow death, because His purpose was to bring great good out of the evil, and, by two sinners, to bring forth a righteous multitude. Therefore He produced slow death, by establishing a law that would work it out. It is like fixing an alarm clock, the mechanism of which is adjusted to the time it is required to go off. The Word of God against Adam made him a mortal man with a mortal body. Look at Adam and Eve, mortal; by-and-by, children; what are they? Just the same: they also are mortal. Could a mortal beget an immortal? Mortal means deathful. The word comes from a Latin word, "*mors*"—death, and is imported into the English language, but in plain Saxon, it is "deathful". Why deathful? Because of Adam's sin.

… He was born that he might die, as the first necessity in the case; for thus was the righteousness of God to be declared, and sin condemned in its own flesh as the foundation of all the goodness to come afterwards. … All these aims required that the sacrificial victim should be a perfectly righteous man, as well as a possessor of the nature to be sacrificially condemned—who should do no sin himself, while "made sin" and treated as sin for us; who should be just and holy, obedient in all things, while yet "numbered with the transgressors and making his grave with the wicked"[Isaiah 53:9-12]. (pages 9- 11)

Being made of a woman, he was of our nature—our condemned and weak and mortal nature: but being begotten of God and not of man, he was in character spotless "holy, harmless, undefiled, separate from sinners" [Hebrews 7:26]. Sin had hold of him in his nature, which inherited the sentence of death from Adam: but it had no hold of him in his character: for he always did those things that were pleasing to his Father. When he died, "he died unto sin once". But God raised him because of his obedience, and "being raised from the dead, he dieth no more: death hath no more dominion over him" (Romans 6:9, 10). (pages 11-12)

It is the grace of God then,—the act of God—that we see in the introduction of Christ upon the scene to open a way for mercy conformably with wisdom and justice. This required that he should appear in the nature of Abraham and David, which was sinful nature. How then, some say, was he, with sinful flesh, to be sinless? God's relation to the matter is the answer. God did it. The weak flesh could not do it. Jesus was God manifest in the flesh, that the glory might be to God. … (pages 18-19).

It was a spiritual necessity that he should partake of our nature. It is expressly said that he did, and John says that any man who denies it, as many did in his day and many have done since, denies the truth and is indeed anti-Christ. He is strong in maintaining that Jesus came in the flesh, that is, the flesh of the children, the flesh of David—flesh mortal because of sin. Why does he take this strong ground? Because the denial of it cuts at the root of God's arrangement of wisdom and righteousness. It destroys the very principle that made it impossible that the blood of bulls and of goats should take away sin. The object was that God's righteousness might have full play in advancing to our salvation. Christ could not righteously die if death had no dominion over him, and it could not have this dominion except through Adam, through Abraham, David, and his mother, for he had no sin of his own: it was the sin of others that was on him. It was his mission to take this away: how could he do this if it were not on him? "The Lord hath laid on him the iniquity of us all" [Isaiah 53:6], a figure of speech, because God proposed to forgive us all for Christ's sake. Still, in this very real sense, our sins are considered as being laid on him, and the beginning was made by making him of the same death-inheriting nature from Eden. The whole process was conducted in harmony with God's plan of righteousness in every item. The plan required that the sufferer while himself in the channel of death so far as nature was concerned, should himself not be a sinner, that he should be the Lamb of God, without spot, undefiled. Such an one could only be provided by what God did. God went out of His way to provide such a man. The man produced through Mary, by the Spirit of God, combined the two essential qualifications for a sacrifice; he was the very nature condemned in Eden, and therefore wrong was not done when he was impaled upon the cross. "It pleased the Lord to bruise him" [Isaiah 53:10]. Would it please the Lord to do iniquity? Nay. Therefore, it was right. But how could it be right unless he were the very condemned stock? (pages 12-13)

… Thus the meaning of the death of Christ falls easily within the definition that has been supplied to us in the words of inspiration. That definition satisfies all the demands of the understanding, reconciling every apparently discordant element in the case. It occurs twice in the course of Paul's letter to the Romans— in two different forms that exhibit the whole case. Both forms have been frequently on our lips in the course of these remarks; but they bear repeating. In the first, he says it was to "declare His (God's) righteousness for (and in order to) the remission of sins that are past, through the forbearance of God" (Rom 3:25), and in the second, he says it "condemned sin in the flesh" (Rom 8:3). The crucifixion of Christ as a "declaration of the righteousness of God" and a "condemnation of sin in the flesh", exhibited to the world the righteous treatment of sin. It was as though it was proclaimed to all the world, when the body was nailed to the cross: "This is how condemned human nature should be treated according to the righteousness of God; it is fit only for destruction". The shedding of the blood was the ritual symbol of that truth; for the shedding of the blood was the taking away of the life. Such a declaration of the righteousness of God could only be made in the very nature concerned; a body under the dominion of death because of sin. (page 16)

And now we have to consider in what sense did Christ come in sinful flesh. There are two things involved in these expressions that require carefully separating in order to understand their bearing on the questions that have been raised. Sin, in the primary and completest sense, is disobedience. In this sense, there was no sin in Christ. But where is the source of disobedience? In the inclinations that are inherent in the flesh. Without these, there would be no sin. Hence it is (because they are the cause of sin) that they are sometimes spoken of as sin. As where Paul speaks in Romans 7 of "Sin that dwelleth in me" and "The motions of sin in my members" etc. These inclinations are so described in contrast to the Spirit nature in which there are no inclinations leading to sin. It is only in this sense that Christ "was made sin", which Paul states (2 Corinthians 5:21). He was made in all points like to his brethren, and therefore of a nature experiencing the infirmities leading to temptation: "Tempted in all points like them but without sin". All this is testified (Hebrews 2:17; 4:15).

He has also come under the dominion of sin in coming under the hereditary power of death which is the wages of sin. He was in this sense made part of the sin constitution of things, deriving from his mother both the propensities that lead to sin and the sentence of death that was passed because of sin. He was himself absolutely sinless as to disobedience, while subject to the impulses and the consequences of sin. The object was to open a way out of this state, both for himself and his brethren, by death and resurrection after trial. It pleased God to require the ceremonial condemnation of this sin-nature in crucifixion in the person of a righteous possessor of it, as the basis of our forgiveness (pages 20-21)

Robert Roberts, *An Open Letter to Readers of The Christadelphian*, The Christadelphian, vol. 33, 1896, p. 263
At one or two points some had been turned aside by the sophistries of one George Cornish. … It is reached in the case of the truth, through a plausible theory to the effect that we do not inherit death from Adam by any physical law, but merely by denial of access to the tree of life: that the sentence of

death took no effect on Adam's body, and therefore is not in ours: that in fact we are the "very good" and uncursed Adamic nature that God formed from the ground in the first case; that our nature is not an unclean and sinful nature; that there is no such thing as sin in the flesh, or sinful flesh, or "sin that dwelleth in us" [Romans 7:17-23].

… Renunciationism[188], while denying Christ as the bearer of sin for its abolition through death and resurrection, did at least admit that the race was under condemnation. But this "ism" denies the very first fact of the Gospel testimony, that "By one man, sin entered into the world, and death by sin, and so death hath passed upon all men"[Romans 5:12]. By denying this, it denies the death of Christ in its testified character as God's appointed method of taking away the sin of the world. It declares that "Christ died because he was killed," in destruction of the Gospel testimony that "he gave his life a ransom for many" (Mark 10:45); laid down his life for the sheep (John 10:15); put away sin by the sacrifice of himself (Hebrews 9:26); offered one sacrifice for sins for ever, by which he hath perfected for ever them that are sanctified (Hebrews 10:12–14) through the offering of the body of Jesus Christ once for all (Hebrews 10:10). It reaches these disastrous results through the apparently harmless idea that the body of Adam was unaffected by the sentence of death, and that therefore Jesus was pure and holy and good in body as well as in character.

Robert Roberts, *The Nature of Man and the Sacrifice of Christ,* Diary of a Voyage 1896, pp. 66-69, The Christadelphian, vol. 33, 1896, pp. 339 - 442[189]

1) That death entered into the world of mankind by Adam's disobedience. *"By one man sin entered into the world, and death by sin" (Romans 5:12). "In (by or through) Adam all die" (1 Corinthians 15:22). "Through the offence of one many are dead" (Romans 5:15).*

2) That death came by decree extraneously to the nature bestowed upon Adam in Eden, and was not inherent in him before sentence. *"God made man in his own image ..... a living soul (a body of life) .... very good" (Genesis 1:27; 2:7; 1:31). "Because thou hast harkened unto the voice of thy wife .... unto the dust shalt thou return" (Genesis 3:17, 19).*

3) Since that time, death has been a bodily law. *"The body is dead because of sin" (Romans 8:10). "The law of sin in my members ..... the body of this death" (Romans 7:23, 24). "This mortal ...... we that are in this tabernacle do groan, being burdened" (1 Corinthians 15:53; 2 Corinthians 5:4). "Having the sentence of death in ourselves, that we should not trust in ourselves, but in God who raiseth the dead" (2 Corinthians 1:9).*

4) The human body is therefore a body of death requiring redemption. *"Waiting for the adoption, to wit the redemption of our body" (Romans 8:23).*

---

[188] Renunciationism refers to the teachings of Bro Edward Turney, who in 1873 "renounced" his previous beliefs, and taught that *"the body of Jesus did not inherit the curse of Adam … was therefore not mortal; that his natural life was "free" … and might, if he had so chosen, have avoided death, or even refused to die upon the cross and entered into eternal life alone … his death being the act of his own free will, and not in any sense necessary for his own salvation …".* See *The Christadelphian, vol 10. 1873, pp. 460-468.*

[189] This article was reprinted by both Bro CC Walker and Bro John Carter. See *The Christadelphian*, vol. 44, 1907, pp. 458-459, and vol, 74, 1937, pp. 552-554.

"He shall change our vile body that it may be fashioned like unto His own glorious body" (Philippians 3:21). "Who shall deliver me from the body of this death?" (Romans 7:24). "This mortal (body) must put on immortality" (1 Cor 15:53).

5) That the flesh resulting from the condemnation of human nature to death because of sin, has no good in itself, but requires to be illuminated from the outside. *"In me (that is in my flesh) dwelleth no good thing" (Romans 7:18). "Sin dwelleth in me" (Romans 7:20). "The law of sin which is in my members" (Romans 7:23). "Every good and perfect gift is from above and cometh down from the Father of Lights" (James 1:17). "Out of the heart proceed evil thoughts" (Matthew 15:19). "He that soweth to the flesh shall of the flesh reap corruption" (Galatians 6:8). "Put off the old man which is corrupt, according to the deceitful lusts" (Ephesians 4:22).*

6) That God's method for the return of sinful man to favour required and appointed the putting to death of man's condemned and evil nature in a representative man of spotless character, whom He should provide, to declare and uphold the righteousness of God, as the first condition of restoration, that He might be just while justifying the unjust, who should believingly approach through him in humility, confession, and reformation. *"God sent His own Son in the likeness of sinful flesh, and for sin condemned sin in the flesh" (Romans 8:3). "Forasmuch as the children are partakers of flesh and blood, he also himself took part of the same, that through death he might destroy that having the power of death, that is, the devil" (Hebrews 2:14). "Who his own self bare our sins in his own body to the tree" (1 Peter 2:24). "Our old man is crucified with him, that the body of sin might be destroyed" (Romans 6:6). "He was tempted in all points as we are, yet without sin" (Heb 4:15). "Be of good cheer, I have overcome the world" (John 16:33). "Whom God hath set forth to be a propitiation through faith in his blood, to declare his righteousness for the remission of sins that are past through the forbearance of God, to declare, I say, at this time, his righteousness, that he might be just, and the justifier of him that believeth in Jesus" (Rom 3:25-26).*

Robert Roberts, *True Principles & Uncertain Details*, The Christadelphian, vol. 35, 1898, pp. 182-189

MAN'S STATE AFTER CREATION

GENERAL PRINCIPLE.—He was a living soul or natural body of life, maintained in being by the action of the air through the lungs like us, but unlike us, a "very good" form [Genesis 1:31] of that mode of being, and unsubjected to death.

Uncertain Detail.—Would he have died if left alone, unchanged, in that state if he had not sinned? Who can tell? The testimony is that death came by sin: but the fact also is that, not being a spiritual body, he was presumably not immortal. Are we going to insist upon an opinion on a point like this, which no man can be certain about? We shall act unwarrantably if we do so. It is sufficient if a man believe that Adam after creation was a very good form of flesh and blood, untainted by curse. The uncertain points must be left to private judgment.

Robert Roberts – The Christadelphian, vol. 35, 1898, pp. 196-200

… The body continues mortal as ever, notwithstanding our relation to *"The law of the Spirit of life in Christ Jesus"* [Romans 8:2] - a law *in Christ* and not in us, and a law of immortal life, not animal life; and a law that will only come into force with regard to us when "Christ who IS our life shall appear" [Colossian 3:4]. Till then, we are waiting for the adoption, to wit, *the redemption of the body*, as Paul mentions in our morning's chapter [Romans 8]. The body will then be no longer "dead because of sin" [Romans 8:10]. It is so as yet—dead because of ancestral sin—mortal by inheritance from the first sinner. It will remain in this dead state till changed in a moment when the Lord, our life and glory, returns from the heavens. Then "this mortal"—this deathful—will put on immortality, if the Lord and Judge think well to grant this unspeakable privilege. Then we shall finally part company with the first Adam. We are in process of this redemption, and in process only. The process will be complete with "the redemption of the body." There has been much unskilful and obscuring talk on this subject.

Robert Roberts, *Why Did Adam Sin?* The Christadelphian, vol. 35, 1898, p. 343

Adam was in the 'very good' state before he sinned [Genesis 1:31]. He was not in the state his descendants are in. They are heirs of death; he was not. They have the sentence of death 'in themselves' (2 Corinthians 1:9); he had not. Paul had to say, 'sin dwelleth in me'; 'I see a law in my members warring against the law of my mind' (Romans 7:17,23); Adam could not have said this. …

Sin, as disobedience, arose in their case from a wrong opinion concerning a matter of lawful desire, and not from what Paul calls 'sin in the flesh'. It became sin in the flesh when it bought fourth that sentence of death that made them mortal, and all their children with them: that is, this sentence, passed because of sin, affected their bodily state and implanted in their flesh a law of dissolution that became the law of their being. As a law of physical weakness and death, it necessarily became a source of moral weakness. That which originated in sin, became a cause of sin in their posterity, and therefore accurately described by Paul as 'sin in the flesh'. It may shock you to think that such a condition attached to the Lord Jesus in the days of his flesh. But there is no cause where a full enlightenment prevails. He partook of our very nature that in him it might be redeemed and perfected. He did no sin, but he was physically "made sin for us who knew no sin." He was sent forth in the likeness of sinful flesh that sin might be condemned in him: that through death he might destroy that having the power of death. It is so testified (2 Cor 5:21; Romans 8:3; Hebrews 2:14), and we have nothing to do but believe the testimony, even if we could not see through it. But in point of fact, reason discovers a sublime beauty in this the highest of the works of God with man.

Robert Roberts – The Law of Moses, 1898, pp. 170-173

The position of men was that they were under condemnation to die because of sin, and that not their own sin, in the first instance, but ancestral sin at the beginning. The forgiveness of personal offences is the prominent feature of the apostolic proclamation, because personal offences are the greater barrier. Nevertheless, men are mortal because of sin, quite independently of their own transgressions.

… We see Jesus born of a woman, and therefore a partaker of the identical nature condemned to death in Eden. We see him a member of imperfect human society, subject to toil and weakness, dishonour and sorrow, poverty and hatred, and all the other evils that have resulted from the advent of sin upon the earth. We see him down in the evil which he was sent to cure: not outside of it, not untouched by it, but in it, to put it away. 'He was made perfect through suffering' (Hebrews 2:10), but he was not perfect till he was through it. He was saved from death (Hebrews 5:7) but not until he died. He obtained redemption (Hebrews 9:12) but not until his own blood was shed.

Robert Roberts – The Law of Moses, 1898, pp. 264-265

From this ceremonial shadow, we easily go to the substance. The ashes of a slain heifer applied to a man defiled by death, was a curing of death by death. This is precisely what happened in anti-type: Christ, "through death, destroyed that having the power of death, that is, the devil" (Hebrews 2:14). How could he do this if he had not in himself the power of death to destroy by dying? He has destroyed death. But in whom? In himself alone as yet. Believers will obtain the benefit by incorporation with him at the resurrection: but at the present time, the victory is his alone. The fact is plane to everyone. Some who admire Christ are horror-struck at the idea of his having being a partaker of the Adamic condemned nature – a nature defiled by death because of sin. Their horror is due wholly to too great a confinement of view. They fix their attention on the idea of "defilement" without remembering that the defilement was undertaken expressly with a view to removal.

We must have God's revealed object in view. The power of death was there that it might be destroyed. If it was not there, it could not be destroyed. This is the mischief of what may be truly called the Papal view. By denying that Jesus came in the very dying flesh of Adam, it changes the character of the death of Christ into a martyrdom or a punishing of the innocent for the guilty: instead of being what it is revealed to have been—a declaration of the righteousness of God that he might be just, while the justifier of those who have faith in it for the forgiveness of their sins (Romans 3:24–26).

LB Welch

LB Welch, The Christadelphian, vol. 29, 1892, pp. 139-142

When we go to the Edenic record, we find a very innocent pair in the persons of our first parents; as innocent, confiding, simple, and chaste in their minds and person as the little, simple, confiding child, with the exception that their nature never would have felt the motions of sin had they remained obedient, which the child will in time because it has inherited the nature of Adam after sin had been implanted in it by transgression. How happy were they in those the days of their innocency and companionship of the angels, or Elohim!

... By the testimony we learn that sin opened the eyes of Adam and Eve (Genesis 3:7) to the knowledge of good and evil by introducing them to a personal experience of evil, by developing in them fleshly impulses not before felt, and expressed by a consciousness of disobedience of law, and, therefore, an evil conscience (Hebrews 10:22); and also bringing upon them a still greater evil, the cutting-off of their life, or the bringing upon them of the sentence of death (Genesis 3:19). Sin, evil, death!

LB Welch, The Christadelphian, vol. 32, 1895, pp. 219-224

Of late I have been pondering over the two phases "in Adam" and "in Christ", in connection with which it is said, "in Adam all die," and "in Christ shall all be made alive" [1 Corinthians 15:22]. There is a very beautiful truth embodied in those two phrases, but an amount of haze has recently been developed around them. A few simple reflections may tend to dissipate it.

There is a certain fate awaiting all who abide in Adam. That fate is death and dust. We learn from the Bible that what constitutes our being in Adam is the being of his nature. We learn from the same source that the sentence of death rests upon the nature; that it is therefore a nature of death, or a body of death, and finally returns to the dust. We also learn that all begotten in and born of that nature are but propagations of it, heirs of all belonging to it, and therefore in Adam. It is not necessary to our purpose at present to enquire why death is the fate of Adam's nature, and therefore the fate of all who are of his nature. It is enough to know that being of his nature they are in him and suffer all the consequences arising out of being in him. The nature is Adam, and there is no escape from Adam as long as one possesses his nature; nor is there any escape from the consequences of his transgression in Eden, as long as we are of his nature, or in him.

Though saints are "in Christ," it is only in a preliminary sense. Christ is glorious nature. No one can be in Christ as he is in Adam till he is of Christ's nature. This is a self-evident truth. The inference to be drawn from it would clearly be that the phase "in Christ" cannot have the same import as the phase "in Adam" until a future event takes place. "In Christ shall all be made alive." This is yet in the future. We must therefore be in Christ as we are now in Adam (that is by nature) before we are truly alive. It is in Christ we are made alive; that is, by being of his nature. The nature Christ now has is a life-nature, while Adam's is a death-nature. It is clear that at present we can be made alive in Christ only prospectively. Our being actually made alive can be only when we are in Christ as we are now in Adam, or of him as we are now of Adam. Surely this ought to be clear to the simplest mind. At present our being in Christ is, and can be, only a state or condition of relationship. By baptism into his name we are brought into a relation of reconciliation, or favour, with God, whereby we stand related to a full adoption in Christ by the redemption of our nature and its exaltation to the nature Christ now has.

It is a serious blunder to interpret the phrase "in Christ" otherwise than simply one of relationship; that is, it would be wrong to interpret it as expressive of present results, or to say that as soon as we are baptized into the name of Christ, we have entirely left Adam and entered Christ. …

… Who is Christ? He is the Son of God, but not the eternally begotten Son of God. No one can understand who Christ is until he first understands God's purpose with Adam's race, and how He proposes to carry out His purpose. The Bible tells us how the race has its origin in Adam, and how it has been condemned to death and dust in him. The Bible further tells us that God's purpose is to take out of that condemned race a people to inherit the earth for ever. We also learn from the Bible that not one of that condemned race is able to deliver himself from sin and from the condemnation under which he rests. In this helpless state of the race, and for the carrying out of His purpose, God puts forth His own hand to bring salvation to a perishing people. He does it by begetting a Son in the sinful and condemned nature from which he is developed, and out of which he is born, in due time, a member of the race. To the commands of God he rendered a perfect, a sinless obedience. In his nature, God condemned sin by his death in the shedding of his blood. This was the redemption of the sinful and condemned nature from sin and death and dust. It was all accomplished by the power of God manifested in and through the condemned nature. Afterward, in three days, the nature was brought from death and the grave, and changed to spirit nature. That was redemption and glorification of Adam's sinful and condemned nature. The person through whom this was all accomplished is called the Son of God, and his name is the very embodiment of his great work. We behold him in two states, to wit: That of the flesh, and in the state of great humiliation; and that of the Spirit, and in the state of the exaltation and glory.

… On the other hand, when we see that disobedience produced a state of sin, and that the wages of sin is death, then we can see the force of condemning Adam and his race in him to death and dust in the way all go to death and dust. A state of sin exists with the race by reason of Adam's sin, into which all are born. But how is the race to escape the sinful state and the condemnation to death and dust? God shadowed forth the escape in the sacrifice in Eden. He promised the seed of the woman as the destroyer of sin, but that he would have to be first bruised in the heel (put to death in the flesh of sin) by sin [Genesis 3:15]. To typify this shedding of his blood for the condemnation of sin, animals were slain in Eden [Genesis 3:21]. The shedding of blood in the animals slain pointed out to Adam how sin would be condemned in the seed of the woman, and thus atoned for. It was a sacrifice in type prophetically pointing to Christ's sacrifice; …

CC Walker

CC Walker, The Christadelphian, vol. 36, 1899, p. 71

"*Explain Paul's meaning in Romans 8:20.*"—Paul's words are: "The creature (or creation) was much subject to vanity, not willingly, but by reason of him who hath subjected the same in hope." The "vanity" is the evil condition of mortal life and the death that terminates it, that has come upon the race through sin. The "not-willingly" feature is obvious when we consider our helpless entry into this evil case. Paul had alluded to this in Romans 5:12–14. The "subjection" of the creation to evil is explained in the history of Adam's sin given in the book of Genesis, and in the apostolic comments thereon in this and other places. The "hope" you know is the hope of life in Christ that was introduced even in Eden, and made plain in the Apostles' days by their preaching remission of sins in His name after He had triumphed over vanity and death in His own person by reason of obedience. Paul's words in Romans 5 will perhaps best explain his allusion in Romans 8:20.

CC Walker, The Christadelphian, vol. 42, 1905, pp. 320-321

QUESTION NO. 1.—Is it scriptural to believe that the sentence of death which was passed on Adam did not produce any change in Adam's physical constitution?

QUESTION NO. 2.—Has a belief "that the death sentence produced no change in Adam's physical constitution" any bearing on the nature of Christ? If so, how?

ANSWER TO NO. 1.—No, it is not scriptural, as may be seen from the apostolic references to human nature—"this body of death" (Romans 7:24); "creation groaneth . . . waiting for the redemption of the body" (Romans 8:18–23). These things could not be affirmed of Adam before he sinned; they could afterwards. ... The connection between sin and "change in physical constitution" is well seen in the works of the Lord Jesus. To say to the paralytic, "Son, thy sins be forgiven thee," was equivalent to saying, "Arise, take up thy bed and walk" (Matthew 9:5). A "change in physical constitution" immediately followed, and the man walked off rejoicing. ... It is because of the "change in the physical constitution" of Adam that David says: "Behold I was shapen in iniquity, and in sin did my mother conceive me" (Psalm 51:5). The same could have been said of every son of Adam, from Cain downwards; and if any object that it could not be said of Jesus, he has to face the explicit declaration of Paul that God "made him to be sin for us" (2 Corinthians 5:21), which is equivalent to "made him to partake of flesh and blood" (Hebrews 2:14). The Scriptures thus describe human nature after Adam's transgression as "sin"; because the new conditions of evil were referable to transgression.

ANSWER TO NO. 2.—The bearing upon the nature of Christ of a wrong conclusion concerning the result of Adam's sin is obvious. If there were "no change in Adam's physical constitution" because of sin, then sin hath not the power of death, and Jesus could not put it away in crucifixion. There is then no real reason why he should not have partaken of angelic nature. ... And therefore we go on pointing out that for Jesus to "put away sin by the sacrifice of himself" [Hebrews 9:26] he must have borne "sin" in bearing the condemned nature of Adam after the fall.

CC Walker, The Christadelphian, vol. 42, 1905, p. 569

The Word knows nothing of a "mortal constitution which is yet not subject to death"! It makes no such statement concerning Adam. The Word always uses the term "mortal" with the meaning "subject to death," and we decline participation in the enterprise of putting another meaning on it. That is how the apostasy arose, which proclaims as its fundamental doctrine, that man is "mortal in constitution, but not subject to death," i.e., in the inward part, the immortal soul.

But if the I.O.O.F. brethren, and brother Bell among them, we presume, now affirm that Adam was made "mortal in constitution, but not subject to death," what are we to make of the Shield's warm approval of the following:—"Now, I will give proof positive that it was a mortal body before he sinned. 'Mortal' means 'subject to death.' Proof that Adam was mortal before he sinned: Genesis 2:17—'Thou shalt surely die.'" Thus a brother writes in the Shield for June last, p. 117, and brother Bell, on the same page, calls it shining truth! The grave fallacy of the statement is that it misrepresents God, for the statement of Genesis 2:17 is "In the day that thou eatest thereof thou shalt surely die." Death was contingent upon disobedience, as also says the apostle, "death by sin" (Romans 5:12). How, then, does this brother say that Adam was subject to death before he sinned? How, also, do those who upheld him now affirm the very opposite? This is only one of many illustrations of the distressing confusions that have arisen. If Adam's destiny "was not determined until he transgressed God's law," which is perfectly true, how could he be mortal, which means subject to death, before transgression? Let the I.O.O.F. brethren first tell us exactly what they understand by "mortal." And then let them adhere to the definition given, and one step will be made towards re-union.

CC Walker, The Christadelphian, vol. 43, 1906, pp. 502-503

Throughout the Word briers and thorns are a constant symbol. They stand for the wicked, the useless, wild world-growth, to be rooted up, burned, and destroyed (Nahum 1:10). There is a fitness in the parallel that impresses the mind, from the beginning; even from the garden of the Lord in Eden to the garden of the Lord shown in the apocalyptic revelation. Between these periods runs the time of briers and thorns. Before sin was in the earth there grew none of these noxious weeds; and when sin is finally destroyed, the briers and thorns will have gone for ever. The sin-brought curse of God fell alike upon the ground and the man who came forth from it. Vegetable briers and thorns were its fruit in the one case, and moral briers and thorns--disobedience and rebellion growing up as a root of wickedness in the hearts of men, in the other.

There and then began the world-old struggle. The man, to preserve life, had to combat the tendency of the earth to choke the good fruits with useless, harmful growth; and, in himself, began that grievous fight that is with us yet, against the luxuriant growth of that which lifts itself against the mind of God: the lust of the flesh, the lust of the eye, and the pride of life; the principle of sin in the flesh, the briers and thorns of the natural uncultured, undisciplined mind. Without tendance or care grow these, springing up on any neglected ground, and the better the soil the more will they flourish; flowering, seeding, and spreading fast.

CC Walker, *Current Controversies*, The Christadelphian, vol. 44, 1907, pp. 556-557

As to Adam and mortality, Paul says: "By one man sin entered into the world, and death by sin." If Adam did not "become mortal as the result of transgression," then is *not* "death by sin." We use the word mortal in the Bible sense—subject to death—having the sentence of death in oneself (2 Corinthians 1:9), or the law of sin and death in one's members (Romans 7:23-25; 8:2). Those who teach that Adam was created "mortal" have foisted another meaning on to the term, namely, "capable of dying," but not necessarily "subject to death." We have nothing to do with this. It is not Bible doctrine, and we repudiate it.

As to God "implanting sin in (Adam's) physical constitution as a law of his being," brother J. Y. and others entirely misrepresent the *Christadelphian* and its late and present editor over this matter. They put it as if we believed and said that God personally and individually inserted some physical element into Adam after transgression. Nothing of the kind has ever been said or meant. As to the chemistry of the subject, if we may so speak, we are not called upon to speculate upon it. But as to Bible definition, we point to the form of sound words of the apostles. Could you say that Adam had a law of sin and death "*in his members*" before transgression? You could not. Could you help saying that he had such a law *in his members* afterwards?

You could not if you followed Paul and inspiration. So here was a change in physical constitution consequent upon sin, which at last resulted in death. No man understands the balance of life even in mortality. We cannot hope, therefore, this side the Kingdom of God to understand the precise interference with the balance of life that was Adam's before sin entered the world. All we know (because we are told it by God through an apostle) is that death in relation to man is "by sin."

… It is scripturally declared that God sent forth His Son "in the likeness of sinful flesh" (Romans 8:3); that is as being a partaker of flesh and blood (Hebrews 2:14), which flesh and blood is under condemnation to death because of sin (Romans 5). It is testified that God "gave him for a covenant," *commanding* him to lay down his life *that he might take it again* (John 10:17) that thus *through death*, he might destroy him that had the power of death, that is the devil (Hebrews 2:14), or in other words put away sin by the sacrifice of himself (Hebrews 9:26) and so obtain eternal redemption (Hebrews 9:12) *for himself first* and then for "his people."

We do not say that "God condemned Jesus," for that would imply moral reprobation, which is unthinkable; but we do say that God raised him up in the already condemned line of Adam and David "to put away sin by the sacrifice of himself." …

J. Y. and others ought not to say that the *Christadelphian* holds and teaches "that Christ *was not holy*, harmless and undefiled, and separate from sinners in his mortal lifetime." He ought to know, for he says he has read all sides, that the *Shield* quoted Hebrews 7:26 to attempt to prove that Jesus was "undefiled in every sense," *i.e.*, in *nature* as well as character! It is true that this particular expression has since been dropped; but the idea remains, or at any rate is not repudiated. We believe and teach that the Lord Jesus, in the days of his flesh, *was* holy, harmless, and undefiled in *character*, though burdened with the sin-nature from which he was to be delivered "through death." "The flesh" is a "vile body," or, if the expression be preferred "a body of humiliation" (Philippians 3:21). We can assure J. Y. that we shall never give place to the teaching that it is a clean and honourable thing. We know better, both from the Scriptures and our own distressed experience, internal and external. The present controversy in certain parts of the world is only a recrudescence of the old Renunciationist ideas slightly modified. These things are repeated in every generation.[190]

CC Walker, The Christadelphian, vol. 50, 1913, pp. 259-261

Divine usage is the basis of scriptural language, to which all true interpretation must conform. For lack of observance of this principle endless confusion has been wrought over such terms as "soul," "God," "heaven," and "hell." And it is so with this term "sin." The dictionary definitions given above conform more or less accurately to the divine usage of the term; but this can be discovered direct from the word of God itself. Let us turn to the Scriptures.

---

[190] Note that immediately after this article, Bro CC Walker reprinted Bro Roberts' article titled *"The Nature of Man and the Sacrifice of Christ"* – see page 287.

1. "Sin is the transgression of the law"; literally "Sin is lawlessness." This is the primary definition that is given by the apostle John (1 John 3:4). "All unrighteousness is sin" (1 John 5:17). This lawlessness and unrighteousness is made manifest by the law of God, which is "holy, and just, and good." This is the doctrine of Paul (Romans 7:12–13). "By one man sin entered into the world, and death by sin; and so death passed upon all men" (Romans 5:12). Since that time sin has been so inveterately ingrained in human nature that in divine usage it signifies "an incarnation or embodiment of sin" that is "the flesh."

2. "Sin is a synonym for Human Nature" (*Dr. Thomas*). Metonymy is that figure of speech by which, as the Greek term signifies, one name or noun is put for another to which it stands in a certain relation. There is a metonymy of cause, of effect, of subject, and of adjunct.

Sin is the cause of punishment and death and hence is sometimes put for these. "Arise, lest thou be consumed in the *iniquity* (margin, punishment) of the city" (Genesis 19:15). "I will pour *their wickedness* upon them" (Jeremiah 14:16), that is the punishment thereof. "This shall be the *sin* (margin), of Egypt" (Zechariah 14:19), that is "punishment," as in the text.

Sin is both the cause and the effect of the flesh, so much so that even the man after God's own heart exclaims: "Behold I was shapen in iniquity and in sin did my mother conceive me" (Psalm 51:5).

CC Walker – *What Is Sin?* The Christadelphian, vol. 73, 1936, pp. 412-414

"Christ ... his own self bare our sins in his body upon the tree, that we, having died unto sins, might live unto righteousness; by whose stripes ye were healed" (1 Pet 2:24).

Here comes in the principle of metonymy, by which "sin" is put for mortal human nature which is the *effect* of sin. Sin and its synonyms are put for the effects or punishments of sin. The angels hastened Lot and his wife and daughters out of Sodom, "lest," said they, "thou be consumed in the *iniquity* of the city" (Genesis 19:16). That is in the punishment thereof, as in the margin of the A.V. See also Psalm 7:16; Jeremiah 14:16; Zechariah 14:19: "This shall be the *punishment* (marg., *sin*) of Egypt."

... These things enable us to understand the like figures in the New Testament. "The body of sin" is "our mortal body" (Romans 6:6: 8:11), mortal because of sin (Romans 5:12). "He hath made him (Christ) to be sin for us who knew no sin; that we might be made the righteousness of God in him" (2 Corinthians 5:21). That is, "God sent his own Son in the likeness of sinful flesh, and for sin (R.V., *as an offering* for sin) condemned Sin in the flesh" (Romans 8:3). Or, again, Christ "himself likewise took part of the same (flesh and blood) that through death he might destroy him that had the power of death, that is the devil" (Hebrews 2:14). "Our old man was crucified with him" (Romans 6:6). "Jesus Christ by whom the world is crucified unto me, and I unto the world" (Galatians 6:14).

Sin is personified as The Serpent, The Dragon, The Old Serpent, The Devil, Satan, The Prince of this World, and so forth.

Henry Sulley

Henry Sulley, The Christadelphian, vol. 50, p. 443, 1913
The result of eating of the forbidden fruit was disastrous to Adam. The effect of eating was first of all a moral sense of disobedience, but the moral sense must have been accompanied by immediate physical results ultimately leading to death. That a physical change must have occurred to Adam and his wife is proved by the opening of their eyes (a physical result), and by the steps which they took to cover their nakedness. … Elsewhere we are told that "By one man sin entered into the world and death by sin, and so death passed upon all men" (Romans 5:12). A statement by an inspired apostle sufficient to settle the question whether a physical change occurred after transgression, bringing death in its train.

Henry Sulley, *The Atonement (1)*, The Christadelphian, vol. 58, 1921, pp. 392-394
In order to understand why the altar in the Temple of the age to come is to be cleansed and purged with blood, one must also be instructed in the means adopted by the Father for deliverance from the consequences of disobedience in Eden. In this connection it is all-important to remember the recorded facts. Adam having transgressed the condition upon which he was permitted the free choice of all the good things in the garden, one inevitable consequence must follow. The penalty for eating of the proscribed fruit, according to the record, was gradual decay ending in death. Thus we read:

"In the day that thou eatest thereof, thou shalt surely die. (Mar., dying thou shalt die"—Genesis 2:17).

"Because thou hast hearkened unto the voice of thy wife, and hast eaten of the tree, of which I commanded thee, saying, Thou shalt not eat of it: cursed is the ground for thy sake; in sorrow shalt thou eat of it all the days of thy life;"

"Thorns also and thistles shall it bring forth to thee; and thou shalt eat the herb of the field;"

"In the sweat of thy face shalt thou eat bread, *till thou return unto the ground; for out of it wast thou taken: for dust thou art, and unto dust shalt thou return*" (Gen. 3:17–19).

From these testimonies it seems we must understand that the moment Adam partook of the forbidden fruit he became a dying creature, just as a man in the dock is "a dead man" the moment the judge pronounces sentence upon him. Hence his sojourn on the earth came to an end before the expiration of *one day* of a thousand years (2 Peter 3:8). Thus it is written: "All the days that Adam lived were nine hundred and thirty years: and he died" (Genesis 5:5).

Henry Sulley, The Christadelphian, vol. 59, 1922, pp. 23-27, *The Atonement (5)*
The foregoing premises and conclusions may now be summarized:

1. Adam sinned by disobeying one command.
2. He suffered the penalty for his disobedience.
3. His descendants became involved in his transgression, so far as the consequences which follow disobedience, viz., a natural tendency to cherish thoughts contrary to God's commandments, leading to sin

and disobedience. Therefore all Adam's descendants are born subject to death, and unable to escape from the power of sin and death, because of the weakness of the flesh.

Henry Sulley, The Christadelphian, vol. 59, 1922, pp. 344-348, *The Atonement (9)*
"SIN IN THE FLESH" (ROMANS 8:3)
This phrase, shorn of its context, has come to express ideas subversive of the truth. When the apostle said that "what the law could not do, in that it was weak through the flesh, God sending His own Son in the likeness of sinful flesh, and for sin, condemned sin in the flesh" (Romans 8:3), he did not mean that God condemned "sin" in the flesh as though *sin* was a something *in* the flesh, but that he condemned *sinful flesh*, for He sent His Son in "the likeness of *sinful* flesh", *i.e.* in the same flesh (Hebrews 2:14), in order to *condemn sin*. "Flesh" was crucified and put to death in Jesus so that all emotions *to sin* arising from it in him should nevermore arise.

Now, when Adam sinned his flesh became "sinful flesh." Its quality then was sinful, although beforetime very good. So after transgression, the emotions of sin became a law, or rule of action, in Adam. Thus he may be said to be "sin made flesh," and *the law of disobedience* its principal attribute. This fleshly condition was transmitted to his posterity, who became incapable of themselves of manifesting any other quality.

Henry Sulley, The Temple of Ezekiel's Prophecy, 1929, pp. 114–117 (Logos Ed.)
… Therefore all his [Adam's] descendants are subject to death, and to the same conditions which supervened when he sinned, *i.e.*, they are naturally born in a state of sin and subject to death unless a way of escape is provided by the Father. Yet Adam's descendants are not *penalised* for his sin. As his descendants they are excluded from the privileges which he possessed in Eden. In this respect they may be likened to the descendants of a prince who by some act has abrogated his title to freedom and becomes a slave. In such case his descendants do not suffer a penalty, but the disability of their progenitor descends upon them. They never had what they would have enjoyed had not their father vitiated his title and by his misdeeds led them into slavery. This is their misfortune, not their crime.

The descendants of Adam also suffer all the consequences of his transgression which are transmissible through their physical relationship to him; much more so than the son of a leper who becomes leprous, or the son of a syphilitic who is syphilitic. By nature they inherit the natural impulses of the flesh set in motion by Adam's disobedience. This would have been an unmitigated evil had not a covering for sin and "a way" to the tree of life been provided.

John Carter

John Carter, Paul's Letter to the Romans, 1931, p. 61
And mankind is involved in the consequences of the "fall" of the "man," and of the "rise" of the "man." "For as in Adam all die, even so in Christ shall all be made alive" [1 Corinthians 15:22]. In Adam—by physical descent from him, by generation—all die. In Christ—by union with him, by

regeneration—shall all be made alive. This defines the "all." For all universally is not meant. While it is true that all absolutely of Adam's posterity by descent from him die, yet here the apostle's thought is concerned only with those who attain to life and immortality. As in Adam they all inherit death, so in Christ they all obtain eternal life. Both death and life are bound up with a federal head—one head leading along the way to death, the other leading along the way to life.

... "By one man" is a phrase governing every clause in Romans 5:12. Through one man sin entered the world; through him came death; through him death passed unto all, for that, or because, all sinned through his sin. Thus amplified, some of the difficulty which has occasioned much strife of words is removed. Adam sinned and was punished with death. His children inherit mortality and also a tendency to sin so inevitable in its sin-producing power that Paul can say that through Adam's sin all sinned, and therefore all die through him.

John Carter, Paul's Letter to the Romans, 1931, pp. 91-92
There is not exemption from suffering for the children of God. Rather, it is a necessity in the case, if it is a suffering with Christ. But the glory far outweighs the suffering, for the glory of the sons of God is the end to which creation looks and for which it waits. By a very striking and impressive personification, Paul in these verses represents creation as looking and waiting for the culmination of the Divine plan. The ground was cursed for Adam's sake (Genesis 3:17), and is thorn and thistle producing. This evil in nature, associated in origin with man's sin, will be removed in connection with the redemption in Christ. The "dominion" given to Adam (Genesis 1:26), and lost by him, is restored in Christ (Psalm 8:6; Hebrews 2:6–8; 1 Corinthians 15:27). ...

Paul says, "For the earnest expectation of the creation waiteth for the revealing of the sons of God. For the creation was subjected to vanity, not of its own will, but by reason of him who subjected it, in hope that the creation itself also shall be delivered from the bondage of corruption into the liberty of the glory of the children of God" (Romans 8:19–21). There is an incompleteness about man's world which cannot be the end of God's purpose with it. And just as Isaiah, in his picture of millennial peace, says that the wild creatures "shall not hurt in all my holy mountain: *for* the earth shall be full of the knowledge of the Lord, as the waters cover the sea" (Isaiah 11:9), so Paul attributes to creation an expectation of this time of restoration which is bound up with the manifestation of the sons of God. And as it was subjected by God to its present vanity, not of its own will or fault, but because of man's sin, so it will experience a deliverance from its bondage and share the liberty pertaining to the glory of the children of God.

John Carter, *Sin, Sins, and Sin-Offering*, The Christadelphian, vol. 75, 1938, pp. 127-138
"Sin is lawlessness," said John; it is a state where law is not recognised and obeyed: hence "everyone that doeth sin doeth also lawlessness." With but one exception all the race of mankind have sinned—have transgressed God's law. Some in John's day professed a regard for God's law but made light of sin; but the apostle dismisses this with the assertion that these are

opposites—sinfulness is lawlessness. Because all needed the forgiveness of sins Jesus was "manifested to bear sins," to do which he must be sinless; hence John adds, "and in him is no sin"—no lawlessness, no disobedience. It is of actions and disposition that John is speaking, as the context both before and after the words show; for John adds, "Whosoever abideth in him sinneth not: whosoever sinneth hath not seen him, neither known him" [1 John 3:4-6]. Jesus is an example, and those abiding in him follow the life exemplified by him.

It is doing violence to John's context to take the words "in him is no sin" as proof that Jesus had not the physical nature which Paul describes as "sin." John is thinking of sin in moral terms; but he does not contradict Paul who uses the word of physical condition. In fact, John makes the belief that the physical nature of Jesus was like ours a test of fellowship. "Every spirit (teacher) that confesseth that Jesus Christ is come in the flesh is of God; and every spirit that confesseth not that Jesus Christ is come in the flesh is not of God," but antichrist [1 John 4:2-3]. "Many deceivers are entered into the world, who confess not that Jesus Christ is come in the flesh. . . If there come any unto you, and bring not this doctrine, receive him not into your house, neither bid him God speed" [2 John 1:7-11].

We must discriminate between "sin," "a sin," and "sins." Paul says God "hath made Jesus *to be sin* for us, who knew no sin" (2 Corinthians 5:21). This does not mean that Jesus was a sinner; Paul excludes that, saying in effect, Jesus was made to be sin but was not a sinner. Neither does it mean that Jesus was made a sin-offering. …while Paul says "for a sin-offering" in Romans 8:3, he says "sin" and not "sin-offering" in 2 Corinthians 5:21. The same is true of Hebrews 9:28: "So Christ also, having been once offered to bear the sins of many, shall appear a second time *apart from sin*, to them that wait for him." He was not "apart from sin" at the first advent when he was offered to bear sins. The reason is evident: if he had not had our physical nature he could not have been the Redeemer.

In what sense then was Jesus "made sin"? In the sense that "he himself likewise took part of the same" flesh and blood as all the other children who are given him. Therefore "he died unto sin," having all his life "condemned sin" so that he might be an acceptable "offering for sin." If we ask where sin was condemned? the apostle says "in the flesh"; on which Dr. Thomas appositely remarks: "Sin could not have been condemned in the body of Jesus if it had not existed there."

John Carter, *The Reign of Death*, The Christadelphian, vol. 75, 1938, pp. 173-174
The theory is being put forward that death belongs inevitably to the body of man as he was created; that Adam in course of time would have died apart from having disobeyed the law of God; and that the sentence of death imposed for sin is "the second death." We die, according to this view, because it is a law of our nature, and not because of any sentence which has been passed by God upon Adam, and which has involved all his descendants.

… In apostolic language, Death reigns. A child is born—it may die during its earliest days before it has known either good or evil, or it may grow to adult life. But we know that in time death will come. Why? Is it for the same reason that other forms of life come to an end? The insect, which is a creature of few days, and the animal whose natural span of life exceeds that of man, alike die. Is there no other cause for man's death than for that of the insect or the animal? We might so conclude if we had no revelation; we should so conclude if we accepted the theory of man's descent from animal origin as set forth by the teachers of evolution. But with revelation to guide us, another conclusion is reached.

Brother Roberts asks the question: Did the Adamic race commence mortal? And says: "Paul's dogmatic assertion that 'by one man (Adam) sin entered into the (human) world' is a settlement of the question. . . .

The apostle puts Adam and the consequences of his act of disobedience in contrast with Jesus and the consequences of his life of obedience. "By man came death; by man came also the resurrection of the dead" (1 Corinthians 15:21). The theme is expanded in a series of comparisons and contrasts in Romans 5:12–21. The need for the redemptive work of Jesus in the grace of God, is traced to the sin of Adam. Death holds universal sway because of that disobedience, but a way of escape is provided: "That as sin hath reigned unto death, even so might grace reign through righteousness unto eternal life by Jesus Christ our Lord" (Romans 5:21). Here are two regnant powers, the one based on sin, the other on righteousness.

No one disputes, whatever explanation of it may be believed, that Jesus had to die as a part of his work. "He was obedient unto death," as Paul says. If Jesus was a member of the race, sharing the nature which is subject to death because of sin, then we can see in his voluntary submission to it a declaration of God's righteousness, which Paul says was necessary that God might be righteous while bestowing righteousness by the forgiveness of sins on those who believe (Romans 3:21–26). We see the grace of God in providing Jesus, but we see the triumph of that grace reached through righteousness.

But if Jesus and all others inherit a nature which is mortal quite independent of Adam's sin, why did Jesus have to die? If it be answered that he died for us, then we can only conclude that the innocent suffered for the guilty upon the basis of substitution; and he should not have been raised while those for whom he died should not die. Further, in that case, it was not necessary that he should have to die for himself in any sense, for how can a nature undefiled by sin need a cleansing sacrifice? It could not, and Jesus would not then be a partaker of the benefits of his own work. But this is contrary to the teaching of Scripture. He was "saved out of death" (Hebrews 5:7); "by his own blood he entered in once into the holy place, having obtained eternal redemption" (Hebrews 9:12). ... "Now the God of peace, that brought again from the dead our Lord Jesus Christ, that great shepherd of the sheep, *through the blood of the everlasting covenant*, make you perfect" (Hebrews 13:20).

The theory under discussion resembles in some respects the Renunciationist error which was put before the brethren in 1873. Both theories, whether the promoters see it or not does not affect the fact, represent God as doing wrong. In the words of the pamphlet, *The Slain Lamb: "This heresy represents God as doing wrong; for it says of the Christ, the Lamb of God, 'here is a free life.' If so, why should a free life die? But Christ, instead of being what is called a free life, was in the condemned nature of the children of Adam. Hence when he died, nothing wrong happened, so far as God's doings were concerned. The obedience of the Son of God led to his resurrection, and the triumph was complete."*

The terminology has changed, but the essential feature of the error remains: and to quote the same writer's words in *The Blood of Christ*, *"it was a spiritual necessity that he should partake of our nature. It is expressly said that he did, and John says that any man who denies it . . . denies the truth . . . He is strong in maintaining that Jesus came in the flesh, that is, the flesh of the children, the flesh of David—flesh mortal because of sin."*

John Carter, The Christadelphian, vol. 76, 1939, pp. 228-230

We believe it is contrary to the meaning of Scripture to say (1) that the words *"Dust thou art, to dust shalt thou return"* described the condition of man when first created, and is therefore not a sentence of death subsequently passed by God upon Adam as a result of transgression; and (2) that the "death which has come by sin" is not the death common to all men, but the second death. The true teaching of the Bible, we assert, is that we are dying creatures, inheriting a nature which is "evil" (Matthew 7:11), in which *"evil is present,"* which evil is further described as *"a law in our members,"* *"the law of sin in our members"* (Romans 7:23). Such phrases could not be used of Adam before he sinned.

John Carter, *Give Attention To Reading*, The Christadelphian, vol.79, 1942, pp. 4-5

The early chapters of Genesis are essential to a correct understanding of later events. We cannot understand God's work in Christ if we reject the record of the formation of man, and of his sin, and of the sentence which consigned him to death. There are certain consequences which affect us all which have their causes in the early history of the race. Death has passed through to us because of Adam's sin. The creation has been made subject to vanity; it does not in its present form realise the end God had in view. It is a state of groaning and travail, says Paul; but yet not a state without hope. God has indeed subjected it to evil, but He has given hope of deliverance, even from this bondage of corruption, and has promised freedom, "the liberty of the glory of the children of God" [Romans 8:20-23].

John Carter, The Christadelphian, vol. 79, 1942, p. 227

… But if Adam's nature unchanged by sin, and if the nature we bear is not a dying nature *because of sin*, then the death of Jesus could not exhibit God's righteousness. On the contrary, in such a case, since Jesus was free from personal transgression, he could not be related to death as the wages of sin in any way, and to require his death would be unrighteousness. The need for Christ's sacrifice is to be found finally in the transgression in Eden. The law of sin and death then introduced was overcome and finally set aside by the obedience of Jesus unto death, even the death on the cross. We are sure our Australian brethren approve these remarks, and understand that we are with them in opposition to the error.

John Carter, *Winds of Doctrine*, The Christadelphian, vol. 80, 1943, p. 195

The apostle Paul says that *'by man came death'* and, *'in Adam all die'* (1 Corinthians 15:21-22). The same matter is stated in greater fullness in Romans 5:12: *'By one man sin entered the world, and death by sin; and so death has passed upon all men, for that all have sinned'*. If death came 'by man', and 'by sin', it was not present in the world of man before he sinned. This death was the result of the sentence *'unto dust thou shalt return'*; and in the words of Brother Roberts, *'death came by decree extraneously to the nature bestowed upon Adam in Eden, and was not inherit in him before sentence'*. This expresses his view at the end of his life when he was controverting the meaning put upon some of his words written in his younger days, and which now are being reproduced. Dr. Thomas's, general teaching is clear, whatever ambiguity may attach to a few of his phrases. *'Man's defilement was first a matter of conscience and then corporeal'. 'The great principle to be encompassed (for the taking away of sins) was the condemnation of sin in sinful flesh, innocent of actual transgression. This principle necessitated the manifestation of one ... (who) would be Son of God by origination; and Son of Man by descent, or birth of sinful flesh'. 'Sin was to be condemned in sinful flesh'. 'Sinful flesh being the hereditary nature of the Lord Jesus, he was a fit and proper sacrifice for sin; especially as he was himself innocent of the great transgression, having being obedient in all things.'*

John Carter, *Prophets After the Exile*, 1945, pp. 66-67, 80 (1962 Edition)

We are all mortal independently of personal sin; and that mortality is an inherited one, and its ultimate cause is the sin **at the beginning of human history**. All Adam's posterity are involved in the consequences of his transgression, Jesus being no exception. If our mortality is in no way a consequence of sin, and simply something that belongs to the human organization as created (as some have taught), then the nature of Jesus was likewise unrelated to a mortality which was a consequence of sin. In that case unrighteousness and not righteousness would be shown by his death . . .

John Carter, *The Heretics*, The Christadelphian, vol. 83, 1946, pp. 9-10

A pamphlet written by E. Brady, attacking the articles by bro. Collyer in *The Christadelphian* for July and August, 1945, has been widely circulated by a small group of onetime Christadelphians, now self-styled Nazarenes, and by inference in the title of the pamphlet "The Heretics". ...

We should get at the facts. Death has come by sin. Sin is rebellion against God, the setting up of man's will against the will of God, thereby challenging God's supremacy. God therefore punished Adam with death. "By one man sin entered the world, and death by sin", says Paul; and again, "By man came death". These are basic statements of fact—they give the reason why man dies: for Paul continues, "and so death passed upon all men, for that all have sinned" [Romans 5:12]. He proves this by pointing out that death reigned from Adam to Moses, yet men during that period were not living under a penal code. Their death was not the result of any imposition due to broken law, just as in the Christian dispensation there is no divine penal code which inflicts death for disobedience. But the law of Moses had a penal code—for certain transgressions a man had to be stoned: but the absence of such a penal code during the period from Adam to Moses, shows that individual death was not due to individual sin, but to inherited mortality. Paul could hardly cite the Christian dispensation, which would have served his argument equally well, in view of the time he was writing.

The antithesis in 1 Corinthians 15:20-23 shows that the death that has come "by man" is the death which terminates the present life. Paul does not talk of forfeited life: man dies. To treat of "life" as something that could be paid as in commercial transactions, is to obscure the facts. Life is not a separable thing from the man as if it were a part of him that could be dealt with apart from the man as a whole. The Bible deals with the man as a physical being, whose life is terminated by death. And as death has come by man, so "by man came the resurrection of the dead". The death from which Christ rose is the death that has come by man. From this death the gospel offers us deliverance. But instead of these simple facts we are invited to believe, on one page of the pamphlet, that there is "only one penalty for sin, namely death . . . the effect upon a sinner is extinction, final, complete and utter destruction", on another that "if Adam had borne the penalty himself he would have remained dead"; and yet that "death that is the penalty (is) the actual suffering of death and not the fact of remaining dead". So do the necessities of a false theory lead to contradictions.

Christ rose "the firstfruits"; he is alive for evermore. God has highly exalted him because he was obedient even to the death on the cross: he has the keys of the grave. By his voluntary death he declared God's righteousness in involving all in death because of sin; God's supremacy is upheld in Christ by the willing offering of a sinless man who shared the consequences which have come by sin. God's holiness and righteousness is thus upheld, God invites us to identify ourselves with Christ in the symbolic rite of baptism which itself speaks of death. We acknowledge the moral principles of divine action, and for Christ's sake God forgives.

John Carter, *God's Unfolding Purpose*, God's Way, 1947, pp. 80-83

When Adam had transgressed God's law he was sentenced to die—to return to the dust of the ground (Genesis 3:19) He was at the same time prevented from partaking of the "tree of life" while in his sin-stricken condition. And the Lord God said, Behold, the man is become as one of us, to know good and evil and now, lest he put forth his hand, and take also of the tree of life, and eat, and live for ever. Therefore the Lord God sent him forth from the garden of Eden, to till the ground from whence he was taken. So he drove out the man, and he placed at the east of the garden of Eden cherubims, and a flaming sword which turned every way to keep the way of the tree of life" (Genesis 3:22-23).

The First Promise – Genesis 3:15

... "I will put enmity"—God imposed an antagonism between the way of disobedience and the way of obedience—the serpent and its seed standing for the one and the woman and her seed for the other. This conflict has pursued an uninterrupted course throughout men's history. Men of faith and righteousness have opposed and been opposed by men of unbelief and of sin but the climax of the strife is to be seen in the conflict in and about Jesus of Nazareth in the days of his flesh, and in its sequel in the ultimate accomplishment of the purpose of God. As this will be developed in the following chapters in detail, let it suffice here to say that the promise of "the seed of the woman" suggests that the seed is none other than the Son of God, who would be divinely begotten. The seed was not to be the seed of man humanly begotten; but as seed of the woman he inherited all the frailty and tendency to sin which is the lot of all Adam's descendants. In this conflict he yielded a temporary triumph to the sin-power, being wounded in the heel in his death but recovering from this, he gave the death blow to sin by his resurrection and attainment to immortality. This complete personal triumph-thus far seen only in himself - will through him result in the complete removal of every curse and every ill that has followed sin.

John Carter, *Our Representative*, God's Way, 1947, pp. 134–135

Jesus is described as "the last Adam" (1 Corinthians 15:45). Between the first Adam and Jesus there is a parallel and also a contrast, which Paul unfolds in Romans 5. Christ's redemptive work is there explained by reference to the universal need which has its origin in the events narrated in Genesis 2 and 3, previously examined. The sin of the first Adam brought death; the obedience of the last Adam brought forgiveness of sins, and justification, and life; by the first man's disobedience many are "made sinners"—by the obedience of Christ, many are "made righteous" (Romans 5:12-21). The same contrast between Adam and Christ is succinctly expressed by Paul in 1 Corinthians 15:21: "Since by man came death, by man came also the resurrection of the dead".

But the effects of the sin of Adam come upon all by birth—by natural generation; the righteousness of Jesus Christ comes by re-birth—by re-generation. This re-birth requires a response on the part of man which all will not give. Recognizing that all do not respond to God's approach in Christ, in his statement of the results of the work of the two Adams, Paul, therefore, breaks away from what would be a literal parallel and states what is fact: "If by one man's offence death reigned by one; *much more they which receive abundance of grace and of the* gift of *righteousness shall reign in life by one, Jesus Christ*" (Romans 5:17). God's mercy is freely available for men: man on his part must accept it. Receiving God's grace, and with it the gift of righteousness, a man admits his insufficiency of personal righteousness, and finds the grace and truth in Jesus Christ by which he will "reign in life". He also recognizes that "as sin hath reigned unto death, even so might grace reign through righteousness unto eternal life by Jesus Christ our Lord" (Romans 5:21).

John Carter – Unity Book, 1958, p. 20

Through Adam's sin the original very good state was lost, and his posterity inherit a nature with a tendency to sin to which all have succumbed. Because this inherited tendency is so evident a characteristic of human nature, and because it is the result and cause of sin, Paul by the use of metonymy can describe it as sin: "It is no more I but sin that dwelleth in me." He gives it other names as well, such as "*a law – evil present with me*", the "*flesh*", "*a law in my members*" (Romans 7:17-25).

A similar usage of metonymy is found in 2 Corinthians 5:21, where Paul says that 'Him who knew no sin God made to be sin, that we might be made the righteousness of God in him'. This statement is one of a whole series of paradoxes in 2 Corinthians 5. Christ the sinless was made to be sin in sharing in the effect of sin in his life, and by his death providing the conditions for the forgiveness of sins and, finally, the removal of all the effects of sin. The same usage occurs in Hebrews 9:28 which declares that Jesus will appear the second time *"apart from sin"* unto salvation. It is a fallacy in reasoning to say that what is affirmable of sin literal must apply to sin used in this metonymical way. We are blameworthy for our sins, but we cannot help the possession of the natures with which we are born. Sins need forgiving and our nature needs changing. Sins are forgiven now for Christ's sake but the change of nature takes place when our Lord comes." *"The most outrageous statement that has been made (in the Andrew controversy) is the one that men are objects of divine anger because they are flesh" (The Christadelphian 1894, p. 466).*

John Carter – Unity Booklet, 1958, p. 28-32

But sufficient to notice that they experienced a sense of shame and the sentence was passed that 'dust thou art, and unto dust shalt thou return'. Here death came, as the Apostles say, into the world through sin. But by and by children are born. What is it that they inherit? This nature related to death, that had now become the lot of Adam and his wife.

….. What is it that is within us, that the apostle describes as sin? Clearly there are the impulses that lead to sin. There are impulses there that are the result of sin at the beginning, which we have by inheritance.

John Carter – Unity Booklet, 1958, pp. 78-81

At the same time it was rightly insisted that Jesus shared our nature with its sorrows and temptations, but always overcame every trial. As Brother Roberts wrote (1875, p. 376):

> *'He was a sufferer from the hereditary effects of sin; for these effects are physical effects. Death is a physical law in our members implanted there through sin ages ago, and handed down from generation to generation. Consequently, partaking our physical nature, he partook of this, and his own deliverance (as 'Christ the first fruits') was as necessary as that of his brethren. In fact, if Christ had not first been saved from death (Hebrews 5:7), if he had not first obtained eternal redemption (Hebrews 9:12), there would have been no hope for us, for we obtain salvation only through what he has accomplished in himself, of which we become heirs by union with him. He overcomes and we share his victory, by uniting with him, if he at the judgement seat permit.'"*

… It was Adam who sinned; it was Adam who was condemned; it was the dust formed organisation that was sentenced to return to the ground. It was the physical man that sustained such changes as brought shame and fear and a defiled conscience, a defilement which then became, in Dr. Thomas' word, 'corporeal'. But the opposite error is now being taught. 'Sin' used by metonymy for the fleshly impulses, is now being separated from the individual and is being made of itself a reason for alienation and estrangement.

… In 1874 (p. 88), Bro. Roberts answered the question, "What do you mean by "sin in the flesh", which some speak of as a fixed principle?"

> *"Answer: … There is a principle, element, or peculiarity in our constitution (it matters not how you word it) which leads to the decay of the strongest or the healthiest. Its implantation came by sin, for death came by sin; and the infliction of death and the implantation of this peculiarity are synonymous things."*

Islip Collyer

Islip Collyer, The Christadelphian, vol. 33, 1896, pp. 99-102
Because sin is defined as "the transgression of the law" [1 John 3:4], some
have supposed that those who are not under law in a definite specific sense
cannot sin. This is obviously incorrect. In the second chapter of Romans the
apostle declares that those who have sinned without law shall also perish
without law; while those who have sinned in the law shall be judged by the
law [Romans 2:12]. This passage demonstrates the fact that sin is possible
apart from being in any direct way under divine law. The explanation is
that in a certain sense all men are related to law. If, after Adam had sinned,
God had ceased to interfere with the human race all would have been
"without understanding," and, consequently, "like the beasts that perish."
Since, however, God introduced a law for man's redemption certain
commands were made to the race, and, consequently, all who do things
contrary to that law may be said to have sinned; although, being without
understanding, they are not held responsible.

Islip Collyer, *The Meaning of Sacrifice*, Principles & Proverbs, 1938, pp. 94–100
… Transgressions of the divine law can only be put away by the forgiveness
and forbearance of God. Physical uncleanness of nature can only be put
away by the power of God. The sacrifice of Christ is the divinely appointed
basis in which God in mercy and forbearance offers forgiveness and
redemption to sinners (Romans 3:23-24; 4:7; Ephesians 1:7; Colossians 1:14;
1 John 1:9; 2:12).

If we desire to probe further and ask the question why did God require
such a sacrifice as the basis of the forgiveness offered to humanity, we shall
never find any answer through the various interpretations of the law or by
talk of the penalty due to sin. Divine law is simply an expression of divine
will. It was not the will of God that man should sin, but it was the will of
God that man should be a free agent and that death should be the wage of
sin. It was the will of God that the human race having been defiled by sin
should have no access to His holy presence except on the basis of a perfect
sacrifice. And it is the will of God that we should respond to the gracious
invitation and be saved on the basis He has provided (1 Thessalonians 5:9).
If we ask why God required such a sacrifice, we must seek a moral
explanation. It is no answer to quote the law which expresses His will.

Guided by Scripture we can find a moral explanation that satisfies every
demand that the intelligence can make. The perfect sacrifice was required
that the flesh might be effectively repudiated, that sin might be conquered
and condemned, that the righteousness and holiness of God might be
declared, and that sinful man should be humbled without a particle of
ground for boasting being left to him (Romans 3:23-27; 8:3; Ephesians 2:1-9).

… Christ bore just this same defiled nature that we bear or he could not
have been tempted as we are and therefore could not have condemned and
conquered sin. Christ bore this quality in the flesh, but he never allowed it
to conceive even to the point of sinful thought. Therein was the most terrific
struggle and the most portentous victory of all human experience. It is easy
to understand that with his ideals, and his standards of rectitude, the

weakness of the flesh would be so distressing that even the most startling language of the Psalms is comprehensible.

… Some have caused confusion by arguing whether Christ's offering for himself was "only a matter of obedience to God" or whether it was something more. What do they mean? Obedience to God is carrying out the will of God. What can be required beyond this? Surely we are all agreed that Christ, "the beloved son", "the servant in whom God delighted", and the one who "always did his Father's will", needed no forgiveness. Surely we are also agreed that he needed cleansing from the sin-stricken nature in which he wrestled with and conquered the diabolos. There could be no forgiveness for personal sinners except on the basis of the perfect sacrifice, for this was the will of God. There could be no cleansing and immortalizing, no entry into the Most Holy by any of Adam's race except on the basis of the same perfect sacrifice, for that also was the will of God. Christ came to do God's will, he was obedient in all things even unto death, and so with his own blood—in other words, on the basis of his perfect offering—he entered the Most Holy "having obtained eternal redemption" [Hebrews 9:12].

Islip Collyer, *As We Grow Older*, The Christadelphian, 1946, vol.83, pp. 3-8
It would clear away much confusion of thought if all could remember the simple truth that death reigns because of sin. Man is under a law of mortality because of sin. Only by inheritance could death pass upon all men, as taught by the Apostle. As the Lord Jesus said, "That which is born of the flesh is flesh" [John 3:6]. It would have been an injustice far from the character of God if all men had been held guilty of Adam's sin, but there is no injustice whatever in our being born of faulty flesh any more than in a dog being born a dog. We should never hold children guilty of a parental sin in which they played no part, but if the error of the parents lost the original family fortune, the children would grow up in an impoverished house. …

The Bible supplies the explanation. Man was originally designed for something better than animal life. By man sin entered the world, and death by sin. So death has reigned even over those who, not having come under law, have "not sinned after the similitude of Adam's transgression" [Romans 5:14]. They have been born of mortal flesh, and therefore are mortal flesh. We all like the Apostle have "the sentence of death in ourselves" [2 Corinthians 1:9].

… At the first man was very good. There came a time when even children went astray, "speaking lies". The heart of man was described as "deceitful and desperately wicked" [Jeremiah 17:9]. Finally, we have the Apostle in that much abused seventh of Romans putting the matter so plainly that it is quite probable that enemies in his day would sneer at him, and suggest that he was a great sinner. We know quite well that far more than most men he succeeded in keeping his body under, and bringing it into subjection. He describes a struggle, however, which is experienced by all who make a serious attempt to subdue the flesh and bring every thought into captivity. The Apostle did not say that at one time there was a law of sin in his members but that when he put on Christ it departed. He speaks of that other law in our members warring against the mind, and tending to bring it in captivity to the law of sin [Romans 7:17-25]. There could not be such mental warfare unless the law of the enlightened mind and the law of sin were present at the same time. It is a matter of physical inheritance which is not changed by our entering the Covenant. We put on the new man which is renewed day by day by the Word of God, but the flesh remains. Some who began well, some "for whom Christ died", may be "destroyed" through relapsing into fleshly ways.

… It is fair to presume that all Christians recognize the truth that Christ is the only sinless one. If men stood now in precisely the same condition as the first Adam, it would seem strange that after seeing the consequences of so much sin, none should succeed in being perfectly righteous. We are not in that original condition. Human nature is "so much the worse for six thousand years of sinning". The more the flesh pleases itself, the more impatient it is of restraint. We thankfully recognize that training and environment may effect much, but we have to recognize that heredity plays a large part too, as many foster parents have discovered to their sorrow.

In their fallen condition many men have been able to lead decent lives. Ish-bosheth was described by David as a righteous man, and there have been many others who were righteous and "blameless" for the standards of mortal life, but all have "fallen short of the glory of God" [Romans 3:23]. We need not be surprised that a degraded being should so fall short. It brings us again to the wonder of the Lord's achievement in taking hold of this nature and by his perfect life and death destroying that which has the power of death.

WF Barling

**WF Barling, *Redemption in Christ Jesus: The Differences Stated*,
The Christadelphian, vol. 83, 1946, pp. 21-22**

1. Adam's sin made him a mortal (i.e., dying) creature, sinfully inclined.
2. Jesus, as a representative, died to uphold the Edenic sentence of death on human nature, as a basis for the justification of men before God.
3. Jesus, as the son of Mary, was identical in nature with all humanity, in order to share Adamic condemnation with those whom he came to save.
4. Jesus, being begotten of God, was enabled to conquer sin.
5. The term "sin" in Scripture, while signifying literally "the transgression of law", is also generally personified to represent the innate sinfulness of human flesh as a consequence of Adam's disobedience.

**WF Barling, *Redemption in Christ Jesus: 2. Death By Sin*,
The Christadelphian, vol. 83, 1946, pp. 38-40**

… The record informs the reader of Adam's nature – that he was formed of dust, and taken out of the ground (Genesis 2:7). But no question of his return to the earth arose until he sinned. Here again, if he was, regardless of transgression, destined to return to dust, God's pronouncement is robbed of all its points and purpose as an expression of displeasure: it becomes merely gratuitous. A respect for the structure of the chapter, however, makes it clear that God's words to Adam were intended to reveal to him the physical affect, for himself and his posterity, of his sin.

… The N.T. gives the significance of the skin covering. Adam set the law of sin and death in operation; God in His mercy, instituted the law of the spirit of life in Christ Jesus. In a whole series of antitheses the N.T. contrasts the effect of Adam's sin with that of Christ's obedience. Two familiar examples might be given.

1. By man came death, by man came also the resurrection of the dead (1 Corinthians 15:21).

2. As sin hath reigned unto death, so might grace reign unto eternal life (Romans 5:21).

Here are touchstones by which to test the rival interpretations of Genesis 2:17. Both schools of thought accept the first clause, believing that by Adam came death, and that due to him sin reigned unto death: but they differ in their conception of that death. If the second clause is, however, accepted candidly as the antithesis of the first, the very contrast requires that in each case the term "death" should mean that which takes a man inevitably to the grave.

… Death was no enemy of Adam's until his sin introduced it into the world. God made him a living creature: his sin made him a dying creature.

WF Barling, *Redemption in Christ Jesus: 4. The Death of the Cross*, The Christadelphian, vol. 83, 1946, pp. 65-67
The Nazarene contention that Jesus was not made 'Sin', but 'a sin-offering', destroys the antithetical balance of this verse (2 Corinthians 5:21). Men naturally know no righteousness, but are 'made righteousness' when they identify themselves with Jesus. Similarly, because of the identity existing between him and them on account of a common sinful nature, he who knew no sin was 'made Sin'. That is, God, in His mercy, accepted Christ's 'body of sin' as representative of all other human flesh, in which Sin dwells. So though Christ died on a literal cross where we need not (a difference of experience which the Nazarene Fellowship misuses and magnifies into a rigid theory of substitution), yet nevertheless we are "crucified *with* him". He represented us, for if he were our substitute we could not be "buried *with* him". This he did because "sin, in the flesh" (the cause), which in all others has led to transgression (the effect), was in his person regarded by God as representative of men's iniquities.

WF Barling, *Redemption in Christ Jesus: 5. Implications Examined*, The Christadelphian, vol. 83, 1946, pp. 82-84
Nazarene authors declare that transgression altered only Adam's position in relation to law, and "did not cause his flesh to be changed". They therefore regard man as still "very good", and to be "just what the Creator made him". The Scripture that every man is *enticed to sin* by his own lust (James 1:14) is made "to include Adam in Eden" to the extent that the impulses which led Adam to eat unlawfully are defined as "God-implanted natural desires". Logic is invoked to prove this. It is emphasized first that Eve—sinless as yet—experienced "the lust of the flesh, the lust of the eyes, and the pride of life" in as real a sense as any man since (Genesis 3:6). From

this it is inferred, secondly, that if these impulses are sinful now, they were also sinful in Eve who has transmitted them to posterity. Lastly, since these impulses must (it is claimed) in the first place be attributed to God who endowed man with them, we are expected to conclude that "there is not in fact one inclination in all the human mind but what, when you consider it, is good in itself". Otherwise, it is argued, "if any of the senses or faculties of man are sin, then God is the author of sin".

Such reasoning is contrary to Scripture. John explicitly declares the lust of the flesh, the lust of the eyes and the pride of life to be 'not of the father, but of the world' (1 John 2:16). There could be no more emphatic testimony that these 'lusts' are not desires which can be attributed initially to God; but sinful propensities which only came to exist as a result of the first offence. The "lust of the world" and "the will of God" are essentially antagonistic (1 John 2:17). Disciples should therefore "no longer live to the lusts of men, but to the will of God" (1 Peter 4:2), for, far from being "God-implanted", lusts are "of Diabolos" (John 8:44).

By their voluntary belief in, and consequent obedience to, the first lie, their nature was vitiated so that they hid themselves from God (Genesis 3:7-10), and their simplicity, or innocence, was corrupted (2 Corinthians 11:3). Ever since, this moral corruption has persisted as an evil property of human nature, part of the vanity to which God made creation subject until the day of salvation (Romans 8:20-25).

If the Nazarene denial of this fact be true, and human nature is not sinfully inclined, then, theoretically, it should not be hard to do good, nor yet easy to do evil. But it is implicit throughout Scripture that, in practice, to be imperfect is dangerously easy. Disciples must *take heed lest* they sin (Luke 21:34), *fear lest* they come short (Hebrews 4:1), *beware lest* they be not steadfast (2 Peter 3:17). From the use of such language one must infer that man is initially disposed to do wrong. Conversely, it is not easy for him to acquire the inclination always to do right, for disciples must *strive* to enter in at the strait gate (Luke 13:24), *press* toward the mark (Philippians 3:14), *be diligent* to be found without spot and blameless (2 Peter 3:14).

There is thus a bias to evil within man which has to be offset by an acquired tendency to do good (Colossians 3:1). This bias must either have been implanted at Creation, or be the direct consequence of Adam's transgression. The first proposition is inconceivable; the second states the facts.

AD Norris

AD Norris, *The Universal Consequences of the Sin of Adam*, Acts and Epistles, pp. 425-427

Romans 5:12: First of all we have the plain fact that we are all descended from the first created man, Adam, and that it was his sin that involved us in the situation in which we find ourselves. It brought death to him, and to all his descendants, of whom it is true, for each one severally, that "his breath goeth forth, he returneth to his earth. In that very day his thoughts perish". Death comes to all, for the same seed of sin is present in all. That seed in itself brings death, but the actual indulgence of sin means that death is personally deserved as well as inevitable by heritage. (Genesis 2:9, 16-17; 3:17-19; Psalm 146:1-4; 1 Corinthians 15:21-22)

Romans 5:13: Sin existed, we must add, before the Law of Moses was given; and though it is true that sin can only be committed when law is violated, we have already shown that the eternal power and godhead of God were plainly seen of men of all ages, and at all times, men have violated that which their minds had every opportunity to perceive. Even though Adam's sin in the partaking of the forbidden fruit was unique, and even though the specific requirements of the Law of Moses had not risen until Moses himself received them from God, there is evidence enough that God's will was open to knowledge even during this intervening period. Thus, Cain sinned in the matter of his offering; the 'sons of God' in Noah's day sinned against the knowledge they had of their duty before God; the men of Babel flouted divine authority; and the men of Sodom were sinners before God exceedingly (to name only a few). All the evidence shows that all the poison inherited from Adam's fallen nature had permeated human nature, and led men inevitably into sin. Adam is the true fleshly forefather of a sinful race, and provides a fitting figure for another who was to be the true spiritual forefather of a race pledged to righteousness. (Romans 1:20-25; Genesis 4:1-15; 6:1-8; 11:1-9; 13:13)

AD Norris, *Where Science and Religion Meet: 7. The Creation and Fall of Man*, The Christadelphian, vol. 102, 1965, pp. 148-150
… It is our fallen race which lusts, and envies, and slays in anger and with guile. It is ourselves who do wrong things, think wrong thoughts, and endure disquieted consciences because of it. "From within, out of the heart of man, proceed" all the things which are as typically human as our much-boasted attainments. Our power to worship is matched only by our inborn reluctance to accept the whole consequences of the worshipful God whom that power acknowledges. The record of the third chapter of Genesis provides a complete explanation of this. It provides the only basis which prepares us for the historical fact of the coming of the Lord Jesus, the historical reality of his death, and the historical crowning miracle of his resurrection.

AD Norris, *Our Heritage: An Appeal For Faithfulness and Calm*, The Christadelphian, vol. 102, 1965, pp. 176-177
If I were put in the position of having to discuss relations in fellowship with one whose views were different from my own, I should want to say, in effect, to him: (1) I believe that you are mistaken; but, (2) Do I understand that you accept fully the inspiration and reliability of the Scriptural records? (3) Do you, as the Scriptures and our Statements say, also accept the true innocence of man and woman as created? (4) Do you believe that they truly underwent a unique Fall, committing the sin which resulted in their expulsion from the Garden, in their subjection to death, and in our own heritage of temptation and desire?

And if I received positive answers to the questions there put, I think I should have to add: Then, despite our difference on this topic, we do have the same outlook on the sanctity of the Word of God, on the nature of our first parents, on the Fall and on our own nature, and therefore we do hold the same elements of the one Faith

LG Sargent

LG Sargent, The Christadelphian, vol. 78, 1941, pp. 13-14

It is the teaching of Dr. Thomas in Elpis Israel that Adam before the fall was capable of death, but not subject to death: and in that we believe he faithfully and logically interprets Scripture. …

… The word "immortal" is taken to mean "incapable of death"; and "mortal" might be expected to mean its simple opposite, "capable of death": whereas in fact it is used in the sense of "subject to death, destined to die"—a more restricted meaning which has the support of dictionaries. …

If, then, we take "immortal" to mean "incapable of dying" (as Dr. Thomas does in the passage quoted), we must say that Adam in his novitiate was not incapable of dying, therefore capable of dying, and therefore "mortal" as a simple antithesis to immortal, and using the widest sense of an ambiguous term. There is a class, "incapable of dying"; all not included in it must be included in the class "capable of dying"; but the latter class may be divided into two sections: (A) those in whom death is only a capacity— a latent capacity, as we might say; and (B) those in whom it is an active condition. Both are included in one wide classification, "not-immortal": but it is the sub-class in whom death is an active principle who are, on a stricter definition of terms, called "mortal", because they are "subject to death, destined to die". Adam was always within the class, "capable of death", but on the sentence of God he passed from the sub-class in whom it is a latent capacity to the sub-class who are actively subject to corruption as a law of their being; and in that class all his posterity have remained—all save One, who has been "made perfect".

LG Sargent, The Christadelphian, vol. 101, 1964, pp. 205-210

MAN'S NEED: From what does man need to be delivered? Paul states the facts with unsurpassed brevity: "By one man sin entered into the world, and death by sin; and so death passed upon all men, for that all have sinned" [Romans 5:12].

All suffer the consequences of one sin, yet it is no arbitrary sentence imposed by despotism, for all are sinners; heredity and environment combine, their inherent tendency finds opportunity, their impulses are stirred, and they sin. …

SIN, DEATH, CONDEMNATION: In this connection there are three facts to be taken into account. The first is the fact that death "reigns" [Romans 5:17]; all alike, the innocent babe and the aged sinner, are subjects of the dark despot. True though it is that men are constituted as the animals by nature, Paul's teaching is that as a fact in the history of man death came into man's experience as the consequence of the one man's disobedience. It came as judgment by a divine sentence that he must return to the dust. All his progeny suffer in consequence; they suffer because the mortal cannot produce the immortal, and because the sinner cannot produce the sinless. Sin is a universal fact in human nature, and even the babe of a week old possesses the nature which is prone to sin, though it may not be an actual sinner. Of the race as a whole it can be said comprehensively, "all have sinned" [Romans 3:23], and therefore death has passed upon them not by an arbitrary *fiat*, but as a necessity of the righteousness of God.

LG Sargent, *The Faith of the Christadelphians*, The Christadelphian, vol. 101, 1964, pp. 262-264,
… Christadelphians therefore believe without any equivocation in the Fall of Man. They believe that moral evil has its source in man's fallen nature; and consequently they do not believe in any principle or entity of evil outside of man and striving against God. It is man's own impulse, his unregulated desire, his self-assertive pride, which is adverse to God and to man's own good: and Christadelphians believe that the "Devil" and "Satan" are scriptural personifications for this principle in man's nature and its various manifestations in society.

As a necessary consequence of his nature, man is mortal, subject to death. In the universe of a holy and omnipotent God, who is also God of love, there is no place for immortal rebels or deathless sinners. Thus, when we read the words of Paul, "The wages of sin is death, but the gift of God is eternal life through Jesus Christ our Lord" (Romans 6:23), Christadelphians take these words simply and literally: death is earned, and in Paul's words death "passed upon all men" (Romans 5:12); life is a gift granted through the channel whom God has appointed, who is His Son. And the teaching of all the New Testament is that deathless life is given on the ground of faith in Christ Jesus—a living faith which bears fruit in obedience and which endures to the end.

Edward Whittaker

Edward Whittaker, *The Genesis Record of Creation*, The Testimony, vol. 39, 1969, pp. 131-133
God intended that Adam should be lord of all created things on the earth—"over the fish of the sea, and over the fowl of the air, and over the cattle and over all the earth, and over every creeping thing that creepeth on the earth" (Genesis 1:26). But because he sinned he forfeited the "dominion" and brought down God's curse on all the world of nature, so that disharmony now reigns among all living creatures and the animal kingdom is in a continual state of war, "red in tooth and claw". Psalm 8:5-8 has been explained by the Christian prophets (1 Corinthians 15; Hebrews 2, etc.) as a remarkable prophecy of the ultimate victory of our Lord, when God "has put all things under his feet, all sheep and oxen, yea, and the beasts of the field; the fowls of the air, and the fish of the sea, and whatsoever passeth through the paths of the sea." At his return, Christ will deliver his people from the bondage of corruption, and also deliver "the whole creation which groaneth and travaileth together in pain until now" by restoring harmony and balance to the world of nature (see Isaiah 11:6-9; 65:25).

Edward Whittaker, *The Antediluvian Patriarchs*, The Testimony, vol. 41, 1971, p. 16
By the offence of one many were made sinners" (Romans 5:19), and, ever since, 'a fixation of sin' has inhered in Adam and his posterity, producing a murder as early as the first generation.

Peter Watkins

Peter Watkins, *The Cross of Christ*, The Christadelphian Magazine and Publishing Association Ltd (UK)

… Genesis 3 continues the narrative. It tells of the disobedience of Adam, and the consequences of this disobedience. God pronounced the death sentence upon Adam:

"In the sweat of thy face shalt thou eat bread, till thou return unto the ground; for out of it wast thou taken: for dust thou art, and unto dust shalt thou return" (Genesis 3:19).

The effect of this upon the rest of humanity is stated by Paul: *"By one man sin entered into the world, and death by sin; and so death passed upon all men, for that all have sinned"* (Romans 5:12).

Like begets like. Adam disobeyed and became a sinner, and all his children follow him in the way of sin. The Scriptures declare, and we know from personal experience, that there is in all human beings a strong tendency to defy the law of God. Adam was condemned to death, and his descendants, the sin-stricken human race – all who are "in Adam", to use a Scriptural expression – are likewise subject to death: "Death passed upon all men, for that all have sinned."

The Scriptures themselves emphasize the fact that man is subject to death because of sin. Romans 5:12, quoted above, is just one of many passages that stress this relationship between sin and death. The oft-quoted Scripture, *"The wages of sin is death"*, occurs in the next chapter of Romans 6:23, and in the chapter after that it is stated that *"the motions of sins, which were by the law, did work in our members to bring forth fruit unto death"* (Romans 7:5).

… When God pronounced the death sentence on mankind in Eden He was upholding His own righteous law. If He were to waive this sentence, He would, in effect, be saying that sin does not really matter after all. So the sentence of Eden stands and God requires that each of us must die.

… But why does the Lord compare himself to a serpent, of all creatures? [John 3:14-15] The Son of God came in human form. In character he was perfect, yet he had inherited from Adam a "serpent" nature – a nature which could be tempted to sin. This nature was the cause of the trouble. It had to be cursed and crucified.

To hang a person on a tree, pole, or cross, was a symbolic act. It was the Hebrew way of cursing the one who was "lifted up". In the words of Scripture: "He that is hanged is accursed of God" (Deuteronomy 21:23). In comparing himself to the serpent on the pole, the Lord was teaching that salvation from death could only come by cursing and destroying human nature with its potential for rebellion against God's authority. The Lord Jesus, an innocent bearer of this rebellious nature, showed what to do with it. He crucified it, and he invited others to do the same.

… The brazen serpent symbolizes the destruction of what is evil, and the paschal lamb symbolizes the giving back to God of what is good. Together they sum up all that was accomplished by the death of Jesus, and all that is required of his followers. Human nature is evil and offensive to God. It must be destroyed. This is the lesson of the brazen serpent. But life itself, and every good gift, has come from God and must be given back to him in sacrifice. This is the lesson of the paschal lamb.

Peter Watkins, *The Tree of the Knowledge of Good and Evil*, The Christadelphian, vol. 101, 1964, pp. 500-503
We say that the act of eating forbidden fruit made Adam and Eve sinners. Did the act of disobedience defile or debase their nature in any permanent sense?

From time to time we hear assertions that Adam's transgression did not, in itself, carry any far-reaching consequences. It is argued that Adam committed an isolated act of sin that did not vitiate his nature; and that its physical effects were not transmitted to his progeny. But let us examine the record.

Let us note, in the first place, the contrast between Genesis 2:25 and Genesis 3:7:

> "And they were both naked, the man and his wife, and were not ashamed."

> "And the eyes of them both were opened, and they knew that they were naked; and they sewed fig leaves together, and made themselves aprons."

Before the transgression Adam and Eve were not ashamed of their nakedness; after the transgression they were ashamed. Why the difference? Why should the knowledge of their nakedness reveal a condition that caused shame?

If we define nakedness as man's natural state the account becomes easier to understand. Before sinning, Adam and Eve were not ashamed of their natural state; after sinning, they were ashamed. We cannot escape the conclusion that, in some way, the act of sin affected their natural state and made it shameful even to themselves. Clearly then, the act of sin must not be thought of as an isolated act that did not affect Adam's nature.

So greatly were Adam and Eve concerned about their changed condition that they took steps to conceal that which was offensive, even to themselves. They made clothes to cover their nakedness. So deeply were they affected that they still felt naked—even after covering themselves with clothes. They hid amongst the trees of the Garden. Indeed, Adam confessed to God that he had hidden himself amongst the trees because of his nakedness, although he was already clothed when he looked for concealment. Obviously physical nakedness was only a part of the trouble. There was a spiritual nakedness that neither clothes nor shady trees could conceal. The nature of Adam and Eve was so much defiled by the act of disobedience that only God could provide an adequate covering for their nakedness. Sacrifice was necessary. Coats of skin were provided.

… We have seen that the act of disobedience of our first parents made an indelible impression upon the transgressors themselves. And because none can bring a clean thing out of an unclean, the defiled Adamic nature is transmitted to all the children of Adam and Eve.

… All human beings inherit a defiled nature from Adam and Eve. There is abundant scriptural confirmation of the fact that humanity is stricken by sin. A number of passages come to mind immediately, such as:

"The imagination of man's heart is evil from his youth" (Genesis 8:21).

"The heart is deceitful above all things and desperately wicked: who can know it?" (Jeremiah 17:9).

"From within, out of the heart of men, proceed evil thoughts, adulteries, fornications, murders, thefts, covetousness, wickedness, deceit, lasciviousness, an evil eye, blasphemy, pride, foolishness: all these evil things come from within, and defile the man" (Mark 7:21–23).

"Every man is tempted when he is drawn away of his own lust, and enticed" (James 1:14).

Alfred Nicholls

The Committee of The Christadelphian, *For Whom Christ Died*, The Christadelphian, vol. 108, 1971, pp. 358-363

The Bible is very plain. Of the nature of Adam after he fell there is no doubt. In the day that he sinned he was condemned to death. From that moment he was as good as dead. "By one man sin entered into the world and death by sin." All of us, save One, actually do sin and all, without any exception at all, are faced with the urge to do so, which is part and parcel of our fallen nature.

History shows it: the Fall of Adam was followed by the murder of Abel, and then by the multiplication of wickedness which arose from the indulgence of "every imagination of the thought of man's heart".

Genesis 3; Romans 5:12; Romans 3:23; Hebrews 4:15; Genesis 4; Genesis 6:5

Precept shows it too: the last quotation was almost a statement of what man's heart is like, and immediately following the Flood God pronounces that "the imagination of man's heart is evil from his youth", a very plain statement of where sin springs from, stating equally plainly that we are not only tempted to sin from without: the temptation is there, powerful and urgent within. As James puts it, "Every man is tempted when he is drawn away of his own lusts, and enticed." The same root source of all our sinning is found in Jeremiah's statement, "The heart of man is deceitful above all things, and it is desperately sick." …

Genesis 8:21; James 1:14; Jeremiah 17:9; Romans 1:24, and throughout chapters 1–3; 7:1–24; Romans 8:3; James 4:1; Galatians 5:19–21.

We need only the Lord Jesus' own confirmation of our position. And this he provides when he rejects the idea that defilement comes from outside, and tells us quite plainly whence come all our promptings to evil:

"That which proceedeth out of the man, that defileth the man. For from within, out of the heart of men, evil thoughts proceed, fornication, thefts, murders, adulteries, coveting, wickedness, deceit, lasciviousness, an evil eye, railing, pride, foolishness: all these evil things proceed from within, and defile the man" (Mark 7:20–23).

So there we have our human nature: through no fault of our own each one of us inherits desire contrary to the will of God. This is the "law of sin in our members". When we indulge it we actually commit sin. Our nature can only be like that of Adam after the Fall; nor can it be said that terms like "clean" or "undefiled" are in accord with the Scripture teaching set out above. So long as this nature is with us we are unfit for the Kingdom of God. That is why a man needs to be born again, and why the Lord Jesus Christ died and rose again to make this possible.

John 3:3–5; Galatians 5:21; 1 Corinthians 6:10-11.

The Committee of The Christadelphian, *In Adam or In Christ*, **The Christadelphian, vol. 112, 1975, pp. 390-403**

THE PRINCIPLE OF RESPONSIBILITY

"By one man sin entered into the world, and death by sin." Paul's statement in Romans 5:12 emphasises the fundamental importance of the Genesis record for our study, since in the experiences of the "one man" the principles of responsibility and judgement are laid down.

… Salvation begins with the renewing of the mind, followed by the sanctification of the spirit and is completed by the resurrection of the body; condemnation affected man in the same order: he was affected in mind and conscience first, then in bodily sensations, and finally he was to die. …

CONDEMNED BY GOD

The sentence which God pronounced was immediate and terrible: some aspects of it had arisen instantly as a result of their bad conscience—the sense of nakedness, the fear, the shame. The rest were to follow in their now degenerate life before their physical decay brought them to the grave.

We can now examine further the relationship between salvation and condemnation. Just as Paul draws an analogy between the sin of one man which brings the death of all, and the righteousness of one man by which all can be saved, so it is possible to see the parallel between the process of the Divine sentence and its removal. Evidently Adam's conscience had been affected and some of the consequences of his sin were already active within him, as he felt his nakedness and was ashamed before God. He was condemned already, in the sense of knowing he was guilty, by his own act and out of his own mouth. Nevertheless, God condemned him to death and ensured that there was no way of evading that penalty (Genesis 3:23). In the same way, the man obedient to God's command can first render "the answer of a good conscience", "be transformed by the renewing of the mind"; and sanctify God in both body and spirit. His release from the bondage of corruption, however, is the last stage in the process of his salvation.

Genesis 3 throughout; 1 Peter 3:21; 1 Corinthians 6:20; 2 Corinthians 7:1

JUDGEMENT AND CONDEMNATION

It is important to stress, even at the risk of some repetition, one aspect of the judgement on Adam which has a bearing upon the whole principle of judgement we are considering. There were immediate consequences of his sin and the life of joyful fellowship was evidently over, since Adam tried to hide from the presence of God in the garden. But there was still a definite, formal "hour of judgement", when Adam and Eve were brought before God, and the sentence, both in such effects of their transgression as they had already experienced and in its ultimate issue in their death, was unmistakably seen to be the sentence of God, formally pronounced in their presence.

Genesis 3:9, 10, 16–19

ALIENATED FROM GOD

Although "the Lord God made coats of skins and clothed them", which in view of later records we are justified in interpreting as the institution of sacrifice as a means of approach to God, the man and his wife were nevertheless excluded from the garden. The actual words of the Lord God are: *"Behold, the man is become as one of us, to know good and evil: and now, lest he put forth his hand, and take also of the tree of life, and eat, and live for ever; therefore the Lord God sent him forth from the garden of Eden"*. So Adam and Eve, both by personal transgression and by divine edict were alienated from the life of God as they had formerly experienced it. There could be no possibility of their continuing as "one of us" and sharing a divine fellowship, for their life was to be one of shame, fear, pain and sorrow, and theirs was to be a "living death" until physical death brought it to an end. Yet there was a "way of the tree of life", which though not yet opened up, offered hope of eventual restoration to those who should be granted the privilege of treading it because they had overcome.

Genesis 3:22–24; Revelation 2:7

We must carefully distinguish between the two periods of Adam's life, and avoid drawing conclusions about our own case from one period which properly belong to the other. The transgression that allowed sin into the world, bringing with it the spiritual and physical death that were its punishment, took place in the Garden of Eden. It was unique in being the first and only such transgression, and it was unique in its far-reaching consequences for Adam's seed. In the garden also the judgement took place and the sentence was pronounced. After Adam's expulsion from the garden and exclusion from the tree of life, his life was lived in the conditions produced by his transgression and in relation to the arrangements for worship and the covenant God had made with him. It is to this period alone therefore that any questions of Adam's *future* judgement and relation to eternal life—his "probation" in our terms—must be referred. For the Scripture is thenceforward concerned with Adam and all his descendants on the basis of their mortality and their own sinfulness and their relationship to God's promises, whereby they could become partakers of the divine nature if they escaped the corruption that is in the world through lust. Adam and Eve had first been alienated from God by their transgression, but had become separated also by their nature. They were what they were because they had sinned: and because of what they had become they would never be free of the propensity to sin and the possibility of sinning until that nature was destroyed.

2 Peter 1:2–4

… The first man had alienated himself from God in the garden because he became a stranger to the life of God by his own will. Thereupon, being expelled from the garden, he had been condemned to live with the consequences he had brought about. His progeny were not only living with those consequences but had become, of their own will, strangers from God.

… So in the day they sinned, Adam and Eve were "without God", and as we have already seen, their expulsion from the garden showed how complete was that alienation from the life of God. They were under "the wrath of God", having chosen wicked works, being wilfully ignorant, not of the specific commandment, but of the mind and purpose of God. So would they have remained had it not been for the hope, the sacrifice and the covenant of promise. The basis of any future acceptability with God was faith, the manner of their approach was through sacrifice; the infirmity of their fleshly nature, however, would remain until the consummation of all things in Christ. How Adam and Eve fared in this new sphere of probation we do not know and we gain nothing by speculation.

… The term "flesh" in Scripture, with reference to sin, refers to "deeds done in the flesh" for which man's mind and heart are responsible. "Flesh" merely as a physical substance has no will and cannot therefore be considered as guilty; nor is it of itself an evil substance. Since the days of Adam's sin, to partake of "flesh and blood", however, is to feel within oneself the motions of a will not naturally subject to the law of God.

Romans 7:18; Romans 8:13; Galatians 5:19–21

In Adam All Die

Thus "by one man sin entered into the world and death by sin, and so death passed upon all men, for that all have sinned." Thus was inaugurated the universal reign of sin and death: sin "came in" and death "came upon" all men as a consequence of one man's action, declares Paul in his fundamental statement in Romans 5:12. It is a plain statement of the relationship of all men to Adam, since the Apostle is not here speaking of the personal share which the man and the woman had in the original transgression, as he is in 1 Timothy 2:14: "Adam was not deceived, but the woman being deceived was in the transgression". The Romans passage deals with the man as involving the succession of the race for "he begat a son in his own likeness and after his own image".

Romans 5:12; Genesis 5:3

… In the disobedience of one man all are involved by natural birth and without their own volition. In the perfect obedience of one man all can become involved by a new birth. But in the process of being begotten into perfection and life, our faith and voluntary obedience are an essential part.

Romans 5:12–20; John 3:3–5; 1 Peter 1:22-23.

For the moment, however, we are still concerned with the consequences of being "in Adam". "Sin entered . . . all have sinned". Here is sin seen both as something in which all men are involved, and as something which develops itself in our conduct: it is both the propensity to sin and the habit of sinning. The very metaphors Paul uses emphasise its universal character: all are "under sin" (Rom 3:9) and "sin has reigned" (Rom 5:21). All men are subjects of the same powerful monarch. And since it "reigns unto death", then Paul can also say that death reigns too, for the law of sin and death was pronounced in Eden when the Lord God said unto the first man: "In the day thou eatest thereof, *thou shalt surely die*".

In the effects of sin on the first human pair is to be seen a pattern of the disorders, mistrusts and passions that would henceforth continue to ravage human life and society. "Desire" and "dominion" entered into relations between the sexes; man was banished from God's presence and was afraid to seek his Creator, and he had to battle against evil in the created world; while on the physical level life was a painful and ultimately hopeless struggle to renew and sustain its basic processes. For the whole human race was born outside the garden, alienated from the life of God. "The carnal mind is enmity against God, for it is not subject to the law of God, neither indeed can be. So then, they that are in the flesh cannot please God." Indeed, "flesh and blood cannot inherit the kingdom of God" and in his parallel phrase Paul tells us why: "neither doth corruption inherit incorruption". Corruption is both physical decay and all that is associated with the life and morality of man born of corruptible seed, the servant of corruption—corrupt manners, corrupt deeds, corrupt speech. In short, the image of Adam, the earthy.

Gen 3:16–19; 4:4; Rom 8:7, 8; 1 Cor 15:50; Gen 6:5,11,12; Eph 4:22; Jude 1:10

"As is the earthy, such are they also that are earthy", and in Adam all die. "By the offence of one, judgement came upon all men to condemnation." In dealing with the things of God which lie so completely beyond our understanding except by His revelation, we are not spiritual but carnal if we construct rival or mutually exclusive theories of God's judgement and mercy based on our own use and usage. The fact is, in Scripture there is both a racial and an individual condemnation, as can be clearly shown. The former is the consequence of being born "in Adam", the other of personal transgression. The unique responsibility of Adam derived from the fact that he was the ancestor of the human race, and had been created to have dominion over the works of God's hands. The command to be fruitful and multiply and replenish the earth meant that everything subsequently hung upon his obedience to the explicit command relating to the tree of knowledge. What the earth would have been like peopled by the offspring of a spiritually mature Adam we cannot know. We do know that "the whole creation groaneth and travaileth together in pain until now", since not only man but all else has been involved in the consequences of Adam's transgression. Again, we get a glimpse of this principle in reverse, so to speak, in Isaiah's vision of the harmony of the beasts and the removal of hurt and destruction when righteousness reigns upon the earth.

Isaiah 11:1-9; Romans 8:20–23

CORPORATE INVOLVEMENT IN TRANSGRESSION

… Thus, Adam was not merely an individual man, but the progenitor of the human race of which he and his wife were then the sole representatives. In his phrase that "By one man sin entered into the world, and death by sin; and so death passed upon all men, for that all have sinned", Paul is therefore saying more than that all men have sinned personally, true though that is, with the single exception of Christ.

We have, however, already pointed out that there are overtones of moral guilt and estrangement involved in terms like "condemnation" and "alienation". The involvement of the race in the punishment of Adam, is not the same thing as imputing to all the guilt, as distinct from the consequences, of his iniquity. Again, the analogy of Israel helps us here. Caleb and Joshua were forced to wander forty years in the wilderness, being members of the sinful nation condemned so to do. But being alone judged personally faithful to the Lord and His covenant, they did not perish with the rest, but entered into the promised Land. … Also, in the case of visiting "the iniquity of the fathers upon the children", we must not ignore the qualification "of them that hate me". Hereditary and environmental factors resulting from a father's dissolute way of life involve innocent children, but there is mercy (unto a thousand generations, not just three or four) for children who forsake their father's ways and "love me and keep my commandments". For we, like Israel, are forbidden to say, "The fathers have eaten a sour grape and the children's teeth are set on edge", thereby imputing guilt to subsequent generations for something not particularly their transgression. So while Scripturally there was an original sin, the consequences of which lie heavily upon all men, there is no such thing as "original sin" for which subsequent generations are to be accounted morally guilty.

Exodus 20:4–6; Joshua 7:1, 11; Romans 5:12

THE LAW OF SIN AND DEATH

We must now consider the varied relationship of men to God in their life "in Adam", since all are born of his line. Again we must be careful to distinguish things that differ: Paul's theme in Romans 5 is the comparison between the way sin, and therefore death, entered into the world and the revelation of God's righteousness which brings life: both were by one man. So since the point at issue in this passage is not the ground of God's final judgement, which is a matter of personal and individual responsibility, only those effects of Adam's transgression which are transmitted to all his posterity are brought into the comparison. These effects were the inheritance of death and of a sin-disposed nature.

Paul's succinct phrase for the human condition is: "*Death* reigned"; and the reason: "*Sin reigned unto death*". He distinguishes also between "sin" and "transgression": transgression is disobedience to a specific commandment, *a* sin indeed, whereas since the entry of sin into the world, men sin where there is no specific commandment to transgress. Sin was in the world before the law (and the context in v. 14 demands that we understand "the law of Moses"), but the law served to reveal the true nature of sin—it is the condition of those who are "not subject to the law of God" as well as those who actually transgress it, or to use Paul's language, sin was made to appear "exceeding sinful" [Romans 7:13]. So "death reigned from Adam to Moses, even over them that had not sinned after the similitude of Adam's transgression" [Romans 5:14], not because they were held guilty for what Adam had done, but because they were his race, the human race, an organic whole, who could not be free of the tendency and the possibility of sinning except by the work of the other "one man". "Death passed upon all men, for that all have sinned", and we both "have sin" and "have sinned" according to the Divine record.

... Remembering that "*sin* entered" by Adam's *transgression* inside the garden, for which he was formally judged and sentenced, and that the total consequences of his transgression, his condemnation, have become the lot of all begotten of him outside the garden ...

IN CHRIST

"As in Adam all die, even so in Christ shall all be made alive". Here we return to the twofold theme of "the one man": the one through whose righteousness grace and life abounded just as through another's transgression sin entered and death came upon all. It is important to grasp Paul's meaning in this passage in 1 Corinthians 15, since its bearing on the question of resurrection is fundamental. The whole chapter is concerned not with a mere coming out of the grave, an *anastasis* which is of itself neutral as regards acceptance in judgement, but with *resurrection to life eternal*, which is the sense of the expression *"raised incorruptible"*. He is not dealing in this chapter with the question of resurrection to condemnation, and makes no more than a brief allusion to the Epicurean philosophers' denial of it in verse 32. Their doctrine was that dead men never rise again and there is therefore nothing to fear from a judgement to come; so there is no need for restraint upon self-indulgence: "Let us eat and drink; for tomorrow we die" (cf. Acts 17:32). Paul's word for "made alive" in 1 Corinthians 15:22 is *zōopoieō*, to quicken, a term certainly not applicable to "the resurrection of condemnation". His sense is not "all those in Adam die, *but* only those in Christ ever come to life again"; but "just as death is certain for all the seed of Adam, so eternal life is assured for all who are Christ's." The context again demands that for "in Christ" we do not read "all who have ever been baptized into Christ's name", but "all they who are truly Christ's" (v. 23), whether they "wake or sleep" at his coming.

1 Corinthians 15:26, 54; John 5:24–29; Romans 5:10

Alan Hayward

Alan Hayward, God's Truth, 1973, *Chapter 24 – The Problem of Suffering*
Take a Bible and read the first three chapters of Genesis for yourself. … you will find a simple account of how the first man was given freedom of action, and a chance to use his freedom wisely. He lived in a world described as "very good", and he had the chance to live a very pleasant life. But poor Adam misused his opportunity: he chose to disobey God. Through this choice he started a sort of habit, the habit of sinning, which has gripped the human race like a python ever since.

Their Maker told the first human pair that two tragic consequences would follow from their sin. First, that they and their children would experience "sorrow"-which in modern English we would call "suffering". And secondly, that they must suffer death - the greatest and most final form of suffering there is.

So Genesis tells us how suffering came into the world, when the first man chose to disobey God. Because we are Adam's children we inherit his sinful tendencies. And so we too must suffer, and we too must die.

… The Book of Genesis reveals that God was ready with a plan to bring great good out of the disaster in Eden. And in this plan, suffering plays a very important part. God began by sentencing the whole sinful race to death. Not to immediate death, though; He allows us to live a while, before we suffer the just penalty of sin. This is really a great act of mercy on Gods part. Every single day we live is an unearned, undeserved, gift from God.

Alan Hayward, *The Real Devil*, Christadelphian Bible Mission, 1975, pp. 3-4
The first three chapters of the first book, Genesis, tell us how God created this world and the first human beings, Adam and Eve. He gave them a law to keep, but they disobeyed Him.

… So the message of Genesis, and of other Bible writers who refer to Genesis, is plain. Don't blame a fallen angel for the sinfulness of human nature. Put the blame where it belongs: on Adam, and on his sinful children—including ourselves.

Alan Hayward, Creation and Evolution, 1985, pp. 198-199
After Adam and Eve sinned, this 'very good' creation was cursed. ... What Genesis 3:15-24 actually tells us is that the Fall had four main consequences. (1) It brought punishment to the creature that tempted Eve to sin. (2) It affected the physical nature of woman, so that childbearing became more painful than it otherwise would have been. (3) Agriculture was adversely affected, so that man's life became more of a struggle than it need have been. (4) Above all, it caused the human race to be alienated from God and subjected to death.

... Consequently, conservative evolutionists generally treat the story of the serpent, and the record of the curses upon the land and upon woman, as pure allegory. They regard the sentence on Adam as 'spiritual death', instead of physical death. This they justify by noting that God had warned Adam, 'In the day that you eat of it you shall die' - whereas Adam did not die physically until long after.

But this is very questionable exposition. The New Testament concept of spiritual death is never found in the early books of the Old Testament. The only kind of death the ancient Hebrews spoke of was physical death. Even in the New Testament the death that Adam brought into the world is treated primarily as physical death; in 1 Corinthians 15, for example, it is contrasted with Christ's resurrection, which all conservatives agree was a physical fact.

HP Mansfield

HP Mansfield, *How the Gospel Relates to Salvation, Romans 8*, Logos Magazine, vol. 32, 1965, pp. 143-144
"There is therefore now no condemnation to them in Christ" [Romans 8:1] — Paul is now contrasting the benefits derived "in Christ" with the state of things obtained "in Adam" (cp. Romans 5:16). "In Christ" there are only benefits derived, whereas "in Adam" the condemnation of mortality rests upon his posterity. Paul is not referring to the Judgment Seat of Christ, nor is he teaching that one who has embraced Christ but who has wandered out of the way of righteousness will not be condemned; he is teaching that "in Christ" there are found only benefits, and they are discernible 'now' and not only in the future.

HP Mansfield, *"What is Sin?"*, Logos Magazine, vol. 36, 1970, pp. 459-462
... Consider the use of "sin" in the following places, and try to align them with the definition: "Sin is transgression of law."

> • "By one man's disobedience many were made sinners" (Romans 5:19).

Were many "made" transgressors of the law by the disobedience of Adam? To teach so, would be to accuse God of unrighteousness, as suggesting that the descendants of Adam were considered as actual transgressors of the law merely because *he* disobeyed.

When, however, we understand "sin" as a synonym for fallen human nature, we can interpret the passage without adversely reflecting upon the righteousness of God. Through one man's disobedience many became related to sin by possessing the condition of human nature that came through sin.

- "Sin hath reigned unto death" (Romans 5:21).

Does an individual act of transgression reign as a king? Of course not! What, then, reigns? The answer is sinful flesh. Again "sin" is related to fallen human nature, with its proneness to transgress, and its state of mortality.

What is the "body of sin" (Romans 6:6), but the body of human nature? What is meant by the term "ye were the servants of sin" (Romans 6:17), but that we were once slaves of the flesh. What is the "sin that dwelleth in me" (Romans 7:17) but the promptings of human nature? But give these places the definition of active transgression, and they fail to make sense

HP Mansfield, *"Adamic Condemnation: Legal or Physical?"*, Logos Magazine, vol. 37, 1971, pp. 134-137

A careful consideration of the evidence will reveal that Adamic condemnation is physical, and not legal or moral. If it were the latter, it would imply the imputation of guilt on every person born without him or her doing anything to deserve that guilt. That would make God unjust. Physical condemnation, however, constituted the carrying out of the death penalty on Adam by bringing him under the curse of mortality. The mortality inflicted on Adam was inherited by his descendants. They are mortal because of sin, and in this weakened physical state, inherit a nature which is dominated by the lusts of the flesh, which were aggravated, or inflamed, by sin in the first instance.

So mankind is no longer in the "very good" state of original creation (Genesis 1:31), but as described by God in Genesis 8:21, as "evil from youth".

This, as Brother Thomas declares in *Elpis Israel*, is our misfortune not our crime. It is something we must try to conquer in the strength derived through Christ (Philippians 4:13). We are only held accountable when knowing the means devised by *Yahweh* to control its influence, we refuse to use them. When a person knowingly and blatantly rejects the Truth he will be brought up from the dead for judgment.

Let us clarify these matters in our minds, so that we may see the principles of the Atonement simply and clearly. In The Christadelphian for October, 1896, p. 398, Brother Roberts makes reference to a group of "new errorists", who, among other things, taught: "That our mortality in Adam is not an affair of physical heredity, but a legal decree."

Obviously, a "legal" or "moral" defilement must carry with it a personal stigma of some kind, so that the one bearing it would appear personally abhorrent to God merely because of his nature.

Brother Roberts repudiated this concept of the Atonement, and clearly showed that the nature of the defilement was physical. This, however, had its reaction upon man's mental condition, for, as a result of sin, he inherited "a nature prone to sin." This "proneness to sin" is so strong, that despite all efforts to the contrary, the most faithful have succumbed to it apart from the Lord Jesus. He did not do so, for he was strengthened of God (Psalm 80:17) to succeed, in the mission of mercy initiated by the Father for the salvation of those who will come unto Him in faith.

HP Mansfield, *An Appeal to Troubled Brethren*, Logos Magazine, 1972, vol. 38, pp. 351-358

Thus the Unity Book directs attention to the BASF, and the doctrines therein, including those referred to above. One cannot accept the unity basis without accepting the Statement of Faith, and it should be noted that it requires that the latter be accepted "without reservation". However, it does attach an explanation of Clauses 5 and 12 which reads as follows [CCA quoted in full – see page 30].

We find nothing wrong with this. True, it does not specifically use the word "defiled," nor the phrase "the condemnation of sin in the flesh," for the simple reason that it has stated already that the doctrines *"believed and taught by us, without reservation, are the first principles of the One Faith as revealed in the Scriptures, of which the BASF (with positive and negative clauses) gives a true definition,"* and these terms are found therein.

A nature that has inherited mortality (which it did not originally possess) and which has become "prone to sin," has obviously become "defiled" from its original "very good" state. We can acknowledge that it is "unclean" without going further and claiming that possessors of this fallen nature are alienated from God.

We believe that the book issued by the Concord Ecclesia is incorrect in such statements as the following:

> "The Carter-Cooper Addendum represents an important concession as it restricts defilement to conscience" (p.6).

We fail to see how that anybody, fairly reading the Addendum, can come to such a conclusion, unless they see in the word "defiled" some different significance to what the BASF teaches. The clause in the Statement of Faith declares:

> "Adam broke this law, and was .... sentenced to return to the ground from whence he was taken — a sentence which defiled and became a physical law of his being, and was transmitted to all his posterity."

This, the Unity Book states, is part of that teaching which must be accepted "without reservation," in the light of the explanation given. Thus the Addendum states:

> "Adam .... was sentenced to return to the dust. He fell from his very good state and suffered the consequences of sin - shame, a defiled conscience and mortality. As his descendants, we partake of that mortality that came by sin and inherit a nature prone to sin ... "

Does not a "mortality that came by sin," and "a nature prone to sin," express a very real "fall" from the original "very good" state? Is not such a nature physically "defiled"?

How else can the Addendum be read? The booklet does not find this completely satisfactory because, we believe, it sees something more in the term "defilement" than the physical law of mortality and proneness to sin which we inherit in consequence of the fall of Adam. It defines "'defilement' as a state of alienation by nature.

But "defilement" and "alienation" are two different things. The former is a misfortune; the latter is a moral condition brought about by a fault. The former relates to "the law of sin and death which is in our members"; the latter comes about by giving way thereto. It is essential to acknowledge the former in order to correctly understand the true nature of flesh; but to claim that the latter is imposed upon us because of our physically defiled state that is our inheritance at birth, is to lay the foundation for widespread error if it is carried to its logical conclusion.

Logos Magazine, 1974, vol. 40, The Ecclesial Calendar, June 1974, p. 2
MEETING OF THE AUSTRALIAN CHRISTADELPHIAN FELLOWSHIP COMMITTEE AND THE CHRISTADELPHIAN INTER-ECCLESIAL ADVISORY COMMITTEE (SA) HELD IN ADELAIDE ON SATURDAY 4th MAY, 1974.

The following representatives were present:

DJ. Caudery, A.C. Dangerfield, P.B. Hurn, J. Kingston, EJ. Russell, J.A Watson, W.C. Gurd, C. Kempster, B.Luke, J.Luke, M.Lund, *H.P.* Mansfield, J. Martin. Present as an observer: J. Rosser.

It was unanimously agreed that the Unity Basis of Fellowship as set out in the Unity Booklet pages 13 to 15 is a completely adequate Basis for Inter-ecclesial Fellowship.

It was also agreed unanimously that the following eight extracts from the Cooper/ Carter Addendum would provide a satisfactory basis for discussions on the subject of the Atonement between representatives of the two Committees and representatives of those ecclesias in the Brisbane area experiencing problems in their inter-ecclesial relationships in regard to this subject. The comments following some of the extracts are general expressions amplifying the extracts as a basis of discussion. It was agreed that there is no intention or desire to have these comments added to the already agreed and adequate Basis of Fellowship. However, these extracts and the comments upon them were considered to form a satisfactory Agenda for proposed meetings in the Brisbane area.

1. **Adam was made of the earth and declared to be very good.**

2. **Because of disobedience he was sentenced to return to the dust.**
   Comment: His death being the punishment for sin referred to in Gen 2:17 and 3:17-19.

3. **He fell from his very good state and suffered the consequences of sin — shame, a defiled conscience and mortality.**
   Comment: Mortality (subjection to death) entailed a change in the condition of Adam's nature which caused him to be physically destined to death.

4. **As his descendants, we partake of that mortality that came by sin, and inherit a nature prone to sin.**
   Comment: Proneness to sin has been inherited by all Adam's race, but was not part of Adam's nature before sin.

5. **By our actions we become sinners and stand in need of the forgiveness of sins before we can be acceptable before God. Forgiveness and reconciliation God has provided by the offering of His Son.**

Comment: Human nature does not alienate from God, though it is the root cause of the sins which do.

6. **Though Son of God, he (Jesus) partook of the same nature - the same flesh and blood as all of us, but did no sin.**
   Comment: As a consequence of Adam's sin Jesus also inherited mortality and proneness to sin and was not in the same condition as' Adam before sin.

7. **In his death he voluntarily declared God's righteousness; God was honoured, and the flesh shown to be by divine appointment rightly related to death.**

8. **To share in God's forgiveness, we must be united with Christ by baptism into his death, rising from baptism, dead to the past, to walk in newness of life. The form of baptism is a token of burial and resurrection, and submitting to it we identify ourselves with the principles established in the death of Jesus, who "died unto sin," recognising that God is righteous in decreeing that the wages of sin is death, and as members of the race, we are rightly related to a dispensation of death.**

In conclusion, it was agreed that as a result of the degree of unanimity, we are hopeful of being able to arrange discussions with representatives of the ecclesias in the Brisbane area involved in this matter. However, it was thought desirable to have preliminary discussions with the individual ecclesias before finalising arrangements for a combined meeting of representatives of all groups involved.

- Bro. P. Hurn, Chairman of the Meeting

HP Mansfield, *Psalm 8 – The Glory of Yahweh In The Son*, Logos Magazine, vol. 41, 1975, pp. 247-253
… Philippians 3:20-21 comprises a key passage of the Epistle, it discourses upon heavenly citizenship, the return of Christ, the change of nature to be granted the righteous and the subduing of "all things" unto the Lord Jesus. The statement, "Subdue all things unto himself' refers back to Psalm 8:6; Genesis 1:28.

Why should Paul cite the Creation Decree as evidence of these matters? In what way does it illustrate that "our vile body" or "the body of our humiliation" must be changed? Because the state of our bodies was conditioned by the Fall, and the accomplishment of the Decree was delayed by the manifestation of sin. Adam's disobedience of the Edenic Law revealed him as unfit in that state, to exercise the promised domination.

HP Mansfield, *Made Sin for Us*, Logos Magazine, vol. 43, 1977, pp. 74-78
Although Jesus was "without sin" in the sense of transgression, he possessed a nature identical with that of those whom he came to save: a nature that is the seat and origin of sin: "That which cometh out of the man, that defileth the man. For from within, out of the heart of men, proceed evil thoughts, adulteries, murders, thefts, and so forth all these evil things come from within, and defile the man" (Mark 7:20-23). The same nature that erupts into actual transgression on the part of mankind was possessed by the Lord, but he kept in check its impulses, by drawing upon the strength

made available to him from God. In that way his crucifixion resulted in the destruction of the "body of sin;" the "putting away of sin by the sacrifice of himself" (Hebrews 9:26); or the destruction of that "which was the power of death, that is the devil" (Hebrews 2:14). He conquered the devil in life, and silenced it through death.

… Although Jesus was "without sin" in the sense of transgression, he possessed the nature which is the root cause of sin, which is, itself, subject to death because of sin at the beginning. In this sense, his crucifixion was a putting of death of the "body of sin" (Romans 6:6), or the destruction of that "which has the power of death, that is the devil" (Hebrews 2:14).

HP Mansfield, *"Stages in the Work of Redemption"*, Logos Magazine, vol. 43, 1977, pp. 244-248
Brethren sometimes speak or write as though mankind needs forgiveness for sin's flesh, or as though the guilt of Adam's transgression rests upon his descendants, and, therefore, they are in a state of alienation from God because of their nature. The Bible does not speak in that way. It shows that men are alienated from God through ignorance, or through wicked works (Ephesians 4:18), and it is because of these that they need enlightenment or forgiveness.

Nevertheless, our nature stands as a barrier to eternal life, and will bring us ultimately to the grave there to remain forever, unless brought into a relationship to God's way of redemption. Moreover, our nature is a barrier to us rendering perfect obedience to God, even when drawn to Him by the truth. This is because, as a consequence of transgression in the beginning, a bias towards sin was developed in the flesh, which will inevitably produce its fruit in us. There was not so much a change of nature in man, as a change of condition. The flesh was no longer "very good" (Genesis 1:31), no longer "in healthy being," as Bro. Thomas expresses it in *Eureka*. The bias in the flesh that leads to sin, had become active in man, and now needs to be restrained, disciplined, quelled. Otherwise it will inevitably produce its fruit in us.

… Christ's offering reveals that the flesh cannot effect its own salvation, and that the only way to life is through death. The Law of Moses as well as the Law of Grace taught that principle. It was impossible for the Lord to keep the Law of Moses perfectly without dying, for he figuratively had to put to death the flesh to do so, and was he not the antitype of the very sacrifices that had to be offered "according to the Law?" How then was it possible for him to obey the Law perfectly, without enacting the very part that that Law revealed in type he must accomplish? Christ did not "suffer the punishment due to sin," as is sometimes alleged, nor did he die that we might obtain forgiveness for sin's flesh, as others have said. He died that a way of redemption might be opened for humanity as a whole through a change of nature; and in order that the sins men commit might find forgiveness in their acknowledgement of the principles involved. In benefiting himself from his offering justice was done, and in extending forgiveness to man who acknowledged the principles of the atonement, justice was blended with mercy. Thus through divine grace man is able to rise to heights absolutely impossible outside of Christ. Thanks be to God for His unspeakable gift!

HP Mansfield, Story of the Bible, vol. 1, pp. 47-52 (1992 ed.)
However, the tree remained, a token to Adam and Eve of the hope of eternal life. But how were they to attain unto that seeing that sin had brought them to a state of mortality (Romans 5:12)? Moreover, they were conscious of their weakness, and felt the stirring of sin within them. They felt spiritually naked, and recognised the need for a proper covering. And God proceeded to show what was required.

Meanwhile, the very good condition of creation had been spoiled by sin. It had aroused in Adam and Eve desires that were contrary to the will of God, and brought them under the power of death. Their destiny was now the grave, and only through the mercy of God, and by a resurrection to eternal life could they escape from the penalty of mortality that already began to work in them.

… Now we agreed that the woman had told the serpent the Truth What would have happened if she had never listened to the serpent? She would have obeyed God, and not sinned. Has there ever been anyone who has obeyed God in every way? Only Jesus Christ. He can well be called "the seed of the woman". Did Jesus die? Yes. He died that others might live. In this He was "bruised" by the serpent power (Isaiah 53:5). But did he remain in the grave? No. God raised him from the dead. By that means he was healed from the mortal nature that is the heritage of all the descendants of Adam and Eve.

Harry Whittaker

Compilers Note: EC advocates often refer to Bro. Harry Whittaker's book, *Genesis 1-2-3-4*, in a bid to establish that he believed that Adam was created mortal and there was no change in the condition of human nature after the fall. The relevant quotations from pages 58 and 67 of *Genesis 1-2-3-4* are presented immediately below, followed by other quotations from Bro Harry on this same subject.

Firstly, it is important to note that Bro Harry states that "mortal" means "subject to death" as per the Oxford English Dictionary (OED) definition. He did not teach that before sin Adam was in a state like us today that was unconditionally subject to death.

Although Bro Harry taught that Adam was created mortal, on page 58 he qualifies this by saying *"but of course with an opportunity of being sustained in being indefinitely…."*. We do not have this opportunity. We are unconditionally subject to death.

Then on page 67 he taught that, *"during his probation Adam's mortality was kept in abeyance by his eating of the leaves of that tree"*. We are not in a state today, where mortality is kept in abeyance. We are not able to eat the leaves of the tree to arrest the process of mortality. Bro Whittaker did not teach that Adam was mortal (subject to death) because mortality was kept in abeyance.

So he clearly taught that the condition of Adam's natural body of life was different from mankind's present mortal state. He did not teach that God created Adam in a state of mortality that was subject to death. He taught that post his sin and losing access to eat the leaves, he became mortal without qualification – as per the Oxford English Dictionary definition of the word – "subject to death". We are all "in Adam". As his descendants we too have no access to eat from the leaves of the tree to arrest the process of mortality. So he is teaching that Adam introduced mortality without any qualifications (a state of being subject to death) for a as a consequence of his sin.

We can be sure of this, because throughout the rest of *Genesis 1-2-3-4* Bro Harry explains: on page 68 that Adam and Eve's *"essential nature was changed"* as a result of their sin; on page 93 that *"their nature had been vitiated"*, on page 107 that Jesus was born subject to *"the curse of Eden in every detail - sorrow, sweat, eating bread, thorns and thistles, a return to the ground"*; on page 112 that the *"evil"* Adam and Eve came to know after partaking of the tree of the knowledge of good and evil *"was the curse of labour and mortality"*.

Other quotations from Bro Harry included in this section confirm that he taught that the mortality of man is linked with the fact that he is a fallen creature, and that the temptations of Jesus originated or found an answering strain in the **marred** human nature which he inherited.

In this regard, his understanding of "mortality" is similar to that expressed by LG Sargent – who divided "mortality" into two different classes: *"(A) those in whom death is only a capacity— a latent capacity, as we might say; and (B) those in whom it is an active condition"*. [See page 313 to read this article in context] Bro LG Sargent therefore taught that the condition of the 'natural body' that Adam was created with before the fall was different from the condition of that same body after the fall. It is the second of these two natures that we inherit with its changed condition of being subject to death and having a nature with a predisposition to sin. With this conclusion, the vast majority of Christadelphian authors agree.

Harry Whittaker, Genesis 1-2-3-4, Biblia, 1986, pp. 58, 67

The question is often raised: Was Adam created mortal or immortal? Important theological conclusions have rather foolishly been made to depend on the answer supplied. (As though an incorrect answer to such a question could invalidate a man's Christian baptism!).

Clearly Adam was not immortal, or he would still be alive. The glib answer not infrequently heard: "Neither mortal nor immortal, but very good" is meaningless, for (a) "very good" is far too vague to be useful, without further definition; (b) every living being in the universe is either mortal or immortal, for the two states are mutually exclusive. "Mortal" means "subject to death" (OED), and Paul's handling of this passage in 1 Corinthians 15 declares emphatically that **Adam was created mortal (but of course with an opportunity of being sustained in being indefinitely until his Maker either made him immortal or condemned him to the grave)**. (p. 58)

"Of every tree of the garden thou mayest freely eat," except the tree of knowledge, fairly plainly implies that eating of the tree of life was not forbidden. This consideration leads to an interesting sequence of ideas:

> a. Adam was made mortal:
>> (i) for he was certainly not made immortal;
>> (ii) like the animals he was made "a living soul"(1:30; 2:7);
>> (iii) the sequence of antitheses in 1 Corinthians 15:42-50 (see p.33) makes Genesis 2:7 (v45) equivalent to "natural body"

> b. Since, in Revelation 22:2, "the leaves of the tree (of life) are for the healing of the (mortal) nations," **it is reasonable to suppose that during his probation Adam's mortality was kept in abeyance by his eating of the leaves of that tree. (p. 67)**

Harry Whittaker, Genesis 1-2-3-4, Biblia, 1986, pp. 68, 93, 107, 112, 123

But when the sin was committed, Adam and his wife did not die in the very day in which they ate. Quite a variety of explanations have been advanced to cope with this problem:

> a. They died spiritually. If by this is meant that **their essential nature was changed, this is true**. From the time of the Fall human nature has been sullied with a humanly incurable bent towards evil. Every

> innocent little baby grows up to be a naughty child, a self-willed teenager, a chronic moribund sinner. (p. 68)

This is the first mention of fear, and the explanation given was an evasion, Adam's euphemism for "because I know myself to be a sinner." Only a little while before, they were both naked and were not ashamed (2:25). The fact that shame was now their natural condition shows that **their nature had been vitiated** (this was one of Peter Watkins' insights). From now on "nakedness" (except in the sense of destitution) is a close associate of "shame" (Exodus 32:25; John 19:23; Hebrews 12:2). (p. 93)

The Man whose Name is The Branch was brought forth out of the cursed soil of the human race, a soil where spiritual thorns and thistles are prolific. But on him, The Branch, **came the curse of Eden in every detail - sorrow, sweat (Luke 22:44 only), eating bread, thorns and thistles, a return to the ground**. He was a man of sorrows (the gospels give no hint of a laugh or even of a smile on his face), in Gethsemane the perspiration on his brow (on a particularly cold night) was a sweat like great drops of blood; it was his food and drink to do the will of his Father; he was crucified crowned with thorns; and that day he returned to the ground from which the first Adam was taken. (p. 107)

"Cain" was Messianic in flavour. But by the time of his brother's birth (this must have been some years later, and probably with the birth of daughters intervening), it was already evident to the parents that evil propensities were now built not only into their own nature but into all their family. So with a despairing swing to the other extreme, the second son was called *Hebel*, vanity, worthlessness (in the English Bible the aspirate has got lost through adoption of LXX spelling - Greek has no letter H). Already it was easy to see that Adam was begetting sons "in his own likeness, after his image" (5:3). (p. 122)

Harry Whittaker, The Christadelphian, vol. 99, 1962, p. 173
The doctrine of the mortality of man has always been a good Christadelphian chopping-block, and it must so continue as long as the immortality of the soul continues to be the biggest lie in the Christian world. Today, as for centuries past, people learn their theology from popular hymns, not from the Bible; and in the last hundred years the hymns have hardly changed at all. It is desirable, surely, **to link this mortality of man more firmly and more evidently to the Bible doctrine of the nature of man—that he is a fallen creature with a will and propensities which are warped, perverted, twisted.**

Harry Whittaker, The Christadelphian, vol. 99, 1962, p. 266
In particular, there is need for repeated stress on the truth that Jesus really and truly shared our nature, knew our weaknesses as his own, and fought our battles—and overcame gloriously where we fail dismally. ...

Yet this fact about Jesus is the best of all touchstones of truth. "Many false prophets are gone out into the world. Hereby know ye the Spirit of God: Every spirit that confesseth that Jesus Christ is come *in the flesh* is of God: and every spirit that confesseth not that Jesus Christ is come *in the flesh* is not of God: and this is that spirit of anti-christ" (1 John 4:2). Here, as almost uniformly throughout the New Testament, the phrase "in the flesh" means "in very human nature with all its weakness"; compare the familiar words "the world", "the flesh", and "the devil".

Thus the best of all tests of a true teacher is: Does he teach truth concerning the nature of Christ? And in this respect Christadelphians stand alone. All others fail by this test, mostly insisting on what has come to be known among us as the "Clean Flesh" heresy (the phrase is a clumsy one, but it spotlights the first and worst heresy of all).

Harry Tennant

Harry Tennant, *Living to Die*, The Christadelphian, vol. 100, 1963, pp. 56-57
… The Bible gives a clear explanation. Adam did not want to die. Eve's choice depended on the truthfulness of the serpent when it said, "Thou shalt not surely die". And she discovered all too late that she had believed a liar. Death was imposed on Adam and Eve by God. There had been a direct clash of wills. God the author of life had given life to Adam and Eve for so long as they looked to Him and believed by being obedient. The creatures rebelled against the Creator and thereby lost all claim to the right to live. They had chosen the words of death instead of the living God.

Mortality is not merely a fact: it is a principle. Sin is an offence against God and is thereby an abuse of the privilege of living. There is but one answer to it—death. Thus Adam and Eve left the garden of God for the wilderness of men. All their children were born outside the garden and were the offspring of sinners, dying men. No sop was offered concerning death; no word to lessen the reality—if that is the right word—of the end of life. It is foolishness to play fast and loose with the clear word of God concerning death: such talk is a repetition of the serpent's "thou shalt not surely die", by telling God that He does not mean what He says.

Harry Tennant, The Christadelphian, vol. 100, 1963, pp. 215-217
The day came when man and God parted company. … Strife entered into the world: man against God and God against man. A warfare of wills began which would leave the flower of manhood strewn upon the field of battle. Every man born into the world would be involved in it whether he would know it or not. The Spirit would lust against the flesh and the flesh against the Spirit. Every man born into the world would be born of "the will of man", of "the will of the flesh", and would seek by nature his own will and purpose. There was no way back. Man would seek the glory of man and learn at the last that "All flesh is grass, and all the glory of man as the flower of grass. The grass withereth, and the flower thereof falleth away."

… When Christ goes out to die, his victory is complete. He is king over sin. The impulses born into humanity by Adam's self-will are stilled forever in the Son of God. His resignation is perfect even to the last moment when life itself would ebb away, not held back by self-preservation, but as it were lifted by his last weak strength and placed in God's care: "Father, into thy hands I commend my spirit."

Harry Tennant, The Christadelphian, vol. 106, 1969, pp. 538-540
It has been remarked often enough that man's sins spring from a wrong use of good gifts. Adultery is an unlawful relationship of which marriage is the good counterpart: idolatry is the perversion of the innate capacity of man for worship: drunkenness is over-indulgence of a natural appetite. In their innocence, Adam and Eve had not misused their lawful desires. Not until the serpent had implanted the seeds of rebellion did things go wrong. Then, Eve bent the proper and acceptable God-given appetites against their Maker. She "saw the tree was good for food, and it was pleasant to the eyes and a tree to be desired to make one wise". From thenceforth the three basic desires lost their innocence and are now lodged in the heart of man as part of his equipment by which he produces evil thoughts, murders, adulteries, fornications, thefts, false witness and blasphemies (Matthew 15:18–19). John describes them as "all that is in the world, the lust of the flesh, and the lust of the eyes, and the pride of life", which are "not of the Father" but of the world (1 John 2:16).

Harry Tennant, The Christadelphian, vol. 107, 1970, pp. 10-12
… When sin cast its shadow across their conscience, "they knew that they were naked; and they sewed fig leaves together and made themselves aprons" (Genesis 3:7). Their nakedness was a token of their sin and they knew it. God had planted in them by their transgression a sense of need for a covering. The nakedness of man had become a sign that Adam and his progeny would need a garment for sin. God speaks in the same terms at intervals throughout history as given in His word:

> "Thou shalt make them linen breeches to cover their nakedness … that they bear not their iniquity, and die" (Exodus 28:42–43).

> "Blessed is he that watcheth, and keepeth his garments, lest he walk naked, and they see his shame" (Revelation 16:15).

Harry Tennant, *The Christadelphians – What They Believe And Preach*, 1986, pp. 6-9
… The first man consisted of "dust" and "the breath of life". In his entirety he was called "a living soul". Notice that in this verse man is not so much said to possess a soul as to be one. In total, therefore, man was in the image and likeness of God and consisted of dust and the breath of life. But beyond all this, was man in fact like unto the angels, to die no more?

One thing is clear: there is nothing in the creation record to tell us that there was a part of Adam which could not die. Take another look at him in Eden in those days when all was well. Was he at that time subject to the fear of death, the certainty of dying, as is the common lot of all mankind at this present time? The answer is, No. Adam had no fear of that kind and he enjoyed the felicity of life in Eden untrammelled by cares, fears, tears or arduous toil.

… But how was Adam to have a truly free choice in his obedience to God? Since God clearly did not want mindless and loveless obedience, but an intelligent willingness, how was this to be made possible? Unlike us, Adam enjoyed a mind which was uncorrupted by evil; there was no taint within and only "goodness" outside.

Harry Tennant, *The Christadelphians – What They Believe And Preach*, 1986 pp. 134-137

SUFFERING AND DISEASE

… The very first evils following the sin of Adam and Eve were brought about by God – death and the curse on the ground. The adverse conditions in agriculture were of God:

> *"Cursed is the ground for thy sake; in sorrow shalt thou eat of it all the days of thy life; thorns also and thistles shall it bring forth to thee."* (Genesis 3:17-18)

… The Lord Jesus Christ demonstrated his power over all kinds of disease when he carried out healings of every kind. These included those cases which are attributed to demons or unclean spirits, …

In addition to his supremacy over disease and death, the Lord Jesus exercised sway over the elements when he stilled the storm on Galilee. It is evident that the Scriptures are teaching us to look to Jesus the Son of God as the divine remedy for the world's ills. Evils occur within the containing power of the Lord God. They are not out of control or brought about by evil powers outside of the human sphere. Sin is the root cause of all our problems. It is an evil, and all other evils – fear, disease, poverty, natural disasters, and death itself – have come as a consequence of sin and a punishment for it. All these evils – sin and its effects – will be removed by the Lord Jesus Christ when he returns to the earth.

Harry Tennant, *The Christadelphians – What They Believe And Preach*, 1986 pp. 137-138

CONSEQUENCES OF SIN

When God created man and placed him under a clear command, He granted him freedom of choice. Thus Adam and Eve were told what would happen to them if they disobeyed. Nevertheless, they were allowed to choose for themselves what they would do. It is implicit in this arrangement that a wrong choice, freely arrived at, would result in very serious consequences for the sinners and for their progeny in due course. These consequences included:

> Fear of death
> Death itself
> Sorrows, together with hard toil because of the cursed ground, as long as life lasted.

All of these evils came from God. They were God's response to sin which is the greatest evil of all. Some people have found it difficult to accept that God creates evil. He does, and the following verses illustrate this fact:

> *"I (God) form the light, and create darkness: I make peace, and create evil: I the Lord do all these things."* (Isaiah 45:7)
> *"Shall there be evil in a city, and the Lord hath not done it?"* (Amos 3:6)

Evil came into the world because of sin. Whilst we may wonder at the extent of the evil, we can at least understand why it is there. What we are pursuing, however, is the feeling of outrage against our sense of "fairness", when evil falls on good people or on children

Harry Tennant, *The Christadelphians – What They Believe And Preach*, 1986, pp. 147-153

When Adam and Eve sinned, by surrendering to desires aroused by the words of the serpent, they brought death into the world. Paul expressed it in this way: *"Sin ... deceived me ... and slew me"* (Romans 7:11). Death was not introduced by some outside evil power; it was the direct result of sin. The command given by God contained its own penalty clause which God brought into effect. No one else was involved. In the same way it is God who will finally remove sin from the face of the earth at the end of the millennium. In other words: when sin came, death came: when sin goes, death goes.

Harry Tennant, *The Nature of Christ*, The Testimony, vol. 58, 1988, pp. 234-237

... All of these things are summed up in such well-known words as, 'God sending His own Son in the likeness of sinful flesh" (Romans 8:3); and "He hath made him to be sin for us, who knew no sin" (2 Corinthians 5:21).

We have all inherited the downward pull of the flesh towards sin and death. Indeed, this has been the great dilemma of mankind, the impasse from which man had no escape. All men have cried, with Paul: "who shall deliver me from the body of this death?" (Romans 7:24).

It appears to have been from a mistaken regard for the person of Christ that some brethren have shrunk from applying these words to Jesus; or, if they have applied them, they have sought to redefine 'sinful flesh' by saying that we do not inherit a bias toward sin. We believe that this is to misunderstand both the nature of Christ and the nature of his atoning work. It is to confuse the character of the Lord Jesus Christ with the background against which it was achieved. In fact, it diminishes the magnitude of the victory of Christ and the glory which now attaches to him.

On the other hand, there have been those who wholly accept the teaching concerning 'sinful flesh', and are prepared to say that the Lord fully shared this infirmity; but they want to go further and say that all mankind is subject to some additional condemnation or uncleanness simply because of the flesh we bear; and that this would rest also on Christ. The Truth is set out in our *Statement of Faith:*

> Clause V. —That Adam broke this (Edenic) law, and was adjudged unworthy of immortality, and sentenced to return to the ground from whence he was taken—a sentence which defiled and became a physical law of his being and was transmitted to all his posterity".

By birth we suffer from no legal impediment or guilt other than that which we physically inherit. This was true also of Christ.

All erroneous teaching complicates doctrine and makes even the refutation of it a matter which is far from easy. The truth is simple: as a result of his transgression Adam was condemned to die; his "very good" nature became evil. We physically inherit the *results,* but not the guilt, of that condemnation. When we sin we come under personal condemnation, and deservedly so. The condemnation in our physical natures cannot be removed by baptism, by faith, by law or by anything other than a change to immortality at the hand of Christ should we be found faithful. The condemnation because of sin, however, *can* be removed by forgiveness through faithful baptism into the death of the Lord Jesus.

Sinful flesh is flesh inherited from the sinner, Adam. It is flesh in which the consequences of his sin are working towards death, and in which "the motions of sins" (Romans 7:5; RV, RSV, NIV, sinful passions) are at work. The promptings and urgings of the flesh are not themselves sin until they are yielded to, and then they bring forth sin. This is the difference between temptation and actual sin (James 1:14-15). Every man before and since Christ has sinned; that is, has been overcome of sin and is personally a transgressor.

Harry Tennant, *The Crisis of the Cross of Christ – Why Did Jesus Die?* The Christadelphian Magazine and Publishing Association Ltd (UK), pp. 9-17

But where did our evil hearts come from? This a fair and searching question. Obviously, we can say that we are what we are from our parents and they from their parents and so on. What does the Bible say? There is no mention of the evil heart of man until after Adam and Eve were expelled from the garden of Eden because of their sin. Sin brought evil consequences. Later on, when the world had become filled with wickedness prior to the coming of the Flood, the scripture says:

> "And God saw that the wickedness of man was great in the earth, and that every imagination of the thoughts of his heart was only evil continually." (Genesis 6:5)

This is exactly what Jesus said. Man's heart is responsible for all the wickedness in the earth. Once this basic Bible teaching is understood and we cease to lay the blame elsewhere, we are ready to begin to understand the crisis of the cross.

WHERE DID DEATH COME FROM?

Death was the consequence of Adam and Eve's disobedience in the garden in Eden: "In the sweat of thy face shalt thou eat bread, till thou return unto the ground; for out of it wast thou taken: for dust thou art, and unto dust shalt thou return" (Genesis 3:19). They became mortal creatures, and finally they died - "For the wages of sin is death" (Romans 6:23), as the Apostle Paul tells us.

Death was therefore God's answer to sin. Sinners cannot live for ever, God will not allow it. Adam was not executed but he was henceforth different because death worked in his body and would finally cause him to die. Also, sin had become part of his thinking and would always affect him and all his descendants.

Paul describes this condition. He talks of wishing to serve God but finding that the wish to do good was challenged within him by a natural urge to do otherwise:

> "I delight in the law of God after the inward man: but I see another law in my members, warring against the law of my mind, and bringing me into captivity to the law of sin which is in my members. O wretched man that I am! who shall deliver me from the body of this death? I thank God through Jesus Christ our Lord." (Romans 7:22-25)

Adam's sin brought death into the world and the legacy for his children is mortality (death at work in us) and a natural urge to do 'our own thing' whatever God commands.

... In his sacrifice it was not just his body that Christ was rejecting, for his body was fearfully and wonderfully made. It was that inner fault-line, inherited from Adam, from which sprang temptation and the possibility of rebellion against God, that was lamented. Jesus gave himself so that the fault- line might be removed. The fault-line was righteously there because of Adam's sin and God's condemnation of it. It was now to be righteously removed by Christ's sinlessness and his resurrection, and by the consequent God provided bestowal of immortality.

Michael Ashton

Michael Ashton, Studies in the Statement of Faith, *The Saving Work of Christ - Clauses XII-XIV*, The Christadelphian, vol. 127, 1990, pp.164-166
Two distinct, but connected, consequences had arisen for Adam's descendants because he had been disobedient to God's law. They were all born dying creatures - mortality was part of their physical nature - and temptation to sin was also constantly present with them. The two go hand in hand, for: "By one man's disobedience ... sin entered into the world, and death by sin" (Romans 5:19, 12).

... Jesus' unique parentage made wonderfully possible the removal of these two consequences of Adam's sin. As a *sinless* sharer of man's condemnation, his death allowed God righteously to abrogate (i.e. cancel) the "law of sin and death" in his case. His perfect obedience (possible only because he was God's only begotten Son) allowed God to raise him from the dead. Jesus thus declared by his life and in his death that God's condemnation of sin was wholly just. Sin had to be destroyed on the territory it had claimed when Adam and Eve disobeyed God's command. Only in Jesus was this accomplished.

Michael Ashton, *The Beginning*, The Christadelphian, vol. 136, 1999, p.104
... Genesis explains that God's creation was all "very good"[Genesis 1:31], and goes on to reveal that when Adam and Eve chose to follow earthly thinking they became sinful dying creatures. The LORD God's assessment of their descendants a few generations later was stark: "GOD saw that the wickedness of man was great in the earth, and that every imagination of the thoughts of his heart was only evil continually. And it repented the LORD that he had made man on the earth, and it grieved him at his heart" (Genesis 6:5-6).

The New Testament comment reinforces this: "By one man sin entered into the world, and death by sin; and so death passed upon all men, for that all have sinned" (Romans 5:12). What was implied in Genesis is thus stated explicitly by the Apostle: before man sinned, death was not experienced by the human creation. Adam was not created a dying creature: for "the Lord God formed man of the dust of the ground, and breathed into his nostrils the breath of life; and man became a living soul" (Genesis 2:7).

Mortality was therefore the direct consequence of man's disobedience, for God said: "in the day that thou eatest thereof thou shalt surely die" (Genesis 2:17). The certainty of these words expresses a further truth—that man's situation was changed both immediately ("in the day that thou eatest thereof") and irrevocably ("thou shalt surely die"). Left to himself, man was powerless to alter this. Obedience was harder for him as a dying creature than it was in his condition before he fell. This caused Solomon to conclude when he was praying at the dedication of the temple, "there is no man that sinneth not" (1 Kings 8:46).

This was also the Apostle's conclusion, "death passed upon all men ... all have sinned" (Romans 5:12). Picking up and extending the thought of that last phrase, he also wrote, "all have sinned ... and come short of the glory of God" (Romans 3:23).

… The two situations—life in Eden and mortality outside the garden—could hardly have been more different. Added to this was another factor: "Behold, the man is become as one of us, to know good and evil" (Genesis 3:22). The combination of these factors explains why God "drove out the man". As a dying creature, living in a harsh environment and weakened by mortality and liable to sin, it was merciful—as well as righteous—to place a barrier between the man and the tree of life. Access to the tree would only prolong the inevitable conclusion, and this was unacceptable to a righteous God—His provision for man's future life was to be based on grace and not on man's grasping for something which was not rightfully his.

… Subsequent generations proved the rightness of God's judgement, for all Adam's descendants missed the mark and fell "short of the glory of God" (Romans 3:23). Like him, after he was cast out of the garden, they were dying creatures sharing a condition which originally arose through disobedience. Our physical state is called by the Apostle "sin's (or sinful) flesh" (Romans 8:3) primarily because its condition arose through Adam's sin.

This common heritage of the human race is explained in Genesis when we are told that Adam at the age of 130 years, "begat a son in his own likeness, after his image" (Genesis 5:3). And the New Testament comment continues the idea when we read, "That which is born of the flesh is flesh" (John 3:6). Like begets like. Adam's new condition was shared by all his descendants, without exception.

The description of that condition as 'flesh of sin' is helpful in two respects. First, as we have seen, it expresses the truth about its origin; but secondly it explains that there is in every individual a predisposition towards sin. This predisposition is so strong that every child born to two human parents sins. Weakness of mind or body results in temptations constantly arising and diverting attention from the need to "seek the Lord" and His glory.

Tecwyn Morgan, Studies in the Statement of Faith, *Concerning Mortal Man - Clauses III-IV*, **1991, pp. 20-24** (originally published in The Christadelphian in 1990).

"AS IN ADAM..."

It is a matter of historical record that God created Adam from the dust of the ground and breathed into him the breath of life (Genesis 2:7), whereupon he became a "living being". Having been made "in the image of God" (Genesis 1:27), he was "very good" (Genesis 1:31), as was all God's creation. This condition of being was clearly not the same as perfection, else there would have been no scope for expansion and further development; but neither was he flawed in any way, nor was the earth in which he lived. He and Eve had every opportunity and blessing that they needed, including the challenge to develop mentally and emotionally.

God put them to the test, by introducing the law of the Tree, so that their affections and desires could be developed, and then demonstrated. The tragedy was that they first learned to love themselves above all else. Thus Eve wanted what she saw: she would not wait for the eternal realities (2 Corinthians 4:18). The Tree was desired as a source of wisdom without effort; it offered God-likeness outside of the discipline of law (Genesis 3:6). And while its very existence had provided the pair with a knowledge of right and wrong, after eating of the fruit they had experience of what evil meant, and the taste was bitter indeed. Now they were to discover that God's Word was irrevocable law, and that the warnings He had given were not idle threats, but intended for their good, to keep them from evil.

Eve did not originate the idea that she should eat of the tree. The record is quite clear that she was prompted to experiment by the subtle, guileful serpent, who deceived her (Genesis 3:1-5; 2 Corinthians 11:3). The temptation came from without, not within. The implication is that it would never have occurred to her to eat of the fruit, had it not been suggested.

And, just as the serpent put the idea into her mind, Eve put the idea – or rather the fruit – to Adam "and he did eat". She ate while under the influence of the serpent's deception; Adam ate wilfully (1 Timothy 2:14). It seems that he deliberately chose to stay with her, rather than choose separation. In so doing, he declared a preference for human companionship rather than Divine fellowship and so became the author of human misery. He might have been able to act as Eve's saviour or redeemer, had he remained in the Garden. Banished, they became partners in sin and inevitably victims of death.

"AS BY ONE MAN ..."
Scripture does not merely record Adam as a sinner, or even as the first wilful sinner; it declares him to be the father of sin and death, who begat many sons after his fallen likeness. ...

From the outset, Adam's transgression was seen as something with far reaching significance: it was not simply that it introduced death into the world. Mortality was a physical consequence of Adam's sin. We shall later consider the moral implications. Death had been the deterrent that God presented to Adam: "Of the tree of the knowledge of good and evil, thou shalt not eat of it: for in the day that thou eatest thereof thou shalt surely die" (Gen 2:17). That came to pass. On the day of the transgression Adam was assured that he would die (Gen 3:19), for when God's judgement was delivered there was no possible doubt about the eventual execution of the sentence. From then on there was no doubt about Adam's death, which eventually came when he was 930 years old (Genesis 5:5).

The curse placed upon him has two interesting aspects in this respect. First, death is the last thing to be mentioned. Second, it is manifestly clear that God expected Adam to live for a long time before his death"

> "Cursed is *the ground* for thy sake; in sorrow shalt thou eat of it *all the days of thy life;* thorns also and thistles shall it bring forth to thee; and thou shalt eat the herb of the field; in the sweat of thy face shalt thou eat bread, *till thou return* unto *the ground;* for out of it wast thou taken: for dust thou art, and unto dust shalt thou return" (Genesis 3:17–19).

It has been argued that in those words God was anticipating the outcome of sacrifices that were to be offered that day for Adam and Eve (Genesis 3:21), and was therefore able to ignore the death sentence that would otherwise have come into immediate effect. But the more likely explanation is that the earlier warning, "in the day that thou eatest thereof thou shalt surely die", did not mean summary execution on the day of the transgression – that would have ended human existence almost before it had begun and would have made barren any process of salvation. Rather, God's words indicated the beginning of a process of death: that Adam would become a dying creature, from that day on. There is an interesting parallel in 1 Kings 2:37-42, where Solomon had placed Shimei under a prospective sentence of death, which was eventually fulfilled.

After his sin, Adam's condition was different from his earlier created state, which was described as "very good". He now knew and felt the corruption of mortality. He was physically flawed, where previously he had not been.

Tecwyn Morgan, Studies in the Statement of Faith, *Concerning Mortal Man - Clause V*, 1991, pp. 24-29 (originally published in The Christadelphian in 1990)

GOD'S SENTENCE ON MANKIND

This is how the Statement of Faith explains what happened:

> V—That Adam broke this law, and was adjudged unworthy of immortality, and sentenced to return to the ground from whence he was taken—a sentence which defiled and became a physical law of his being, and was transmitted to all his posterity.— Genesis 3:15-19, 22, 23; 2 Corinthians 1:9; Romans 7:24; 2 Corinthians 5:2-4; Romans 7:18-23; Galatians 5:16-17; Romans 6:12; 7:21; John 3:6; Romans 5:12; 1 Corinthians 15:22; Psalm 51:5; Job 14:4.

THIS accords with the wide ranging effects of the curse we have already noted: there was much more involved than simply the passing of the death sentence upon Adam himself. For example, Eve was not expressly told that she would die, yet she did. Adam was obviously a representative man for the purposes of the judgement on sin, as he had been for the act itself – a sort of federal head, a representative, for all mankind. And the sentence was universal: the curse permeated the whole of God's created earth, man's existence and nature included.

This is how the apostle Paul understood the position, as he explained it in his letter to the Romans. There he explains how all have come under the dominion of sin (3:9-18); how all, save Christ, have failed to achieve perfect obedience (3:23, 24); and how all this came about because of Adam's transgression (5:12-19).

Death gained control of the world, claiming all earth's creatures as its victims, and condemning them to suffer its dominion. Paul makes it clear that Adam was not subject to death before he ate of the tree, though that obviously does not mean that he was then immortal, else he could never have died. Death came because of sin and it was "passed on" to all men down the human chain. As a result of Adam's sin many have therefore subsequently died because:

    a. they inherited Adam's dying nature and,
    b. they too have sinned.

We die because our nature is such that we cannot live for ever. When we commit sinful acts and deeds which demonstrate our wilful association with Adam we show that God has justly condemned mankind to death.

ALL CREATION CURSED

Paul sees the full effects of the Adamic curse as permeating the whole of human existence. In Romans 8:18–23 he describes those effects as blighting all creation.

At some length, Paul had spelled out, in Romans 7, how he was himself subjected to frustration, from the very core of his being and, as Romans 8:23 makes clear, this working of sin "in his members" (Romans 7:23) was his post-baptismal experience, not that of his previous Pharisaic life. In summary, Paul's letter to the Romans supplies a full analysis of the origin, the effects and the conditions of sin. It attributes them to Adam's initial act, showing that a belief in the special creation of this "son of God" answers the otherwise unanswerable moral issues of life.

A SENTENCE WHICH DEFILED . . .

We are now a dying race: that is an inescapable part of our experience. Death is "a physical law of our being". But in what sense can the sentence that was passed upon Adam be regarded as something that "defiles" us? Does this terminology imply that we are to blame for the nature we bear, that we are in some way guilty before God from the beginning of our conscious existence?

In addition to the physical condition of his body, making the grave his certain destiny, Adam's sin also created in him something which affected all his future actions. Once he had made a wilfully wrong choice, his "knowledge of good and evil" was awakened. Before, he had known what "evil" was by definition – it was the breach of God's Law. After, he knew about evil by his experience, and it left a bitter after-taste. He could never again have the guileless innocence that existed when he was created. He was immediately ashamed of his actions; they "hid themselves from the presence of the LORD God amongst the trees of the garden" (Genesis 3:8), and this separation from God featured in all of his future life. Henceforth temptation would arise both from without and from within. Just as mortality became the experience of all human life, the inner tendency or propensity to please self rather than God was also passed on to all his descendants, for Adam's knowledge of good and evil was inherited by all his children: now it is invariably the case that, "every man is tempted, when he is drawn away of his own lust and enticed" (James 1:14).

For these reasons Scripture styles the nature we bear "sinful flesh". It has been inherited by all mankind, as Scripture testifies frequently. Consider Jeremiah 17:9; Mark 7:20-22; Psalm 51:5; Romans 7:18,24; Galatians 5:17; James 1:14-15)

It is important to recognise that we are not to blame because of these tendencies: they are inherited, and not our fault. In the same way, we die because our bodies have an inbuilt obsolescence; we are dying creatures from our birth onwards. The sentence of death that was first passed upon Adam will be carried out on us too, in due course, for we are mortal. Paul is careful to observe that "by one man sin entered into the world, and death by sin". This is the physical result of Adam's sin. But then he goes on to deal with the moral dimension. He adds that "death passed upon all men, for that all have sinned" (Romans 5:12).

THE DIVINE INITIATIVE

The nature of man was, and is, such that there has never been any prospect of our being able to rescue either ourselves or our brothers from the prison house of death. The ransom is too great to pay (Psalm 49:7-9), the task is insurmountable. By thus submitting to the urgings of our sin-prone condition, we are shown to be "children of wrath", "alienated and enemies in (our) mind by wicked works", separated "from the life of God" (Ephesians 2:3; Colossians 1:21; Ephesians 4:18). Continually exposed to the temptation to sin, we are in need of redemption by Divine intervention.

Just as the desperate consequences of the sentence passed upon Adam, which have been inherited by all his descendants, have two aspects, physical and mental, so there are two aspects to our redemption. We can transfer from Adam to Christ now, by renewing our minds after the pattern of the Son's. But fully to restore the relationship with God terminated by Adam's sin, our lowly bodies must be transformed – as was the Lord's, for "flesh and blood (with its enduring propensity to sin) cannot inherit the kingdom of God" (1 Corinthians 15:50). There must be a transformation in the way we think: no longer like Adam, but like Christ. Then, when Christ returns, we can be "clothed upon"; "this mortal (shall) put on immortality" (2 Corinthians 5:2; 1 Corinthians 15:53). In short, we must all be changed, within and without.

Chapter 27
The Devil – Personification of Fallen Human Nature

John Thomas

John Thomas, The Herald of the Kingdom, vol. 2, 1852, pp. 180-185
That *diabolos,* rendered *devil* in the Common Version, is SIN, appears from the expressions of Paul in various parts of his writings. He says "that having *the power* of death is *diabolos"* [Hebrews 2:14]. The power of death is that which causes death. In a venomous serpent the *to kratos,* or power of death, is its fang or sting. Remove this, and the most deadly reptile is perfectly innocuous. It has lost its power, not of locomotion, but of inflicting death. So if the power that makes death work strongly within us could be removed, we should never die. It is that *power* that Paul styles *diabolos.* It is not death; but the death-producing power, which is in every man, young and old, saint and sinner; therefore *diabolos* is in every human being. . .

Now, this exceedingly great sinner, Sin, working death in a man, the scripture styles diabolos: and it may be pertinently asked, Why is it so called? The following I conceive to be the reason. The attribute most characteristic of Sin's character is deceitfulness; as it is written, "Exhort one another daily lest any of you be hardened through the deceitfulness of sin"[Hebrews 3:13]; "Sin taking occasion through the commandment deceived me" [Romans 7:11]; "Eve being deceived was in transgression" [1Timothy 2:14]; and "the Serpent beguiled her through his shrewdness" [2 Corinthians 11:3]. Eve being deceived, the Serpent's part in the transaction was finished. He held no conference with Adam, who, the apostle says, "was not deceived." Sin, the Seducer, approached him through Eve, whose eyes were open to evil. Sin incarnate in Eve was Adam's tempter. "With her much fair speech she caused him to yield, with the flattering of her lips she forced him"[Proverbs 7:21]. She gave him of the tree, and he did eat; and eating, fell. Thus Sin caused him to fall in casting him across the law-line; and therefore it is called diabolos.

John Thomas, The Herald of the Kingdom, vol. 2, 1852, pp. 200-201
We have ascertained satisfactorily, because scripturally, as it appears to me, that the thing, styled in the Greek New Testament "diabolos," and rendered "devil" in the English version, is SIN IN THE FLESH - he that "walks according to the flesh" "serves sin," diabolos or the devil [Romans 8:3]. The Mortal body is "the body of sin" [Romans 6:6] or Sin Incarnate, which with its affections, lusts, and transgressions, is styled "the Old Man," than whom no imaginary devil can be more wicked, and defiant of God and His Law. The Old Man in his individual, social, and political manifestations is the diabolos, or devil, or the New Testament mystery (1 Timothy 3:16), and treated of accordingly.

... "Diabolos" had no existence before the formation of man, but the Serpent had. Moses gives not the slightest hint of the existence of a Devil before the creations of the sixth day. The Serpent first, then man; afterwards, woman; and lastly, "diabolos," or Devil. This is the scriptural order of their manifestation, the revelation in the flesh of the incitant to transgression, or "diabolos," being coeval with the Fall. Man existed before the Devil, and will flourish in eternal glory after his destruction, when Sin and all its works are eradicated from the earth.

John Thomas, Elpis Israel, 1866, p. 74

Probation before exaltation, the law of the moral universe of God—The temptation of the Lord Jesus by Satan the trial of his faith by the Father—The Temptation explained—God's foreknowledge does not necessitate; nor does He justify, or condemn, by anticipation—The Serpent an intellectual animal, but not a moral agent, nor inspired—He deceives the woman—The nature of the transgression—Eve becomes the tempter to Adam—The transgression consummated in the conception of Cain—A good conscience, and an evil conscience, defined—Man cannot cover his own sin—The carnal mind illustrated by the reasoning of the Serpent—It is metaphorically the serpent in the flesh—God's truth the only rule of right and wrong—The Serpent in the flesh is manifested in the wickedness of individuals; and in the spiritual and temporal institutions of the world—Serpent-sin in the flesh identified with "the Wicked One"—The Prince of the World—The Kingdom of Satan and the World identical—The Wiles of the Devil—The "Prince" shown to be sin, working and reigning in all sinners—How he was "cast out" by Jesus—"The works of the Devil"—"Bound of Satan"; delivering to Satan—The Great Dragon—The Devil and Satan—The Man of Sin.

John Thomas, Elpis Israel, 1866, pp. 76-77

This enemy within the human nature is the mind of the flesh, which is enmity against God; it is not subject to His law, neither indeed can be (Romans 8:7). The commandment of God, which is "holy, just and good", being so restrictive of the propensities, which in purely animal men display themselves with uncontrolled violence, makes them appear in their true colours. These turbulent propensities the apostle styles "sin in the flesh", of which it is full; hence, he also terms it "sinful flesh". This is human nature; and the evil in it, made so apparent by the law of God, he personifies as "*pre-eminently* a sinner", χαθ' ὑπεϱβολὴν ἁμαϱτωλός (Romans 7:12-13,17-18). This is the accuser, adversary, and calumniator of God, whose stronghold is the flesh. It is the devil and satan within the human nature; so that "when a man is tempted, he is drawn away of his own lust and enticed". If a man examine himself, he will perceive within him something at work, craving after things which the law of God forbids. The best of men are conscious of this enemy within them. It troubled the apostle so much, that he exclaimed, "O, wretched man that I am! who shall deliver me from the body of this death" (Romans 7:24), or, this mortal body? He thanked God that the Lord Jesus Christ would do it; that is, as he had himself been delivered from it, by God raising him from the dead by His Spirit (Romans 8:11).

John Thomas, *The Carnal Mind*, Elpis Israel, 1866, p. 94

Now, they who do the works of the flesh are the children of the Wicked One, or of sin in the flesh; on the like principle that those Jews only were the children of Abraham who did the works of Abraham. But they did not the deeds of Abraham, but evil deeds. They were liars, hypocrites and murderers: therefore, said Jesus, "Ye are of your father the devil, and the lusts of your father ye are willing to do. He was a murderer from the beginning, and stood not in the truth, because there is no truth in him" (John 8:39-44). We have seen in what sense this is affirmed of the Serpent, the unaccountable and irresponsible author of sin. Every son of Adam is "conceived in sin and shapen in iniquity", and therefore "sinful flesh"; on the principle that "what is born of the flesh is flesh." If he obey the impulses of his flesh, he is like Cain, "of the Wicked One"; but if he believe the "exceeding great and precious promises of God", obey the law of faith, and put to death unlawful obedience to his propensities, he becomes a son of the living God, and a brother and a joint-heir of the Lord Jesus Christ of the glory to be revealed in the last time.

John Thomas, *The Prince Of This World*, Elpis Israel, 1866, pp. 95-99

Sin made flesh, whose character is revealed in the works of the flesh, is the Wicked One of the world. He is styled by Jesus ὁ ἄρχων τοῦ χόσμου τούτου the Prince of this world. *Kosmos*, ordered world in this phrase, signifies, that *order of things* constituted upon the basis of sin in the flesh, and styled *the kingdom of Satan* (Matthew 12:26), as opposed to the kingdom of God: ... Satan's kingdom is the kingdom of sin. It is a kingdom in which "sin reigns in the mortal body", and thus has dominion over men.

... The kingdom of Satan is manifested under various phases. When the Word was embodied in sinful flesh, and dwelt among the Jews, the *Kosmos* was constituted of the Roman world, which was then based upon the institutions of paganism. ... The lord that dominates over them all from the days of Jesus to the present time is SIN, the incarnate accuser and adversary of the law of God, and therefore styled "the Devil and Satan".

... If a man embrace one of the religions of Satan's kingdom, he is still "dead in trespasses and sins", and walks according to the course of the world (Ephesians 2:1-2). In brief, anything short of faith in the gospel of the kingdom, and obedience to the law of faith, is walking according to the course of the world. To walk in sin is to walk in this course. Hence, the apostle terms walking according to the course of the world, walking according to *the Prince of the Power of the Air*—ὁ ἄρχων τῆς ἐξουσίας τοῦ ἀέρος: which he explains as "*the Spirit now working* in the children of disobedience". The "*power of the air*", or aerial power, is *the political power of the world*, which is animated and pervaded by *the spirit of disobedience*, which is sin in the flesh; and styled above, the Prince of the Power of the Air. This is that prince of whom Jesus spoke, saying, "Now is the judgment (χρίσις) of this world; now shall the Prince of this World be cast out" (John 12:31), that is, "judged" (John 16:11). The key to this is suggested in what follows: "And I, if I be lifted up from the earth, will draw all unto me. This he said, signifying *what death he should die*."

... They bruised him in the heel (Genesis 3:15). ... But here the serpent-power of sin ended. It had stung him to death by the strength of the law, which cursed every one that was hanged upon a tree. Jesus being cursed upon this ground, God "condemned sin in the flesh" through him (Galatians 3:13; Romans 8:3). Thus was sin, the Prince of the World, condemned, and the world with him according to the existing course of it. But Jesus rose again, leading captivity captive; and so giving to the world an earnest, that the time would come when death should be abolished and sin, the power of death, destroyed. Sinful flesh was laid upon him, "that through death, he might destroy *him* that had the power of death, that is, the devil", or sin in the flesh (Hebrews 2:14): for, "*for this purpose* the Son of God was manifested, that he might destroy the works of the devil" (1 John 3:8).

John Thomas, *The Works Of The Devil*, Elpis Israel, 1866, pp. 99-100
The works of the devil, or evil one, are *the works of sin*. Individually, they are "the works of the flesh" exhibited in the lives of sinners; collectively, they are on a larger scale, as displayed in the polities of the world. All the institutions of the kingdom of the adversary are the works which have resulted from the thinking of sinful flesh. …

Among the works of sin are the numerous diseases which transgression has brought upon the world. The Hebrews, the idiom of whose language is derived from the Mosaic narrative of the origin of things, referred disease to sin under the names of the devil and Satan. Hence, they inquired, "Who sinned, this man or his parents, that he was born blind?" A woman "bowed together with a spirit of infirmity for eighteen years", is said to have been "bound of Satan", or the adversary, for that time; and her restoration to health is termed "loosing her from the bond" (Luke 13:10–17). …

John Thomas, *Deity Manifested in Spirit*, Eureka, vol. 1, 1861, pp. 106-107
For this cause, "Jesus was made a little lower than the angels for the suffering of death; … that he, by the grace of the Deity, might taste death for every man." For this cause, and forasmuch also "as the children (of the Deity) are partakers of flesh and blood, He also himself likewise took part of the same; that through death he might destroy that having the power of death, that is, the *diabolos*," or elements of corruption in our nature, inciting it to transgression, and therefore called "Sin working death in us"— Romans 7:13; Hebrews 2:9, 14.

John Thomas, *The Diabolos*, Eureka, vol. 1, 1861, pp. 246- 251
The Spirit clothed himself with weakness and corruption—in other words, "Sin's flesh's identity"—that he might destroy the *Diabolos*. It is manifest from this the *diabolos* must be of the same nature as that which the Spirit assumed; for the supposition that he assumed human nature to destroy a being of angelic nature, or of some other more powerful, is palpably absurd. The Diabolos is something, then, pertaining to flesh and blood; and the Spirit or Logos became flesh and blood to destroy it.

Now, whatever flesh-and-blood thing it may be, Paul says that "it hath *the power* of death"—that is, it is the power which causes mankind to die. If, then, we can ascertain from Paul what is the power or cause of death, we discover what the thing is he terms the Diabolos; for he tells us that the Diabolos has the power of death.

... In Romans 5:12, he says, *"Death by sin."* He does not say, "By the Devil sin entered into the world;" if he had, this would have given "the Devil" existence before Sin: but he says, "By one man, or Adam, sin entered into the world." This agrees with Moses, who tells us that there was a time after the creation was finished when there was nothing in the world but what was "very good"—"and Elohim saw *all* that He (the Spirit) had made, and behold, it was very good"—Genesis 1:31. Man is, therefore, older than Sin, and, consequently, older than the Diabolos. Man introduced it into the world and not an immortal devil, nor God. Neither God, then, nor such a devil, was the author of sin; but the authorship was constituted of the sophistry of the serpent believed and experimented by the Man, male and female.

... By this time, I apprehend, the intelligent reader will be able to answer scripturally the question, "What is that which has the power of death?" And he will, doubtless, agree, that it is "the exceedingly great sinner SIN," in the sense of "the Law of Sin and Death" [Romans 8:2] within all the posterity of Adam, without exception. This, then, is Paul's *Diabolos*, which he says "has the power of death;" which "power" he also saith is "sin, the sting of death."

But why doth Paul style Sin *diabolos?* The answer to this question will be found in the definition of the word. *Diabolos* is derived from *diaballo*, which is compounded of *dia*, a preposition, which in composition signifies *across, over*, and answers to the Latin *trans;* and of *ballo* to *throw, cast;* and intransitively, *to fall, tumble.* Hence, *diaballo*, is *to throw over or across;* and intransitively, like the Latin *trajicere*, to *pass over*, to *cross*, to *pass.* This being the signification of the parent verb, the noun *diabolos* is the name of *that which crosses*, or *causes to cross over*, or *falls over*. DIABOLOS is therefore a very fit and proper word by which to designate the law of sin and death, or Sin's flesh.

... But *diaballo* has secondary and ternary significations. It signifies *to traduce*, to *attack character*, to *slander*, to *libel;* and thirdly, to *deceive, mislead, impose upon.* Hence, *diabolos* will also signify a *traducer, slanderer, deceiver, imposter.* In this sense, Judas is styled a *diabolos*—John 6:70. So also the pious scribes and Pharisees, priests and rulers, who, though as priests, officially holy, were as Jesus said, "of father the Diabolos, and the lusts of their father (the flesh) they would do. The same was a man-killer from the beginning, and stood not in the truth, because truth is not in him. When he speaks a lie he speaks of his own things, for he is a liar, and the father of it"—John 8:44. And "he that committeth sin is of the Diabolos, for the diabolos sinneth from the beginning"—1 John 3:8. All this is perfectly intelligible when understood of Sin's flesh, in which dwells no good thing, and which *of itself* can neither do right nor think aright. Man's ability to do either is derived from a higher source—*from the truth indoctrinated into him.* When this is declared and reasoned into him, and he comes to understand it, to believe it, and to love it, a power is set up within him called "the law of the Spirit of life," which is counteractive of "the law of sin and death," and brings the man to "the obedience of faith," by which he is manifested to the skilful in the word as a son of God. The disobedient are all of father Diabolos; and his spirit, which is the spirit of the flesh, works in them. Hence the clergy, Jewish and Gentile, are all of what they call "the Devil," being ignorant, and consequently disobedient of the gospel of the kingdom.

But, Diabolos is discoursed of in scripture in its imperial as well as racial manifestations. John says, "For this purpose the Son of God was manifested, that he might destroy the works of the Diabolos"(1 John 3:8). When the Diabolos and his works are destroyed "every curse will have ceased" (Revelation 22:3). The works of the Diabolos are the Works of Sin. Look into the world, ecclesiastical and civil, and the reader will see Sin's works on every side. The thrones, dominions, principalities, and powers … are all the works of Sin, which festers and ferments in all "the children of disobedience." They are all based upon the transgression of the divine law; and are all officered and sustained by the children of the Diabolos. The Messiah's mission is to destroy them all. John, the baptizer, proclaimed this in pointing to Jesus, and saying, "Behold, the Lamb of God who takes away The Sin of the world!" which, by Paul and John the apostle, is interpreted as the Son of God that destroys the Diabolos and his works—the flesh and all its institutions: for the time comes at the end of the Thousand Years, when flesh and blood nature will be abolished from the earth; and by consequence, all evil and death, "the last enemy" [1 Corinthians 15:26], which are its wages in all the earth.

John Thomas, *The Old Serpent Eureka*, vol. 4, 1866, pp. 66-76
In the beginning, the Serpent-World consisted of no more than two sinners—Adam and his wife; yet small as was its extent, all the evil that has since manifested itself, was latent in them. Their symbol was the Serpent, or Dragon, and *represented falsehood, unbelief, and rebellion against the Deity*. Wherever these three have been found politically organized, and in conflict with the saints, there is the Serpent which was in the beginning—"the old serpent." Of this serpent-world the Scripture saith, "Love not the world, neither the things that are in the world. If any man love the world, the love of the Father is not in him. For all that is in the world—the lust of the flesh, and the lust of the eyes, and the pride of life—is not of the Father, but is of the world. And the world passeth away, and the lust thereof; but he that doeth the will of the Deity abideth for ever" (1 John 2:15–17).

In after times, far distant from the beginning, the serpent-world acquired an immense development. From two persons it had increased to myriads of millions. …

John Thomas – Phanerosis, 1869, pp. 35-36 [Logos 1969 Edition]
The Old Man of Sin's Flesh, who is the Devil, cannot be converted. His destiny is destruction; "for this purpose was the Son of God manifested that he might destroy *the works* of the Devil," or the works of the flesh, which are the same things: and "forasmuch also as the children (of his Father) are partakers of flesh and blood, He (the Son) himself, likewise, took part of the same; that through death he might destroy him that had the power of death, that is, *the Devil*" (1 John 3:8; Hebrews 2:14). Hence the Old Man of the Flesh and his deeds are doomed to extirpation from the earth at the hands of Jesus and his brethren.

John Thomas, The Christadelphian, vol. 11, 1874, pp. 156-160[191]

EVIL: Seven attested propositions on the origin and the operation of evil in relation to the human race.

Proposition VI
This principle of evil, which reigns in flesh and blood, is styled "an exceedingly great sinner;" and all that is affirmed of the devil in the Scriptures is predicated of the evil that dwelleth in man, as expressed in his individual actions, and through the political and ecclesiastical organizations of the world.

> JOHN 8:44.—The devil from the beginning abode not in the truth, because there is no truth in him. When he speaketh a lie, he speaketh of his own, for he is a liar, and the father of it.

Here Jesus fixes the origin of falsehood where Moses placed it in his account, as originating in the subtlety of the serpent whom he styles the devil or suggester. "When he speaketh a lie, he speaketh of his own, for he is a liar." Give him speech, as did the Lord God, and he will express only subtlety; for deceivableness, artfulness, and cunning are the characteristics of his physical organization. He was the father of lies, and all liars are, therefore, his seed.

> 1 JOHN 3:8.—The devil sinneth from the beginning.

"The *beginning*" here indicated is the time fixed by Moses in Genesis 1:1, 31, when "the heavens and the earth were finished, and all the host of them." The devil sinneth. The evil suggested by the serpent found place in the mind of man; and these having conceived a desire to do what God had forbidden, transgression was the result. This the apostle personifies as the devil which sins from the beginning, even till now in all the disobedient.

> JOHN 8:44.—The devil was a murderer from the beginning.
> 1 JOHN 3:12.—Cain was of that wicked one, and slew his brother.
> VERSE 8.—He that committeth sin is of the devil.
> VERSE 15.—No murderer hath eternal life abiding in him.

Cain proved himself to be of the number of the serpent's seed, "*because his works were evil.*" Hence he is said to be "of that wicked one," "the devil." Cain was not the devil, though Jesus styles the devil "a murderer;" and the only murderer in the beginning was Cain. But the evil principle which entered into his parents when they ate of the tree of the knowledge of evil was transmitted to him congenitally. This was the word or corruptible seed of the serpent, as opposed to the word or "incorruptible seed of God," which was in him. The Lord God had required a *sin-offering* from those who came to him. The word of God having no place in him, Cain followed the suggestions of his own corrupt nature when reasoning on the commandment of God, which told him it was unnecessary. Thus the evil within him, in its nature essentially hostile to the law of God, conceived, and brought forth transgression. …

---

[191] Published by Bro. Roberts with the comment: "Found in an old MS. of Dr. Thomas, which, so far as we know, has never been published."

Thus in Cain's case *"the devil"* was the evil latent within his nature, which revived under the holy, just and good commandment of God; he yielded to its suggestions and gave expression to its murderous emotions, and thus brought upon himself "the end of these things which is death." "No murderer hath eternal life abiding in him." Hence "THE EXCEEDINGLY GREAT SINNER" [Romans 7:13], who is innate in flesh and blood, that is, "THE DEVIL," nor the man who yields himself servant to obey him in the lust of the flesh, have any glory, honour, incorruptibility, or eternal life abiding in them, which sufficiently proves the absolute destructibility of the devil and his seed.

Proposition VII
The devil is not immortal.

> HEBREWS 2:14.—Forasmuch, then, as the children of God are partakers of flesh and blood, Jesus also himself took part of the same, that through death he might destroy him that had the power of death, that is, THE DEVIL."

What is it in flesh and blood that had the power of subjecting the body to death? The evil principle of corruption within man, termed by Paul "the law of sin in the members" [Romans 7:23,25], "the law of sin and death" [Romans 8:2], "sin in the flesh" [Romans 8:3]. This then is "the devil, that had the power of death."

The evil principle, which entered into man when he ate of the tree of the knowledge of evil, and which is inherent in all the descendants of Adam being proved to be the devil in the passage adduced, it follows that he is not immortal, unless it can be affirmed that evil, lust, sin, &c., are in themselves essentially incorruptible, and, therefore, indestructible and immortal, which would be the *ne plus ultra* of absurdity.

Robert Roberts

A Declaration Of The First Principles Of The Oracles Of The Deity, 1867[192]

XXIII - THE DEVIL OF THE BIBLE

The Devil - Who is he? It is of great consequence to understand this question, because the Son of God was manifested *expressly for the purpose of destroying the devil and his works* (I John 3:8; Hebrews 2:14). The mission of Christ is, therefore, imperfectly understood when the nature of the Bible Devil is not comprehended. We affirm that the devil is not (as commonly supposed) a personal, supernatural agent of evil, and that in fact, there is no such BEING in existence. The devil is a *Scriptural personification of sin in the flesh*, in its several phases of manifestation - subjective, individual, aggregate, social and political, in history, current experience, and prophecy; after the style of metaphor which speaks of wisdom as a Woman, riches as MAMMON and the god of this world, sin as a Master, etc.

---

[192] Bro. R.C. Bingley was the author of this document published by Bro. Roberts. Importantly, since this first edition in 1867, it has served as a standard Christadelphian pamphlet outlining essential first principles of the Bible, even the one true faith as taught by the apostles in the first century, which Christadelphian consider as essential for salvation.

Hebrews 2:14; Romans 6:23; Hebrews 9:26; James 4:7; Hebrews 12:4 John 13:2; John 6:70; Acts 5:3,9; James 1:14-15; Ephesians 2:2; 1 Timothy 5:14-15; 1 Timothy 1:20; Matthew 16:23; Mark 8:33; Luke 4:8; 1 Thessalonians 2:18; Revelation 2:12-13; 1 Peter 5:8; Revelation 2:10; Romans 16:20; Genesis 3:15; Psalm 68:21; Jeremiah 51:20; Revelation 12:13,17; Revelation 20:2; Psalm 110:6; Daniel 2:44

Robert Roberts, *Christ Saved From Death*, The Christadelphian, 1874, pp. 481-482

Now that Jesus was, in this respect, made like unto those for whom he died and rose again, is evident from what Paul tells the Hebrews 2:14-15: "Forasmuch as the children are partakers of flesh and blood, he also himself likewise took part of the same, that through death he might destroy him that had the power of death, that is, the devil; and deliver them who, *through fear of death, were all their lifetime subject to bondage.*" The devil (serpent) is here said to have the power of death, that is, over all who have Adam's nature, and since the Book does not tell us that he had this power over man *before* he sinned, but quite the contrary, as is taught by Paul (Romans 5:12), it follows that Jesus having that nature, feared lying under the power of death (Hebrews 5:7), after death had passed upon it, being as a son of man, in the same condition as those who are declared to have been all their lifetime *subject to bondage.* The Father hearkened to his dear Son's supplication, and delivered him from death. The Son asked life and the Father gave it unto him, even the length of days forever and ever. - (Psalm 21:4). Let us give thanks for this, for IF CHRIST BE NOT RAISED, *our faith is vain, we are yet in our sins, and they who have fallen asleep in Christ ARE* PERISHED [1 Corinthians 15:18].

Robert Roberts, Christendom Astray from the Bible, 1884, pp. 192-203

… [The Devil] is that which personifies the great principle which lies at the bottom of the rupture at present existing between God and man, as pre-eminently the accuser and striker through with a dart—the calumniator of God and the destroyer of mankind. First, let the fact of this personification be demonstrated. The evidence of it makes a powerful beginning in Hebrews 2:14, where we read as follows:—

> "Forasmuch then as the children are partakers of flesh and blood, he (Jesus) also himself likewise took part of the same, that *through death* he might destroy *him that had the power of death*, that is, the Devil."

… John says, "For this purpose the Son of God was manifested, *that he might destroy the works of the devil*" (I John 3:8) … The devil Christ has come to destroy is sin.

Christ, through death, destroyed, or took out of the way, "the sin of the world". In this, he destroyed the Bible devil. He certainly did not destroy the popular devil in his death, for that devil is supposed to be still at large, but in his own person, as a representative man, he extinguished the power of sin by surrendering to its full consequences, and then escaping by resurrection, through the power of his own holiness, to live for evermore. This is described as "God sending His own Son in the likeness of sinful flesh, and for sin, condemned *sin in the flesh*" (Romans 8:3). Sin in the flesh, then, is the devil destroyed by Jesus in his death. This is the devil *having the power of death*, for it is sin, and nothing else but sin that causes death to men. Does anyone doubt this? Let him read the following testimonies:—

> "By one man sin entered into the world, *and death* by *sin* (Romans 5:12).
> "*By man* came death" (I Corinthians 15:21).
> "*The wages of sin* is death" (Romans 6:23).
> "Sin hath reigned *unto death*" (Romans 5:21).
> "Sin ... *bringeth forth death*" (James 1:15).
> "The sting of death is Sin" (I Corinthians 15:56).

Having regard to the fact that death was divinely decreed in the garden of Eden, *in consequence of Adam's transgression*, it is easy to understand the language which recognises and personifies transgression, or sin, as the power or cause of death. The foregoing statements express the literal truth metonymically. Actually, death, as the consequence of sin, is produced, caused or inflicted *by God*, but since sin or transgression is the fact or principle that *moves God to inflict it*, sin is appropriately put forward as *the first cause* in the matter. This is intelligible to the smallest intellect. ...

... Every man is tempted when he is drawn away of his own lust, and enticed. Then when lust hath conceived, *it bringeth forth sin*, and sin, when it is finished, bringeth forth death" (James 1:14, 15). This agrees with a man's own experience of himself; sin originates in the *untrained natural inclinations*. These, in the aggregate, Paul terms "another law in my members, warring against the law of my mind." Every man is conscious of the existence of this law, whose impulse, uncontrolled, would drive him beyond the restraints of wisdom. The world obeyeth this law, and "lieth in wickedness." It has no experience of the other law, which is implanted by the truth. "All that is in the world" John defines to be *"the lust of the flesh, and the lust of the eyes, and the pride of life"* (I John 2:16).

... There is no devil but his own inclinations, which tend to illegitimate activity. These are the origin of sin, and sin is the cause of death. Both together are the devil. "He that committeth sin *is of the devil*" (I John 3:8).

... The individual serpent itself has long since passed away in the course of nature, but the fruits remain, and the principle lives. The idea instilled by it into the minds of our first parents has germinated to the production of generations of human serpents. Mankind has proved but an embodiment of the serpent idea; so that they are all calumniators of God in disbelieving His promises, and disobeying His commandments. ... All who are in the first Adam, are "the children of the devil" [1 John 3:10], because they are the progeny of a serpent-devil contaminated paternity. Their mortality is evidence of this, whatever be their moral qualities, because mortality is the fruit of the serpent-devil conceit operating in Adam to disobedience. But those who, upon a belief of the promises of God, are introduced into "the second Adam" (who in his death destroyed the bonds of the devil in taking away sin), are emancipated from the family of the devil, and become sons of God.

Progeny is according to paternity; like produces like; "Children of the devil" must be devil; and hence it is that the world of human nature as a whole is regarded as the devil, because it is the embodiment of the devil principle. ... the abstract principle which lies at the bottom of human misery and mortality is personified. Hence, Jesus destroying the devil and his works, is Jesus taking away the sin of the world, which will ultimate in the complete abolition of human nature on the Adam or serpent basis, and the swallowing up of death in victory.

Robert Roberts – The Christadelphian Instructor, 1886

57.   What are we to understand by the statement of Paul quoted in proof of the answer to Question 55 that Jesus died that through death he might destroy him that had the power of death, that is, the devil? Who is this devil?

Answer: The devil, or Satan, is the Bible name for sin in its various forms among men. Christ took away sin by the sacrifice of himself. Sin is the death-power. There is no such being as the personal immortal devil of popular religious belief. The belief in such a being is due to the misunderstanding of certain figures and symbols in the Bible. The Bible devil has many shapes; but all these have their origin in the insubordination of flesh and blood to divine law. He presents himself in our own feelings, and in the persons of those who would draw us into wrong ways. In his largest shape, he exists in the present political constitution of things upon the earth.

Proof: *Hebrews 2:14; 9:26; Romans 6:23; James 1:14-15; 4:7; Hebrews 12:4; John 13:2; 6:70; Acts 5:3-9; Ephesians 2:2; 1 Timothy 5:14-15; 1 Timothy 1:20; Matthew 16:23; Mark 8:33; Luke 4:8; 1 Thessalonians 2:18; Revelation 2:12-13; 1 Peter 5:8; Revelation 2:10; Romans 16:20; Revelation 12:3, 17; 17:9,12; Revelation 20:2.*

Robert Roberts, The Law of Moses, 1898, pp. 178-179

This is the whole principle: redemption achieved in Christ for us to have, on condition of faith and obedience. It is not only that Israel are saved from the law of Moses on this principle, but it is the principle upon which we are saved from the law of sin and death, whose operation we inherit in deriving our nature from Adam. Christ partook of this nature to deliver it from death, as Paul teaches in Hebrews 2:14, and other places: "Forasmuch as the children are partakers of flesh and blood, he also himself likewise took part of the same that through death he might destroy him that had the power of death, that is, the devil".

Understanding by the devil, the hereditary death-power that has reigned among men by Adam through sin, we may understand how Christ, who took part in the death-inheriting nature, destroyed the power of death by dying and rising. We then understand how "He put away sin by the sacrifice of himself". We may also understand how "our old man is crucified with him, that the body of sin might be destroyed" (Romans 6:6) and how he "died unto sin once", but now liveth unto God, to die no more (verses 9–10).

LB Welch

LB Welch, The Christadelphian, vol. 29, 1892, pp. 171-174

To the English mind, and according to English idiom, the full import of the noun diabolos would be expressed in the following terms: "That which causes to cross over," "that which causes to fall." It may be illustrated in this way: If a line of obedience be laid down, and one be forbidden to cross over it, then whatever would cause one to cross over and thus fall from obedience would be a diabolos. Such is the Greek idea conformed to English idiom. But the term diabolos has other significations, not so much philological as the character of whatever or whoever is employing the first characteristic of the term, thus: "traducer," "culminator," "accuser." These terms are not really radical significations of the term diabolos, but they show the real and true attitude of that or him acting the part of a diabolos, so that they come to be inseparably associated with the term as secondary significations.

There is another term employed in the Bible, which is supposed to signify an "impersonal devil." The term is Satan, and is purely Hebrew. It is the term used in the Old Testament, diabolos (which is Greek) not being found there. Satan or Satanas, means "an adversary," "one who stands against or opposes." Anyone giving adverse counsel would be a satan, as Peter was to Jesus (Matthew 16:23). … Although not of the same philological import as diabolos, yet, as just said, it has been employed to signify the same agency or agencies in the line of disobedience of God's commandments, or sin in the impulses, workings, and counsels of sinful flesh whether manifested in self-promptings of the flesh or through other parties. The term "serpent" is also used in the same sense, because it is the name of the agent first inciting to transgression or sin, but is more particularly applied to serpent-minded flesh as expressed through the machinations of corporate or embodied power politically enthroned in governments based upon mere fleshly promptings, thinkings, reasonings, or wisdom. The serpent-mind is thus emphatically the mind of mere flesh ("Carnal mind," of which Paul speaks,) expressed in the channel of disobedience of God's law, whether individually or politically manifested in Adam's race.

You thus perceive, honest learner, that the entire development of diabolical and satanic power in all its channels of manifestation, whether racially (in individuals of the race) or politically (in governmental function) expressed, is enrooted in the serpent-mind, serpent-reasonings in the channel of disobedience of God's law, and carries us back to the Edenic transgression for its origin. … Since he (Sin, or the Devil) belongs exclusively to human nature, or flesh and blood nature, Jesus was the Spirit-Word's manifestation in that nature that he might destroy him (Sin, or the Devil) by cleansing the nature of sin, and redeeming it from death caused by sin. If the flesh and blood nature of Adam ceases as such, then the serpent-mind in that nature must also cease to exist; and there could then be no serpent reasoning, no sin, no devil, and no death. The devil and all his works would then be destroyed. Now, this is just what the death and resurrection of Jesus is to accomplish when his work is completed in his presenting to the Father an immortal family of children, developed from Adam's race through faith and obedience in him and his sacrificial, atoning blood which was poured out to destroy him (Sin, or the Devil), having the power of death (Hebrews 2:14.)

CC Walker

CC Walker, The Christadelphian, vol. 50, 1913, pp. 259-261

Sin is personified. He is a Master who has "servants" (John 8:34; Romans 6:6, 17, 20), and pays terribly bad "wages" (Romans 6:23). He is a King who "reigns" (Romans 5:21; 6:12, 14). He "reigned unto death"; "had the power of death" and is therefore "the devil" (Hebrews 2:14). Jesus died that *through death* he might "destroy him," "put him away," "cast him out," which he did in the initial stage when he rose again from the dead, and will do completely hereafter when he abolishes sin and death from the earth. Sin is a Warrior whose "instruments" (margin, arms, or weapons), are the "members" of his "servants" (Romans 6:13).

CC Walker, The Christadelphian, vol. 50, 1913, p. 539

... we conclude that the phrase, "the Devil" (quite properly with the capital) is expressive of *a title* and *a Power*, and *not* of an individual. It is like the titles, "The Tirshatha," "The Governor," "The Pope," "The Czar," "The Kaiser," in so far as these expressions define a Power and Office rather than an individual. The individual Devil, Pope, Czar, etc., may die, but the Power lives on, though it is not immortal.

The Devil is *a bad Power*—ALWAYS—a seducing, corrupting, opposing, betraying, murdering, lying, oppressing, ensnaring, slandering, falsely accusing, killing, sinning, dragon-serpent POWER! These epithets are simply set down from the Word of God as quoted in the foregoing schedule, and they focalise unerringly in one word: SIN.

> "The Devil is a scriptural personification of Sin in the flesh, in its several phases of manifestation—subjective, individual, aggregate, social, and political—in history, current experience, and prophecy, after the style of figure which speaks of Wisdom as a Woman, riches as Mammon and the god of this world, Sin as a Master, etc."[193]

This old Christadelphian definition is palpably true, and does not need revising; and no exception to its application can be made in Hebrews 2:14, where it has actually been proposed to interpret "the devil" by "the law," *i.e.*, the law of Moses, which is apostolically declared to be "holy and just and good" (Romans 7:12). In view of the foregoing complete list of passages, try to imagine a "holy and just and good" Devil!

G Pearce – *Principles of Redemption (Part 1)*, The Christadelphian, vol. 73, 1936, pp. 203-207 (Edited by CC Walker)

... The Diabolos causes to cross over God's law or causes to transgress. This characteristic of Diabolos is expressed in 1 John 3:8: "*. . . for the Devil sinneth from the beginning.*"

The passage just quoted also informs us how long the Diabolos has been active—*i.e.*, "*from the beginning.*" Our minds are directed to Adam and Eve in the Garden of Eden. In seeking here for the operation of the Diabolos we are also guided by the words of Revelation 20:2: "*And he (the Angel) laid hold on the Dragon, that old Serpent, which is the Devil and Satan . . .*", from which

---

[193] Bro CC Walker is quoting from *"A Declaration"*, first published in 1867. See page 351.

we learn that the Devil is that old Serpent of the Garden of Eden. In harmony with the characteristic of the Eden serpent as a beguiler we read further on in Revelation 20:3,10 *"And the Devil that deceived the nations . . ."* Perhaps it may be remarked in passing that as is general throughout the Apocalypse, these words of Revelation 20:2 are not to be taken literally, but are symbols (or Personification.—ED., C.) expressive of principles or qualities. This then we have found: The Devil is spoken of as a deceiver; it causes to transgress God's law; it is called *"a sinner from the beginning"*; and it is another term for what is to be understood by *"the old Serpent."*

Let us look at the first transgression and the serpent in the Garden of Eden. The serpent had much in common with Adam and Eve. Both were from the dust, were organized into flesh and blood, were animated by God's spirit and pronounced very good. The serpent had powers of observation, hearing and speech. He was intelligent (*"be ye as wise as serpents,"* Christ said) and was able to reason upon what he heard and saw. He only differed from man and woman in having no moral faculties, and was not placed under Divine law. Man and woman, besides propensities and intellect, had sentiments such that their intellect could appreciate and respond to God's law.

The serpent having no appreciation of obedience or responsibility to God, reasoned in the manner given in Genesis 3 and presented his reasoning to the woman. His reasoning was what we term the thinking of the natural mind or *"the thinking of the flesh,"* aiming at the gratifying of the animal instincts. This reasoning of the natural mind in the serpent was not culpable, or contrary to his description at creation as *"very good."* But in the woman it should have been suppressed because it was at enmity with the law of God. Instead of being suppressed the serpent reasoning took a hold in her mind and worked upon her desires—desires of the flesh, the eye and of life. This reasoning finding strong support from her natural desires was accepted by her mind and resulted in the action that was transgression.

From this it is seen that the transgression had its inception in the serpent reasoning and this, co-operating with her natural desires, caused the unlawful act. These then—the serpent reasoning and the desires of the flesh—were in her the diabolos, "causing to cross over" God's law. Only in such a way can the words *"The Diabolos sinneth from the beginning"* be understood. Clearly the Diabolos is not transgression itself but the cause of it as shown above. In the serpent the false reasoning was not a Diabolos because he was under no law to God. It existed in Eve as soon as she believed the serpent reasoning. Until the serpent beguiled her she had thought truthfully and so had remained obedient. The evil arose when she accepted the serpent reasoning and the idea then represented the thinking of her own mind.

We must conclude that the Diabolos did not exist in her from creation from another consideration. We are told that the Diabolos has the power of death (Hebrews 2:14); and Adam and Eve were not originally subject to death, for Paul says (1 Corinthians 15:21), *"By **man** came death"*; and again (Romans 5:12), *"Wherefore as by one man **sin** entered into the world and **death by sin** . . ."* Clearly while they were not subject to death the Diabolos was not in them.

That the Diabolos in man is the result of serpent reasoning operating on the natural desires is expressed by Christ in John 8:44: *"Ye are of your father the devil and the works of your father ye will do. He was a murderer from the beginning and abode not in the Truth, because there is no truth in him. When he speaketh a lie, he speaketh of his own, for he is a liar and the father of it."* The serpent reasoning was a lie—the original lie. As we have seen, in his reasoning arose the Devil and so Christ says *"he is a liar and the father of it."* Again the serpent reasoning enflamed the natural desires—hence Christ speaks of "the lusts of the Devil." Christ's condemnation of those around him was the same as that of Adam and Eve—that instead of overcoming the lusts, they did them, that is, they sinned. The passage continues: *"He was a murderer from the beginning."* In that the Diabolos caused transgression it brought the penalty attached to disobedience, *"Thou shalt surely die."* Thus it was a murderer; or as elsewhere expressed it had the power of death.

We accept, then, the Diabolos as that principle or way of thinking that established itself in Adam and Eve and caused transgression. After transgression it became a characteristic of their nature and is transmitted to all their descendants. This is the next proposition we have to establish. Considering the matter apart from scriptural evidence, is it not a matter of experience with every one of us that our mind and body tend to go contrary to God's law? And turning to the teaching of the scriptures it must be directly inferred from Paul's statement in Romans 5:19 that the Diabolos is an inherent quality of human nature: *"For as by one man's disobedience many were made sinners, so by the obedience of one shall many be made righteous."* *"Were made sinners"* is more correctly translated *"were constituted sinners"*; which must mean that after the transgression our nature was so organized or constituted as to make us inevitably sinful. ... Now if we are constituted sinners by Adam's transgression this must of necessity require the *cause* of sin to be in us, for every effect needs a cause. From which we must conclude the Diabolos is in all the descendants of Adam. The establishment of the Diabolos as a law in the flesh is all sufficient to constitute every son of Adam a sinner, for if there is no opposing force of the law of God, the Diabolos will lead to sinful action; and as the law of God is not natural to us, but comes by enlightenment, we perceive that the Diabolos at first does reign supreme in all that are born, and sin is the inevitable result.

Again, Paul's discourse in Romans 7 shows clearly the existence of this principle in all flesh. He sums the matter up in Romans 7:23, where he speaks of this sin-causing principle as *"the law of sin in my members."* His earlier remarks (verses 15–23) show that he regarded this Diabolos as an innate quality of his flesh.

A further proof of the Diabolos being inherent in Adam's descendants is found in considering our mortal nature. If we are willing to admit Adam's descendants to be mortal, then they must possess the Diabolos, because the writer to the Hebrews (2:14) says it is the Diabolos that has the power of death.

Besides wielding the power of death in Adam and all humans, the Diabolos was the cause of further physical evil in Adam and Eve as laid down in the sentence God passed against them. Up till transgression Adam and Eve had only known good. After transgression they knew—*i.e.*, experienced—evil as well as good. They and their surroundings were so organized that they were subject to evil—pain, disease, weakness, sorrow, and as already mentioned, death. These evils are our common lot and inheritance from our first fathers. This is scripturally expressed in two places: First, Romans 5:18, *"Therefore as by the* **offence of one** *judgment came upon* **all men** *to* *condemnation, even so by the righteousness of one the free gift came upon all men to justification of life."* This passage informs us that all men are condemned by God through Adam's transgression. ...

With such a scriptural understanding of the Diabolos we may now turn to the work accomplished by Christ, expressed in Hebrews 2:14: *"Forasmuch then as the children are partakers of flesh and blood he also himself likewise took part of the same; that through death he might destroy (R.V., bring to nought) him that had the power of death, that is, the devil."*

From this we learn that he destroyed the Diabolos; (*a*) by partaking of flesh and blood and (*b*) by dying.

The first qualification was necessary so that he should himself be a possessor of the Diabolos; for as we have shown it existed in Adam at transgression and afterwards in all his seed. How otherwise could Christ destroy the Diabolos by dying? Clearly he did not then remove the Diabolos from other men, for since that time the principle has flourished mightily in godless men. The only alternative is that he destroyed it in himself and thereby made it possible for the complete destruction of this evil in the future, as given symbolically in Revelation 20.

The destruction of the Diabolos in Christ himself is clearly seen in Paul's words, Ephesians 2:14: *"(Christ) having abolished in his flesh the enmity, even the law of commandments, . . . and that he might reconcile both unto God in one body by the cross, having slain the enmity thereby (margin, in himself)."*

The enmity (made manifest by the law of commandments as Paul argues in Romans 7:7–12) takes us back again to the Edenic sentence (Genesis 3:15), *"And I will put enmity between thee and the woman and between thy seed and her seed and it shall bruise thy head and thou shalt bruise his heel."* The enmity was between the woman and the serpent. This is not literal but in a figure expresses principles. As we have seen, the lie that was according to the flesh and that resulted in transgression, arose from the serpent and so this way of thinking in men is appropriately typified by a serpent. This is at enmity with the principles of truth, faith and obedience, typified by the woman. It is the enmity expressed by Paul in the passage at which we have already looked (Romans 7:21–25), where he speaks of two laws warring against each other— the law of sin in his members and the law of God. Now in such an antagonism the enmity could only be abolished by destroying the serpent and if Christ abolished the enmity in his flesh, the serpent must have existed there. ...

Our understanding of the existence and destruction of the Diabolos in Christ is greatly helped by the typical teaching of an incident in the journeyings of the children of Israel—the lifting up of the brazen serpent. Christ directly applies this incident to himself and makes it certain that the serpent nature or Diabolos was in Christ and was destroyed at his crucifixion. Christ says (John 3:14): *"As Moses lifted up the serpent in the wilderness, even so must the Son of Man be lifted up; that whosoever believeth on him should not perish but have everlasting life."*

Turning to the record in Numbers 21 we find that the children of Israel murmured because of the hardness of the way. God sent fiery serpents that bit them so that many died. The rest repented, acknowledging their sin, and were saved from dying from the serpent bite by looking upon a similar fiery serpent lifted up on a pole by Moses. We read, "And Moses made a serpent of brass and put it upon a pole and it came to pass that if a serpent had bitten any man, when he beheld the serpent of brass, he lived" (Numbers 21:9).

The parallel between this deliverance and the salvation of man is striking. The fiery *serpents "had the power of death"* to these people and their salvation was through faith in the uplifted replica of what had bitten them. Drawing the parallel the serpent principle has bitten all of us through Adam and so our salvation is through beholding the uplifted serpent; which from the analogy must be a crucified Christ possessing serpent nature, for Christ directly associates his crucifixion with the uplifted serpent. *"As Moses lifted up the serpent so must the Son of Man . . ."* Is not this conclusive as to the serpent nature being in Christ? There must be some meaning in the analogy Christ draws and our conclusions are surely straightforward and definite.

… Partaking of flesh and blood he possessed the Diabolos and in his life and death he "brought it to nought." His death was a necessity in doing this. In his life he brought it to nought by the constant application of the Word of God, thereby always overcoming the evil tendencies. But eventually, without his cutting off, this life of overcoming would be of no avail for that evil principle he constantly checked would have operated in him to death and would still be the victor—God's judgment in Eden operating to condemnation as in all mortals. But by the deliberate act of cutting off his life and pouring out his blood, the mainspring of this evil was destroyed and so the evil itself was destroyed. His death was necessary in order that he might be delivered from the serpent principle that claimed his life. This, however, was the full extent of its power. When his blood was poured out, the impulses to evil could no longer operate and the Diabolos was destroyed. Not being marred by any transgression, God could raise him to life and incorruption.

In this then, we see the necessity for Christ to die to gain his own salvation. This necessity of his own salvation from death is directly expressed by Paul (Hebrews 5:7): *"Who in the days of his flesh, when he had offered up prayers and supplications with strong crying and tears unto him that was able to save him from death, and was heard in that he feared."* Christ was under the dominion of death through inheritance of the Diabolos and he was saved by being strengthened by God to bring it to nought. This having been accomplished it could be said *"death hath no more dominion over him"* (Romans 6:9).

The statement of Paul in Hebrews 2:14 already referred to leads us to the same conclusion. He partook of flesh and blood that through death he might destroy the Diabolos and deliver them who through fear of death were all their lifetime subject to bondage. This shows to us the fundamental position occupied by the Diabolos in relation to our need of salvation—a position we have already appreciated from looking at the original occasion of disobedience. In the wisdom and justice of God he regarded the destruction of the Diabolos as a vital necessity before deliverance from death was possible. As then Christ himself possessed the Diabolos, was not his death which destroyed this, necessary to himself?

G Pearce – *Principles of Redemption (Part 2)*, The Christadelphian, vol. 73, 1936, pp. 257-260 (Edited by CC Walker)
Clearly then there is in man what is styled Sin, which precedes transgression. We might well ask why the Diabolos should be styled sin. Does not the application of the word sin to the Diabolos show that God regards the Diabolos as the fundamental, as the root cause of alienation from Him. This is in harmony with our previous conclusion in relation to Christ's redemptive work, that the destruction of the Diabolos was the essential required by God and accomplished in Christ

If now we have understood this other scriptural use of sin we are able to understand the ascription of sin to Christ, and the several passages which are viewed by many with difficulty as they stand, are seen to be capable of simple and straightforward application. In the sense shown in the previous paragraph Christ had sin. Thus Paul says (2 Corinthians 5:21): "For he made him (to be) sin for us who knew no sin, that we might be the righteousness of God in him." …

Again Paul's statement (Hebrews 9:28): "So Christ was once offered to bear the sins of many, and unto them that look for him shall he appear the second time without sin unto salvation," implies that the first time he had sin—which is to be understood as in the passage just quoted.

… In Romans 6 Paul speaks of this body in which dwells the Diabolos as a body of Sin, and that as Christ at his crucifixion destroyed the body of Sin, we also are to regard ourselves as freed from Sin through association in baptism with his crucifixion. Thus Rom 6:6: "Knowing this, that our old man is crucified with him, that the body of sin might be destroyed, that henceforth we should not serve Sin."

Paul enlarges on this destruction of the body of Sin at Christ's crucifixion in Romans 8:3. He speaks of the matter already mentioned, that it was God's action primarily that made Christ able to overcome the law of sin. The law of commandments did not prove a sufficient power to do this because it was weak through the flesh—that is weak because flesh was so exceeding sinful. Hence he says: "God, sending his own son in the likeness of sinful flesh, and for Sin, condemned Sin in the flesh." The law was not adequate to condemn or overcome the sin principle but God in Christ did this, bringing to nought the Diabolos in his life and death.

… All Adam's descendants are born under a condemnation arising from Adam's transgression. They are subject to disease, pain, sorrow and death and have an innate tendency to think and act contrary to God's law—a condition which is all the result of inheriting that evil principle called the Diabolos, serpent nature, or sinful flesh. Natural man is born without any "divine light within" and inevitably sin reigns and he obeys it in the lust thereof. This evil tendency is, as it were, an ever present weight in the balance of conscience which decides for right or wrong. Enlightenment by the Word of God brings to bear an opposing force and is a weight in the other pan of the balance. But though this law of God wars against the law of sin in our members it is not able entirely to overcome it and man still sins and is alienated from God. As the law of God was weak through the flesh it required God's intervention;—God's arm brought salvation by providing one who by his divine conception and the rich indwelling of the Holy Spirit was able to overcome completely—to be sinless. In him was manifested God's will—His requirements of perfect obedience and the exhibition of the true worth of human nature or sinful flesh. In his life this later requirement was manifest in the contrast between the sinless character of Jesus and the sinful character of the men and women around him begotten of the will of men. In his death this was more certainly manifested, in that God, without injustice could require the "lifting up" of such a sinless man, because he possessed that evil nature resulting from Adamic condemnation. In this Christ wrought salvation for himself and for us. For himself in that he was freed from the claims of his inherited nature—he destroyed the body of sin. And for us—when we faithfully and humbly acknowledge this representative treatment in Jesus and associate ourselves with his crucifixion by baptism, God is willing to accept us, and abide with us if we seek to serve Him and not to serve the former lusts of our flesh.

Henry Sulley

Henry Sulley, The Christadelphian, vol. 50, 1913, pp. 148-152
Jesus also furnishes us with an illustration of his own relationship to sin, saying: "As the serpent was lifted up in the wilderness, so must the Son of Man be lifted up" [John 3:14]. ..._Why should those who had sinned be delivered from death by looking upon the brazen serpent? Was it not because the serpent represented their sin, the biter in the case, for the sting of death is sin? What, then, by the parallel, do we see affixed to the tree in the person of Jesus. Was it not that which brought death to the human race? Whence cometh sin? From the flesh. Hence we see flesh crucified upon the tree in the person of Jesus. Thus it is written: "Forasmuch as the children are partakers of flesh and blood, he likewise himself partook of the same, that through death he might destroy him that had the power of death, that is, the Devil" (Hebrews 2:14). The Devil, or adversary, is sin. How could the adversary be destroyed by the death of Christ if sin was not in, or did not take hold of the flesh of Jesus? Therefore, it is written: "He himself bare our sins in his body on (or to) the tree" (1 Peter 2:24). When we look at Jesus impaled upon the tree, as we are commanded to do, we see sin's flesh, the cause of sin, put to death; and the power of that flesh to sin, destroyed by dying, or, as the Apostle puts it, "The adversary destroyed through death."

Henry Sulley, *The Atonement (9),* The Christadelphian, vol. 59, 1922, pp. 344-348
From this record, quite apart from the question who was the *agent* of temptation, it will be seen that the "devil" which tempted Jesus was *in his flesh,* because it is written that he partook of flesh and blood "that through death he might destroy that which had the power of death, that is, the devil" (Hebrews 2:14). We have already seen that until death no one is free from temptation to sin, which has the power of death in those who yield to its impulses. Natural impulse—or inclination to sin—is the devil which has to be destroyed. Therefore those who yield to temptation are of the devil. Hence Jesus said to the Jews, "Ye are from beneath; I am from above" (John 8:23), a statement more readily comprehended by his further definition. "Ye are of this world" (*ibid*), "Ye are of father the devil, and the lusts of your father ye will do" (John 8:44). ... in this case he referred to the original cause

of sin, *i.e.*, the desire to eat the pleasant fruit of the forbidden tree, which arose in Eve in consequence of the lying suggestion of the serpent, whom Jesus said was a liar and murderer from the beginning. Hence he said, "Ye are of your father the devil, and the lusts of your father ye will do." "Ye do the deeds of your father" (John 8:41). "I speak that which I have seen with my Father: and ye do that which ye have seen with your father" (*ibid*, verse 38). "Ye are from beneath; I am from above" (*ibid*, verse 23).

… The Devil, or Sin, which Jesus came to destroy by dying, is inherent in the flesh, which is "sinful."

Henry Sulley, The Temple of Ezekiel's Prophecy, 1929, pp. 114-117 (Logos Ed.)

Who his own self bare our sins in his own body on, or to, the tree (1 Peter 2:24).

Seeing that Jesus could not have borne our personal sins in his own body; seeing that he did not commit sin in the sense of personal transgression, the only admissible inference is that sin was crucified in the *person* of Jesus. This conclusion is supported by the illustration which Jesus himself furnished of his own relationship to sin, saying:

As Moses lifted up the serpent in the wilderness, even so must the Son of man be lifted up (John 3:14).

Here we have a parallel which may be readily understood by those unspoiled by philosophy. *First*, as to the type. The children of Israel sinned. Fiery serpents bit them, and caused death, in consequence of their sin. Those who looked upon a representative, of that which caused death, fixed upon a pole, were healed from the serpent's bite. What then do we see in looking upon Jesus impaled upon the tree? The Apostle Paul shall answer:

Forasmuch then as the children are partakers of flesh and blood, he also himself likewise took part of the same! that through death he might destroy him that had the power of death, that is, the devil (Hebrews 2:14).

What is it that has the power of death? Again the Apostle shall answer:

The sting of death is sin: and the strength of sin is the law (1 Corinthians 15:56)

Whence cometh sin? Another Apostle shall answer:

Every man is tempted when he is drawn away of his own lust, and enticed (James 1:14).

These testimonies conclusively show that, physically, Jesus was related to sin just as are all the children of Adam, yet without question, Jesus did not sin, for he was "holy, guileless, undefiled, separate from sinners" (Hebrews 7:26). But like the High priests under the Mosaic economy he *offered for his own sins*. Thus we read:

Who needeth not daily, like those high priests, to offer up sacrifices, first for his own sins, and then for the sins of the people; for this he did once for all, when he offered up himself (Hebrews 7:27).

Now since impulse to sin arises from the flesh (James 1:14) in response to the wiles of the tempter, the motive power of which is provided by the life blood coursing through the arteries of the body, the only way to abolish such impulses is by death, as saith the Apostle:

> *He that is dead is freed from sin (Romans 6:7).*

In this way the source from which sin comes, its fountainhead, is destroyed. This occurred in the crucifixion of Jesus, who not only destroyed the adversary in Himself by dying (Hebrews 2:14; Ephesians 2:15–16), but will also destroy the power of sin in others (1 John 3:8.)

John Carter

John Carter, *The Destroyer of the Devil*, God's Way, 1947, pp. 138-142
The explanation in the Bible of the work of Jesus is closely connected with the Bible doctrine of the devil, and some reference to this subject is necessary. In the Letter to the Hebrews, the writer shows the necessity for the redeemer of men himself to be perfected through suffering, for him to have the same nature as those who share in his redemption. With pronounced emphasis Paul expresses the identity of Jesus with the redeemed, saying: "Forasmuch then as the children are partakers of flesh and blood, he also himself likewise took part of the same; that through death he might destroy him that had the power of death, that is, the devil" (Hebrews 2:14). Mark the words "also", "likewise" and "himself", and it is evident that the writer is stressing the fact that Jesus possessed the flesh and blood common to all men. The reason given is: "that he might destroy him that had the power of death, that is, the devil". As Jesus had to share our nature in order to destroy the devil through his death, it is evident that there is some connection between human nature and the Bible devil. What is this connection? The answer appears when we ask another question: what has the power of death? The Bible answer, as we have before found in many testimonies, is that sin has the power of death, in that sin by divine decree is punished by death. A few of the statements in support of this may be briefly repeated. "The wages of sin is death" (Romans 6:23). "Sin hath reigned unto death" (Romans 5:21). "The sting of death is sin" (1Corinthians 15:56). "By one man sin entered the world, and death by sin" (Romans 5:12). This connection of sin and death is also asserted by Jesus when he said that certain of his listeners should "die in their sins" (John 8:24).

… A comparison of the passages cited shows that by "the devil" Paul means the sin-tendency which dwells in every member of the human race and which, when God's commandment becomes known, is revealed in its opposition to righteousness. In the language of personification Paul speaks of this evil propensity of the flesh as "Sin", as when in Romans 7:9-25 he refers to "Sin that dwelleth in me", which frustrated his efforts to achieve holiness. "With the mind I serve the law of God, but with the flesh the law of sin". In the 8th chapter of Romans the same personification of Sin is used concerning the work of Jesus in a statement which provides a strict parallel in meaning to the language in Hebrews 2:14. "What the law could not do, in that it was weak through the flesh, God, sending his own Son in the likeness of sinful flesh, and for sin (R.V., as an offering for sin), condemned sin in the flesh " (Romans 8:3). "Sin" which was condemned in the flesh of Jesus was "the devil" which it was his mission to overcome and destroy. It becomes further evident from such statements as Hebrews 9:26, and Romans 6:10: "In that he died, he died unto sin once: but in that he liveth, he liveth unto God". He came under the dominion of death, but was raised from the dead, and now "Death hath no more dominion over him".

As the result of Christ's victory over sin, he has been raised from death: and he will yet remove all the effects of sin—disease and evil in every form—from the earth. This is comprehensively expressed by the apostle John "For this purpose the Son of God was manifested, that he might destroy the works of the devil" (1 John 3:8).

The recognition that the devil of the Bible is sin in some form or other makes clear its usage in all passages. ….

Islip Collyer

Islip Collyer, The Christadelphian, vol. 33, 1896, pp. 99-102,
In view of these facts it would be obviously inconsistent to imagine that sins committed after baptism could not be covered. If the act of entering covenant relationship effected any change in human nature, the case would stand in a different light. If coming into association with the sacrifice of Christ removed that tendency towards evil which is characteristic of Adam's flesh, we should naturally suppose that subsequent perfection would be required. Baptised men would then stand in a much more privileged position than did the first Adam, for, in addition to being "very good" physically [Genesis 1:31], they would have the history of centuries of sin and misery to warn them. No diabolos within their flesh, and a most effective object lesson in the shape of the world's history to assist them in antagonising suggestions from without.

The case, however, does not stand so. Such a change of nature indeed would destroy the principle of salvation by faith, and leave a margin for the flesh to "glory." The only change effected by baptism is one of relationship. We still have "this body of death" to contend with, we still have a law of sin in our members, and men are just as prone to sin after baptism as before. Seeing then that believers often pass through a probation of greater duration than Christ's entire mortal existence, it would be obviously inconsistent with divine principles that absolute perfection should be required. God recognises human frailty, and provides a means of forgiveness, apart from which salvation would be impossible.

Islip Collyer, *The Meaning of Sacrifice*, Principles & Proverbs, 1938, pp. 94–100
…. When we speak of "sin" in the flesh we use the phrase just as the Apostle used it in Romans 7:17-25. Obviously, it is a derived or secondary sense of the word, for the primary meaning of sin is transgression of divine law. It is a similar extension of meaning to that of the word "death" for poison when they said, "there is death in the pot". The Apostle speaks of a law in his members which wars against the laws of God and leads to transgression. He calls this physical weakness "sin" in the flesh or "sin" that dwelleth in me. It is the diabolos in human nature, the natural desires of the flesh which, if they

are allowed to "conceive", "bring forth sin". We need not argue as to whether there is such a law. We all know it only too well. We are born with it and if we give way to any sin we correspondingly strengthen the evil desire in that direction and thus make "sin" in the flesh more active.

WF Barling

WF Barling, Law and Grace, 1952, p.195

He was led up of the Spirit into the wilderness with the heavenly voice still ringing in his ears, "This is my beloved Son, in whom I am well pleased". For six weeks almost, he withstood the temptations of the devil—those impulses inalienable from human nature since Adam's fall—fasting the whole while.

WF Barling, *Redemption in Christ Jesus: 3. Our Outward Man*, The Christadelphian, vol. 83, 1946, pp. 52-54

… So, in Paul's usage, Sin which deceived him into sinning, is clearly an active force, existing independently of law since it takes occasion by the commandment.

Such a force was not part of Adam's nature, or of Eve's, when God made them; God made man upright. The significant difference between Paul's language and that of Genesis indicates that this indwelling transgression–tendency is the legacy of Adam's first transgression. For it was Sin which deceived Paul (Romans 7:11), where it was the serpent which beguiled Eve (2 Corinthians 11:3). The difference is striking. In Eve's case the serpent tempted from without; in Paul's case sin was indwelling. Eve was deceived by the enticing speech of the outward tempter who aroused in her a desire to disobey; in Paul the desire existed already, and functioned spontaneously when the commandment came, for it was his own lust which enticed him (James 1:14). This can mean but one thing; after the first transgression Diabolos was inward, not external. Thus sin, in Paul's argument, is not some legal overlord, but a transgression-tendency dwelling in the literal flesh of man.

WF Barling, *Redemption in Christ Jesus: 4. The Death of the Cross*, The Christadelphian, vol. 83, 1946, pp. 65-67

His [Jesus'] baptism was a token of this fact. Anticipating his crucifixion, Jesus declared, "I have a baptism to be baptized with" (Luke 12:50). Previously at Jordan, whereas all others came to John confessing their sins, he came with none to confess, but insisting nevertheless that John should baptize him. He knew the import of John's testimony that all flesh is grass (Isaiah 40:3–8), and that he himself, though a sinless bearer of flesh-nature, had nevertheless to be baptized. That is, Jesus had to submit to a ceremonial condemnation of his nature in anticipation of the literal condemnation which he would later suffer, and by which he would destroy Diabolos (Hebrews 2:14), or Sin in the flesh, the power which reigns unto death (Romans 5:21). So "to them that look for him shall he appear the second time without Sin unto salvation" (Hebrews 9:28).

WF Barling, *Redemption in Christ Jesus: 5. Implications Examined*, The Christadelphian, vol. 83, 1946, pp. 82-84

John explicitly declares the lust of the flesh, the lust of the eyes and the pride of life to be 'not of the father, but of the world' (1 John 2:16). There could be no more emphatic testimony that these 'lusts' are not desires which can be attributed initially to God; but sinful propensities which only came to exist as a result of the first offence. The "lust of the world" and "the will of God" are essentially antagonistic (1 John 2:17). Disciples should therefore "no longer live to the lusts of men, but to the will of God" (1 Peter 4:2), for, far from being "God-implanted", lusts are "of Diabolos" (John 8: 44).

… Paul speaks of the snares and wiles of Diabolos (1 Timothy 3:7; Ephesians 6: 11). James bids us resist him (James 4:7). Diabolos is defined by Jesus as the wicked one who defeats the work of the Sower (Matthew 13:19, 38-39). John says that Diabolos put into the heart of Judas Iscariot to betray Jesus (John 13:2), and that whoever commits sin is of Diabolos (1 John 3:8).

The use of personification in these and similar Scriptural statements is obvious, but so also is the fact that what is personified as Diabolos is an active beguiling force. Since it tempts men to sin, it is also called Sin by metonymy, so that in so far as a man resists Diabolos he also avoids being "hardened through the deceitfulness of Sin" (Hebrews 3:13). Finally, Diabolos is described literally as "the spirit that now *worketh* in the children of disobedience" (Ephesians 2:2), and so contrasts with "the Word of God which effectually *worketh*" in those that believe (1 Thessalonians 2:13). This can only mean that Diabolos (or Sin, as the cause of transgression) is, in Scripture, an active spirit of disobedience, hostile to God's Law. For that reason, the language of active deception befits it, whereas such language is grotesquely inappropriate when applied to the devil postulated by the Nazarene Fellowship, who is a pure invention.

The Scriptures leave us in no doubt where the true Diabolos resides and operates. In order that by his death he might destroy Diabolos Jesus partook of flesh and blood (Hebrews 2:14). "Now if I do that I would not", declares Paul, "it is no more I that do it, but Sin that dwelleth in me" (Romans 7:20). "Do ye think", asks James, "that the Scripture saith in vain, The spirit that dwelleth in us lusteth to envy?" (James 4:5), and he attributes strife to lusts that war in the members (James 4:1). These and other apostolic pronouncements make it abundantly clear that Diabolos must be located in man's physical constitution.

AD Norris

AD Norris, *The Cross and the Devil*, Understanding the Bible, 1948, pp. 84–90,
… The devil is, in fact, sin in all its forms, and the promptings of sin whenever they arise. It is very frequently personified, for sin cannot be manifested without a person in which to appear, but it is impossible to attribute any consistent activities to the person. In one case "your adversary the devil, as a roaring lion, goeth about seeking whom he may devour" [1 Peter 5:8], or tries disciples and casts them into prison; and evidently carries out these activities upon the faithful. Yet these same faithful are exhorted to "resist the devil, and he will flee from you" [James 4:7]. Clearly

it is not always the same devil. Sometimes it is a persecuting authority, opposing the will of God by casting His faithful saints into prison; sometimes it is a prompting of sin within their minds, which needs only to be resisted to be repelled—as it was by Jesus in the Wilderness.

Because the world which will not serve God is given over to sin, the world and the devil are often equated, or the wrongdoing which characterises the world is summed up in this same personification. So we hear of "the prince of this world," "the spirit that now worketh in the children of disobedience," "the evil one."

But the true nature of the devil whom Jesus destroyed can be indicated by considering in parallel two passages from the letter to the Hebrews:

"Through death He might destroy him that hath the power of death, that is, the devil."[Hebrews 2:4]

"Once in the end of the world hath He appeared to *put away sin* by the sacrifice of Himself." [Hebrews 9:26]

to which we should add one from the Letter of James:

"Sin, when it is finished, *bringeth forth death."* [James 1:15]

Sin causes death, and the devil causes death. The devil was destroyed by the death of Jesus, and sin was destroyed by the death of Jesus. Surely we can therefore only conclude that the devil is bodily sin.

All then becomes clear: Jesus, by resisting the power of sin, and by giving up to the Cross the body in which sin must always remain a peril, destroyed for ever the power of sin over Himself. As we shall see, this made possible for Him the first resurrection to immortality. What He achieved for Himself is made available to others who give their assent to His work (as partly suggested in the last chapter, and to be elaborated later), and so the dominion of sin and death has already been destroyed in principle, and a period set to its survival.

AD Norris, *The Death of the Cross*, The Christadelphian, vol. 90, 1953, pp. 170-174
2.—"Forasmuch as the children are partakers of flesh and blood, Jesus also Himself likewise took part of the same, that by death he might destroy him that had the power of death, that is, the devil, and deliver all those who, through fear of death, were all their lifetime subject to bondage" (Hebrews 2:14–15).

This passage indeed repeats the message that it became Jesus to die because he had a nature like our own, but it puts the truth in another way. There we, who are men and women, were exhorted to have minds like his: here he, who partook of our nature, is said to have done so, so that we might gain the benefit of his death. Indeed, we must go further than this: his death was only able to bring about its triumph *because* he partook of the same nature as we. It was only thus that he could destroy the devil, and liberate the devil's slaves from their bondage of fear. …

3.—"As Moses lifted up the serpent in the wilderness, even so also must the Son of man be lifted up, that whosoever believeth in him should not perish but have eternal life" (John 3:14–15).

This is more closely connected with the subject than might be imagined. For the Israelites before whom Moses erected his serpent of brass (Numbers 21:4–9) had grievously sinned before God, and were dying of snake-bites for their punishment. The erection of the brass snake was doubtless the token that God had conquered their plague, and the act of looking upon it was a gesture of faith in his work. And Jesus in making comparison between those former Israelites, and those whom he now addressed, was plainly intending to bring out two resemblances: the first between the snake-bitten then and the sin-bitten now; and the second between the serpent on the pole and himself "lifted up".

… The serpent was the symbol of sin, and therefore the serpent on the pole was the symbol of sin conquered. But Jesus "lifted up" is to be like that serpent, and since there is no doubt that "lifted up" meant crucified (see John 12:32–33), he is telling us quite calmly that his crucifixion will be the conquest of sin. Nor does this quite exhaust the intimacy of the comparison: we are told, not merely that sin will be conquered *by* his death, but that sin will be conquered *in* his death—that he, dying, will be like the brass effigy hoisted up as a symbol that God had conquered what it signified.

Reverent minds might well recoil from this suggestion: for it implies that Jesus was sin; and it might be taken to imply that he was a sinner, whereas we know that he was nothing of the kind. "He did not sin"; "He was tempted in all points like as we are, yet without sin"; "Which of you convicteth me of sin?" How can we compare the innocence of Jesus on the Cross with the tempter in the garden, or with the vile forms which sin takes in all our human race?

We acknowledge his sinlessness gladly, but are constrained to insist that this is what the parallel means. For, after all, is it not the same message as that of our second passage, put in another way? In this former, his death is the conquest of the devil; now it is the triumph of God over the anti-symbolic serpent: plainly there is no difference, as all will realize who remember that graphic expression of the Book of Revelation, "that old serpent, called the devil and satan" (Revelation 20:2). All, in different words, express the sin of our race in one or other of its manifestations.

And in any case the Scriptures leave us with no alternative than to admit this comparison. God —made him to be sin for us, who knew no sin", shows that in the death of Jesus it is possible to associate sin with the body of one who did no wrong. "What the law could not do in that it was weak through the flesh, God, sending his own son in the likeness of sinful flesh, and for sin, condemned sin in the flesh" (Romans 8:3) establishes all that we have so far urged: that Jesus is associated with sin because of "sinful flesh", or "sin's flesh", which he bore; and that the death of Jesus did in reality what the erection of the brass serpent did in symbol and condemned sin—in the flesh, in Jesus' flesh.

… He himself hints at this, and says nothing to contradict it. He is not prepared to allow an enthusiastic young man to describe him as *"good Master"*; for there is none good but God. He speaks of perfection in himself not as a present condition, but as a goal before him: "I do cures today and tomorrow, and the third day I shall be made perfect"[Luke 9:22] — as though he were consciously comparing the healing of other men's fleshly illnesses with the ultimate healing of the infirmity which was an inescapable part of his own fleshly heritage. And though the Letter to the Hebrews several times uses the word "perfect" of Jesus, it is always of what he became through suffering and death, and never of what he was while mortality was still upon him (Hebrews 2:10; 5:9; 7:28 R.V.).

We can state simply the conclusion to which we are led: Jesus was made of our nature so that, by his willing obedience, he might conquer its infirmity ....

Men in all ages who look upon the Cross are thus taught to see there, not merely the malice of wicked men who took and slew him, but also the determinate counsel and foreknowledge of God who so showed before men the exceeding sinfulness of sin, whose flesh must be thus ignominiously shamed. "There was no beauty that we should desire him" [Isaiah 53:2] sets out the essential ugliness of the spectacle in which flesh was displayed with all the bitter curse that Jesus willingly bore to show its nature and its due destruction.

LG Sargent

LG Sargent, The Christadelphian, vol. 101, 1964, pp. 262-264,
Where then is the source of evil and imperfection? It is to be found in the wayward will of man. "Every good and every perfect gift is from above, and cometh down from the Father of lights"; but "Every man is tempted when he is drawn away of his own lust, and enticed. Then when lust hath conceived it bringeth forth sin: and sin, when it is finished, bringeth forth death" (James 1:14–15, 17). Without free will man could not truly love God; yet with free will there must be the possibility of sin. Christadelphians therefore believe without any equivocation in the Fall of Man. They believe that moral evil has its source in man's fallen nature; and consequently they do not believe in any principle or entity of evil outside of man and striving against God. It is man's own impulse, his unregulated desire, his self-assertive pride, which is adverse to God and to man's own good: and Christadelphians believe that the "Devil" and "Satan" are scriptural personifications for this principle in man's nature and its various manifestations in society.

LG Sargent, The Christadelphian, 1966, vol. 103, p.126
As the Epistle to the Hebrews shows, Christ shared to the full the life and nature of the men he came to save—sons of Adam subject to the consequences of the Fall—in order that he might "suffer, being tempted", tempted in all points like them; and it was through this that he was able "through death to bring to nought him that had the power of death, that is, the devil". Only by this means could he bring the deliverance of "all them who through fear of death were all their lifetime subject to bondage" [Hebrews 2:14-15].

Peter Watkins

Peter Watkins, The Devil, the Great Deceiver, 1976, p. 9
The ultimate devil is man himself – not the man who was created in the image of God, but the man who, by disobedience, marred that image and was condemned to death.

Peter Watkins, The Devil, the Great Deceiver, 1976, pp. 21-25
Ungodly Lusts - It is submitted that the following definition removes the problems: the devil is a symbol of ungodly human desires. There is no want of Scriptural support for this definition, and we shall discuss it later. Our immediate purpose, however, must be to see how this definition fits the account of the wilderness temptation, and the teaching of Hebrews 2:14.

"In all points . . ." The devil that tempted the Lord Jesus was his own human desires. That is the proposition that we must examine now. It hardly needs saying that there is a mass of evidence, particularly in Hebrews, that the Lord Jesus possessed a nature just like ours. Again, we refer to Hebrews 2:14—to the first part of the verse: "Forasmuch then as the children are partakers of flesh and blood, *he also himself likewise took part of the same . . ."* The words, "also", "himself" and "likewise" are put in to stress the fact that the Lord Jesus really did possess a nature like ours. Verse 17 of the same chapter repeats the point: "Wherefore in all things it behoved him to be made like unto his brethren"; and Hebrews 4:15 says that "he was in all points tempted like as we are, yet without sin". We do not dishonour Christ when we say that he was tempted as we are. We honour him the more, because we acknowledge that, although he was tempted as we are, he did not sin. In this he was unique.

... Hebrews 2:14 again - The human desires that were frustrated in the wilderness were destroyed at Calvary. As long as there was an Adamic nature, there was the possibility of temptation. It was not enough to frustrate the human desires that opposed the will of God. They had to be destroyed. And how else could this be done but by the destruction of the source of these ungodly desires—the nature inherited from Adam? Thus the Lord Jesus destroyed sin in the place where it resided. He destroyed sin in the flesh [Romans 8:3].

This is the message of Hebrews 2:14. Jesus came in our nature that he might die; that, by his death, the devil, or ungodly human desires, could be destroyed at their source. "He put away sin by the sacrifice of himself" (Hebrews 9:26).

Peter Watkins, The Devil, the Great Deceiver, 1976, p. 82
The theme of the devil is a sustained New Testament parable about sin-stricken human nature

Alfred Nicholls

Alfred Nicholls, *For Whom Christ Died*, The Christadelphian, vol. 108, 1971, pp. 358-363

When Paul speaks of Jesus as coming "in the likeness of sinful flesh" (or flesh of sin), or "in the likeness of men", he cannot be understood as meaning that Jesus' make-up resembled these things, but was in reality different. In both cases he clearly means that, though our human nature left to itself had failed to overcome sin, when God sent His own Son born in the same human nature the victory was achieved. That the Lord's fleshly nature was that of Adam after he fell, is seen in the fact that he offered up prayers "with strong crying and tears, unto him that was able to save him from death: and was heard in that he feared. Though he were a Son, yet learned he obedience by the things which he suffered." There is no need to rush to the Lord's defence as though there were any discredit to him in having been born with a nature prone to sin. This was his lot, which he accepted and overcame. Far greater was the triumph of battling against sin in a body where a fallen nature was entrenched, than would have been the case had he commenced in innocence with a human nature unspoiled by heritage from Adam. And far greater was his brotherhood in affliction and now in mediation, with his brethren, when we acknowledge that he conquered that very nature, with all its urge to turn away from God, which we know in our own consciences so well. There is real meaning in the words "to put away sin by the sacrifice of himself" when this is acknowledged; and in the fullest possible sense he destroyed the devil through death on the cross when, after the pattern of the serpent which Moses lifted up in the wilderness, he finally put away the power of sin from himself, and became the priest who can lead us in ultimate victory over the same power.

(*Romans 8:3; Philippians 2:7; Hebrews 5:7–8; 9:26; John 3:14; Numbers 21:9*)

Alan Hayward

Alan Hayward, *The Real Devil*, Christadelphian Bible Mission, 1975

According to this other view that is what the devil really is—an enemy inside us. In other words, when the Bible speaks of the devil it is using a kind of parable. The devil of the Bible represents all the wickedness that is within the hearts of men and women (page 2).

The first three chapters of the first book, Genesis, tell us how God created this world and the first human beings, Adam and Eve. He gave them a law to keep, but they disobeyed Him. (page 3)

So the message of Genesis, and of other Bible writers who refer to Genesis, is plain. Don't blame a fallen angel for the sinfulness of human nature. Put the blame where it belongs: on Adam, and on his sinful children—including ourselves. (page 4)

But as soon as we accept that the devil is our fallen human nature, all these problems vanish (page 17)

What Jesus had done was to "bind" the "Satan" of human nature that was inside him. He did this every day, by conquering every temptation that came to him and thus living a sinless life. (page 18)

But now let us try the key that has already explained so many difficult passages. There is no *person*, besides God, who holds the power of death. But there is one *thing* that holds it: human sinfulness. Here are two verses that say so: "The wages of *sin* is *death*" (Romans 6:23). "Sin when it is full-grown brings forth *death*" (James 1:15). Without any doubt, therefore, the devil of Hebrews 2:14, the devil that had the power of death, was human sinfulness. (page 19)

Now to return to the first sentence of the verse we were looking at, Hebrews 2:14. Notice how it says that, in order to destroy the devil, Jesus needed to "share our human nature" …… take note of this verse's teaching that Jesus *died* so as to destroy the devil. But what can a man destroy by dying, except his own human nature, or his own self? (page 19)

Now that we know the devil *is* human nature—actually is that evil thing we call "SELF", or selfishness—all is beautifully clear. Of course Jesus had to share our human nature. Otherwise, there would have been no "devil" inside him to be destroyed. Of course he had to die. Otherwise he would never have completely destroyed "self". (page 19)

With the right key in our hands everything in this verse fits together and makes perfect sense. Self, the human-nature devil, is too strong for you and me; it has the power of death over us; it destroys us. But the Lord Jesus Christ was the one and only human being who conquered every temptation that his human nature could hurl at him. And he went on doing so, right up to his dying breath. Had he done his own will and run away from the cross, the devil of human nature would have destroyed him. But he did no such thing. Instead, he did his Father's will. He went forward bravely to an agonising death. And thus he destroyed the devil. (page 19-20)

HP Mansfield

HP Mansfield, *Dr Thomas and the Mortality of Man*, Logos Magazine, vol. 16, 1950, pp. 266
The Devil or adversary to be destroyed being "sin's flesh", Brother Thomas shows that Christ possessed this nature, and by emerging morally undefiled from the fierce controversies against this power, through death destroyed sin in the flesh. Brother Thomas is careful to point out that the triumph of Christ was more than a mere triumph of will-power, and emphasises the Spirit-anointing result of the conceiving of Christ, whereby he became morally a manifestation of the Father, being Deity manifest in the flesh (1 Timothy 3:16). "God was in Christ reconciling the world unto himself" (2 Corinthians 5:19). Brother Thomas expresses the matter with great clarity in the following sentences:

> "Jesus claimed to be the seed of Abraham and God, while he charged them (the Jews) with being seed of Abraham and sin — they were, in other words, begotten of sinful flesh, while he was begotten of God,

> sinful flesh being the matrice (mould) of both parties. One thing may resemble another without being identical in every particular. This was the case with Christ's flesh. It was sin's flesh so far as its maternity was concerned, but not as to its Fatherhood."

These words are very clear. Christ was, by reason of his birth, in the Adamic line, a form of sin's flesh. This maternal inheritance was ever-present and an occasion of groaning and tears (Hebrews 5:7), until his resurrection. The moral manifestation was then related to a glorious setting of the eternal nature, and he became "the Lord, the Spirit". In comparing Christ with Adam before the fall, Brother Thomas writes: "His flesh, however, was still reduced in strength below that of Adam's original nature, because of its maternal defilement".

HP Mansfield, *Made Sin for Us*, Logos Magazine, vol. 43, 1976, pp. 74-78

Although Jesus was "without sin" in the sense of transgression, he possessed a nature identical with that of those whom he came to save: a nature that is the seat and origin of sin: "That which cometh out of the man, that defileth the man. For from within, out of the heart of men, proceed evil thoughts, adulteries, murders, thefts", and so forth, "all these evil things come from within, and defile the man" (Mark 7:20-23). The same nature that erupts into actual transgression on the part of mankind was possessed by the Lord, but he kept in check its impulses, by drawing upon the strength made available to him from God. In that way his crucifixion resulted in the destruction of the "body of sin;" the "putting away of sin by the sacrifice of himself" (Hebrews 9:26); or the destruction of that "which was the power of death, that is the devil" (Hebrews 2:14). He conquered the devil in life, and silenced it through death.

For the devil is the term expressive of the lusts of the flesh, to which the Lord never gave way. When his body hung lifeless upon the cross, so also did the desire of the flesh. Having figuratively put them to death in life, he literally did so in submitting to crucifixion. His sacrifice was representative, on our account, graphically setting forth the ideal towards which we must strive. Therefore, Paul taught: "They that are Christ's have crucified the flesh with the affections and lusts" (Galatians 5:24).

Although Jesus was "without sin" in the sense of transgression, he possessed the nature which is the root cause of sin, which is, itself, subject to death because of sin at the beginning. In this sense, his crucifixion was a putting to death of the "body of sin" (Romans 6:6), or the destruction of that "which has the power of death, that is the devil" (Hebrews 2:14)

Harry Whittaker

Harry Whittaker, The Christadelphian, vol. 99, 1962, p. 266

Here, as almost uniformly throughout the New Testament, the phrase "in the flesh" means "in very human nature with all its weakness"; compare the familiar words "the world, the flesh, and the devil".

Thus the best of all tests of a true teacher is: Does he teach truth concerning the nature of Christ? And in this respect Christadelphians stand alone. All others fail by this test, mostly insisting on what has come to be known among us as the "Clean Flesh" heresy (the phrase is a clumsy one, but it spotlights the first and worst heresy of all).

Harry Whittaker, *Tempted of the Devil*, Studies in the Gospels, 1984, pp. 68-69
The interpretation suggested here requires acceptance also of the view that the temptations either originated or found an answering strain in the marred human nature which Jesus inherited. This apparently drastic conclusion is entirely in harmony with all that Scripture teaches regarding human nature and, more particularly, regarding the nature of Jesus. He shared fully the fallen human nature which he came to redeem.

Harry Tennant

Harry Tennant, *The Christadelphians – What They Believe And Preach*, 1986, pp. 145-147

JESUS' TEMPTATIONS IN THE WILDERNESS

What then of the New Testament? In the first place, there is a considerable change of emphasis. The words Devil and Satan are given a prominence which is not found in the Old Testament. When Christ appears, the words are used with deliberate intent in the inspired Word of God. It is as though the two words have a special significance in relation to him. Here are some of the Scriptures:

> "Then was Jesus led up of the Spirit into the wilderness to be tempted of the devil." (Matthew 4:1)

> "And he was there in the wilderness forty days, tempted of Satan; and was with the wild beasts; and the angels ministered unto him." (Mark 1:13)

> "Forasmuch then as the children (the people whom Jesus came to save) are partakers of flesh and blood, he also himself likewise took part of the same; that through death he might destroy him that had the power of death, that is, the devil; and deliver them who through fear of death were all their lifetime subject to bondage." (Hebrews 2:14-15)

From these verses we gather that:

> In the temptation of Christ, the words Devil and Satan are interchangeable. The meanings "accuser" or "adversary" would certainly describe the nature of the temptation.

> Jesus is joining battle with the Devil or Satan. The battle is in respect of temptation. There is no sense of a display of power, or any application of it, by the Devil during temptation.

> In order to "destroy the devil", Jesus shared our nature, flesh and blood. It is impossible not to conclude that there must be a relationship between flesh and blood, temptation and the Devil; and, furthermore, the destruction of the Devil is achieved through death which must indicate that death and the Devil are related.

Our next step must be to examine the New Testament teaching about temptation. What is the main source of man's temptation? Here are the clear teachings of Scripture — Romans 7:17-25; Galatians 5:17-21; 1 John 2:16, 17; 1 John 3:8; and James 1:13-15.

… The Scriptures quoted above, and there are many more, tell us plainly the facts about the seedbed of lust and sin. It is the flesh. The flesh has its own natural appetites which are flesh-centred, self-centred, and therefore opposed to God. All of the world's evils described in Galatians 5 above are "works of the flesh", and these are described in 1 John 3 as, "the works of the devil". This must mean that there is a strong connection between "the flesh" and "the devil". If the Devil has its roots in the flesh, which is the only reasonable conclusion from these verses, it follows that the way to overcome it is to enter into conflict with it on its own ground, flesh and blood. This is exactly what the Lord Jesus Christ is described as doing when he "partook of flesh and blood" that he might "destroy him that hath the power of death, that is, the devil" (Hebrews 2:14).

Harry Tennant, _The Christadelphians – What They Believe And Preach_, 1986, pp. 147-153

THE CONQUERING OF SIN

… There is little wonder then, to find his temptations described as a battle with the Devil or Satan. It was. He was engaged in mortal combat with the natural instincts of his nature and with the comprehensive sinfulness of a whole world of sinners. The world was ruled by Sin, and Christ was come to bring deliverance, to break the power of sin and death, to "destroy him that hath the power of death, that is, the devil".

But how does "the devil" have the power of death? The Scripture tells us that God inflicted death on Adam and Eve. In what way does the Devil have that power? Scripture is crystal clear (see Hebrews 2;14; John 8:44; Romans 5:12, 17, 21; 6:23; 1 Corinthians 15:56).

We now have an unmistakable connection linking lust, the flesh, the Devil, sin and death. It is impossible to escape this Scriptural conclusion. The Devil is responsible for death. Sin is responsible for death. The flesh is responsible for death:

> _"Be not deceived; God is not mocked: for whatsoever a man soweth, that shall he also reap. For he that soweth to his flesh shall of the flesh reap corruption …"_ (Galatians 6:7-8)

We must conclude from Scripture that flesh is fundamentally disposed to sin. Our natural urges or lusts (described in 1 John 2:16 as _"the lust of the flesh, and the lust of the eyes, and the pride of life"_) will, if allowed full expression, produce sin, which ends in death. This explains why human nature is described as _"sinful flesh"_ (Romans 8:3), and why the same part of Scripture says, _"If ye live after the flesh, ye shall die"_ (Romans 8:13). How, then, do we explain the words "the devil", and the comment we have read that _"he was a murderer from the beginning"_ (John 8:44)?

There can be but one answer to meet all the known facts: the Devil and sinfulness are so interrelated that we must conclude that, in the context of the Scriptures we have quoted, they are describing the same thing. Man's capacity for sinfulness is the Devil; and *"by one man sin entered into the world, and **death by sin**"* (Romans 5:12).

When Adam and Eve sinned, by surrendering to desires aroused by the words of the serpent, they brought death into the world. Paul expressed it in this way: *"Sin … deceived me … and slew me"* (Romans 7:11). Death was not introduced by some outside evil power; it was the direct result of sin. The command given by God contained its own penalty clause which God brought into effect. No one else was involved. In the same way it is God who will finally remove sin from the face of the earth at the end of the millennium. In other words: when sin came, death came: when sin goes, death goes.

We conclude therefore that the basic sinfulness of man, his natural selfish disposition, is the true meaning of "the devil", in the passages we have been considering. In one sense that meaning is true for the word "Satan", as well. Sinfulness is the direct adversary of God. But we must proceed to look at the two words a little further, because they are not always interchangeable. We shall discover that while the Devil is satisfactorily described, at least in a substantial part, by human sinfulness, it also has some clear extensions of meaning in a wider sense; and Satan has some particular significances also. ….

… We believe that Satan is the sum total of everything in the world which has to do with mortality, including all the ills to which man is heir. Among men, sin reigns as king and his empire is characterised by disease and mortality. The sum total of these things is Satan. It includes human sinfulness, and all the consequences of sin, and the total corporate and cumulative wickedness of man.

Harry Tennant, *The Crisis of the Cross of Christ – Why Did Jesus Die?* The Christadelphian Magazine and Publishing Association Ltd (UK), pp. 9-17

THE DEVIL AND DEATH

We learned from the verses from Hebrews that "the devil" has the power of death. But how can this be? It was God who brought death into the world because of Adam's disobedience. How then could the devil be said to have that power?

Look at these phrases from scripture and see whether you can make sense of them: "The wages of sin is death" (Romans 6:23). "The sting of death is sin" (1 Corinthians 15:56). "He that hath the power of death, that is, the devil" (Hebrews 2:14). Three things emerge from these verses: sin brings death, sin is the sting of death, and the devil has the power of death. Man committed sin and brought death into the world. This is exactly what Paul says:

> "By one man sin entered into the world, and death by sin; and so death passed upon all men, for that all have sinned." (Romans 5:12)

The devil is therefore sin at work in us and is expressed in the world around. Sin's work brings death. The Bible quotations we have just looked at make no sense at all if the devil is a supernatural being, as some believe. The "devil" is personified in Scripture, but is not a living person: there can be no rival to God.

How did Jesus deal with the devil? The Bible has already given us the answer - Jesus was flesh and blood in which death works and where sin is produced, and Jesus shared that nature with its evil potential.

This is the key to Christ's redemptive work. The bliss of Eden was destroyed by Adam's sin, and Adam's life was slowly but surely destroyed by death. Sin reigned like a king over all Adam's descendants, none was free from sin and all would die. How could the vicious circle be broken and thereby bring deliverance from death? Redemption and salvation could come only from God. But how could it come righteously from God? In other words, how could God's righteousness be vindicated in providing a Saviour, whilst sin was not ignored but truly condemned?

> "He saw that there no man, and wondered that there was no intercessor: therefore his arm brought salvation unto him; and his righteousness, it sustained him." (Isaiah 59:16) (pages 13-14)

THE STRONG MAN OF SIN

To all appearances, sin was unassailable within its fortress - all mankind. God created man in the first place and it was not His purpose to abandon man to his misery but instead to provide a wonderful Deliverer. Sin was to be defeated on its own territory. Jesus said, "No man can enter into a strong man's house, and spoil his goods, except he first bind the strong man; and then he will spoil his house" (Mark 3:27). That was the key: to enter the house of the strong man of Sin and bind him, and then spoil his goods.

The strong man's house was human nature in which sin had reigned ever since Adam sinned. How then could sin be bound within its own house? It was done by Christ entering the strong man's house. He was born of a human mother and thereby shared her-our-nature. This meant that he would inevitably suffer temptation like all men; and, by sharing Mary's nature, flesh and blood, Christ would himself be mortal; death would be at work in him. (Page 14-15)

This was the greatest battle in human history. Other battles have been between sinners of one kind and another and every victor was himself in the end beaten by the last enemy, death. But this battle was to be astonishingly different. Temptation and Sin were to be defeated on their own ground! In the very nature which resulted from Adam's sin, Sin was to be crushed and mortally wounded. A seemingly mysterious word of prophecy spoken by God in Eden after Adam and Eve had sinned was thus realised:

> "I will put enmity between thee and the woman, and between thy seed and her seed; it shall bruise thy head, and thou shalt bruise his heel." (Genesis 3:15)

Having no human father, Jesus was truly the seed of the woman. Sin was mortally crushed by Jesus through his sinlessness, but in that process, Christ himself died. The last enemy, death, appeared to have the final triumph.

THE BI-FOCAL PERSPECTIVE

The root of temptation lay in Jesus - as in all of us - in the nature he inherited from his mother. As Paul said, he had a "law in his members, warring against the law of his mind" (Romans 7:23). The only way to eliminate that law was to die, not simply by growing old and dying, but by the deliberate choice of death, the total rejection of the seat of rebellion by willingly dying. That was the Great Triumph, the Ultimate Victory. The Cross was not a defeat, it was the final mastery, the complete vanquishing of Sin.

All who looked on Jesus saw a crucified, dying man put to public shame and unspeakable ignominy. But, was that all the picture? Is rejection by humankind and the degradation of the Son of God what it was all about? Not at all! Far from it!

Look more closely and see the surpassing beauty of what was done. God was served to the limit by the sacrifice of God's own Son, so that the way of salvation could be opened for us all.

Michael Ashton

Michael Ashton, *He Himself Hath Suffered, Being Tempted*, The Christadelphian, vol. 125, 1988, pp. 385-386
He [Jesus] was in the wilderness, and *alone*. To show the intimate connection between temptation and a nature related to sin and death, it was "the devil" that tempted him. Described later in Scripture as having "the power of death" (Hebrews 2:14), because death resulted from sin, the absolute correspondence between the physical nature of Christ and those he came to save is thus declared most evidently by the temptations he endured. So, like us, "he suffered, being tempted".

Michael Ashton, The Christadelphian, "Studies in the Statement of Faith", vol. 127, 1990, p.127
Alongside the important position accorded in Bible teaching to the mortality of man must be placed a true understanding of "the devil". Because this is a subject so widely misunderstood by so-called "Christians" groups it is necessary to define carefully what the scriptures mean. While the first part of the Statement of Faith explains the holy nature of God and the fallen condition of man, something which became "a physical law of his being", it would be possible to believe in the existence of a "supernatural personal (evil) being". This belief is roundly rejected in No. 11 [of Doctrines to be Rejected].

Michael Ashton, *The Beginning*, The Christadelphian, vol. 136, 1999, p.107
"Like unto his brethren"
So when the Apostle explains the Lord's victory, he starts by showing the relationship between Jesus and Adam's race: "Forasmuch then as the children are partakers of flesh and blood, he also himself likewise took part of the same; that through death he might destroy him that had the power of death, that is, the devil" (Hebrews 2:14).

"The children" are flesh and blood, dying creatures, caught in the web of sin and unable to free themselves from its "power". The wonder of the work of God through His Son is that Jesus fully shared that condition in order to battle against sin on its own territory. This was the greatest battle that has ever been fought, and the most important result was at stake—the redemption of the world.

… Unless Jesus fully experienced the condition of the rest of mankind, he could not "destroy him that had the power of death". Born of a human mother, the Lord was a dying creature, living in surroundings which provided a constant reminder of sin. But there was more involved even than that. Jesus was not an interested spectator of the problems which affect his brethren and the rest of the world, he was a full partaker, living under the effects of that which "had the power of death". The Lord was therefore aware at all times of the compelling tendency towards disobedience which leads men and women to sin. He said to his disciples during one of the most testing times of his ministry, "the spirit indeed is willing, but the flesh is weak" (Matthew 26:41). And he gave his disciples a practical exhortation of how that weakness can be resisted: "Watch and pray, that ye enter not into temptation".

Throughout each phase of his battle against Sin, Jesus called on His Father for help: "not as I will, but as thou wilt" (Mathew 26:39). The salvation of the world rested completely on his success or failure. Anything less than Jesus' complete identification with the problems experienced by the rest of mankind would make his work a masquerade or a sham. Hence Paul was inspired to record with what might otherwise appear extravagant explanation, that Jesus was tempted "in all points" like his brethren, that "he also himself likewise took part of the same" nature as them; and that through his death—the death of a mortal, yet sinless, man—he destroyed the devil.

SECTION 7

FURTHER READING

"Now I beseech you, brethren, by the name of our Lord Jesus Christ, that ye all speak the same thing, and that there be no divisions among you; but that ye be perfectly joined together in the same mind and in the same judgment." (1 Corinthians 1:10 KJV)

Further Reading

Association of Australian Christadelphian Ecclesias, Final Paper: *"Bible Teaching on Creation"*, response to Motion 8 Brisbane Conference, 2018 (distributed 6 May, 2020)

Allfree, M. and Davies, M., *The Deception of Theistic Evolution* Bible Study Publications, Nottinghamshire, UK 2017

Burges, David, *Wonders of Creation: The works of the Divine Designer*, The Testimony Birmingham 2017

Cresswell, P., *The Genius of Creation*, CSSS Adelaide, Australia 2017

Heavyside, P., *Genesis 1-2: A harmonised and historical reading*, Ascent Publications, 2018

Perry, P., *Theistic Evolution Refuted*, CSSS Adelaide, Australia 2019

Storey, M., *The God We Worship*, The Christadelphian, Birmingham 2019

Walker, A., *The Genesis of Blessings*, The Christadelphian, Birmingham, 2017

Wang, A. and Larsen J., *Taipei Christadelphian Ecclesia Timeline*, distributed to all ACBM Regional Committees and the ecclesias they represent, 25 October 2016 http://cbmresources.org/forums/index.php?/topic/1162-taipei-christadelphian-ecclesia-timeline/

The Bible Magazine

Vol. 22, 2009	October	Billington, Paul	In the beginning God created …
Vol. 27, 2014	April	Billington, Paul	The power of creation
		Kidd, Ron	The Bible challenges theistic evolution
	July	Kidd, Ron	The challenge of theistic evolution
Vol. 28, 2015	January	Carter, John	Oracles of God (extract from book)
		Houghton, Terry	Evolution or the Bible? What do we tell the Children?
		Billington, Paul	Creation, the Bible & the Vatican
		Billington, Paul	Deceived & being deceived
		Abel, Frank	Theistic Evolution?
Vol. 30, 2018	April	Burt, Bernard	Theistic evolution & inspiration
	July	Burt, Bernard	Theistic evolution & the doctrine of the atonement

The Christadelphian Magazine

Vol. 152, 2015	January	Levett, Sid	Genesis Foundations: Creation – a sense of immediacy
	February	Harrison, Allan	Genesis Foundations: The power of God's wisdom in creation

	March	Talbot, Robert	Genesis Foundations: I believe in creation because…
	April	Hellawell, John M	Genesis Foundations: Halting between two opinions
	May	Godber, Andrew	Genesis Foundations: Evolution, education and the believer
	June	Morris, John	Genesis Foundations: The way God works
	July	Watkins, Peter	Genesis Foundations: Genesis in all the scriptures
	August	Palmer, Stephen	Genesis Foundations: Creation or evolution – the integrity and truth of scripture
	September	Palmer, Stephen	Genesis Foundations: Creation or evolution – debating with evolutionists
	October	Palmer, Stephen	Genesis Foundations: Creation or evolution – implications for the atonement
	November	Pople, John	Genesis Foundations: The Genesis account of creation – seeing God's signature
	December	Bramhill, Andrew	Genesis Foundations: And God Said…
Vol. 153, 2016	March	Cave, Lawrence	Challenges from the world
	December	Bramhill, Andrew	Editorial: "The desire for life".
Vol. 154, 2017	July	Walker, Andrew	A sign of authority
Vol. 155, 2018	January	Cresswell, Paul	Christ our intercessor
Vol. 157, 2020	January	Morris, John	Book Review: "The Fool hath said in his heart .. there is no God"
	April	Talbot, Kevin	Radiometric Dating of Fossils: Science or Blind Faith"?
		Nightingale, Tom	Book Review: The Deception of Theistic Evolution
	May	Vincent, Mark	"Yes…but…" (Part 5): God of the Gaps
	June	Vincent, Mark	"Yes…but…"Part 6): Modern Scholarship
	July	Vincent, Mark	"Yes…but…" (Part 7): In What Ways Is the Bible The Word of God
	August	Dean, Simon	"Yes…but…" (Part 8:): Science and Belief in God

The Lampstand Magazine

Vol. 2, 1996	November	Evans, David	The Australian Unity Agreement
Vol. 13, 2007	March	Luke, Jim	Editorial: "Evolution and Inspiration"
Vol. 14, 2008	January	McDermott, Kevin	Changing Alliances: How Science turned from being the champion of Christianity to its embittered opponent
		Martin, John	Significance and Meaning of the Cooper-Carter Addendum
		Thiele, Rob	The Unity Book – Fellowship Clauses
Vol. 19, 2013	May	Lampstand Committee	Creation - emphatic of scriptural teaching
		Lampstand Committee	Evolution and our statement of faith
		Lampstand Committee	Creation and evolution
Vol. 20, 2014	January	Thiele, Rob	Did Moses write the Pentateuch, the first five books of the Bible?
	May	Roberts, Robert	"The First Man" reprint of article from The Christadelphian
Vol. 21, 2015	January	Luke, Jim	If the foundations be destroyed
	March	Lines, Tony	Re-affirmation statement concerning creation and the fall of man
Vol. 23, 2017	March	Larsen, James and Jamieson, Matt	Death – the last enemy (Part 1)
	May	Larsen, James and Jamieson, Matt	Death – the last enemy (Part 2)
	July	Larsen, James and Jamieson, Matt	Death – the last enemy (Part 3)
Vol. 24, 2018	May	Book Review	Burges, David, Wonders of Creation, The Testimony, Birmingham, 2017
Vol. 26, 2020	January	Mansfield, James	Fellowship (Part 1): Biblical Fellowship and the Importance of the Statement of Faith
Vol. 26, 2020	March	Luke, Brian	Fellowship (Part 2): The Last Appeal of Our Lord
		Kidd, Ron	The World of the Ungodly (1)
	May	Thiele, Rob	Fellowship (Part 3): Fellowship
		Kidd, Ron	The World of the Ungodly (2)

	July	Lampstand Committee	Fellowship (Part 4): Open Fellowship – The Truth
Vol. 26, 2020	September	Lampstand Committee	Fellowship (Part 5): Open Fellowship – Questions and Answers
		Parry, Carl	Fellowship in the Gospel

The Testimony **Magazine**

Vol. 82, 2012	February	Nicholls, John	Instinct deals a heavy blow to evolution: review of pdf e-book
		Alleyne, Wilfred	*How Does Instinct Evolve? The question Evolution Cannot Answer.*
Vol. 83, 2013	May	Various authors	Special Edition: *Genesis: Seedbed of the Bible*
	November	Penn, Gary	Genesis and Darwinism
Vol. 84, 2014	October	Hammond, Kel	The Bible, Science, evolution and creation
Vol. 85, 2015	January	Burt, Bernard	Gems from early Genesis (1)
		McCann, James	Through death
	February	Burt, Bernard	Gems from Genesis (2)
	March	Burt, Bernard	Gems from Genesis (3)
	August	Burt, Bernard	Gems from Genesis (4)
	September	Heavyside, Peter	Genesis 1-2: Jesus' reading of Genesis 1-2
	October	Heavyside, Peter	Genesis 1-2: The duration of creation
	November	Perry, Andrew	Problems with theistic evolution (1)
	December	Perry, Andrew	Problems with theistic evolution (2)
Vol.86, 2016	February	Heavyside, Peter	Genesis 1-2: Portrayals of the beginning
	April	Heavyside, Peter	Genesis 1-2: Order and content
	July	Hammond, Kel	Evidence, reason and faith
	August	Hammond, Kel	Evidence, reason and faith (1)
	September	Hammond, Kel	Evidence, reason and faith (2)
		Heavyside, Peter	Genesis 1-2: Different literary styles
	October	Hammond, Kel	Evidence, reason and faith (1)
	November	Hammond, Kel	Evidence, reason and faith (2)
	December	Hammond, Kel	Evidence, reason and faith (1)
		Heavyside, Peter	Genesis 1-2: Different views of God

Vol. 87, 2017	January	Hammond, Kel	Evidence, reason and faith (2)
		Henstock, Geoff	Is Genesis plagiarised?
	February	Hammond, Kel	Evidence, reason and faith (1)
		Heavyside, Peter	Genesis 1-2: God's names
	March	Hammond, Kel	Evidence, reason and faith (2)
		Byrnes, Colin	Eve, Temptation and the serpent
	April	Hammond, Kel	Evidence, reason and faith
	July	Hammond, Kel	Evidence, reason and faith
		Heavyside, Peter	Genesis 1-2: Different methods of creating
	September	Jamieson, Matt	Destroying strongholds
	October	Heavyside, Peter	Genesis 1-2: Different views of humanity
	December	Heavyside, Peter	Genesis 1-2: Concluding remarks
Vol. 88, 2018	September	Genders, Paul M.	Genesis in the light of modern discovery
Vol. 89, 2019	January	Allfree, Mark	Genesis 1-2: Inspiration and Honesty
	October	Whittaker, Jamie	Theistic evolution and the meaning of creation
	December	Brown, Michael	Harmonising Egyptian History with the Old Testament. Putting the case for historical revision: 1. The Scale of the Exodus
Vol 90, 2020	January	Brown, Michael	2. The Historical Background to Genesis and Exodus
	March	Thomas, Jeremy	A Matter of Honesty (1)
		Brown, Michael	3. The Curious Pattern of Biblical Archaeological Evidence
	April	Thomas, Jeremy	A Matter of Honesty (2)
		Brown, Michael	4. Why are there two dates for the Exodus?
	August	Brown, Michael	5. Patterns of Evidence
	September	Brown, Michael	6. The Amarna Letters – crucial evidence (1)
	October	Brown, Michael	7. The Amarna Letters – crucial evidence (2)

Scripture Index

Topical Index